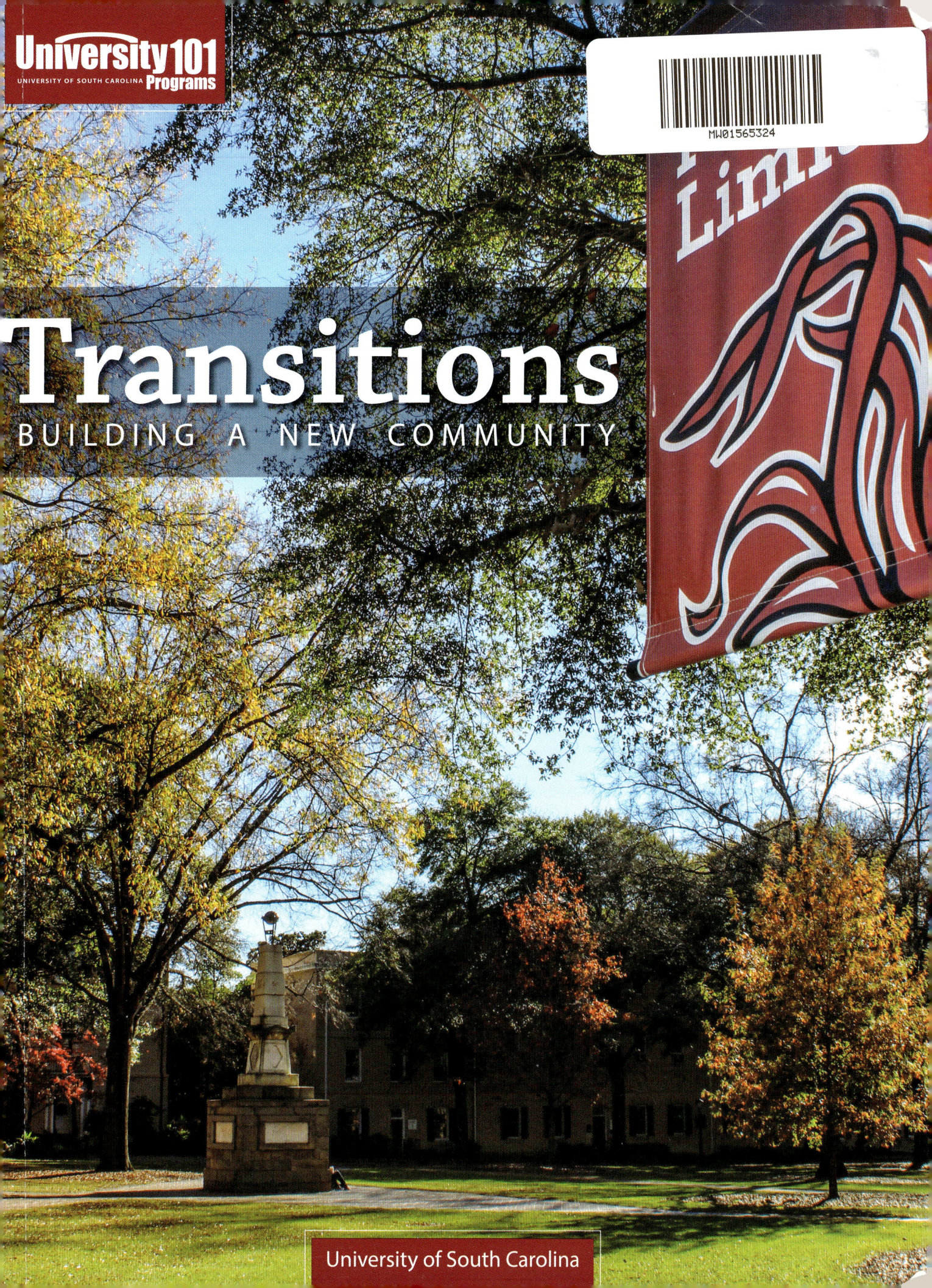

Mary Elizabeth Sewell, Dan Friedman
Editors

Dottie Weigel
Copy Editor

Erin Morris
Design, Layout

Carly Edwards
Cover Photo

We would like to acknowledge the special contributions of our dedicated and knowledgeable authors without whom we could not produce this publication:

Chapter 1: **Dan Friedman**, Director, *University 101*

Chapter 2: **Jennifer Latino**, former Associate Director, *University 101 Programs*

Chapter 3: **Jimmie Gahagan**, Director & Kimberly Dressler, Coordinator, *Office of Student Engagement*, **Irma Van Scoy**, Executive Director, *USC Connect*

Chapter 4: **Dan Friedman**, Director, **Jaime Shook**, former Graduate Assistant, *University 101*, **Mary Elizabeth Sewell**, Associate Director, *University 101*, **Maureen Grewe**, former Practicum Graduate Student, and **Paul Millard**, former Graduate Assistant, *University 101*

Chapter 5: **Jaime Shook**, former Graduate Assistant, *University 101*, **Mary Elizabeth Sewell**, Associate Director, *University 101*, **Eric Moschella**, Director, *Student Success Center*, **Claire Robinson**, Associate Director, *Student Success Center*

Chapter 6: **Mike Hix**, Associate Director, *Career Center* & **Dawn Traynor**, former Coordinator of Cross Campus Advising, *Student Success Center*, **Mary Stuart Hunter**, Associate Vice-President, *University 101 Programs and the National Resource Center for The First-Year Experience and Students in Transition*, **Sandra Smith**, Coordinator of Cross College Advising, *Student Success Center*.

Chapter 7: **Karen Brown**, Reference Librarian, *Thomas Cooper Library*, **Dan Friedman**, Director, *University 101*, **Timothy Simmons**, First-Year Experience Librarian, *Thomas Cooper Library*.

Chapter 8: **Mary Elizabeth Sewell**, Associate Director, *University 101*, **Michelle Burcin**, former Director, *Healthy Carolina*, **Debbie Beck**, Executive Director, *Student Health Services*, **Jessica Johnston**, Director, *Healthy Carolina*, **Marguerite O'Brien**, Director, *Campus Wellness*, **Frank Anderson**, Pastor, *Student Life*, **Gwen Geidel**, Director, *Environment and Sustainability Program, Research Professor, and Undergraduate Director, School of the Earth, Ocean, and Environment*; **Katherine Robinson**, Adjunct Faculty, *Department of Philosophy*; Sustainable Carolina's Curriculum Team

Chapter 9: **Jennifer Keup**, Director, *National Resource Center for The First-Year Experience and Students in Transition*, **Mary Elizabeth Sewell**, Associate Director, *University 101*, **Rodrick Moore**, Director, *Office of Multicultural Student Affairs*

Introductory letters and scenarios for each chapter were written by current University 101 Campus Partners. We thank the following professionals for their contributions: **Dr. Dan Friedman**, Director, *University 101*(Chapter 1), **Dr. Dennis Pruitt**, Vice President for Student Affairs, Vice Provost and Dean of Students, *Office of the Vice President* (Chapter 2), **Anna Edwards**, Director of Student Services, *Student Life* (Chapter 3), **Dr. Christy Friend**, Associate Professor, *Department of English*/Director, *Center for Teaching Excellence* (Chapter 4), **Dr. Eric Moschella**, Director, *Student Success Center* (Chapter 5), **Dr. Helen Doerpinghaus**, Vice Provost and Dean, *Undergraduate Studies* (Chapter 6), **Timothy Simmons**, First-Year Experience Librarian, *Thomas Cooper Library* (Chapter 7), **Marguerite O'Brien**, Director, *Campus Wellness* (Chapter 8), **Dr. John Dozier**, Chief Diversity Officer, *President's Office* (Chapter 9)

How to cite this text:
Sewell, M.E. & Friedman, D. B. (Eds.) (2014) Transitions: Building a new community. Columbia, SC: University of South Carolina.

Copyright © 2014 University 101 at the University of South Carolina. All rights reserved. No part of this work may be reproduced or copied without written permission from the University of South Carolina.

Transitions was printed responsibly by using a certified FSC forestry management chain of custody paper processed in acid-free and chlorine-free manufacturing conditions and made with 30% post-consumer waste, 50% total recycled fiber, and elemental chlorine free pulps.

CONTENTS

List of Assessments, Figures, and Tables v
How to Use This Book. vi

Chapter 1
An Introduction to University 101 . . . 1
About University 101 at the University of
South Carolina 3
University of South Carolina – The National and
International Leader in First-Year Seminars 4
University 101 Goals and Learning Outcomes 7
Your University 101 Instructors. 8
University 101 Peer Leader Program 8
University 101 Sponsored Awards. 9
University 101 Programs. 10

Chapter 2
Discovering Carolina 15
Keeping It Cocky Since 1801: A Chronological History . 17
The History of the Horseshoe. 20
Carolina History 23
Noteworthy Moments in University History. 24
Current Carolina Traditions 29
The Carolina Culture 33
Carolinian Creed 36

Chapter 3
Exploring YOUR Carolina 41
USC Connect 43
What is Engagement?. 45
Student Engagement Plan. 48
Engagement Pathways. 48
Research 53
Community Service 55
Global Learning 56
Other Opportunities 59
Discover Columbia 61
Scenarios From College Life: A Little Too Involved. . . . 76

Chapter 4
Managing Your Time 79
Time Management 81
Aligning Your Goals and Values. 83
Goal Setting. 83
Procrastination 84
Multitasking. 86
Scheduling Tools. 87

Chapter 5
Academic Skills 99
Staying on Top of Your Academic Work Load 101
Note-Taking. 107
Listening Skills 112
Reading Comprehension 112
Test Preparation and Test Taking. 113

Chapter 6
Charting Your Path 125

Major Exploration and Career Planning 128
Career Decision Making: Four-Step Model. 128
Suggested Career Planning Timeline 133
Academic Advising 139
Academic Planning Strategies 139
Course Planning 144
Academic Policies and Procedures 146
Scenarios From College Life: It's Your Choice 152

Chapter 7
Searching for Knowledge: Information Literacy and Academic Integrity . . . 155

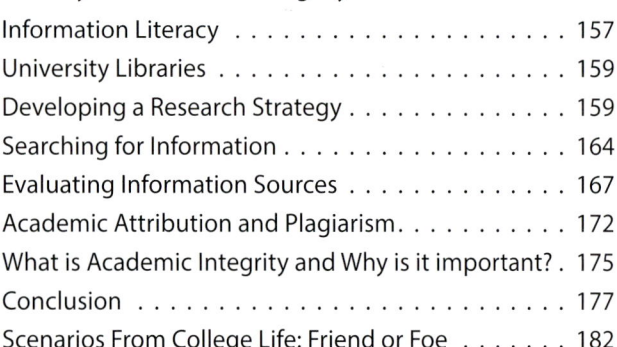

Information Literacy 157
University Libraries 159
Developing a Research Strategy 159
Searching for Information 164
Evaluating Information Sources 167
Academic Attribution and Plagiarism. 172
What is Academic Integrity and Why is it important? . 175
Conclusion 177
Scenarios From College Life: Friend or Foe 182

Chapter 8
Making Healthy Decisions 185

Physical Wellness. 189
Eating Healthy on Campus 192
Physical Activity 193
Health Care 194
Sexual Health 201
Social Wellness 206
Interpersonal Violence: Staying Safe and Standing Up 206
Safety. 211
Protecting Your Property. 213
Emotional Wellness 214
Intellectual Wellness 222
Spiritual Wellness 223
Occupational Wellness 225
Environmental Wellness 225
Scenarios From College Life:
    A Roommate with a Secret. 233
    A Night of Letting Loose 234

Chapter 9
Value of Diversity 237

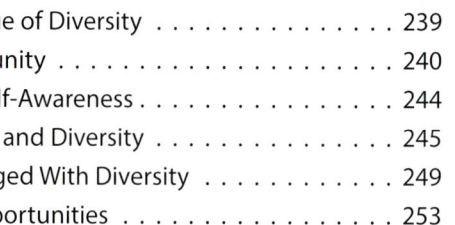

Educational Value of Diversity 239
Carolina Community 240
Diversity and Self-Awareness 244
Communication and Diversity 245
Becoming Engaged With Diversity 249
Community Opportunities 253
Scenarios From College Life: You Believe What? 254

Appendix:
The University of South Carolina Campus Map . .257

Index 261

ASSESSMENTS, FIGURES, AND TABLES

Chapter 1: An Introduction to University 101
By The Numbers 6

Chapter 2: Discovering Carolina
History of the Horseshoe. 20
Carolina History 23
Other Noteworthy Moments in University Other Noteworthy Moments in University 27
Carolina Traditions. 28
Student Reminders from 1930s Student Handbook. 34
The Carolinian Creed 36
Outstanding Alumni 38
The USC Bucketlist 39

Chapter 3: Exploring YOUR Carolina
How to Make the Most of your Educational Experience 46
Your USCConnect 47
Campus Engagement. 49
Athletic Team Schedules 60
Student Engagement Plan. 66
    SEP Part 1: A Pathway to Discovering High-Impact Practices and Campus Resources 66
    SEP Part 2: Student Engagement Inventory 67
    SEP Part 3: Personal Reflection 69
    SEP Part 4: Knowing Campus Resources 70
    SEP Part 5: Creating Your Plan for Engagement 72
    SEP Part 6: Mapping Your Academic and Beyond-the-Classroom Experiences. 75

Chapter 4: Managing Your Time
It's A Matter of Time. 82
Academic Goal Setting Sheet. 90
Where does my time go?. 91
Values Inventory 92
Syllabus Mapping 94
Semester at a Glance 96
Weekly Schedule. 97

Chapter 5: Academic Skills
Dos and Don'ts of Faculty office Hours 102
Memory Curve 104
Communicating With Your Professors. 105
Assessing Your Note-Taking Skills 107
Academic Success. 108
Test-Taking Strategies. 115
Identifying Your Academic Strengths 118
E-mail Etiquette 119
Test Anxiety Inventory 120
GPA Calculator 122

Chapter 6: Charting Your Path
What's right for you? 135
Gathering More Information 135
First-Year Student Resume. 136
Senior Resume 137
Developing Your Career Path 138
Advisee/Advisor Responsibilities. 141
USC Advising Quick Facts 142
Carolina Core 145
Four-year Curriculum Plan. 147
Academic Policies 148
Advising Preparation Sheet 149
Registration Worksheet. 150
Schedule Worksheet 151

Chapter 7: Searching for Knowledge
Information Literacy Framework. 158
Beginning Research-Breaking Down a Topic 160
Evaluate Your Own Research Question 161
Comparing Magazines and Journals 163
Types of Sources 163
Possible search terms for "narcotic trafficking" 166
Google Scholar 168
Useful Terms 169
Information Literacy & Academic Integrity 171
To Cite or Not to Cite 178
Is This a Violation of the Honor Code?. 179
Comparison of APA, Chicago, MLA, and CSE styles 180

Chapter 8: Making Healthy Decisions
Top Ten Impediments to Academic Success. 188
Are You Nutrition Savvy?. 189
Healthy Choice Icon. 192
Health and Well-Being Offices on Campus. 195
USC Alcohol & Drug Consequences 199
Signs of Drug Misuse 200
Sexually transmitted infections and diseases and Their Symptoms. 202
Types of Contraception. 203
Tips for Communicating with your Partner about Sex 204
Personal Relationship Quiz 210
Shuttle Cock. 212
Top 10 Strategies Successful People Employ When Experiencing Stress 216
Making Healthy Choices 218
Healthy Sleep Habits 221
Carolina Recycling Guide 227
Wellness Wheel Inventory 228
The Student Stress Scale 232

Chapter 9: Value of Diversity
Diversity Quiz. 211
Diversity at Carolina. 214
Diversity and Inclusion Terms. 216
Values Clarification 222

ON THE WEB

Each chapter contains On The Web boxes intended to provide you direct links to several online resources related to the content of the chapter.

Consider This

In the Consider This boxes, you will find reflection prompts to help you connect what you will read or have just read to what you already know about a topic or idea.

Peer Leader Advice

Throughout the book, you will meet some of the great students who served as Peer Leaders for University 101. The Peer Leader Advice boxes contain the words of wisdom, perspectives, expertise, and advice on the topics discussed in the chapter.

Check yourself

You will also have opportunities to Check Yourself using assessments or quizzes to gauge your current behaviors or attitudes toward particular concepts.

HOW TO USE THIS BOOK

Transitions 2014-2015 is just as much a resource guide as it is a textbook. It includes advice, information, and strategies designed to make your academic career and extracurricular or personal interests more productive and enjoyable. Your University 101 instructor(s) will direct 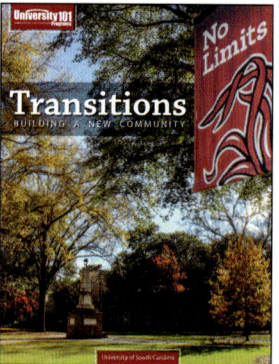 your attention to several sections of this textbook to facilitate your progress in defining and reaching your personal and academic goals.

Each chapter has been written with you in mind! They each contain information specific to the University of South Carolina-Columbia, including the history, campus involvement opportunities, programs and services provided for students, and important information you should know as a new member of the university community. The chapters also contain information and advice applicable to your extracurricular life as a student. We hope that you thoughtfully take note of these lessons and then selectively act upon them.

Additionally, each chapter contains important contact information to enable you to connect with valuable resources mentioned throughout the chapter. This allows you to jump immediately to the end of a chapter if you are looking for a specific office location, web site, or phone number. We also include a campus map at the back of the book.

Transitions will only be helpful to you if you use it. Use it not only as your instructor directs, but also as a personal resource, reference, and handbook. If you do so, we know this student success book will serve you well! Above all, *Transitions* 2014-2015 is intended especially for you to be "Your Book!"

An Introduction to University 101

Chapter One

Dear First-Year Student,

Congratulations on your acceptance to the University of South Carolina and your decision to enroll in our nationally recognized University 101 course. By signing up for UNIV 101, you have made a commitment to your own success and have paved the way for a smoother transition to college and a more rewarding first-year experience.

You probably have heard that University 101 has been consistently recognized by *US News and World Report* as "A Program to Look For," along with other schools, such as Princeton, Stanford, North Carolina, Michigan, and Yale. Back when US News ranked first-year seminars, South Carolina was selected as the #1 program in the country. You should be proud to attend a school that is continually recognized as the leader in the nation in helping students make a successful transition to college.

The University 101 course is designed to help you achieve academic success, discover all the resources Carolina has to offer, engage in the academic and cocurricular life of the University, and build important relationships with students and faculty. It will provide you with the tools and resources needed to succeed. I anticipate that this will be one of the most rewarding, meaningful, and engaging courses you will take as a college student.

As with most things in life, what you get out of this experience will be commensurate with what you put into it. This course, your instructor, and your peer and/or graduate leader, along with this edition of *Transitions*, are here to help you be as successful as you want to be. College comes with many new freedoms, which can be both exciting and daunting. But with these new freedoms come new responsibilities. Discovering how to manage and balance freedom and responsibility are important goals of this course.

If there is anything that I, or others in the University 101 office, can do to support you in this important transition, please do not hesitate to call on us (777-6029). I hope you have a wonderful first-year experience, and I wish you the very best.

Sincerely,

Dan Friedman
Director, University 101 Programs

About University 101 at the University of South Carolina

Welcome to the University of South Carolina! We are excited that you are joining a great institution and have taken the first step to ensure success during your time here by enrolling in University 101. University 101 is essentially an extended orientation, and our goal is to give you the information, resources, and support you need at the time you need it. When you were here for Orientation, you may have been overwhelmed with information or concerned mostly with where you were going to live and what classes you would take. Now that you are a student on campus, you are probably more interested in learning about all the great opportunities this school has for you, how to manage your time effectively, or how to eat well on campus. This course was designed by staff and students to meet these needs.

We know this course will help you be more successful. Students who take U101 earn higher first-year grade point averages (GPAs) than other students, come back for their sophomore year at greater rates, and are more likely to complete their degree at Carolina. In addition, University 101 students are more likely to report that they are satisfied with USC. Over 92% of UNIV 101 students responding to the 2009 National Survey of Student Engagement indicated that they would choose to attend USC again if they had it do to over (compared with 85.5% of participants who did not take UNIV 101).

Past students have raved about University 101. In 2012, over 95% of students said that they would recommend this course to other students. We also know students are tweeting about their great experiences.

We expect that you will have a great experience as well. But as with anything in life, you will get out of it what you put into it. Here are a few tips from former U101 students to having a successful U101 experience:

1) **Keep an open mind.** Some of the activities you do in U101 might seem odd or silly. But trust us, all these activities are intentional and have a purpose.

2) **Attend every class.** U101 is a seminar class, meaning that it is a group conversation. Your opinions, perspectives, and experiences are important.

3) **Take advantage of the small class experience** by getting to know your classmates and your instructor. This class is a great way to meet new friends and to have a resource and mentor in your instructor and peer leader.

> **1st Year Student Quote**
>
> I feel that my University 101 experience was extremely beneficial to my adjusting to life at college. I was informed of all of the available resources located here on campus, and it gave me good advice on what to do and what not to do. It gave me a core group of friends to do things with, and from there I made more friends. To this day I'll see one of my fellow U101 classmates around and we'll always say hi and talk to each other just because we were all there for each other in the beginning.

University of South Carolina – The National and International Leader in First-Year Seminars

New-student seminars have been part of the academic curriculum at American colleges and universities for more than 100 years. A first-year seminar was first offered in 1882 at Lees College in Kentucky, but the popularity of these courses has fluctuated since that time. After almost disappearing in the 1960s, the first-year seminar has enjoyed a gradual and steady rebirth across the nation since the mid-1970s, due largely in part to the model that was created here at the University of South Carolina in 1972. Following Carolina's lead, a majority of American colleges and universities have created similar courses. In fact, data from the 2009 National Survey on First-Year Seminars, sponsored by our very own National Resource Center for The First-Year Experience and Students in Transition, indicated that 87% of responding institutions offered some type of new-student seminar.

Did you know?

seminar |semənär| noun
A class at a college or university in which a topic is discussed by a teacher and a small group of students.

The Impetus for University 101

University 101 at the University of South Carolina was born out of student activism. In the late 1960s and early 1970s, many college campuses experienced student protests against the Vietnam War and social injustices. Notable demonstrations occurred at The University of California at Berkeley and Kent State University. Similarly, student unrest affected the University of South Carolina as students voiced their opinions to the faculty and administration in various ways.

In the spring of 1970, the conflict came to a head when approximately 1,000 students turned out to protest the U.S. invasion of Cambodia in addition to other state and campus issues that had been brewing for months. The governor called out the National Guard, and although no shots were fired, the students responded by storming the office of President Thomas Jones and holding him a virtual prisoner for days (Morris & Cutright, 2005).

Student Protest

President Jones interpreted the students' protests as evidence that the University had "failed its students in some fundamental way, and it was incumbent on the institution to do a better job of assimilating students into university life, specifically USC's history, purposes, and traditions" (Morris & Cutright, 2005). Jones believed that the University could help students succeed during their time in college by enhancing their relationships with faculty and staff. In 1972, he introduced University 101 as a first-year seminar course that would focus on helping students be successful rather than on a specific discipline.

Thomas F. Jones, Jr. was elected the 23rd president of USC in 1962 and served until 1974. He was one of the most influential and innovative presidents in USC history.

University 101 Today

The University 101 course today has evolved from the course Jones introduced more than 40 years ago. However, the spirit of University 101 is the same: to promote student success through a small seminar, taught by caring faculty, and focused on transition needs. University 101 is designed to help students make a successful transition to the University of South Carolina, both academically and personally. It is a unique learning experience in that it is a course for first-year students, about first-year students.

University 101 is an elective for approximately 85% of the students enrolled; however, selected student populations such as Opportunity Scholars, Exercise Science majors, Teaching Fellows, and Capstone Scholars are required by their program to take the course. Annual student enrollment has risen to over 80% of the first-year class.

University 101 is taught in small groups (19 students) by faculty and staff members who have a special interest in first-year students. The small class size allows students to learn directly from each other as they share common experiences and establish personal relationships with a college instructor. University 101 is offered in the fall and spring semesters, although the vast majority of University of South Carolina-Columbia students enroll in the fall. Students with fewer than 30 credit-hours and other students enrolled in their first semester are permitted to register for University 101. Transfer students are also permitted to register, but only in their first term at the university.

Peer Leader Advice

As an out-of-state student I was not familiar with the Columbia area and I did not know a single person attending USC. I was so thankful to have the opportunity to take University 101 because it introduced me to so many great Carolinian traditions and people. I learned about exciting events ranging from Tiger Burn to Chicken Finger Wednesday, and suddenly South Carolina began to feel like home. I can't imagine what freshman year would have been like without a class like U101.

- Niki Schieder
Philidephia, PA • Junior
Accounting

UNIVERSITY 101

BY THE NUMBERS

1972 — THE YEAR UNIVERSITY 101 WAS CREATED AT THE UNIVERSITY OF SOUTH CAROLINA

The percent of colleges and universities across the country that have since created a first-year seminar.

87%

Students enrolled in 212 sections of UNIV 101 in Fall 2013 (up from 3441 in Fall 2010)

3880

186 Faculty and staff teaching UNIV 101 in Fall 2013 (145 in 2010)

- 2012: 93%
- 2010: 57%

Sections that utilized a Peer or Graduate Leader in a team-teaching and mentoring capacity.

3.28 UNIV 101
3.16 No UNIV 101

The average first-year GPA of students enrolled in UNIV 101 was higher than those who did not take UNIV 101 in Fall 2011.

 **Faculty Development Excellence**

In 2011, the National Association of Student Personnel Administrators (NASPA) awarded University 101's Faculty Development Program the Gold Excellence Award.

 **11**

Consecutive years that UNIV 101 and the first-year experience at the University of South Carolina have been recognized by *US News & World Report* as a "program to look for."

 **71.1%** UNIV 101   **64.9%** No UNIV 101

The five-year graduation rate for students who took UNIV 101 was significantly higher than those who did not take the course in Fall 2007.

 **88.0%** / **84.4%**

The one-year persistence rate of students who took UNIV 101 was significantly higher than those that did not take the course in Fall 2011.

 **68%** UNIV 101 / **64%** No UNIV 101

The five-year graduation rate for minority students who took UNIV 101 was higher than the graduation rate for minority students who did not take the course in Fall 2007.

20

Types of special sections of UNIV 101 offered in Fall 2013. These include major-specific sections, as well as sections for special populations.

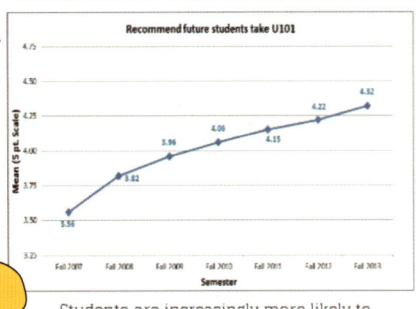

Students are increasingly more likely to recommend that future students take UNIV 101.

92%

UNIV 101 students that reported they would choose to attend USC again if they had to do it over, (compared to 85.5% of non-participants) on the 2009 National Survey of Student Engagement.

University 101 Goals and Learning Outcomes

Each University 101 class may vary in terms of structure and content based on the needs of the students enrolled in the specific course section. Common learning outcomes, however, exist for all sections and are designed to guide student learning around three course goals. The University 101 course is designed to

1. Foster academic success
2. Help students discover and connect with the University of South Carolina
3. Prepare students for responsible lives in a diverse, interconnected, and changing world

These three goals will be achieved through the demonstration of the following 13 learning outcomes.

I. Foster Academic Success

As a result of this course, students will

- Adapt and apply appropriate academic strategies to their courses and learning experiences
- Demonstrate how to effectively evaluate information sources and utilize University libraries and information systems for academic inquiry
- Recognize the purpose and value of academic integrity and describe the key themes related to the Honor Code at the University of South Carolina
- Use written and oral communication to discover, develop, and articulate ideas and viewpoints
- Identify and apply strategies to effectively manage time and priorities
- Have knowledge of relevant academic polices, processes, and procedures related to advising, course planning, and major exploration

II. Help Students Discover and Connect With the University of South Carolina

As a result of this course, students will

- Become familiar with appropriate campus resources and opportunities that contribute to their educational experiences, goals, and campus engagement
- Develop and apply skills that contribute to building positive relationships with peers, staff, and faculty
- Describe what it means to be a Carolinian in context of the history, traditions, and culture of the University

III. Prepare Students for Responsible Lives in a Diverse, Interconnected, and Changing World

As a result of this course, students will

- Examine how their background and experiences impact their values and assumptions and explain the influence these have on their relationships with others
- Be able to articulate concepts of diversity and recognize diverse perspectives
- Describe and demonstrate principles of responsible citizenship within and beyond the campus community
- Identify processes, strategies, and resources related to their overall wellness and explain the implications of their decisions

Your University 101 Instructors

Each University 101 class is taught by a University faculty or staff member and may be cotaught by an outstanding upper-division undergraduate (peer leader) or second-year graduate student (graduate leader) who will serve as a mentor, resource, and facilitator for learning during the semester. There are close to 200 instructors from over 70 departments across campus teaching University 101, and what they all have in common is a desire to help first-year students be successful. University 101 instructors receive extensive training and have a strong desire to provide a high quality learning environment. You can consider your University 101 instructors as primary resources for both academic and cocurricular situations when you need help. If your instructors cannot assist you directly, they will know how to connect you with a campus expert who can.

University 101 Peer Leader Program

The University 101 Peer Leader Program at the University of South Carolina has been an important component of the University 101 course since 1993. Outstanding rising junior and senior students are recruited to help incoming first-year students navigate their Carolina experience by serving as role models, mentors, and facilitators for learning. Peer Leaders model academic success and involvement in the Carolina community for new students, while helping them successfully begin their Carolina experience. A former UNIV 101 student reflected on her peer leader, "She gave great insight because she has been through it and experienced what we are going through now." Look to your University 101 Peer Leader for advice and guidance in the classroom and beyond!

Instructor Quote

As a University 101 Instructor, we are not just a teacher, we are a part of a first-year student's experience. Teaching this course has been one of the most rewarding opportunities of my career.

- Viki Fecas
University 101 Instructor
2013 Teaching Award Recipient

Did you know?

The average GPA for U101 Peer Leaders is a 3.72!

ON THE WEB

For more information about the University 101 Peer Leader Program, visit:

www.sc.edu/univ101/peerleaders

and check them out on Facebook:

 facebook.com/U101peerleaders

University 101 Peer Leaders

Get Involved!

If after this semester you are interested in continuing your involvement with the University 101 program and would like to assist with the teaching of a course in your junior and/or senior year, you are encouraged to apply to become a University 101 Peer Leader. University 101 Peer Leaders exemplify the principles of the Carolinian Creed, have a 3.0 or higher GPA, and are involved in a wide variety of campus groups and organizations.

University 101 Sponsored Awards

Each year, the University 101 Program recognizes and rewards outstanding students, faculty, and staff for their contributions to the first-year experience at Carolina. Students who have successfully completed University 101 in the past year may be nominated for a University 101 Scholarship. Faculty, staff, and students may also be nominated for the Outstanding Advocate for First-Year Students, and University 101 students may recommend their University 101 instructor for the Teaching Award. All scholarship and Advocate Award recipients are recognized annually at the University of South Carolina Awards Day ceremony.

University 101 Scholarships

University 101 scholarships recognize undergraduate students who have made major contributions to their University 101 class and who have incorporated the course ideals and values into their academic and cocurricular experiences. To apply for the scholarship, a student must first be nominated by his or her University 101 instructor. Instructors recommend students based primarily on the impact they have had on the overall success of the class. Nominated students are then invited to submit an essay demonstrating their unique contributions to their University 101 class and to the University community through their academic excellence, campus involvement, and community service. Each spring, the selection committee awards up to 10 recipients a $500 scholarship to apply to their tuition the following academic year. Out of state recipients may also receive a tuition discount for the year as their award.

Outstanding Advocate for First-Year Students Award

Many members of the University community take a very special interest in the welfare and success of first-year students. For the past 19 years, University 101 has given formal recognition to such individuals by honoring them as Outstanding Advocates for First-Year Students. A plaque honoring previous recipients of the award is displayed prominently in the Russell House.

If, during your first year at the University of South Carolina, someone makes an important and positive difference in your academic or personal life, you are encouraged to nominate this individual for the award. In the fall semester, a call for nominations will be posted on the University 101 website and featured on the University home page. Your nominee may be any member of the campus community whom you regard as an exceptional advocate for first-year students.

University 101 Teaching Award

As one way of recognizing the great work of our instructors, University 101 Programs sponsors an award for outstanding teaching in University 101. This award was established to recognize one University 101 instructor annually who demonstrates exemplary teaching and achievement of course outcomes and has made a positive impact on student lives. All University 101 students, peer leaders, and graduate leaders at the USC Columbia campus are invited to nominate their University 101 instructor for this award following the completion of each fall semester. Nominees are notified of their selection and are invited to apply for the award by submitting a curriculum vitae (CV), syllabus, and a brief statement on their philosophy of teaching first-year students. The award recipient is recognized at the annual Building Connections Conference in May and receives a $500 award and a plaque honoring this important achievement.

ON THE WEB

For more information about University 101 Awards, visit: **www.sc.edu/univ101/awards**

University 101 Programs

University 101 Programs is an academic unit at the University of South Carolina that offers four courses that support students' transition into and through their college experience.

In addition to the University 101 course, University 101 Programs offers:

University 201: Fundamentals of Inquiry
This course focuses on the essential components of research. University 201 is designed to challenge students to discover the benefits of inquiry while exploring a variety of subject areas. Topics vary to engage students in current interests and events. Previous UNIV 201 courses have included: *Ever Wonder Why????A Look at Positive Human Behavior, James Bond & Cultural Inquiry, Researching Slang at USC,* and *Service-Learning in South Carolina.*

University 290, Special Topics in Residential College
This one-credit hour course for students in a living-learning community covers topics aligned with the mission and goals of the particular community. Recent courses have included the following communities: Capstone Scholars, Green Quad, Magellan Scholars, Healthy Carolina, Bridge Program, Journalism, and Pre-Health Studies. Students enrolled have travelled to Detroit, Costa Rica, and most recently, Iceland!

University 401, Senior Capstone Experience
This seminar is designed to prepare juniors and seniors for the transition to their career or graduate school following graduation. Students enrolled in specific sections of University 401 usually share the same academic major and/or career goals. The course is designed to assist students in bringing closure to their college experience through systematic, intentional reflection on both the student's major and, in general, their liberal arts education. Recent courses have included: *Graduation with Leadership Distinction, Transitioning to Medical School, Pre-Law, Journalism, Synthesizing the Sciences, Preparing for a Career in Higher Education/Student Affairs,* and *Medical School Application Process.*

ON THE WEB

For more information about these courses, visit:
www.sc.edu/univ101/courses

University 101 Programs is part of a larger department that also houses the National Resource Center for The First-Year Experience & Students in Transition. The National Resource Center serves as the trusted expert, internationally recognized leader, and clearinghouse for scholarship, policy, and best practice for all postsecondary student transitions. The primary purpose of the Center is to support and advance efforts to improve student learning and transitions into and through higher education.

University 101 and the National Resource Center work together as one functionally integrated academic unit to build and sustain a vibrant campus-based and diverse educational community committed to the success of first-year college students and all students in transition. University 101 achieves this through the University 101 seminar and its other academic courses. The National Resource Center carries this mission beyond the University campus by sponsoring a series of national and international conferences, online courses for educators, seminars, and workshops; publishing a peer-reviewed journal, an electronic newsletter, a monograph series, and other publications; and maintaining a resource website and several electronic mailing lists.

If you would like to learn more about the University 101 seminar, our other academic courses, or the work of the National Resource Center, you are invited to visit our office any time during regular office hours.

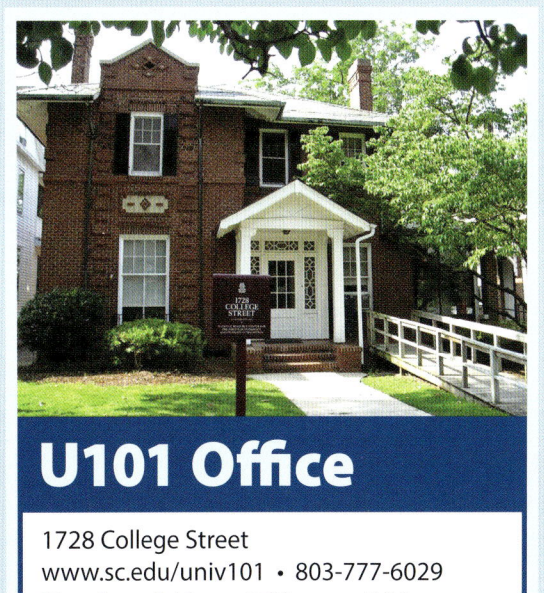

U101 Office

1728 College Street
www.sc.edu/univ101 • 803-777-6029
Monday – Friday • 8:30 a.m. – 5:00 p.m.

ON THE WEB

Meet the University 101 Staff!
www.sc.edu/univ101/contactus

CONSIDER THIS

What do you know about University 101?
What have you heard from other students and University faculty and staff?

___

Why did you take this course?
If the class is required for your major or program, why do you think it is a requirement?

___

What do you expect to learn as a result of your participation in this course?

___

Which University 101 Learning Outcome are you most excited to explore this semester?

___

What expectations do you have for your instructor and peer or graduate leader?

___

CONSIDER THIS

How will you be an engaged and active learner in the University 101 classroom?

How will you share your ideas openly and confidently?

What will you do to be prepared?

In what ways can you intentionally build positive relationships with your classmates and instructor(s)?

REFERENCES

Morris, L.V. & Cutright, M. (2005). University of South Carolina: Creator and standard-bearer for the first-year experience. In B.O. Barefoot, et.al., *Achieving and sustaining institutional excellence for the first year of college* (pp. 349-376). San Francisco, CA: Jossey-Bass.

Page 4 photo - Student Protest: *University of South Carolina Libraries: Caroliniana Columns, 27*, p. 3. Copyright 2010 by the University of South Carolina. Reprinted with permission.

Page 4 photo - Thomas F. Jones, Jr.: http://library.sc.edu/socar/archives/finding_aids/jones.htm

Chapter Two

Discovering Carolina

Dear First-Year Student,

"Carolina feels like home." That is the message we hear from many of our incoming students, some of whom made their decisions to apply to and enroll in the University of South Carolina the moment they first stepped onto the historic Horseshoe. With its tree-lined brick pathways, lush lawn, and federal architecture, there is no denying it is a beautiful spot. But there is more to that feeling of home than simply appearance. There are 200 years of history and tradition that have shaped Carolina into the premier place of learning and living it is today.

Though the students who came before you followed different fashion trends and never imagined sending text messages to celebrate a Gamecocks victory, you have a lot in common. Just like you, generations of Carolinians have studied on the Horseshoe grass, raised a "health" during the singing of the alma mater, pored over *The Daily Gamecock*, and cheered on the Garnet and Black.

This is not to say, however, that we are stuck in the past. Every day at the University of South Carolina, we are generating innovative ideas through research, scholarship, and leadership endeavors. We are forging new traditions, like Alternative Break Service Trips, Parents Weekend, and Graduation with Leadership Distinction.

There are infinite possibilities for you—in your own way—to contribute to Carolina's great legacy by participating in these time-honored traditions and by creating new ones to enhance our vibrant campus culture. Learn about where the University has been and where it is going, then decide how you will be a part of it—how you can be a model for future Carolinians.

Start by reading the *Carolinian Creed*. Written by a group of our students, faculty, and staff, it describes the principles that guide our lives as members of the Carolina community, the attributes that distinguish us from all others. The Creed, quite simply, is what it means to be a Carolinian.

I wish you, a new Carolinian, all the best.

Dennis A. Pruitt
Vice President for Student Affairs,
Vice Provost and Dean of Students

YOU chose Carolina and Carolina chose you! Through the presentation of the University's rich history and an introduction to the traditions that are unique to the South Carolina community, this chapter will help you begin to understand what it means to be a Carolinian. Your journey of discovery will continue as you explore the wealth of opportunities available to Carolina students, take advantage of many learning experiences, and make Carolina your home.

As a student at Carolina, it is important to understand and appreciate the University of South Carolina's history so that you can better understand your role as a member of the community and determine the impact that you want to have on the University's future. There are many traditions at Carolina that are rooted in the past, and as you explore its history, you will begin to understand the culture of your campus and feel a growing connection as you become a true Carolinian!

Keeping It Cocky Since 1801: A Chronological History

(Adapted from http://www.sc.edu/about/our_history/index.php and http://www.sc.edu/about/our_history/ and used with permission.)

The University of South Carolina, chartered on December 19, 1801 as South Carolina College, was a part of an effort to unite South Carolinians in the wake of the American Revolution. South Carolina's leaders saw the new college as a way to promote "the good order and harmony" of the state. The founding of South Carolina College was also a part of the Southern public college movement spurred by Thomas Jefferson. In the antebellum era, South Carolina College was the first university in the United States to be supported continuously by annual state appropriations.

In the years before the Civil War, South Carolina College rapidly achieved a reputation for academic excellence and was known as one of the best endowed and most distinguished colleges in the country. The institution featured impressive faculty, including such noted European scholars as Francis Lieber, editor of the *Encyclopedia Americana*; nationally known scientists John and Joseph LeConte; chemist William Ellet, who produced some of the first daguerreotype photographs (e.g., images made on light-sensitive, silver-coated, metallic plates) in the United States; and Thomas Cooper, a man Thomas Jefferson referred to as "the greatest man in America, in the powers of mind, and in acquired information" (Honeywell, 1931, pp. 90-91). By the 1830s, almost all of the state's General Assembly members were distinguished alumni of the University. James H. Hammond and Wade Hampton III were the most

CONSIDER THIS

Before you begin reading this chapter, take a moment and reflect on the experiences that brought you here to the University of South Carolina:

What first attracted you to the University?

Did you visit campus before attending? If so, how were you welcomed? Were you greeted by a University Ambassador? An Admissions Counselor?

What opportunities did you hear about that made you excited to join the Carolina family?

1801

Governor John Drayton delivers a message to the South Carolina General Assembly recommending the establishment of a state-supported college. With little opposition, the South Carolina General Assembly approved the legislation that established South Carolina College.

Photo courtesy of the South Caroliniana Library

Longstreet Theatre, 1875

Did you know?

The University of South Carolina Columbia campus has grown from one building in 1805, with an enrollment of 29 (all male, all white) and a limited curriculum of mathematics and classical languages, to a diverse enrollment of more than 30,000 students, and more than 324 programs of study.

(Adapted from http://www.sc.edu/uscmap/bldg/buildings_history.html and used with permission.)

prominent of the future governors, senators, judges, and generals who graduated during the pre-Civil War period.

Offering a traditional classical curriculum, South Carolina College became one of the most influential colleges in the South before 1861, earning a reputation as the training ground for South Carolina's antebellum elite. The pre-Civil War campus included Longstreet Theatre and all of the buildings (with the exception of the McKissick Museum) in the area known today as the Horseshoe. When the voluntary enlistment of all its students into Confederate service forced the College to close in June 1862, the buildings were confiscated by the Confederate government for use as hospital facilities. By the time Sherman's army reached Columbia in February 1865, the campus buildings contained several wounded Union soldiers. A fire soon destroyed most of the city, but federal troops helped save the historic Horseshoe from the flames.

State leaders revived the institution in 1866 as the University of South Carolina with ambitious plans for a diverse university that included the first African-American students admitted in 1873. While politically controversial, this development was an extraordinary opportunity for South Carolinians at a time when opportunities for higher education were rare. The University of South Carolina became the only Southern state university to admit and grant degrees to African-American students. The leaders of the university were very conservative and, as a result, closed the university once again in 1877. When they reopened the doors in 1880, the college was an all-white agricultural college and was called South Carolina College of Agriculture and Mechanical Arts. The University faced additional challenges in the 1890s adjusting to the arrival of women and intercollegiate athletics on campus. In 1894, USC agreed to admit women as students, becoming the first collegiate institute in the state to allow coeducation.

Over the next 25 years, the institution became enmeshed in the upheaval of late 19th century South Carolina politics. Carolina went through several reorganizations in which the curriculum frequently changed and its status shifted from college to university and back again. In 1906, the institution was rechartered for the final time as the University of South Carolina. In the early decades of the 20th century, Carolina made strides toward becoming a comprehensive university, and in 1917 it became the first state-supported college or university in South Carolina to earn regional accreditation.

The 1920s witnessed further progress and growth with the introduction of new colleges and degree programs, including the doctorate. The Great Depression temporarily stalled this progress, but the outbreak of World War II launched an era that transformed the university. Carolina hosted U.S. Navy training programs during the war and enrollment more than doubled in the post war era as veterans took advantage of the G.I. Bill. In sharp contrast to the South Carolina College's antebellum elitist philosophy, President William Davis Melton in 1925 expressed a far-reaching principle that emerged in the first quarter of the century saying, "Education is not a special privilege to be enjoyed by a special few." Thus, in its final reorganization, the University of South Carolina developed the institutional objective to provide both liberal and professional education to the people of South Carolina.

In the 1950s, the university began recruiting national-caliber faculty and extended its presence beyond Columbia with the establishment of campuses in communities across South Carolina. On Sept. 11, 1963, Henrie D. Monteith, Robert Anderson, and James Solomon became the first African-American students to enroll at the university in the 20th century; in 1965, Monteith became the first African-American graduate, earning a Bachelor of Science degree in biochemistry.

In the ensuing years, Carolina underwent explosive growth as enrollment stood at 5,660 in 1960, but by 1979 had reached nearly 26,000 students on the Columbia campus alone. To meet the needs of these students and South Carolina's changing economy, the university put new emphasis on research and introduced innovative degree programs as well as a number of new schools and colleges. Carolina had become a true research university.

Since then, dynamic academic expansion and the development of a statewide network of campuses produced highly diverse and innovative educational programs. An increasing commitment to graduate education, along with involvement in major research programs, attracted an outstanding faculty. Moreover, an intense building program resulted in the construction of excellent modern physical facilities as well as the preservation of historic pre-Civil War buildings.

Today, the University of South Carolina, Columbia is not only the state's flagship university but also a rising national star. USC is increasingly an institution of choice among the best and brightest students in the nation. Carolina is 1 of 40 public universities to receive the Carnegie Foundation's highest research designation. The University system serves the entire state and includes, in addition to the Columbia campus, three 4-year campuses (Aiken, Beaufort, and Upstate) and four regional campuses (Sumter, Lancaster, Salkehatchie, and Union). In keeping with its 19th- and 20th-century heritage, the University continues to promote academic excellence while offering progressive educational opportunities to the citizens of South Carolina. With 45,000 students on eight campuses, nationally respected faculty and nearly 260,000 alumni, the University of South Carolina has a bright future to match its rich history.

University of South Carolina— Columbia Campus Mission Statement

The primary mission of the University of South Carolina Columbia is the education of the state's citizens through teaching, research, creative activity, and community engagement. Among America's oldest and most comprehensive public universities, USC Columbia is the major research institution of the University of South Carolina system and its largest campus, enrolling approximately 21,000 undergraduate students and approximately 8,000 students in graduate and professional programs. At the heart of its mission lies the University's responsibility to state and society to promote the dissemination of knowledge, cultural enrichment, and an enhanced quality of life.

(Reprinted with permission from http://www.sc.edu/aboutusc/columbiaMission.shtml.)

Points of Pride

#1

The Undergraduate International Business Program was named #1 in the nation by *U.S. News & World Report*

BEST

The South Carolina Honors College was named Best Public University Honors College in the U.S.

GREEN

Carolina received the highest possible score on Princeton Review's "Green Ratings" for sustainability

The History of the Horseshoe

The buildings on the Horseshoe form the original campus and are now the heart of the University. Listed on the National Register of Historic Places, this modified quadrangle was the next major building project in Columbia after completion of the state capitol. Most of these buildings reflect the federal style of architecture common in the early 1800s.

As in all architecture, climate was the dominant influence in the college's design. Fires were always a threat to the buildings in the winter because fireplaces in each room were the only available means of heating. The buildings were made of brick, which was locally available and inexpensive. Also, the main floors, designed as faculty residences, were above ground level, which promoted air circulation during South Carolina's infamous long, hot summers. Robert Mills, the nation's first federal architect and the designer of the Washington Monument, greatly influenced the architecture of South Carolina College. Mills was involved in the design of Rutledge College, the South Caroliniana Library, and the Maxcy Monument in the center of the Horseshoe, named for the first president of the college, Jonathan Maxcy.

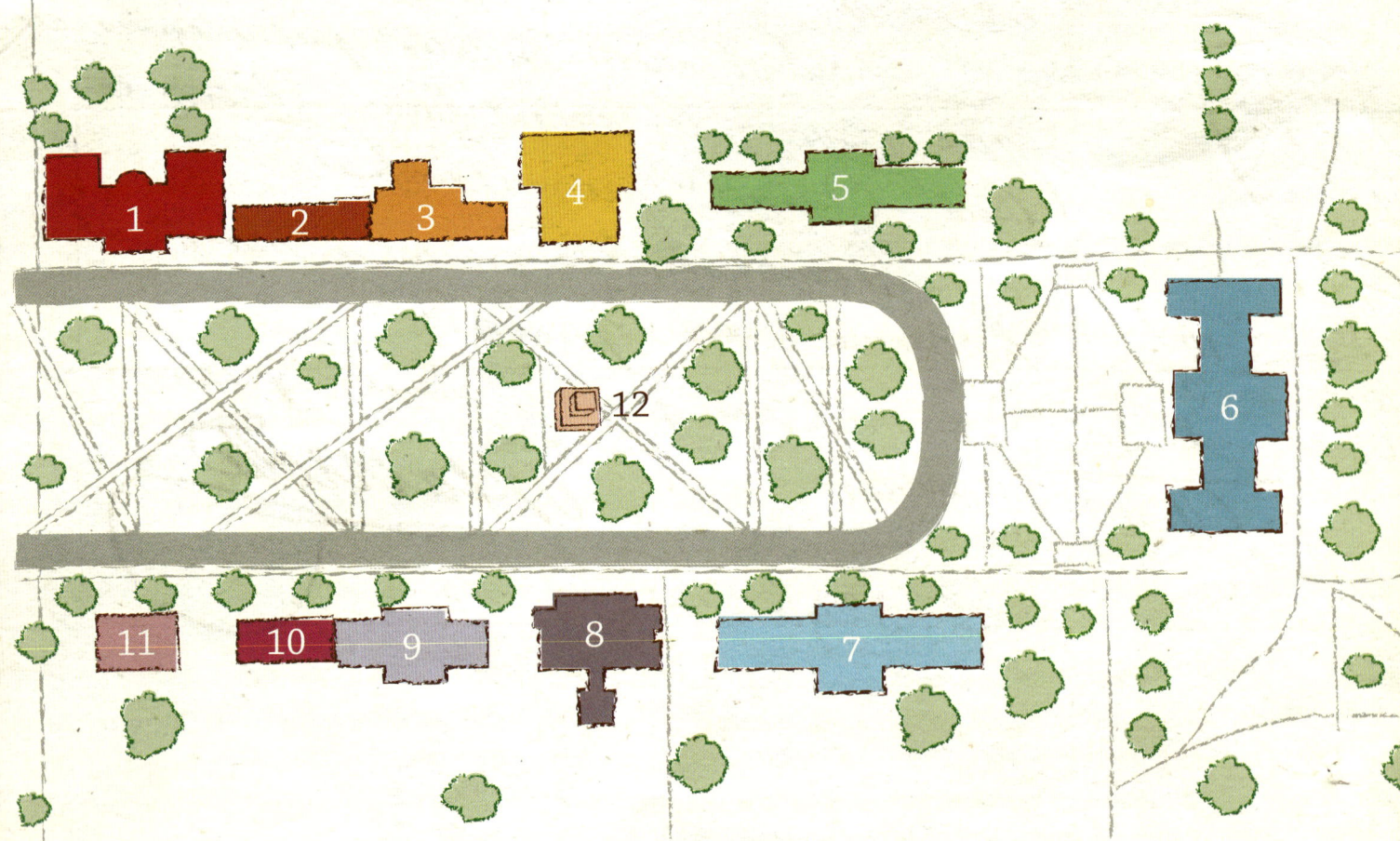

Chapter 2: Discovering Carolina

 **SOUTH CAROLINIANA LIBRARY (1840)**

Then: South Caroliniana served as the main library on campus until the construction of McKissick Memorial Library (now McKissick Museum) in 1940.

Now: The library houses extensive collections concentrating on South Carolina.

Fun Facts: Landmarked as the first freestanding college library in the United States, the South Caroliniana Library is the most architecturally distinctive building on the Horseshoe. The grave in front is that of J. Rion McKissick, president of the University, 1936-1944.

 **ELLIOTT COLLEGE (1837)**

Then: Constructed to accommodate the growing campus, Elliott College served as a dormitory.

Now: Today this building houses students of the South Carolina Honors College.

Fun Facts: It is named for Stephen Elliott (1777-1830), the first president of the Bank of the State of South Carolina. Along with Harper College, Elliott mirrors the Pinckney and Legare buildings across the lawn.

 **HARPER COLLEGE (1848)**

Then: Built to be used as a dormitory, when classes were suspended in March 1862, Harper, along with other campus buildings, was used as a hospital. In 1865, the Federal army used four interior rooms as a military prison.

Now: Now it is home to the Office of Fellowships and Scholar Programs. Elliott and Harper serve as housing for upper-level students in the South Carolina Honors College.

Fun Facts: The building is named for William Harper, Class of 1808, a noted South Carolina judge and U.S. senator. One of the two original student organizations, the Euphradian Literary Society, held its meetings in Harper. The societies died out by the 1980s, but Euphradian Hall, located on the third floor, has been restored.

 **MCCUTCHEN HOUSE (1813)**

Then: McCutchen, Formerly the Second Professors House, was built to house two faculty families.

Now: Home of the School of Hotel, Restaurant, and Tourism Management's student-run restaurant.

Fun Facts: The building is named for William Harper, Class of 1808, a noted South Carolina judge and U.S. senator. One of the two original student organizations, the Euphradian Literary Society, held its meetings in Harper. The societies died out by the 1980s, but Euphradian Hall, located on the third floor, has been restored.

 **DESAUSSURE COLLEGE (1809)**

Then: During the Civil War, DeSaussure College was part of the general hospital. Through the years, DeSaussure was used as a federal military prison and later as the home of the Normal School for the training of secondary teachers.

Now: Home for the College of Social Work and student residences.

Fun Facts: Named for Henry William DeSaussure (1763-1839), director of the U.S. Mint and chancellor of the state of South Carolina, this building is the second oldest on campus.

 **MCKISSICK MUSEUM (1940)**

Then: McKissick Memorial Library served as the primary library until the construction of Thomas Cooper Library (1959).

Now: McKissick is home of the University's Visitor Center and offers outstanding collections, exhibitions, and educational activities in history, natural science, and art.

Fun Facts: Named for J. Rion McKissick, president from 1936 to 1944, and his wife, Caroline. McKissick.

 RUTLEDGE COLLEGE (1805)

Then: Rutledge College contained all college facilities, including faculty and student housing, classrooms, library, chapel, and labs. Gutted by fire in 1855, it was rebuilt immediately.

Now: Home to the Department of Religious Studies, student residences, and a chapel, often used for weddings and funerals.

Fun Facts: The first building to be erected at South Carolina College. Formerly referred to as South Building, Old South Building, Old South, or simply South, it is named for John Rutledge (1739-1800), governor of South Carolina, and his brother Edward (1749-1800), also a governor and a signer of the Declaration of Independence.

 PRESIDENT'S HOUSE (1810, REBUILT 1854)

Then: A faculty residence until the 1940s, it was later converted to a women's residence hall.

Now: In 1952, it was transformed into the official President's House, enhanced by the beautiful downstairs library and the splendid reception room on the second floor. The latest renovation was completed in 2003.

Fun Facts: The home of the president of the University is the most elegant building on the Horseshoe. The second floor contains several public rooms one of which features wallpaper with an oriental theme that dates from 1832. There also includes an alcove with a chair that was specially made for the visit of Pope John Paul II in September, 1987.

 LEGARE COLLEGE (1848)

Then: This building once housed the Clariosophic Literary Society, one of the original student organizations.

Now: Legare houses the Study Abroad Office, Office of Undergraduate Research, Office of Fellowships and Scholar Programs, student residences, and departmental or administrative offices.

Fun Facts: Pronounced "Luh-gree", the building was named for Hugh Swinton Legare, Class of 1814, a U.S. attorney general and founder of the Southern Review.

 PINCKNEY COLLEGE (1837)

Then: Built as a residence hall and a twin to Elliott College across the Horseshoe.

Now: Now serves as a coed, apartment-style residence hall.

Fun Facts: It is named for a family long prominent in South Carolina, one of whom, Charles Cotesworth Pinckney (1757-1824), authored the Pinckney Draft of the U.S. Constitution. A statesman and diplomat, Charles Cotesworth Pinckney also fought with General George Washington during the Revolutionary War and was the first elected board member of the South Carolina College.

 LIEBER COLLEGE (1837)

Then: The Third Professors House, now known as Lieber College, was a duplex home that accommodated two faculty families.

Now: Home to the Office of Undergraduate Admissions.

Fun Facts: The three stories of exposed brick, white trim, austere lines, and small windowpanes are the embodiment of the early architecture of the campus. It was named for Francis Lieber (1800-1872), an illustrious faculty member and editor of the Encyclopedia Americana.

 MAXCY MONUMENT (1827)

Then: The Maxcy Monument in the center of the Horseshoe was built by Clariosophic Society to honor Reverend Jonathan Maxcy, first president of the South Carolina College, from 1805 to 1820.

Now: The Maxcy Monument still serves as a focal point of the historic Horseshoe.

Fun Facts: The Maxcy Monument cost $873 to build and was designed by Robert Mills, the nation's first federal architect and the designer of the Washington Monument. Mills was involved in the design of Rutledge, South Caroliniana Library, and the Maxcy Monument.

Carolina History

1801 to 1850

1801-South Carolina College
The University of South Carolina was chartered in 1801.

1803- University Seal
The seal of the University was adopted.

1852-The Great Biscuit Rebellion
The Board of Trustees refuse to give in to student demands to improve the food on campus.

1805- First Students Attend
The first students entered South Carolina College on January 10, 1805.

1850 to 1899

1862- S.C. College Closes
Voluntary enlistment of all its students into Confederate service forced the College to close in June 1862.

1830's- Distinguished Alumni
Almost all of the state's General Assembly members were alumni of the University.

1866- Institution Revived
State leaders revived the institution in 1866 as the University of South Carolina.

1875- Minority Graduates
The University grants the first bachelors degrees to black graduates.

1902-Tiger Burn
The tradition of Tiger Burn grew from the 1902 feud between University of South Carolina and Clemson University.

1894- Women Admitted
USC agreed to admit women as students, becoming the first collegiate institute in the state to allow coeducation.

1900 to 1950

1908- The Daily Gamecock
The Daily Gamecock was first published in 1908 as a joint venture between the different campus literary societies.

1911- Alma Mater
The University's alma mater was written in 1911 by George A. Wauchope, an English professor, and set to the music of Robert Burns' "Flow Gently, Sweet Afton."

1963- Integration
On Sept. 11, 1963, Henrie D. Monteith, Robert Anderson, and James Solomon became the first African-American students to enroll at the university in the 20th century.

1950 to 2000

1972-University 101
USC introduces the first-year seminar course as a way to help students transition.

1980-Cocky Arrives
Cocky first took action at USC events in 1980.

2001- A Space Odyssey
USC introduces what has been named "the most exciting pregame entry in all of college football". The song was introduced in USC's bicentennial year and is now game day tradition!

2000 to Present

1990 Carolinian Creed
After two years of planning, the Carolinian Creed was created in 1990 as a campus social honor code.

2004- Green Quad Opens
USC opens the world's largest sustainable residence hall-West Quad (172,000 square feet) which uses 45% less energy and 20% less water than other residence halls on campus.

Chapter 2: Discovering Carolina

Noteworthy Moments in University History

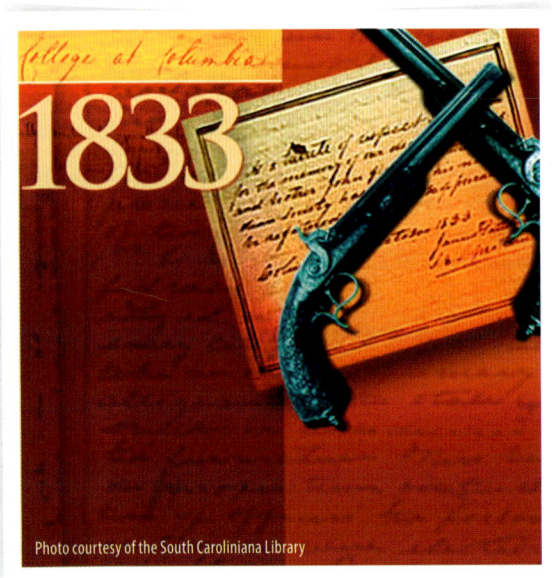

Photo courtesy of the South Caroliniana Library

The history of the University of South Carolina is rich with events and stories that have significantly impacted campus identity today. Ranging from important steps to providing opportunities for any citizen to attend college, to oddities like Barefoot Day and the infamous student duel between A. Govan Roach and James G. Adams, these events help tell the story of how South Carolina College became the University of South Carolina.

Student Duel

College students have historically engaged in playing pranks or mischievous behavior. Common student misbehaviors on the University campus during the 1800s included throwing rocks through the windows of the President's residence (this behavior prompted the administration to enforce a glass tax to help supplement the cost of replacing broken glass) or stealing livestock from the surrounding neighborhoods. Fortunately, typical student misconduct did not result in much harm; however, the shenanigans of an infamous student duo, best friends A. Govan Roach and James G. Adams, met a fatal end in 1833. The tradition of the steward's, or dining hall, was that when a man got hold of a dish of bread, or any other dish, it was his. Unfortunately, Roach and Govan both caught hold of a dish of trout at the same moment. Adams did not let go; Roach held on to the dish. Roach let go of the dish and glared fiercely at Adams' face, and said, "I will see you after supper." Roach left the dining hall first and Adams immediately followed him. A battle between the two friends outside ensued and Adams was killed. Roach was left permanently lame and drank himself to death two years later (Geiger, 2000, pp. 100-101).

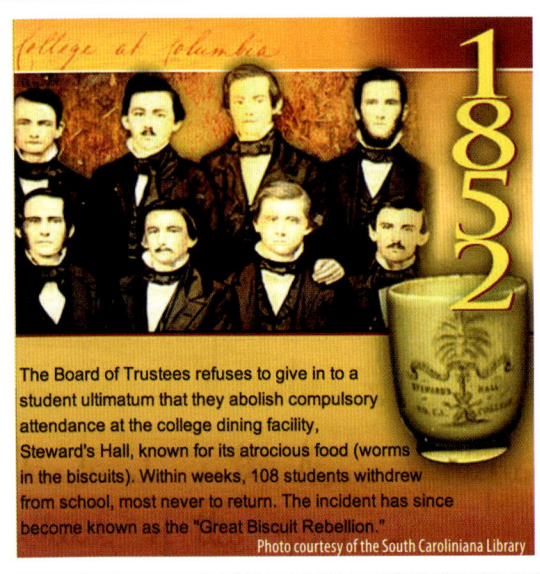

The Board of Trustees refuses to give in to a student ultimatum that they abolish compulsory attendance at the college dining facility, Steward's Hall, known for its atrocious food (worms in the biscuits). Within weeks, 108 students withdrew from school, most never to return. The incident has since become known as the "Great Biscuit Rebellion."

Photo courtesy of the South Caroliniana Library

Campus Dining and the Great Biscuit Rebellion

(Reprinted with permission from Carolinian *[April, 2003])*

The subject of campus food is seasoned throughout Carolina's history, starting in December 1806 when the first college dining hall was completed and all 56 students ate their meals there for $2.50 per week.

Things might have gotten off to a good start at the old steward's hall, as it was then known, but it did not last long. A massive case of indigestion plagued the campus for years, characterized by strikes, civil disturbances, mass disobedience, and declining enrollment, which all were linked to Carolina's poor-quality food in the 19th century. It did not help that dining in steward's hall was mandatory.

The first outright rebellion against campus food occurred in 1827 when a boycott by students led to the expulsion of 41 scholars. Before the action, students had broken into the home of the campus steward and thrown his silver, plates, and furniture into the college well. President Jonathan Maxcy complained that the college "was in yearly jeopardy of being destroyed because of disputes about eating."

Perhaps the most notorious campus unrest happened in 1852 during what came to be known as the Great Biscuit Rebellion. One hundred eight students who were required to eat on campus demanded that they be allowed to eat off campus because they found worms in their biscuits. Trustees were displeased by the ultimatum, but before the impasse could be resolved, the students withdrew from the college, with only a few returning to campus.

The mass withdrawal reduced the junior class in 1852 from 56 to 11 and only 11 seniors graduated in 1853, the smallest class since 1823. The next year the trustees abolished the compulsory dining system.

Integration

The University of South Carolina has been racially integrated twice. In 1873, the Radical Republicans demanded the University accept black students, making it the only state-supported Southern university to integrate fully during the Reconstruction Period. When the Democrats came to power again in 1877, the University was closed, reorganized, and reopened in 1880 as an all-white institution. The University integrated for a second and final time in 1963.

After integration of African American students occurred in 1873, the push for equality in education heightened and was extended to women. Female students were not allowed to enroll at the University until 1895, and the first women graduated in 1898. Most of the students and faculty members did not want women attending the University. One faculty member referred to them as "that monstrous regiment of women" (Monstrous Regiment, 1998, para. 2). However, female students soon proved themselves to be fully capable of competing academically with their male counterparts. Every year since 1981, the University of South Carolina has enrolled more women than men.

Female students

Did you know?
In fall 2013, 54% of first-year students at University of South Carolina were female.

Integration

Rat Cap

Did you know?

If you are interested in learning more about the history of the University of South Carolina or any of the events presented in this chapter, check out these resources:

Caroliniana Library
located on the historic Horseshoe

- Hosts a collection of historical documents and artifacts in the University's rich history

Digital Archives
sc.edu/library/socar/archives

- Links to the *Garnet & Black Yearbook* dating back to 1899
- Photographs and images of the campus and student life
- Exhibits depicting significant events throughout University history

Bicentennial Timeline
sc.edu/bicentennial/pages/
timeline.html

- A digital tour of our history created as part of the University's 200th birthday

Barefoot Day

In the early 1900s, it was customary for upper-level students to haze the newest students on campus. One notable tradition was that first-year students were required to purchase and wear a beanie style cap, known as a rat cap, at all times up until a day late in spring known as Barefoot Day. On Barefoot Day, first-year students were allowed to remove their caps but had to walk barefoot throughout the day. Only the male students were expected to participate in the barefoot activity as it was considered improper during this time period for women to be seen without shoes. In addition to a campus of bare feet, on Barefoot Day upper-level students spent the day hazing the first-year males by ordering them to perform silly or outlandish tasks.

Wednesday, April 6, 1938, marked the end of the Barefoot Day tradition when some upper-level students told a group of first-year male students to kiss the female students as they passed them on campus. Many of the female students were disturbed by this behavior and fled from the men as they chased them in pursuit of a kiss. One first-year student, Hugh Tarte, was credited as the student responsible for much of the chaos that ensued that day. Although he seemed to be the leader of the commotion, Tarte was not the only first-year student that behaved poorly; complaints flooded the administration offices and several female students took legal action against the male students and the University.

President Ron McKissick was deeply disturbed by the behavior of these students and, in an address to the student body said,

> In the years past there have sometime been gross disorder and misconduct here, but I say to you that nothing in all our long past has been so disgraceful, so contemptible, so cowardly, so brutal, so unworthy of gentlemen and so outrageous as what took place in our campus yesterday. (McKissick records, 1938)

As a result of the events of that day, Hugh Tarte was expelled from the University, most of the other male students involved were suspended for the remainder of the semester, and the hazing tradition of Barefoot Day was abolished, although students continued to wear rat caps until the early 1960s.

Other Noteworthy Moments in University of South Carolina History

1896
On November 12 at 11:00 a.m., a rainy Thursday, a football team from Clemson Agricultural College kicks off to a team from South Carolina College on the state fairgrounds in front of a crowd of 2,000. This began the famed Big Thursday football series between South Carolina's two largest public colleges. Carolina won this meeting 12-6.

1909
President William Howard Taft becomes the first sitting president to visit the USC campus.

1957
Senator John F. Kennedy delivered the commencement address at USC.

1963
Henri Dobbins Monteith files suit in federal court seeking to become the first African American to attend USC since 1877. Her suit was ultimately successful, and she and two other students broke the University's 84-year color barrier.

1972
A crowd of 300 students stage a sit-in on Greene Street in order to convince administration to close the street to vehicular traffic. After years of student agitation, a compromise, which closed the street during peak class hours, was finally worked out in 1977.

1980
USC's Longstreet Theater plays host to a debate between candidates for the Republican presidential nomination. Future presidents Ronald Reagan and George Bush participated, along with Tennessee Senator Howard Baker and former Texas Governor John Connally.

1987
Pope John Paul speaks to a crowd of 8,000 gathered in front of the President's Home, declaring "It is wonderful to be young, it is wonderful to be a student, it is wonderful to be a student at the University of South Carolina."

1991
Archbishop Desmond Tutu gives the commencement address in Columbia and receives the honorary degree of Doctor of Human Letters. Tutu won the Nobel Peace Prize in 1984 for his work against apartheid in South Africa.

1998
The National Advocacy Center opens on campus. Located on Pendleton Street, the Center is operated by the United States Department of Justice and used to train federal, state, and local prosecutors and litigators in advocacy skills and management of legal operations.

2001
USC celebrates the 200th anniversary of its charter and concludes its bicentennial year.

2010 & 2011
USC wins back-to-back National Championships in baseball!

2012
The hit heard around the world…Jadeveon Clowney delivers an impressive tackle in the Outback Bowl.

THE Y'S BIRD   19

Carolina Traditions

The following traditions are observed by all Carolina students. Read them carefully and remember them when you come to the campus.

1. All Carolina Freshmen wear a Freshman cap of the Carolina colors garnet and black. This is not a sign of inferiority but a badge of distinction showing that you are a Carolina student.

2. All Carolina students wear Carolina colors during the entire Fair Week.

3. Carolina is a friendly place. All students speak to each other whenever they meet whether they know each other by name or not.

4. Tip your hat and speak to every professor you pass.

5. Always stand at attention with bared heads whenever you hear the Carolina Alma Mater.

6. The Alma Mater is not to be sung as a cheer song but is used only on official occasions.

7. Freshman barefoot day comes in May at the date of the election of the May queen. All Freshmen are required to go barefooted on that day.

8. Carolina students are good sports. They never "boo" an opponent on the athletic field and good plays by our opponent are cheered as well as good plays by our own team.

9. When asked your name by an upper classman, never reply that your name is "Jim" Smith or Mr. Smith but "Rat" Smith.

10. The honor principle is Carolina's oldest and grandest tradition. We were the first college in the United States to operate under this principle. Guard it and cherish it with your utmost effort.

Reprinted from Carolina Traditions -- 1936 student handbook, "The Y's Bird." University Archives.

Current Carolina Traditions

From Carolina Welcome to the Clemson-Carolina rivalry, from Creed Week to Service Saturdays, from the 2001-A Space Odyssey Entrance to Chicken Finger Wednesday, your time at Carolina will be steeped in traditions. As a student at the University of South Carolina, you have an opportunity to participate in many campus traditions that unite the student body and pay tribute to Carolina's history begin as soon as you arrive on campus!

First Night Carolina

First Night Carolina is one of many Carolina Welcome events planned for first-year students. It is a night of food, fun, and noise as the entire first-year class travels to Williams-Brice Stadium for an introduction to campus traditions. An all-star lineup of campus athletes and student leaders walk students across the field (one of the only times students are permitted on the grass at Williams-Brice) to the stands where they cheer on the Gamecocks. The night always ends with one of the best fireworks displays in the Midlands and an opportunity to meet fellow students.

FYRE

The First-Year Reading Experience (FYRE) at the University of South Carolina is a half-day event held each fall before the start of classes. Sponsored by the Office of the Provost, the program introduces students to academics on campus. By bringing students together before the first day of classes to discuss a common reading, the University demonstrates that academics are the top priority at Carolina.

The tradition of FYRE began in 1994 with the idea that students and faculty members should have the opportunity to come together and discuss a common text, outside of the typical classroom environment. As the signature common experience for the first-year class, this event continues to bring students and faculty together in discussion around the selected text, allowing new students to experience a college-level academic discussion, share their own ideas, and hear a diverse array of opinions from their peers, in a nonthreatening atmosphere.

Did you know?

46,600 = The pounds of CHICKEN FINGERS consumed in 2010.

Peer Leader Advice

It is so fun to get wrapped up in the traditions at Carolina. From singing the Alma Mater at the end of every football game, to the Tiger Burn before the Clemson game. Traditions bring a sense of unity to every student.

- Alex Bazin
Charlotte, NC • Junior
Marketing

THE UNIVERSITY OF SOUTH CAROLINA FIRST-YEAR READING EXPERIENCE BOOKS THROUGHOUT THE YEARS

J. Rion McKissick

Tiger Burn

The tradition of Tiger Burn grew from the 1902 feud between University of South Carolina and Clemson University. That year, USC upset Clemson, and Carolina students paraded through the streets near campus carrying a transparency, drawn by USC mathematics Professor F. Horton Colcock, of a gamecock standing over a fallen tiger. Clemson cadets lined up in a battle formation in front of the brick wall on Sumter Street. Mr. Benet, who led the Carolina students in the victory parade earlier that day, intervened and formed a committee of students from Carolina and Clemson to find a resolve. While they were meeting, J. Rion McKissick, a sophomore at Carolina, occupied a spot in the front of the wall. A senior approached McKissick and asked him solemnly, "McKissick, are you armed?"

The sophomore showed him his revolver.

"How many bullets do you have?"

"Five."

"McKissick!" The senior's hand grasped his shoulder in fervent appeal. "Make every shot count!"

Luckily no shots were fired by McKissick, and the committees finally reached the agreement that since the transparency bore an emblem of each team, they would burn the transparency. As the emblem burned, each body of students gave three cheers for the other, and the Clemson cadets retreated. J. Rion McKissick later served as the 19th President of the University.

Each year, students design and construct a 25-foot tiger that is burned at a pep rally before the South Carolina-Clemson football game. Until 1959, this annual gridiron brawl was known as Big Thursday and was always played during the week of the South Carolina State Fair in Columbia. Currently, the annual event is held the week of Thanksgiving before students make their way home for the holiday. Students from the College of Engineering work all semester to design and construct the 50-75 foot tiger as a project for their classes. In recent years, the tiger has been built so that its arms and mouth actually move. The annual event culminates in a mass gathering of students and community members torching the tiger to signify an anticipated win for the Gamecocks.

Mascot and Garnet and Black

(Adapted from http://www.sc.edu/usc/gamecock.html and printed with permission.)

The origins of the University's moniker, Gamecocks, are unknown. A possible link is to one of South Carolina's

colorful military figures, Thomas Sumter. During the War of Independence, Sumter energized South Carolina in its fight against the British. He was known for his fearlessness in battle as well as for the flashy gamecock colors of his hat, coat, and epaulettes-garnet and black; the British referred to this as the South Carolina Game Cock. Another link is to the 1902 South Carolina-Clemson football game. Two weeks after the game and the riots that followed, the state newspaper began referring to the team as the Game Cocks. By 1904, the two words had been joined, and the name stuck.

Cocky first took action at USC events in 1980 and soon won the hearts off all the Gamecock fans all over and now is one of the most recognizable figures to young and old at USC. One of Cocky's trademarks is his 2001 Magic Box entrance. The spectacular performance can be seen at every home football game when the Gamecocks take the field. The Magic Box entrance is one of many things that Cocky does to get the crowd pumped up and cheering for the Gamecocks. Cocky can be seen pepping the crowd up not only at football games, but at men's and women's basketball, volleyball, men's and women's soccer, baseball, softball, swimming, golf, track, and tennis events as well. Cocky also brings his parents to the football game on Parents Weekend!

Fight Song: "The Fighting Gamecocks Lead the Way"

When you attend an athletic event, you will often hear one of the University's talented bands playing the fight song. The music, chosen by former football coach and athletic director, Paul Dietzel, is from the 1967 Broadway musical *How Now, Dow Jones*. Dietzel also wrote the lyrics of the song. Learn the fight song, and show your school spirit the next time you hear it played.

Hey, let's give a cheer, Carolina is here,
The Fighting Gamecocks lead the way.
Who gives a care, if the going gets tough,
And when it is rough, that's when the 'Cocks get going.
Hail to our colors of Garnet and Black,
In Carolina pride have we.
So, go Gamecocks go - FIGHT!
Drive for the goal - FIGHT!
USC will win today - GO COCKS!
So, let's give a cheer, Carolina is here.
The Fighting Gamecocks all the way!

Alma Mater: "We Hail Thee Carolina"

The University's alma mater was written in 1911 by George A. Wauchope, an English professor, and set to the music of Robert Burns' "Flow Gently, Sweet Afton." A March 1911 issue of *The Daily Gamecock* reported that a year or two earlier, the faculty, "realizing we should have a soul-stirring alma mater," offered a prize of $50 for the writing of an alma mater. Of the songs that were submitted, this one became the most popular and, after several years, became known as the official University alma mater. At each Commencement exercise following the awarding of degrees, the audience is asked to rise and sing our alma mater. It is also often sung during athletic events. The custom has arisen over the years of raising the right hand, with the fingers cupped (as if offering a toast), when the phrase "Here's a health, Carolina" is sung. To many alumni, the toast is synonymous with watching the Fighting Gamecocks compete in major athletic events.

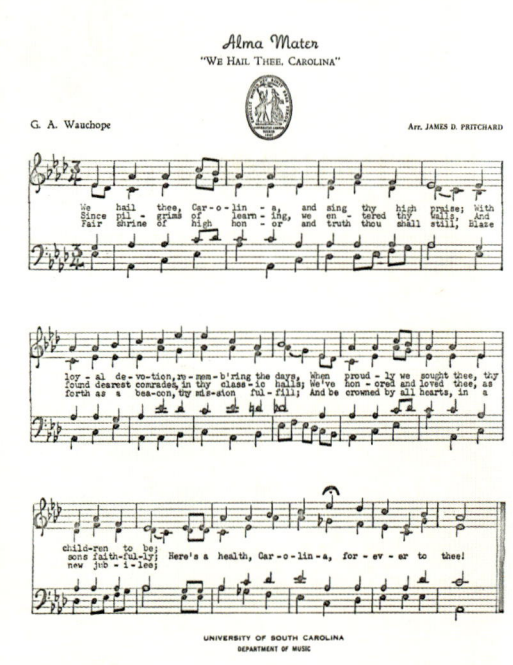

We hail thee, Carolina, and sing thy high praise
With loyal devotion, remembering the days
When proudly we sought thee, thy children to be:
Here's a health, Carolina, forever to thee!

Since pilgrims of learning, we entered thy walls
And found dearest comrades in thy classic halls,
We've honored and loved thee as sons faithfully;
Here's a health, Carolina, forever to thee!

Generations of sons have rejoiced to proclaim
Thy watchword of service, thy beauty and fame;
For ages to come shall their rallying cry be:
Here's a health, Carolina, forever to thee!

Fair shrine of high honor and truth, thou shalt still
Blaze forth as a beacon, thy mission fulfill,
And crowned by all hearts in a new jubilee:
Here's a health, Carolina, forever to thee!

USC Official Seal

The seal of the University was adopted April 26, 1803. The University seal quotes the Latin poet Ovid, "Emollit Mores Nec Sinit Esse Feros," which translated means "Learning humanizes character and does not permit it to be cruel."

Beneath the words stand the figures of Minerva, the goddess of wisdom, and Liberty. Minerva's shield is decorated with the South Carolina state seal. The words and image are designed to remind us that a university education builds not only intellect, but also character. The Latin inscription below the figures is the school name and founding year, 1801.

Class Ring

One of the University's most prestigious traditions, the official University of South Carolina ring, is a time-honored expression of South Carolina pride and is recognized worldwide by University alumni. Designed by students and alumni, the ring forever symbolizes the history and tradition of the University of South Carolina. The design displays the seal of the University, which should be worn to face the wearer while a student at the University. Once a graduate, the ring should be turned so that the seal faces the world. Students with 60 or more credit hours are eligible to purchase a ring through the University of South Carolina Alumni Association. Each semester a Ring Ceremony is held for students who have purchased their ring.

Gamecock Newspaper

The Daily Gamecock was first published in 1908 as a joint venture between the different campus literary societies. The first editor was Robert Elliott Gonzales. Since 1908, The Daily Gamecock has undergone significant changes, but it continues to be the main source of information for Carolina students who want to know more about campus events. This editorially independent student newspaper is published Monday through Friday in both print and online versions. Every year the newspaper changes editors, making it one of the most sought after student media positions on campus.

The Carolina Culture

As in any community, the campus has its own culture and distinct set of rules that govern and distinguish its members. At Carolina, those standards and rules can be found in the Carolina Community student handbook and, particularly, in the tenets of the Carolinian Creed.

Community Standards

College is without a doubt a time where students explore the boundaries while navigating their new found freedom. At the University of South Carolina, students have been doing this since the doors opened. In the past, students were either stealing neighbors' turkeys and chickens in the community or sneaking onto Columbia College campus to visit female students. The student handbook outlined the expectations for Carolina students as well as the policies that governed student behavior on campus. Today, the Carolina Community student handbook is quite different and much broader than the College Laws of 1836. There are no longer rules pertaining to servants or prayer; rather, there are policies concerning issues that students often face today, such as academic integrity, alcohol and other drugs, and matters related to interpersonal relationships.

Each class ring is hand-made and no two are exactly alike!

ON THE WEB

Read *The Daily Gamecock* online:
dailygamecock.com
and check them out on Facebook and Twitter:

 facebook.com/thegamecock

 @thegamecock

STUDENT REMINDERS FROM 1930s STUDENT HANDBOOK

DON'T FORGET—

To write back home—Mother and Dad want to hear from you.

That you have the word "No", in your vocabulary—use it.

That you will never "find" time for anything—if you want time you must make it.

To start studying as soon as you begin to meet classes. Now is the time to prepare for those exams, not the night before.

That when you enter Carolina you are considered a man, and capable of acting as such. You can do as you please about your work and play. Nobody will make you study; you are to be your own "boss". Be honest with yourself and always remember that you are here for a life purpose.

That you will be judged more at Carolina by what you do than by what you say.

To make friends. Do not limit yours to just a few; learn your fellow-students.

That there is a father and mother at home who believe in you. Don't get "wild" and waste your money; be a man.

To bring your courtesy and self-respect with you—you will need them.

To speak to everyone whom you see on the campus, whether a student or a visitor.

To respect the University property. Don't mark and destroy desks, chairs, etc. They belong to the State, and the State belongs to you.

That the type of pictures that are hung in your room denote the type of fellow you are—and the type of thought that goes on in your mind determines your actions.

17

Carolinian Creed

You have probably heard about the *Carolinian Creed* either at orientation, your first hall meeting, or in your University 101 class. It is an integral part of the culture at South Carolina, but have you ever wondered how it came to be?

In the late 1980s, there were several alarming incidents perpetrated against individuals on college campuses across the nation that prompted students and administrators at South Carolina to take action. These violent and hateful acts ranged from sexual assaults on men and women; public displays of sexism, racism, and anti-Semitism; and hazing. In response to these disturbing national events, a group of University students, faculty, and staff were brought together to explore (a) the characteristics that define relationships in the campus community, (b) the expectations of the University regarding student relationships, and (c) suggestions on the most effective way to present these standards and civility aspirations to the student body.

The process took two years to complete and resulted in the creation of the *Carolinian Creed* in 1990 as a campus social honor code endorsed by the Board of Trustees, the National Advocacy Board, the Faculty Senate, and the Student Senate.

Since then, the *Carolinian Creed* tenets have served as the foundation for what it means to be a Carolinian and, most importantly, a contributing member to the community. The *Creed* emphasizes integrity, openness, and the general principles of civility. Students at South Carolina encounter the *Creed* in many places on campus and also before they enter the University. You may remember seeing the *Carolinian Creed* on your application to the University. By reading and signing the *Creed*, students make a commitment to honor and live by the tenents.

As a matter of principle, the *Creed* is infused into all campus life through course work, activities, and service. The *Creed* is officially presented to the first-year class at Convocation.

By defining the qualities valued in others, the *Creed* raises awareness about (a) what is appropriate and acceptable, (b) becoming role models, (c) setting behavioral standards for those around you, and (d) delineating parameters for making difficult and challenging decisions. The *Carolinian Creed* is intended to serve as a guide for living effectively in the University community.

Carolinian Creed and Diversity Week

(Adapted from http://www.sa.sc.edu/creed/whatisit.html and used with permission.)

The *Creed* is a complement to the University's conduct code. It explains why we regulate and restrict what we do. It forms the basis for and serves as a summary of what is expected by the institution.

It has been called our summary of values, a statement of principles, and a statement of standards we hope will govern relationships in the community. Reporters like to call it a social honor code or a code of ethics. We like to call it a teaching tool in the hope that faculty and staff will use it to help students claim the rights and respect they deserve and to understand the obligations and assumptions that come with being a member of the Carolina community.

Since 1997, Creed Day and Creed Week have become part of the annual celebration of the *Carolinian Creed* includes an annual Creed Day breakfast and the *Carolinian Creed* Essay Contest that offers a monetary award. We hope you will come out to all the events to celebrate the *Creed* with your Carolina community!

The history and traditions presented in this chapter will be the foundation for the legacy that you will create while at Carolina. Your challenge as a member of the Carolina community is to continue to explore the history of this remarkable institution while also contributing to the future of the University of South Carolina.

ON THE WEB

For more information about the *Carolinian Creed* and related events, visit:
sa.sc.edu/Creed

Carolinian Creed

The community of scholars at the **University of South Carolina** is dedicated to personal and academic excellence.

Choosing to join the community obligates each member to a code of civilized behavior.

As a Carolinian...

I will practice personal and academic integrity;

•

I will respect the dignity of all persons;

•

I will respect the rights and property of others;

•

I will discourage bigotry, while striving to learn from differences in people, ideas, and opinions;

•

I will demonstrate concern for others, their feelings, and their need for conditions which support their work and development.

Allegiance to these ideals requires each Carolinian to refrain from and discourage behaviors which threaten the freedom and respect every individual deserves.

CONSIDER THIS

When you enrolled at the University of South Carolina, you became part of a legacy of Carolina students spanning more than 200 years. As you begin making Carolina your home, consider what your legacy will be.

How will you impact the community?

What will you be remembered for?

What will you be remembered for?

These questions are what will guide your experience at Carolina. Take advantage of all the opportunities that are presented to you and take pride in what will be your home for the next few years.

Outstanding Alumni

South Carolina has a long history of graduating successful individuals—and employing them too! Many alumni have become TV personalities, corporate executives, star athletes, artists and musicians, and pioneers in research and health care. Take a look below and see how these notable Gamecocks made their mark on the world.

Millie Jean Adams (1898) was the first female graduate of the University of South Carolina.

John Swearingen (1938, chemical engineering) retired chairman, Standard Oil Company, Indiana; namesake of USC's engineering center

W.W. "Hootie" Johnson (1953, finance) was the chairman of the executive committee of Bank of America Corporation and chairman of the Augusta National Golf Club.

Robert McNair (1958, psychology) was founder, chairman, and CEO of NFL's Houston Texans, chairman of McNair Foundation, and founder of McNair Scholar Program.

Andrew Card (1971, engineering) was the White House Chief of Staff under President George W. Bush, 2001-2006; served in the administrations of Presidents Ronald Reagan and George H. Bush; former U.S. Secretary of Transportation; former vice president for government relations, General Motors Corp.

Darla Moore (1975, political science) is a financier and partner in Rainwater Incorporated as well as one of the first female members inducted into the August National Golf Club.

Kaye G. Hearn (1977, law) was the first woman elected chief judge of the South Carolina Court of Appeals

Cliff Hollingsworth (1977, journalism; 1979, master's in education) is a screenwriter for "Cinderella Man," starring Russell Crowe and Renee Zellweger

Leeza Gibbons (1978, broadcast journalism) is a television celebrity and radio personality; three-time Emmy winner for former talk show "Leeza" created the Leeza Gibbons Memory Foundation to support victims of Alzheimer's disease and their families

Gary Parsons (1978, Master of business administration) is the founder XM Satellite Radio; former executive vice president of MCI Communications

David King (1983, mechanical engineering) was the director of NASA's Marshall Space Flight Center, Huntsville, Ala.; recipient of Presidential Rank Award for Distinguished Executives, the highest honor a government employee can receive; former Space Shuttle launch director and director of Shuttle Processing

Rita Cosby (1989, journalism and spanish) is a television news anchor and correspondent, radio host, and best selling author. She is currently a Special Correspondent for Inside Edition.

George Rogers (1989, interdisciplinary studies) was the 1980 Heisman Trophy winner and former NFL number one draft pick.

Charlie Weis (1989, master of education) is the offensive coordinator for the Kansas City Chiefs; former football coach of Notre Dame; and a former NFL assistant coach, winning three Super Bowl rings with the New England Patriots and one with the New York Giants.

Amos Lee (1995, English) is an American singer-songwriter known for his folk, rock, and soul musical style.

Tonique Williams-Darling (1999, business administration) is the University's first Olympic gold medalist, as the 400-meter champion for her native Bahamas in the 2004 Games.

Hootie and the Blowfish (aka Dean Felber, Mark Bryan, Jim Sonefeld, and Darius Rucker) are Grammy award-winning musicians and founders of the philanthropic Monday After the Masters Celebrity Pro-Am Golf Tournament and Hootie and the Blowfish Foundation.

THE USC BUCKET LIST

100 THINGS ALL GAMECOCKS SHOULD DO BEFORE THEY GRADUATE

1. High five President Pastides.
2. Let the good times roll at the Rosewood Crawfish Festival.
3. Keep on your feet during Dance Marathon or Relay for Life.
4. Look like a fool in the Clapping Circle.
5. Strike a pose with Sir Big Spur.
6. Dance on Greene Street during Hip Hop Wednesday.
7. Cruise in the Carolina Cab.
8. Pig out at the Top of Carolina's Friday BBQ Buffet.
9. Explore new topics in an elective class.
10. Reuse a water bottle for a month.
11. Celebrate Thanksgiving at a USC vs. Clemson football game.
12. Talk with someone handing out flyers.
13. Explore your artsy side at a play in the Longstreet Theatre.
14. Go to class on Halloween in a costume.
15. Eat at Groucho's for Sunday lunch.
16. Make a splash in the indoor pool at Strom.
17. Picnic on the Horseshoe.
18. Volunteer during a Carolina Service Council event.
19. Take a date to dinner and a movie in the Gamecock Park/Carolina Theater.
20. Sign up for Cocky's Reading Express.
21. Buy organic at the Healthy Caroilna Farmer's Market.
22. Donate blood or time to the Carolina vs. Clemson Blood Drive.
23. Dine at the McCutchen House.
24. Start the Gamecock Call— "GAME!" "COCKS!"
25. Climb the stairs to the 17th floor of Capstone.
26. Go out of your way to help a stranger.
27. Sprawl on the first floor of T. Coop, the lowest point in Columbia.
28. Visit Clemson's campus wearing a USC shirt from our bookstore.
29. Dress head-to-toe in green for St. Patrick's Day in Five Points.
30. Feel the burn in a group exercise class at Strom (free for the first 2 weeks of class).
31. Rock out at the Homecoming Step Show.
32. Gorge on chicken fingers every Wednesday for a month.
33. Take a snapshot with Cocky.
34. Sing along during an a cappella concert.
35. Treat your professor with the "Out to Lunch" program.
36. Be the subject in a research experiment.
37. Complete the Dining Hall Marathon—17 dining locations, 1 week.
38. As a senior, befriend a freshman.
39. Stargaze from the Melton Observatory.
40. Run or support a 5K for charity.
41. Snap a graduation picture in front of the Horseshoe gates.
42. Shag with friends at Jillian's.
43. Climb Outdoor Recreation's Challenge Course.
44. Skip class to play Frisbee on the Horseshoe.
45. Go on a ghost tour sponsored by University Ambassadors on Halloween.
46. Play a game of pool in the Golden Spur Game Room.
47. Travel with the Carolina Convoy to an away football game.
48. For good luck before your first exam, take a midnight stroll across the Pickens Street Bridge.
49. Say "thank you" to a university employee.
50. Avoid doing laundry for a month.
51. Stroll down the Riverwalk.
52. Scale Strom's rock wall.
53. Kiss on the Horseshoe during a full moon.
54. Visit 10 tables at a Student Organization Fair.
55. Celebrate the holidays by attending USC's Tree Lighting Ceremony.
56. Compete in Cocky's Quest Scavenger Hunt.
57. Paint up for an athletic game.
58. De-stress at Carolina After Dark.
59. Convince a professor to hold class outside.
60. Check out the Columbia Museum of Art or the State Museum.
61. Continue the ring tradition and buy a class ring.
62. Spend a day at the Riverbanks Zoo.
63. Win a coveted intramural sport t-shirt.
64. Study in the South Caroliniana Library.
65. Tube down the Congaree River.
66. Get an autograph from a student-athlete.
67. Drop some lyrics at Spoken Word Wednesday.
68. Tell a professor what you *really* think of his/her class.
69. Ride every USC shuttle route.
70. Get produce from City Roots.
71. Cast your vote in Student Government elections.
72. Attend a Greek function or philanthropy event.
73. Sit in on a class you aren't taking.
74. Learn all the words to our fight song and our alma mater.
75. Sing your heart out at Carolina Ale House's Karaoke Night.
76. Watch the sunset from the top of Horizon Garage.
77. Flip a coin into the T. Coop fountain.
78. Smile for a picture with "Gamecock Jesus."
79. Remember Carolina Cup.
80. Write a letter to the editor of The Daily Gamecock.
81. Check out an event at the Koger Center.
82. Deactivate your Facebook for a week, and use your extra time to have an adventure.
83. See a movie at the Nickelodeon theater.
84. Meet the person who now lives in your freshman room.
85. Plan a weekend excursion to Charleston.
86. Attend BGLSA's Birdcage event.
87. Sightsee with Columbia Carriage Works.
88. Eat something fried at the S.C. State Fair.
89. Apply for a leadership position within a student organization.
90. Grill out at a AAAS Cookout.
91. Grab a coffee and study in one of our local coffee shops—Cool Beans, Immaculate Consumption or The Drip!
92. Study abroad.
93. Swim, sail or chill at Lake Murray.
94. Celebrate diversity by becoming a Safe Zone Ally.
95. Order Beezer's after 2 a.m.
96. Find the Hootie and the Blowfish brick on the Horseshoe and take a picture with their monument.
97. Devour a gyro at the Greek Festival.
98. Grab a coffee from Colloquium and sit out on Gambrell's third-floor patio.
99. Tour the State House, and find all six stars on the exterior.
100. Ignite your football passion during Tigerburn.

Student Government
University of South Carolina Student Life

For more information please visit our website:
www.uscbucketlist.com

@USCBucketList

RESOURCES

Alma Mater
http://www.sc.edu/usc/almamater.html
Annual Giving Programs
http://www.sc.edu/annualgiving/
Bicentennial Timeline of University of South Carolina
http://www.sc.edu/bicentennial/pages/timeline.html
Board of Trustees
http://trustees.sc.edu/
Carolina Callers 777-4705
http://www.sc.edu/carolinacallers/
The Carolinian Creed
http://www.sa.sc.edu/creed/

Carolina Community
http://www.sa.sc.edu/carolinacommunity/
Carolina Dining 777-6339
http://sc.edu/dining/
My Carolina Alumni Association 777-4111
http://www.mycarolina.org/s/842/start.aspx
Office of the President
http://president.sc.edu/
University of South Carolina Archives 777-5158
http://www.sc.edu/library/socar/archives/
University of South Carolina Mission Statement
http://www.sc.edu/aboutusc/columbiaMission.shtml

REFERENCES

Barefoot Day. (1938). McKissick records, Box 1, 1938-39. Retrieved from http://library.sc.edu/socar/archives/finding_aids/mckissick_1938-1939.htm

Geiger, R. (Ed.). (2000). *The American college in the nineteenth century*. Nashville, TN: Vanderbilt University Press.

Honeywell, R. J. (1931). *The educational work of Thomas Jefferson*. Cambridge, MA: Harvard University Press Language.

Monstrous regiment: Establishment of coeducation at USC. (1998, spring). *Caroliniana Columns*. Retrieved from http://www.sc.edu/library/socar/uscs/98spr/coeds.html

Wormy salt meat and no steaks for breakfast: Campus dining in the 1800s. (2003, April). *Carolinian*. Retrieved from http://www.sc.edu/carolinian/features/fea_03apr_01.html

Chapter Three

Exploring YOUR Carolina

Dear First-Year Student,

Welcome to the University of South Carolina! We are thrilled that you have chosen to join us and engage in the Carolina experience, which is something you don't get on just ANY college campus. It is an experience that challenges, entertains, develops, molds, and prepares you. There are many activities and events for students at USC. I encourage you to take advantage of them all and make the most out of being a Gamecock.

As a new student at Carolina, consider your journey here. What will you learn? How will you be challenged as a student, community citizen, student athlete, or student leader? Your final destination (e.g., a degree, a career, a new life direction) is important, but your path toward that goal is equally important. By selecting University 101, you have chosen to be active in this journey and to get as much as you can out of your experience. The course will provide you with opportunities to learn about the University and what it takes to be a successful student.

This chapter covers the many ways to become involved and engaged as a Carolina student. Possibilities are available at every turn on our campus from joining a student organization to pledging a fraternity or sorority to attending athletic events to writing for *The Daily Gamecock*. Involvement is participating, attending, and making a difference. It might be a conversation you have during a Diversity Dialogue or an opportunity to study abroad or explore a research idea through Undergraduate Research. Whatever it may be, make the most of it, and connect with the Carolina experience.

As you plan your career path, consider how student involvement and leadership opportunities can give you the experiences you will need to be competitive for internships, co-ops and full-time positions. Think about the impact you want to make on the Carolina community—what will you do to make a difference? Challenge yourself. Explore new things. Step outside of your comfort zone. Soak it all in. Change the community.

Sincerely,

Anna Edwards
Director of Student Services, Student Life

THE University of South Carolina is an exciting institution presenting unique possibilities to make the most of your college experience. Now that you are here, you will have many opportunities within your residence hall, around campus, and in the Columbia community to participate in activities that interest you and enhance your learning.

With so many opportunities available, it may be overwhelming deciding what to choose. Explore your options and make the most of your time outside of the classroom by committing to organizations and activities that are the most beneficial and enriching to you both professionally and personally. Finding ways to engage with the campus will not only help you academically and contribute to your success as a Carolinian but can also provide new skills and a network of friends and colleagues that you will continue to draw from in years to come.

No matter what your interests are, you can find something on campus or in the community to become involved with outside of the classroom. In this chapter and throughout *Transitions*, the various opportunities for engagement will be highlighted, including USC Connect, the University's newest initiative to help students integrate learning both within and beyond the classroom.

Peer Leader Advice

By getting involved in one of the countless organizations USC has to offer, you can find a passion and purpose for your time here. It's a great opportunity to build relationships with people that can last far beyond your four years and make connections with future employers. Just don't spread yourself too thin and prevent yourself from giving each commitment your best effort. Always pick a group where you are able to grow as an individual and have positive experiences.

- Courtney Enright
Greenwich, CT • Senior
Marketing & Fashion Merchandising

USC CONNECT: Integrating learning within and beyond the classroom

Have you ever felt like you are just checking off boxes in your educational journey? Does it seem like what you study in class has few connections to the rest of your life? USC Connect is about helping you make the most of your education by *connecting experiences in your classes to meaningful activities that you participate in beyond the classroom*. You take an important step toward setting yourself apart by purposefully selecting and engaging in activities that will enrich what you know and can do.

Examples of purposeful experiences might include

- Working with your peers to bring more locally produced foods into campus dining services
- Supporting elementary children and their teachers in creating a poetry and sculpture garden at their schools
- Conducting lab tests and recording data that feed into research on Alzheimer's disease
- Traveling to Scotland to conduct research and write a play
- Raising local health awareness through the campus Health Affairs Committee

You truly make the most of your education and prepare yourself for the future when you (a) integrate your learning by intentionally analyzing and relating your within- and beyond-the-classroom experiences to one another and (b) apply what you have learned to lead the way in your areas of interest.

Finding opportunities outside the classroom helps you tailor your education to fit your needs and reach your goals. Explore experiences that are meaningful to you in your college or major, residential life, or student organizations as well as campus offices (e.g., Career Center, Student Engagement, Study Abroad, Undergraduate Research). You can find opportunities through the USC Connect Searchable Database or by reviewing what experiences are recommended for your major.

Peer Leader Advice

Always remember that what you're learning in the classroom can be applied in every aspect of your life—not just for your future career. Continuously look for opportunities to integrate your classroom learning into everyday life. This will help you not only decide what you want to do with your degree, it will also help you grow as a leader, student, and professional. By applying concepts I learned in my major to my job at the Office of Orientation and Testing, I feel more prepared and motivated to take on projects in my future career.

- Kristine Snyder
Matthews, NC • Senior
Global Supply Chain and
Operations Management and Marketing

ON THE WEB

Visit the USC Connect website for details on Graduation with Leadership Distinction for your graduation year.

sc.edu/uscconnect

CONSIDER THIS

What characteristics do you believe define a leader?

_____

_____

Have you already taken on a leadership role here at Carolina? If so, please describe. If not, what role do you plan to take?

_____

_____

Graduation with Leadership Distinction

One way to choose experiences that can work together for you is to focus on a *pathway* that leads to Graduation with Leadership Distinction. Graduation with Leadership Distinction recognizes students who have completed specific requirements in the core components of USC Connect including within- and beyond-the-classroom experiences, reflection on learning, and application to the future. Whether or not you ultimately choose to complete requirements for earning the distinction for your transcript, all students can use the framework of integrating learning within and beyond the classroom to make the most of their educational experiences.

The pathways in USC Connect and Graduation with Leadership Distinction relate to all majors. Which one is the best match for you?

- Professional and Civic Engagement (combines peer leadership and internships)
- Research
- Community Service
- Global Learning

Within each pathway, students are encouraged to engage in a variety of experiences and learning activities. Think about the categories in the table as your guide for integrating your experiences within and beyond the classroom into a meaningful whole. There are specific requirements in each category to graduate with Leadership Distinction.

Making the Most of Your Carolina Education: Graduating with Leadership Distinction by Class Year

First Year

- Attend the Get Connected Fair. Participate in a USC Connect integrative learning experience in your UNIV 101 class.
- Search the USC Connect Database and talk with others to explore possibilities.
- Try out experiences.
- Check out your academic program's recommendations.
- Complete a Student Engagement Plan for your Carolina years that complements your interests and major.

Second Year
- Focus and expand on experiences you have found to be most rewarding.
    - If you have been participating in community service, consider doing an alternative break service trip.
    - If you have been expanding your global horizons, plan to participate in an international experience (e.g., a faculty-led course or study abroad).
    - If you are focused on research, contact the Office of Undergraduate Research to connect to faculty research projects and check out possibilities for financial support to pursue projects.
    - If you are focused on professional and civic engagement, be sure you are planning for both leadership opportunities and professional work experience/internships.
- Keep records of your experiences electronically (e.g., an e-portfolio), including notes on what you have learned.
- Attend an orientation session for Graduation with Leadership Distinction to make sure you are on track.

Third Year
- Stay engaged in beyond-the-classroom experiences and think about how they relate to your major and course work.
- Continue to build and document your core experience hours.
- Take advantage of enhancement experiences (e.g., lectures, workshops, community events) related to your pathway and keep a record of your participation (e.g., photos, certificates, e-portfolio entries).
- Share your learning in class discussions and use examples from your beyond-the-classroom experiences in class projects and assignments.
- Save samples of your work from class that relate to your pathway in your e-portfolio.
- Present at Discovery Day or publish an article in *Caravel* (USC's Undergraduate Research Journal).

Fourth Year
- Make connections across *all* experiences.
- Consider taking UNIV 401 to continue integrating your experiences and creating an e-portfolio.
- Summarize learning and the skills you have developed in an e-portfolio. Include how you will apply learning to make a difference, to lead, in the future.
- Complete your application for Graduation with Leadership Distinction. Make sure you know how to tell *your* story!

What is Engagement?

Being a student at the University of South Carolina means more than just going to class, meeting with faculty members, and acing those tests! It is essential as a first-year student that you engage yourself both in and out of the classroom. The concept of student engagement is often realized through involvement on campus. While involvement is a critical component, engagement goes beyond simply joining campus groups. True engagement synthesizes classroom knowledge with out-of classroom experiences, enhancing your overall learning experience and reinforcing important information. Getting involved is also a great way to immerse yourself in campus life and culture; gain practical skills and experiences; and form lasting friendships and relationships with other students, faculty, and staff members. Utilize the Student Engagement Plan at the end of the chapter as you make a plan for integrating your in-class learning with your out-of-class experiences.

How to Make the Most of your Educational Experience

Integrative Learning Component	USC Connect	
	For All	**To Graduate with Leadership Distinction**
Core Experiences Beyond the Classroom	Engage in first-hand experiences in Community Service, Internships, Peer Leadership, Global Learning, and Research. Search the USC Connect Database for opportunities and view on-line Recommendations by Major.	Depending on your chosen pathway, complete the following: • 300 hours of Community Service • 300 hours of Professional and Civic Engagement • A semester studying abroad for Global Learning • Two semesters of extensive research for Research
Enhancement Activities Beyond the Classroom	Enhance your understanding of a pathway through special events (e.g., lectures, workshops, conferences, performances) or experiences.	Complete three required enhancement activities related to selected pathway.
Course Work Within the Classroom	Complete courses that provide a theoretical framework or increased awareness of issues related to the pathway. These may already be in your major or Carolina Core requirements.	Complete six course credits from approved list.
Presentation Learning and Application	Integrate examples and learning from your beyond the classroom experiences into course assignments, papers, projects, and oral presentations.	Publicly present at Discovery Day, a professional conference, or an approved department or college event OR publish in a journal (e.g., USC's *Caravel* for Undergraduate Research)
Bring it all Together— Tell Your Story! Learning and Application	Analyze how you are prepared for the future as a result of your experiences within and beyond the classroom. Highlight significant experiences in your resume and be ready to describe what you know and can do as you consider future opportunities. Complete a culminating assignment or seminar (available in many programs or UNIV 401) in which you describe key learning and how you will apply it. Graduate school, fellowship, and job applications/interviews provide opportunities for highlighting your knowledge and skills.	Complete an e-portfolio including sections on learning, analysis, application to the future, and leadership.

www.sc.edu/uscconnect

Did you know?

There are now more than 6,000 student leadership positions and opportunities available at Carolina!

ON THE WEB

To find out more information about the Carolina Leadership Initiative, visit:
leadership.sc.edu

For a complete list of all the Student Organizations at Carolina, visit:
sa.sc.edu/studentorgs

To find out more about Carolina Production's upcoming events or how to get involved, go to:
cp.sc.edu

You can also find them on:

 facebook.com/usccp

 @usccp

 @usccp

Did you know?

Student Organization Fairs are held once a semester on Greene Street. Organizations set up information tables representing various student organizations. These organization fairs are held the first Wednesday in September and the second to last Wednesday in January.

Joining a student organization is a great way to meet new and interesting people and provides an opportunity to enhance your leadership skills. South Carolina has more than 300 registered student organizations including honor societies, sports clubs, service organizations, and a host of religious, cultural, professional, political, and special interest groups. Whether you want to work for *The Daily Gamecock* or become a member of the Pastafarians, there is most likely an organization that will spark your curiosity and help you meet students with shared interests.

Student organizations are also helpful for those students still deciding on their major by providing opportunities to learn about and network within a particular profession or field of study before making a career decision. Likewise, organizations are a way to explore new interests or additional hobbies—things you might not get to do as part of your major or coursework. To discover all the options available to you, refer to the Student Organizations webpage or attend one of the Student Organizations Fairs held each semester. You can also visit the Leadership and Service Center, located on the second floor of the Russell House Union, which houses a variety of offices aimed at getting students involved.

In joining an organization, your level of involvement and leadership is up to you! There are some groups that promote a heavily involved and leadership-driven membership. Those organizations include student government, peer leadership, and residence hall involvement.

If you are interested in getting involved but not quite ready to take on a leadership role, you have options. With more than 400 organizations at Carolina, there are opportunities for you to establish your level of engagement.

Carolina Productions

Carolina Productions is the student programming board responsible for coordinating events in the Russell House University Union and other venues around the University of South Carolina campus. Events include weekly movies in the Russell House Theater, student talent showcases, speakers, comedians, concerts, and much more! Carolina Productions consists of six committees: Cinematic Arts, Comedic Events, Concerts, Daytime Events, Marketing & Promotions, and Special Events. In the past, Carolina Productions has brought Seth Meyers, Young the Giant, Nick Offerman, Chris Young, Nev Schulman, Stephen A. Smith, and many more great acts! There are also opportunities for students to serve on Carolina Productions' Executive Board or as a general member. General members are the heart and soul of the organization as these student volunteers are involved in the planning of all their fantastic events!

CAMPUS ENGAGEMENT
At the University of South Carolina

No matter what your interests are, you can find something on campus or within the community to get involved with.

George Kuh (2003) found that "...the time and energy students devote to educationally purposeful activities is the single best predictor of their learning and personal development"

1250 Study Abroad students from 2012-2013

The 5 most popular destinations were

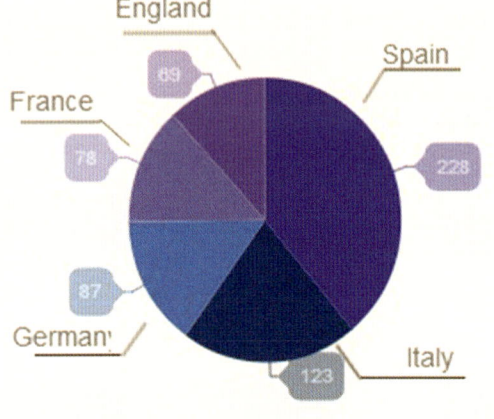

- England: 69
- Spain: 228
- France: 78
- Germany: 87
- Italy: 123

400+ Student Organizations

These include honor societies, sports clubs, service organizations, and a host of religious, cultural, professional, political, and special interest groups.

 472,152  6,000+  $2 Million+

Community	Leadership	Research
service hours completed by more than 30,000 USC Volunteers [2]	opportunities and positions available for students [2]	dollars awarded for Magellan Scholar research [2]

Internships

The Career Center posts Internships available to students of all majors and class levels through Job Mate.

Opportunities include:
- University Ambassadors
- Changing Carolina Peer Educators
- Orientation Leaders
- University 101 Peer Leaders
- Eco Reps... & many more!

976 Internships available in 2012 [3]

30+ Peer Educator Opportunities

Graduate with Leadership Distinction

There are 4 pathways you can choose:
- Community Service
- Global Learning
- Professional & Civic Engagement
- Research

---

[1] Taken from 2012-2013 Overview of Undergraduate Education Abroad: http://studyabroad.sc.edu/index.php?option=com_content&view=article&id=136&Itemid=633
[2] Taken from Undergraduate Admissions View Book
[3] Taken from USC's Career Center Website: http://sc.edu/career/internshipscoops.html

Chapter 3: Exploring YOUR Carolina   49

Did you know?

Research studies have shown that students involved in cocurricular activities and campus organizations perform better in the classroom (Astin, 1993; Pascarella & Terenzini, 1991).

George Kuh (2003), who developed the National Survey of Student Engagement (NSSE), states that "what students do during college… the time and energy students devote to educationally purposeful activities is the single best predictor of their learning and personal development" (p.1).

ACE Coaching

One-on-one coaching is available when developing a personal engagement plan. Stop by the Office of Student Engagement or schedule an appointment with a success coach today!

Visit sc.edu/ACE or call 803-777-5430

Campus locations: Bates House, Columbia Hall, Sims, and Thomas Cooper Library

Faculty Quote

Leadership is not about a position or a title. It's about specific individuals and how they relate to other people in order to make a positive difference in the community. All of us are leaders to some degree. The real question is whether we try to become better leaders tomorrow than we are today.

- Dr. Kirk A. Randazzo
Director of the Carolina
Leadership Initiative

Student Engagement Plan

The Office of Student Engagement, in partnership with Academic Coaching and Engagement (ACE) in the Student Success Center, has developed a valuable tool to help you map your plan for integrating your in-class learning with your out-of-class experiences. The Student Engagement Plan (SEP) should be something you develop early in your career as a student and continue building upon and using as you discover activities and opportunities that appeal to your interests and help you develop new skills.

Engagement Pathways
Professional and Civic Engagement

At Carolina, there are countless opportunities to develop your skills as a leader. Leadership is not about telling other people what to do; it is about who you are and how you relate to the community. Building on a 200-year tradition of educating leaders at the University, President Harris Pastides formed the Carolina Leadership Initiative in 2010 in an effort to provide coordination, support, and vision for the numerous programs on campus that develop leadership skills among our students. The Carolina Leadership Initiative is about

- Inspiring change
- Recognizing individual strengths and opportunities for improvement
- Learning effective communication and interpersonal skills
- Developing integrity and putting ethics into practice
- Valuing diversity and teamwork
- Increasing self-awareness
- Promoting creativity and thoughtful risk-taking
- Developing strategic visions to benefit our communities

Academic opportunities related to leadership include completing a minor in Leadership Studies, becoming a Leadership Scholar, and Graduating with Leadership Distinction. A wealth of opportunities that can help you develop leadership skills are also available through Leadership Programs in Student Life. These include the Emerging Leaders program, Student Leadership in the Workplace, and Skill Builders Workshops. Check out these and more at http://www.sa.sc.edu/leaders.

USC CONNECT

Integrating learning within and beyond the classroom

At the University of South Carolina, we apply what we learn in class to the research we conduct in the lab and in the field. We gain new perspectives from the world around us as we share our experiences in community service projects. We solve problems in new and creative ways. See how we connect.

CANDRA CHAISSON
Biology
Class of 2013

encouraged and mentored by strong female role model/science professor

+ identified her own skill set through extensive campus involvement

+ approached situations with fresh set of eyes after study abroad in Taiwan

= will pursue health disparities research and its application to real-world problems

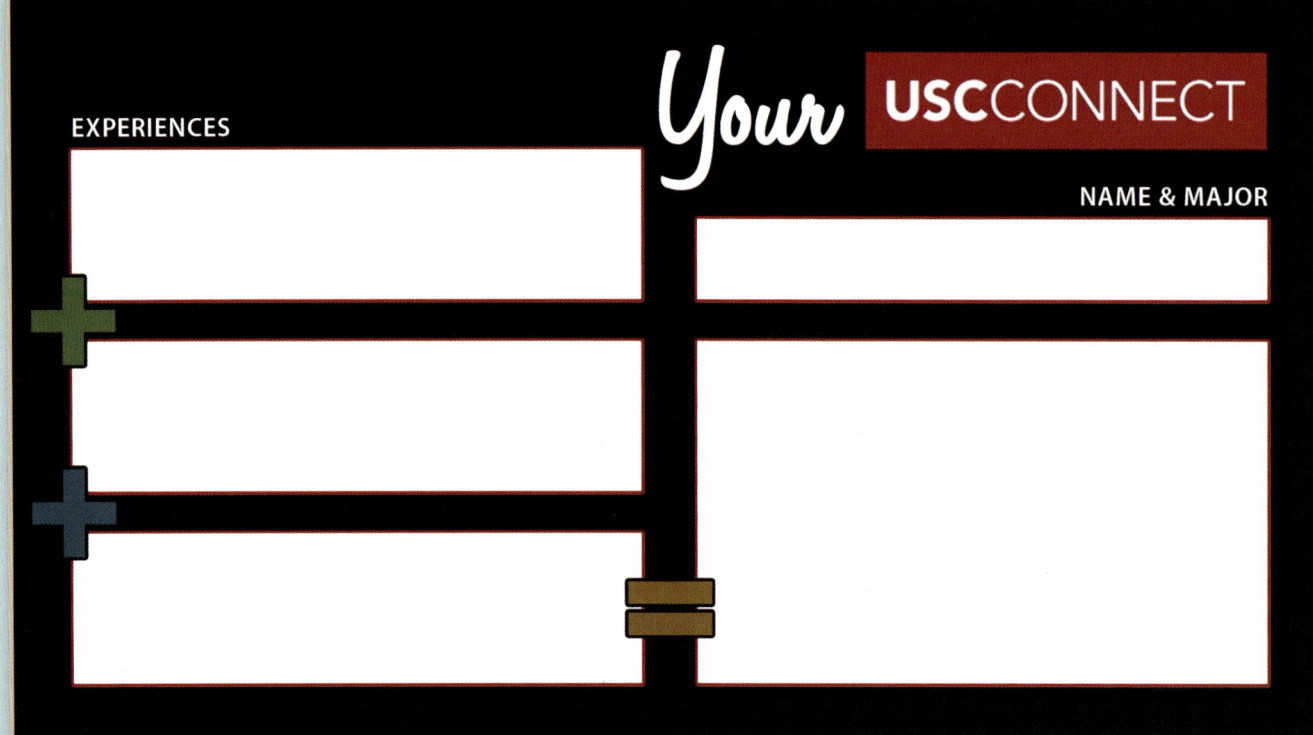

Your **USC CONNECT**

EXPERIENCES

NAME & MAJOR

Student Media

How can you make a major impact on campus, acquire hands-on skills to enhance your learning, and have a great time doing it? Get involved with Student Media. The Office of Student Media includes *The Daily Gamecock*, *Garnet & Black* magazine, WUSC-FM, and Student Gamecock Television (SGTV). You do not have to be a communications major to enjoy working on the paper and spreading the news about the University. Each area is managed by students and provides opportunities to learn about newspaper production, magazine publishing, design, advertising, and broadcast outlets.

Student Government

When you enrolled at the University, you immediately became a Student Government member. Student Government provides the organizational framework to respond to student needs and concerns on a variety of topics and to define student powers and responsibilities by taking issues that affect student life directly. Students can present these concerns to the University administration and various state governing bodies. Within this framework, there are several organizations (listed below) open to students who possess a deeper interest in governance and leadership. Student members serve the student body by managing organizations' registration and renewal and by distributing student activities funds to registered campus organizations. More than 400 students currently hold leadership positions within Student Government.

Freshman Council. One way to become more directly involved with Student Government early is through Freshman Council. The goals of Freshman Council are (a) developing leadership skills and familiarizing members with all the resources and services the University offers as well as (b) unifying the first-year class and presenting the first-year student perspective on ideas, programs, and projects to Student Government. Council members are selected each fall during the months of August and September through an interview and application process.

Executive Officers. The student body president, vice president, and treasurer are elected each February and serve a one-year term. These students represent the student body at faculty, staff, and administrative functions. Eligibility for office is based on a student's GPA and the number of credit hours earned at the University of South Carolina.

Student Senate. Senators are elected from each academic college similar to how U.S. Senators are selected to represent each state. The number of representatives is based on the enrollment in each college. Each senator serves

Did you know?

The Daily Gamecock

South Carolina's student-run newspaper hosts a circulation of 12,000 readers and is available online at dailygamecock.com

Garnet & Black

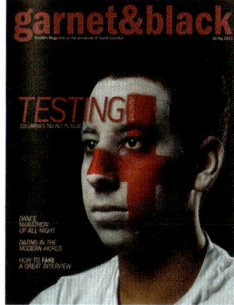

Garnet & Black (G&B), Carolina's student magazine, is free and distributed at more than 80 locations on and around campus.

WUSC-FM (90.5)

WUSC-FM is the noncommercial, free-format student radio station at the University, broadcasting 24 hours a day at 90.5 FM and wusc.sc.edu/.

SGTV

Student Gamecock Television (SGTV) is the student-run cable channel airing on campus cable channel 4.

Staff members of *The Daily Gamecock* and the *Garnet & Black* are always looking for students interested in writing, editing, photography, layout, design, advertising, promotion, marketing, and management.

ON THE WEB

For more information on getting involved with Student Government, visit their website:

sa.sc.edu/sg

You can also find them on:

 facebook.com/UofSCSG

 @UofSCSG

 USCStudentgovt

To learn more about peer leadership and for a list of current opportunities on campus, visit:

housing.sc.edu/ studentengagement/pld.html

Start Your Own Organization!

Not able to find something of interest? Start your own organization! To become registered and recognized by the University, leaders of student organizations must complete an application and petition for registration. In addition, leaders must write a constitution for their organization and have a minimum of 10 interested members.

Did you know?

Approximately 97% of first-year students live on campus!

---

a one-year term. Once elected, each member is assigned to a Senate committee (e.g., academic, athletics, student services) to serve on for the remainder of the year.

Executive Cabinet. The student body president selects students to assist him or her with campus issues and goals. Cabinet members deal with issues, such as parking, housing, safety, and institutional affairs. Most selections are made between the time of elections and inauguration.

University Committees. The student body president nominates individuals to serve on University committees and offer a student voice to faculty and staff members. These students attend meetings, take notes, provide input, and keep Student Government members informed about issues of importance to the student body. University committees address many aspects of campus life, including athletics, health services, disability services, safety, parking, orientation, and retention.

Peer Leadership

A unique way to get involved on campus is through peer leadership. A peer leader is a "student who has been selected and trained to offer educational services to their peers. Each peer leader service is intentionally designed to assist in the adjustment, satisfaction, and persistence of students toward the attainment of their educational goals" (Ender & Kay, 2001, p. 1). In general, peer leaders work one-on-one with students or in a class to share specific information regarding a certain topic or interest area.

Whether serving as a peer educator, peer mentor, or peer tutor, there are nearly 40 different peer leadership opportunities in a variety of offices and organizations you can take advantage of during your time at Carolina. Positions include

- University ambassadors
- Changing Carolina student health educators
- Orientation leaders
- EcoReps
- University 101 peer leaders

...and many more!

Residence Hall Involvement

Living on campus in a residence hall is an important component of your first year at the University of South Carolina. The residence hall is not only a place to eat and sleep, but it is also where you will become part of a community and engage in personal development by taking advantage of the unique opportunity to live and learn with a diverse group of fellow students having varied experiences and backgrounds. Participating in the events planned by the resident mentors, hall government, or your living and learning community will benefit you both academically and personally. Students who live in the residence hall are more involved in campus life and form stronger networks among their peers (Pascarella & Terenzini, 1991). In the residence hall you will find a number of individuals dedicated to making your experience worthwhile, including the resident mentors (RMs) or peer coordinators (PCs), assistant residence life coordinator (ARLC), residence life coordinator (RLC), residence hall director (RHD), and assistant director (AD). The residence hall positions that are staffed by students are excellent opportunities for involvement and leadership.

Resident mentor (RM). These positions are open to first-year students who have completed the fall semester. If you enjoy your experience living in the residence hall, you might want to consider becoming a resident mentor during the spring semester of your first year. Students apply in January to fill positions beginning in the fall of the following year. RMs not only have the ability to make a difference in their residences hall but also enjoy financial perks, such as reduced housing and meal plan costs in addition to a biweekly paycheck.

> ### Peer Leader Advice
>
> I'm proud to say that I have been involved in organizations ranging from the Opera program, to Greek Life, to membership in honor societies. I am also part of a church family that regularly serves the community. Through my involvement, I have met some of my best friends and mentors that are shaping my experience at Carolina. There are so many opportunities here for you, so take advantage of all that USC has to offer!
>
> - Lili Kinman
> Louisville, KY • Junior
> Public Relations

Residence Hall Association (RHA). RHA holds elections within each building in early September to select members for their hall government. RHA is the governing body for all of the individual hall governments and focuses on programming, advocacy, and sustainability within University Housing. Representatives from each hall government attend Senate meetings to assist in achieving the overall mission of RHA. The hall government is responsible for addressing student concerns and serving as an advocate for residents and consists of six executive members: president, vice president, secretary, treasurer, and two senators. In addition, each floor elects representatives to attend hall government meetings. Besides governance duties, most hall governments also plan and host many social and educational programs within their residence hall. Being a part of your hall government is an excellent way to develop your leadership skills and contribute to a positive living and learning environment for yourself and your peers.

National Residence Hall Honorary (NRHH). An organization comprised of the top 1% of campus leaders, NRHH is an affiliate of, and works closely with, RHA. Once you have had some time to establish yourself as a leader on campus, you should consider applying to be a part of this organization. Members of NRHH spend time recognizing individuals and student organizations for their contributions to the University. They also attend regional and national conferences. In addition, members are encouraged to fill out an Of the Month (OTM) to recognize individuals, programs, student groups, staff, or faculty who have made noteworthy contributions to the University for that month. The NRHH selects the OTM winners each month, and many nominees go on to be considered for state, regional, and national recognition. Further, NRHH promotes recognition by hosting numerous appreciation weeks, such as Custodial, Resident Mentor, and Professional/Graduate Staff Appreciation Week. They also host the RHA end-of-the-year banquet.

Research

Research is all about asking questions and finding answers. It is diving into a topic you are interested in and learning more about it. Research happens in all majors but you don't even have to do research in your major. You can explore almost anything that you are interested in!

There are a lot of reasons to get involved in undergraduate research:

- Gaining real-world experience—very important to employers.
- Building your resume for the workplace or for graduate or professional school.
- Working closely with faculty—learning about career options and getting recommendations.
- Strengthening applications for competitive scholarships and fellowships.
- Improving skills and abilities for future success (e.g., communication, critical and creative thinking).
- Spending your time earning money and getting experience in your field. Research can pay!
- Exploring a new major. Research can let you try out a field of study.
- Making the most of your experience. Combine research with study abroad, internships, practica, service, and more!

The earlier you start, the better! Start thinking about research as early as your first semester. You can begin by attending introductory workshops and advising sessions with the Office of Undergraduate Research (OUR). Workshops and advising sessions will introduce you to OUR and its programming. These interactive sessions allow you to learn about research, find potential faculty mentors, and discuss funding opportunities. OUR can help you explore research opportunities through a variety of programs including, Discover Program, Magellan Programming, Discovery Day, and Caravel (USC's undergraduate research journal).

Discover Program. This program encourages and promotes undergraduate research during the first year. This four-week, not-for-credit seminar meets once a week for an hour. You will learn how to take the initial steps to develop relationships with faculty, learn about opportunities for funding and showcasing research, and create a plan for research during your college experience.

Did you know?

- OUR has given over 2.5 million dollars to over 1,000 students
- Magellan programs have funded students on all 8 campuses
- Students have done research on all continents (except Antarctica)

ON THE WEB

For more information about the Office of Undergraduate Research, visit:
sc.edu/our

Magellan Programing. There are several grants through OUR that can help fund your project. From the Scholar to the Mini-Grant, there is something for everyone. Each program has different application deadlines and requirements, but all require working with a project mentor and presenting at Discovery Day.

Discovery Day. Discovery Day is held at the end of April for students (all campuses, all years, all majors) to share any and all scholarly pursuits in and out of the classroom, including study abroad, internships, leadership activities, research/scholarship, service-learning and community service, and national fellowship competitions. Presentations can be: poster, oral, or creative (e.g., art, theater, music, creative writing,).

Caravel. *Caravel* is USC's undergraduate research journal, chronicling student research and creativity. The journal highlights all disciplines and includes articles, poems, videos, and music. See what students have researched and accomplished at http://caravel.sc.edu/.

Community Service

The University's Community Service Programs and service-learning courses provide numerous occasions for developing leadership through community engagement. Community service and service-learning allow students to apply skills and knowledge gained in the classroom to real-world activities, projects, or events. By engaging in service, students develop character and a sense of civic responsibility. Students who participate in community service or service-learning often feel more connected to the community as a result of their involvement. Additionally, students gain confidence in their abilities to make a difference in the world and are energized by the opportunity to use their talents and resources to help others in need. Students who serve in areas related to personal- or career interests also have the opportunity for real-world experiences that may impact their long-term life goals.

Community Service Programs in the Leadership and Service Center and the Office of Student Engagement promote opportunities for students to become engaged in service in and around the Columbia area. The offices support and develop projects and services that address unmet needs and issues in the community; maintain a database of primary community, nonprofit agencies in the Columbia area; serve as resources for student service organizations; provide faculty with support and resources to integrate service-learning into their courses; and act as advocates for community agencies and social issues. There are several service opportunities for students to engage in.

Carolina Service Council (CSC). Carolina Service Council is a student-run organization created to inspire service and leadership in our University. CSC works closely with the community to offer and promote various service projects throughout the year. Their service programs include annual events like Carolina Stocking Stuffers, the Tree Lighting Ceremony on the Horseshoe, Oxfam Hunger Banquet, Alternative Break Trips, and National Volunteer Week as well as new programs created each semester to fit student interest and community need. Participation in all programs is open to all currently enrolled USC students.

Service Saturdays. These volunteer opportunities are offered by various community agencies on select Saturdays throughout the academic year. In the fall, they are offered on football away-game weekends and typically held between the hours of 10 a.m. and 3:30 p.m. On Service Saturdays, students engage in activities such as working with the homeless at the Salvation Army, aiding the Red Cross, renovating a Boy Scout camp, and learning about environmental problems in South Carolina.

Cocky's Reading Express. This on-the-road program's mission is to eliminate illiteracy in South Carolina one schoolchild at a time. Since the project began in 2005, Carolina students have volunteered to visit elementary schools in every corner of the state, reading books aloud to children and sharing the importance of learning to read. Cocky makes an appearance at the end of each story time

Did you know?

By senior year, 65% of Carolina students have participated in community service or volunteer work.

(Source: 2011 University of South Carolina National Survey of Student Engagement)

Did you know?

23,194 USC volunteers engaged in 502,334 service hours in 2012-2013, and raised over $978,736 in donations!

Cocky's Reading Express

Did you know?

The First Lady Michelle Obama visited Columbia and participated in Cocky's Reading Express!

Volunteering in Nicaragua

and has become almost as popular as Santa Claus to the young children! All children receive a book to take home and make a verbal promise to Cocky to read the book to their moms and dads, brothers and sisters—even cats, dogs, and goldfish. Cocky's Reading Express, the only University mascot–sponsored literacy program in the country, gave away its 10,000th book last winter.

Alternative Break Program. Students are offered a meaningful way to spend their fall, winter, and spring breaks. Through these programs, South Carolina students travel together to different locations, most of which are in the United States, to provide service to people in need. Alternative Breaks have included trips to Mississippi, Georgia, Tennessee, Pennsylvania, Louisiana, Florida, and Costa Rica to address problems including homelessness, poverty, and the environment. This program provides a fun and meaningful way to meet and work with other concerned students who share a desire and commitment to make a positive difference in the lives of others.

Service-Learning Courses. These courses intentionally integrate academic coursework and service experiences in ways that are mutually beneficial to both students and the community. These are not classes where students simply clock hours of service; rather, students take what they learn in the classroom and apply it in a real-world setting to address a specific community need. Intentional opportunities for reflection and discussion are built into the course experience. These classes are really a win-win for anyone. Students take classes they need to graduate, learn tangible skills, and give back to the community. Participating in a service-learning course also counts towards one of the requirements of graduating with Leadership Distinction in Community Service. Talk to your academic advisor about service-learning classes or check with the Office of Student Engagement for a current listing of courses.

AmeriCorps Programs. AmeriCorps is a federal program that is a part of the Corporation for National and Community Service. AmeriCorps engages citizens in intensive service each year at nonprofits, schools, public agencies, and community and faith-based groups across the country. Here at USC there are several AmeriCorps*VISTA members working with students to better the community. Students not only have the opportunity to work with these VISTAs, but they can also participate in AmeriCorps Week each spring!

Global Learning

Even though it is your first year at the University of South Carolina, it is not too early to begin thinking about incorporating international study abroad or Domestic Study Away (DSA) into your academic curriculum. Studying away internationally or domestically can provide you with experience that you cannot gain in the traditional classroom through immersion in a new culture.

The cost of study abroad or Domestic Study Away is comparable or equal to campus tuition, not including transportation to the host institution. While housing and food expenses vary by location, many exchange institutions are in areas where the cost of living is similar to South Carolina or at times even less. In addition, if your coursework has been approved in advance, you can apply federal or state-sponsored financial aid and scholarships toward your program expense. If you have private scholarships or aid, you may need to get the approval of your lender to use these towards your experience. In addition, there are also a number of scholarships you can apply for specifically for study abroad.

International Experiences. The Study Abroad Office facilitates study abroad programs and other opportunities for students and faculty to gain leadership skills through cross-cultural collaboration. An overseas experience can give you a competitive edge in the job market as you gain a breadth of knowledge about other cultures, languages, politics, and practices, both across oceans and across the country. You also learn to think critically and problem solve while becoming more self-reliant; skills employers look for. Additionally, it is possible to earn credits that will count toward your major, minor, or elective requirements without delaying graduation. Furthermore, you can improve your foreign language skills by taking courses in another language or taking courses in English while living among non-English speaking natives.

Many students begin planning nine months to a year in advance of going abroad. Allowing sufficient time to plan will enable you to apply for scholarships and financial aid and incorporate your experience into your curriculum to earn credits while studying abroad so you can stay on track for graduation.

ON THE WEB

To find out more information about Alternative Breaks, visit their website at or find them on:

 @UofSCaltbreak

 @servecarolina

There are many more service opportunities for you to get involved with! For volunteer service opportunities visit the Leadership and Service Center's website:

sa.sc.edu/communityservice/

For more information or a complete listing of service-learning courses visit the Office of Student Engagement website:

sc.edu/studentengagement

Alternative Spring Break - Detroit

Typically, students embark upon a study abroad experience during their sophomore or junior year, but you are eligible to apply for the program as early as the spring break of your first year. If you wish to go during your senior year, you will need special permission from your department. Long-term programs, such as those lasting an entire semester, may be best if you are trying to increase your foreign language proficiency. Students with very structured degree programs may find a summer session more suitable for their academic needs, though this is not always the case.

In choosing an international study abroad program, there several options, including Global Exchange, Direct, Partner, and Classroom Programs, which vary in tuition and fee requirements, structure, and institution sponsorship. For the student who would like an international experience, but not necessarily study at another school, there are also teaching, volunteering, working, researching, or interning opportunities.

Domestic Experiences. There are also many options for studying domestically, which includes study in the United States; Canada; or the U.S. territories, such as Guam, Puerto Rico, or the U.S. Virgin Islands. While Carolina students can participate in a number of independent domestic study programs, the most popular choice is the National Student Exchange. Through this program, students pay their tuition to the University of South Carolina, and they can then spend a semester, summer, or year studying at one of approximately 200 schools that participate in the program. More often than not, all financial aid will apply to the program. Students can also enhance their experience by adding an internship in their area, serving as a peer leader on the host campus, or engaging in undergraduate research.

Students can also enroll in courses taught by USC faculty that have a domestic travel component as part of the course. By traveling to Washington, D.C. to learn about policy or to rural parts of South Carolina to learn about poverty, students have the opportunity to learn beyond the typical classroom setting. Domestic courses are available and change each year and are typically offered in the spring semester, Maymester or Summer. Visit www.sc.edu/studentengagement for a current listing of courses.

Conversation Partner Programs. This program pairs English Programs for Internationals (EPI) students with native speakers of English for conversation, giving the international student a chance to meet an American and practice English. This is a great way for students to get to know someone from another country and broaden their cultural experience. Students are paired with international students based upon gender and language preference as well as individual interests. New partners are assigned every nine weeks at the beginning of EPI's terms. The majority of EPI students speak Chinese, Korean, Japanese, or Arabic; however, students who speak Spanish, Turkish, Italian, French, or German are also represented in the program.

International House at Maxcy College. The International House at Maxcy College is the only internationally themed residence hall on the USC campus. Its goal is to bring American and international students together as a community to have the opportunity to learn, experience, and share each other's cultures. This energetic community not only allows people to interact with individuals from around the world, but it also gives residents the opportunity to get involved in numerous internationally focused activities. The French House and Spanish House are also located in Maxcy.

ON THE WEB

For more information on study abroad, visit:
studyabroad.sc.edu

For more information on the National Student Exchange, visit:
sc.edu/studentengagement

For more information about the Conversation Partners program, visit:
fc.epi.sc.edu/cp.html

Other Opportunities
Campus Recreation and Athletics

Campus recreation at the University of South Carolina encompasses a variety of aspects. Not only does the Campus Recreation office maintain both the Strom Thurmond Wellness and Fitness Center and the Solomon Blatt Physical Education Center, but they also provide a number of opportunities for students to get involved on campus while staying fit.

Intramural Programs. Team, individual, and dual sports are offered throughout the year in men's, women's, and co-recreational divisions for sports, including flag football, volleyball, softball, and even bowling. The program emphasizes providing social opportunities through athletics in a fun and safe environment. Consider getting together a team of students from your floor, Greek organization, or student group. You do not have to have a team to be able to play! Simply sign the free agent list at the Campus Recreation office and the staff will place you on a team.

Sports Clubs. Students also have the opportunity to participate in sports clubs. Sports clubs differ from intramural sports in that they are registered student organizations. Sports clubs are formed by students who share a common interest in a specific sport. Clubs include a wide variety of indoor and outdoor sports ranging from soccer to fencing to surfing and chess. Sports clubs play approximately 6-10 games per year against club teams from other universities and at a more competitive level compared to intramural sports. Due to travel expenses, there may be fees to play on a sports club team.

The keys to a successful sports club are student leadership, student input, and student responsibility. As a student-initiated activity, the members of each club play an important role in determining the scope and direction of the club. Sports clubs expose students to new activities, enhance skills already acquired, develop student leadership skills, provide opportunities for students to develop positive interpersonal relationships and an appreciation for cultural diversity, and enhance holistic development through leisure and physical activities.

Outdoor Recreation. This program offers students activities that explore and teach new skills by merging academic and recreational experiences. Students are introduced to the environment through a variety of outdoor recreation activities, including adventure trips in skiing, climbing, backpacking, and mountain biking; wilderness first aid courses; sustainability clinics; and weekly events, such as tubing and slacklining. Participating in one or many of these events is a great way to develop effective team-building and leadership skills while moving beyond self-imposed limitations to discover new strengths within you.

ON THE WEB

For a complete list of current intramural sports, including entry dates and deadlines, visit:
campusrec.sc.edu/intramurals

For more information about Sports Clubs, visit:
campusrec.sc.edu/clubs

For more information about the Outdoor Recreation program, visit:
campusrec.sc.edu/orec

For more information about Student Athletic Tickets, visit :
sa.sc.edu/stlife/studenttickets/

Loyalty Points

Loyalty points are accumulated by students when they attend athletic events (football, men's and women's basketball, and baseball) and other designated events, such as away game tailgates. All students start with at least 3 points. The more athletic events you attend, the more points you accumulate. (1 point – SEC games, 2 points – nonconference games)

Athletics. As a new student at South Carolina, you can show your support for the Gamecock athletic program by attending sporting events and cheering on nearly 500 of your fellow students who compete on University teams. With 19 different teams participating in events throughout the academic year, there is sure to be something you will enjoy watching. Being a member of the Southeastern Conference (SEC) allows Gamecock athletes to play in one of the nation's most competitive collegiate sports conferences.

You must have a current University of South Carolina ID card for entry into Gamecock athletic events. Additionally, student tickets are required for admission into home football, men's basketball, and some baseball games. To be eligible for student tickets, you must be a full- or part-time; fee-paying University of South Carolina, Columbia campus student. Students are not guaranteed a student ticket to each game, only the right to request a ticket as long as tickets are available.

Athletic Team Schedules

Men's Athletic Team	Season	Home Venue
Baseball	February-May	Carolina Stadium
Basketball	November-February	Colonial Center
Football	August-November	Williams-Brice Stadium
Golf	September-April	Cobblestone Park
Soccer	August-November	Eugene Stone III Stadium
Swimming & Diving	October-February	Carolina Natatorium
Tennis	September-April	Carolina Tennis Center
Track & Field	November-May	Weems Baskin Track

Women's Athletic Team	Season	Home Venue
Basketball	November-February	Colonial Center
Cross Country	August-November	Owens Field
Equestrian	September-April	One Wood Farm
Golf	September-April	Cobblestone Park
Sand Volleyball	March-May	Sand Volleyball Courts
Soccer	August-November	Eugene Stone III Stadium
Softball	February-May	Beckham Field
Swimming & Diving	October-February	Carolina Natatorium
Tennis	January-April	Carolina Tennis Center
Track & Field	November-May	Weems Baskin Track
Volleyball	August-November	Volleyball Competition Facility

Cultural Experiences

There are many campus opportunities to explore and learn about people from different cultures. Understanding more about people with diverse backgrounds than your own can open doors for you throughout your life. Consider attending World Night, an event sponsored by the international student community to showcase their traditional food, dress, music, and dance, or a Diversity Dialogue hosted by the Office of Multicultural Student Affairs. Check the Russell House University Union, or even your residence hall calendar, for listings of other cultural events. Exploring diversity can enrich your University experience and help you develop life and professional skills that can serve you in years to come.

Photo courtesy of Columbia Metropolitan Convention & Visitors Bureau

Discover Columbia

To maximize your experience at the University of South Carolina, dedicate some time to familiarize yourself with the Columbia area and all it has to offer. After all, Columbia is going to be your home for the next few years!

Ready for something different? The city of Columbia has it all: films, symphony concerts, jazz, theater, museums, Renaissance art, ballet, avant-garde performance art, stand-up comedy, and even a puppet theater. In addition to these offerings, Columbia also boasts a wide variety of other cultural, historical, educational, and recreational activities and attractions—many within a short walk from campus. The following are just a sample of what Columbia has to offer.

Theater

Columbia is a great theater town and showcase for professional and amateur artists. With 13 theaters in the area producing live shows, there is something exciting for almost everyone. All the theaters have special student prices. During the fall and spring semesters, three to four plays are concurrently performed within two miles of campus. The best part is that you can be either an audience member or artist. Every company is looking for actors, stage managers, and crew members. Opportunities abound for those who have experience or who just

---

Peer Leader Advice

One of the best parts about going to a university in the heart of Columbia, SC is all of the opportunities that you have away from campus to make the most of your time here. There are several rivers and hiking trails if you like the outdoors, numerous nonprofit organizations and community service opportunities with all types of people, as well as plenty of places to explore just a few blocks from our school. One of my favorite things to do during my time at Carolina was to eat at as many local places as I could in Columbia. You definitely have your tried and true chain restaurants, cafes, and coffee shops, but if you're willing to explore, ask around, and go off the beaten path, there's a wide variety of treats to discover!

- Tim Olson
Aiken, SC • Senior
Public Relations

ON THE WEB

Visit these websites for more information about shows, dates, and times!

Koger Center
koger.sc.edu

Trustus Theatre
trustus.org

Workshop Theatre
workshoptheatre.com/info.html

want to get a taste of what it is like to be there when the curtain goes up. Students can also receive academic credit for attending performances or working on productions. Information on theaters and productions in the Columbia area is posted in the elevator area in **Longstreet Theatre** and includes audition and production schedules.

The **Ira and Nancy Koger Center for the Arts** is located on the edge of the Columbia campus. This 2,250 seat, state of the art theatre provides opportunities for students to see traveling Broadway productions of musicals, such as *Hairspray* and *The Producers*; hear musical groups ranging from Nickelcreek to John Legend; enjoy comics (e.g., Jim Gaffigan or Tracy Morgan); and even see live broadcasts by personalities such as Glenn Beck. At the Koger Center, students have the chance to see exciting professional productions at a reduced ticket cost and all within walking distance of most residence halls.

Trustus Theatre, located in the Vista (about a mile from campus), features big comfortable audience chairs with productions that range from classical to innovative theatre. Past productions include *Death of a Salesman, Angels in America, The Rocky Horror Picture Show,* and *Vampire Lesbians of Sodom*. Trustus also has late-night performances of exciting bands and improv comedy. **Workshop Theatre**, located three blocks from campus, presents a wide variety of productions throughout the year, from big musicals to dramatic New York hits. **Town Theatre** is the nation's oldest continuing community theatre. Located less than a block from the Horseshoe, Town Theatre specializes in musicals and traditional American comedies. The **South Carolina Shakespeare Company** produces Shakespeare plays in Columbia parks and throughout the state during the spring and summer. These outstanding presentations are free of charge. You also should not miss the **Columbia Marionette Theatre**, which provides a full season of unique productions and also teaches crafts like marionette, puppet, and mask making.

While Columbia's community is rich with theater opportunities, you do not have to leave campus to get involved. **Theatre South Carolina**, the production arm of the Department of Theatre and Dance, presents a full season of productions that vary from the ancient to the contemporary and experimental. Auditions are held late in the fall and spring. Many of these productions include guest artists from professional companies across the country. These actors and artists give students an opportunity to learn from the best. Each semester, there are a number of student-directed projects and other opportunities to participate as an actor, director, designer, or techie. In addition to Theatre South Carolina, the University hosts several student performance groups. **Puppet Regime** is not about puppets; it is the student production company of the University and produces four shows a year, some of which are original plays by students. **Toast** is an improv comedy troupe that performs on campus and throughout the nation. Once a month, they do a Toast and Jam show on campus that combines outrageous improv with sketch comedy and bands or other kinds of performances.

Dance

Is dance your thing? If so, you will find a wealth of opportunities here in Columbia. The **University of South Carolina Dance Company** presents some of the most exciting work in the region. Each year, this student company presents two productions that combine classical pieces with student-choreographed work in a variety of styles. The company is always looking for dancers and choreographers. **Columbia City Ballet** specializes in classical ballet, but also creates new works, as does **Columbia Classical Ballet**. The **Columbia City Jazz Dance Company** and the **Eboni Dance Theatre**, in contrast, specialize in the production of contemporary works.

Film

Columbia has a number of movie theaters across town. If, however, you want an occasional break from the endless stream of action-packed thrillers and broad comedies coming out of Hollywood, try the **Nickelodeon Theatre**, Columbia's home for classic and experimental films. Bringing back the best of the past and exploring the new, the intellectual, or the innovative, the Nick is a great place to learn about film and meet interesting people, including faculty. You can become a regular member at a low student rate or just attend an occasional flick.

ON THE WEB

For more information on events at The Nick, visit: **nickelodeon.org**

Music

If you are a music lover, no matter what your taste, Columbia has it. Local bands and great food can be found in the Vista almost every weekend. If it is jazz that moves you, join the **Columbia Jazz Club** or read their newsletter for information on local performers. If chamber music is your interest, there is the **Carolina Chamber Players**, which specializes in classical and modern chamber repertoire. Columbia also has its own symphony orchestra, the **South Carolina Philharmonic**, which performs regularly at the Koger Center and often features guest artists. If singing is what interests you, check out the **Palmetto Mastersingers**, a professional choral group with a broad repertoire from Franz Schubert to Paul Simon.

One of the real advantages to being a student on a campus with a first-rate School of Music is that almost every week there are free recitals and miniconcerts on campus. Do not pass them up. The University also offers a wide array of opportunities for you to show off your musical talents. **The University of South Carolina Symphony Orchestra**, conducted by Donald Portnoy, performs regularly at the Koger Center and often features guest artists. **Carolina Alive**, the University's internationally renowned vocal performance company, presents lively and exciting productions of modern popular music. **The University Opera Theatre** produces two operas a year from the best in classical and modern opera. **Township Auditorium** is another great place in Columbia to check out great entertainment. Past shows have included Pretty Lights, R. Kelly, Chris Daughtry, Old Crow Medicine Show, Ron White, and Kevin Hart.

Visual Arts

If you are interested in the visual arts, start with the **Columbia Museum of Art**, located on the corner of Hampton and Main Streets. This museum has a marvelous collection of Renaissance religious art and exciting contemporary works. The museum additionally hosts new exhibitions several times a year. You also can visit **McKissick Museum**, located on the Horseshoe, which not only houses the geology museum and the Movietone News archives but also features traveling exhibitions of special collections of graphic and other visual arts. The **University of South Carolina Department of Art** has a small museum of outstanding works created by its students. There are also several small galleries downtown and in Five Points where you can see what is new and innovative in the world of art. Columbia has more than 40 art galleries with something for every taste.

Parks

For you outdoor enthusiasts, consider visiting one of Columbia's many parks. Several parks are located in or near downtown. **Finlay Park**, a 17.5-acre park in the heart of Columbia's Congaree Vista at Laurel and Assembly streets, features a 1.5-acre man-made lake, a 40-foot cascading waterfall, an amphitheater, and several walking paths. The park hosts many outdoor concerts throughout the year. **Columbia Riverfront Park and Historic Canal**, off Laurel Street, is planned around the city's original waterworks and hydroelectric plant. The park offers jogging, bicycling, and walking paths. **Memorial Park**, located at the corner of Washington and Gadsen streets, is a 7-acre landscaped park and hosts many outdoor concerts and veterans' celebrations. The **West Columbia Riverwalk** is part of a joint effort by the City of West Columbia and the River Alliance to protect our regions' rivers and provide recreational benefits to collective communities. Riverwalk hosts 4.5 acres of the **Three Rivers Greenway**, and is located between Gervais Street and Knox Abbott Drive. Its half-mile path accommodates all levels of physical access, including baby carriages and wheelchairs.

Other parks, further from campus, also offer opportunities for outdoor relaxation and recreation. **Saluda Shoals Park**, a 300-acre park located along the banks of the Saluda River, provides visitors paved and unpaved trails for hiking, biking, and horseback riding; boat, canoe, and kayak launch areas; picnic shelters; and an observation deck overlooking the river. The park also has an 11,000 square foot environmental education center and exhibit hall. **Harbison State Forest**, located only nine miles from downtown, has 18 miles of trails designed for walking, jogging, hiking, and bicycling. A canoe landing located near the Broad River provides access for kayaks and canoes. **Sesquicentennial State Park**, located on Two Notch Road, offers 1,440 acres for camping, picnicking, swimming, fishing, boating, and hiking on nature trails. **Congaree National Park**, located 20 miles from Columbia, offers over 20 miles of marked hiking trails, a 2.3-mile boardwalk loop, 8 miles of marked canoe trails, and picnic areas. The 22,000 acre park is home of the largest intact tract of old-growth bottomland hardwood forest remaining in the United States. You can visit most of these parks free of charge, however some (e.g., Saluda Shoals Park and Sesquicentennial State Park) require small entrance fees that you might want to know about before venturing out!

Historical Sites

Four **Historic Columbia House Museums** are managed by Historic Columbia, a preservation and education foundation dedicated to the cultural heritage of Columbia and its environs. The historic house museums include **Hampton-Preston Mansion and Gardens, Mann-Simons Cottage, Robert Mills House and Park,** and **the Woodrow Wilson Family Home**. Historic Columbia offers tours of the homes as well as educational activities, lecture series, and special exhibitions.

There are several other historical buildings and sites in Columbia, including the **South Carolina State Capitol Building**, located at the intersection of Main and Gervais streets. The Capitol building was built in 1855 and survived Sherman's cannons during attacks by the Union army in 1865. You also may be interested in visiting the **South Carolina Governor's Mansion**, located at the 800 block of Richland Street. The mansion was built in 1855 to house officers of a military academy and has housed governors since 1868. The grounds include two other houses: **The Lace House** and **The Caldwell-Boylston**

ON THE WEB

For more information about the history of South Carolina, visit the South Carolina State Museum! Visit their website for admission information at:

museum.state.sc.us

House. Additionally, you can find out more about South Carolina and its history at the **South Carolina State Museum**, located at 301 Gervais Street. In this renovated textile mill, you will find exhibits of art, history, natural history, science, and technology unique to South Carolina. The museum also offers educational programs, demonstration theaters, and an art gallery and general admission is only $1 per person on the first Sunday of every month.

Photo courtesy of Columbia Metropolitan Convention & Visitors Bureau

Festivals and Fairs

The Columbia area hosts multiple festivals and community celebrations throughout the year. The **Columbia Greek Festival** is held downtown every September at Holy Trinity Greek Orthodox Church. The four-day festival showcases traditional Greek dancers, ceremonies, music, theater, and delicious food. The **South Carolina State Fair** is held each year in October at the South Carolina State Fairgrounds located near Williams-Brice Stadium. This statewide celebration features homemade crafts, demonstrations, livestock shows, rides, games, live entertainment, and fried butter. Columbia is also home to the annual **South Carolina Pride Festival**. Held in September, this statewide celebration of sexual orientation and gender identity is sponsored by the Gay and Lesbian Pride Movement and hosts a variety of local and celebrity entertainment. In the spring, festivals continue with the **South Carolina Cornbread Festival** in March and the **Rosewood Crawfish Festival** in May.

Other Opportunities for Fun

Columbia really does have something for everyone: performing and visual arts, parks, historical landmarks, and seasonal festivals and fairs. If you still are looking for more to do, consider checking out the **Riverbanks Zoo and Garden**. The zoo and garden are located at I-126 and Greystone Boulevard and is home to more than 2,000 animals and 70 acres of scenic overlooks and spectacular gardens. Special events such as Boo at the Zoo and Lights Before Christmas are fun opportunities to visit the zoo during the evening hours. The zoo was the 2002 winner of the Governor's Cup for the Most Outstanding Tourist Attraction in South Carolina.

Photo courtesy of Columbia Metropolitan Convention & Visitors Bureau

As you can see, there are a vast number of opportunities for Carolina students. If you hope to take advantage of all of the things that interest you, start by considering how you can get involved while still leaving time for your academics.

Did you know?

Riverbanks Zoo & Garden welcomes 1 million guests annually.

ON THE WEB

For a complete list of all Columbia has to offer, explore the city's official website:
columbiacvb.com

Name: _____   Year in School: _____

Major/Minor: _____   Date: _____

STUDENT ENGAGEMENT PLAN

Welcome to the Student Engagement Plan (SEP)! Students who fully engage in their academic and social experiences within and beyond the classroom are generally more satisfied and likely to succeed. Additionally, the University of South Carolina provides students with a number of resources that can help them to become more engaged on campus. The purpose of the SEP is to help students become better acquainted with campus resources and understanding high-impact practices that can help them maximize their undergraduate experience.

SEP Part 1: A Pathway to Discovering High-Impact Practices and Campus Resources

At the University of South Carolina, high-impact practices are active learning opportunities that are highly beneficial for enhancing students' undergraduate experiences. Through USC Connect, students can gain educational experiences beyond the classroom and develop skill sets that are critical to their success in college and after graduation. USC Connect includes five different "pathways" of engagement:

Community Service: There are a number of opportunities to give back to the greater Carolina community. Students can participate in monthly Service Saturdays, MLK Service Days, or an alternative break service trip. Additionally, students can enroll in service-learning courses where they will have the opportunity to connect service experiences with academic course outcomes. A full listing and description of service-learning courses available across disciplines can be found at the Office of Student Engagement's website. For further information about service opportunities, please see the Beyond the Classroom Database on the USC Connect website.

Global Learning: A domestic or international study experience can help students develop personally, professionally, and academically by providing opportunities to make new friends and visit a different part of the United States or a country overseas.

Research: Research is as simple as asking a question and finding the answer. The Office of Undergraduate Research helps students answer questions related to their professional field of study or a particular topic of interest and provides them with information about opportunities for research and funding.

Internships: Completing an internship as a student offers great first-hand experience within a major and professional field of interest. There are a number of internship opportunities available within each college and it is important to talk with an academic advisor or the Career Center about planning early. Additional opportunities outside of the Career Center include the "Washington Semester" and the "SC Government." For further information about internship opportunities, please see the Beyond the Classroom Database on the USC Connect website.

Peer Leadership: As a student at USC you have the opportunity to serve as a peer leader. Peer leaders are students who have been selected and trained to offer educational services to their peers. Opportunities for peer leadership include peer education, peer mentoring, peer tutoring/counseling and student leadership within a group or organization. For a list of opportunities, visit sc.edu/studentengagement.

USC Connect
Beyond the Classroom Database
sc.edu/uscconnect/participate

**Service-Learning
Domestic Study Away
Peer Leadership**
Office of Student Engagement,
Patterson Hall, Garden Level
803.777.1945
sc.edu/studentengagement

Study Abroad
Legare College, Third Floor
803.777.7557
studyabroad.sc.edu

Office of Undergraduate Research
Legare College, Room 223
803.777.1141
sc.edu/our

Leadership and Service Center
Russell House, Suite 227
803.777.7130
sa.sc.edu/communityservice

Career Center
Thomas Cooper Library, Fifth Floor
Sixth Floor
803.777.7280
sc.edu/career

SEP Part 2: Student Engagement Inventory

As you fill out this inventory, reflect on your college experience thus far. The goal is to be intentional and selective with your engagement experiences so they have the greatest impact and meet your individual needs over time.

Please circle the appropriate number in regards to each category using the following scale:

		Unfamiliar	No Interest	Some Interest	Interested	Participating
1	Interacting with my professors outside of class on a regular basis	0	1	2	3	4
2	Participating in a practicum, internship, field experience, co-op, or clinical assignment	0	1	2	3	4
3	Doing research in my field of study	0	1	2	3	4
4	Living in a residence learning community with other students who have similar interests such as environmental awareness, languages, the arts, or pre-med	0	1	2	3	4
5	Participating in study abroad for course credit, volunteering abroad, or an internship opportunity or foreign language immersion experience	0	1	2	3	4
6	Participating in a domestic study program such as a faulty-led course or with the National Student Exchange within the United States, Canada, Puerto Rico or Guam	0	1	2	3	4
7	Serving as a peer leader on-campus (e.g., resident mentor, U101 peer leader, orientation leader, academic tutor)	0	1	2	3	4
8	Developing leadership skills by participating in events such as Emerging Leaders Program, LEAP, SLDC	0	1	2	3	4
9	Participating in community service opportunities (e.g., Service Saturdays, MLK Days of Service, or AmeriCorps programming)	0	1	2	3	4
10	Participating in a service-learning class to connect community service experiences with academic course content	0	1	2	3	4
11	Finding employment both on or off campus (e.g., work-study, internships)	0	1	2	3	4
	Please circle the number that appropriately describes your level of agreement with the following statements:	**Strongly Disagree**	**Disagree**	**Neutral**	**Agree**	**Strongly Agree**
12	I am aware of the resources to help support my engagement on campus	0	1	2	3	4
13	I am confident that I will get involved in educationally purposeful activities on campus	0	1	2	3	4
14	I am aware of the resources to help support my involvement on campus	0	1	2	3	4

Scores:

Your scores on the Student Engagement Inventory are intended to assist you and your ACE Coach/advisor/instructor with narrowing down engagement opportunities that will be most purposeful for you based on your interests, major and career aspirations. Keep in mind that it is important to be intentional about the timing of certain engagement activities in order to maximize their impact during your time at USC. Additionally, the goal is not to over-commit yourself with a large quantity of activities, but rather focus on the quality of time you commit to meaningful engagement in select areas.

Fours — **You are ACTIVELY PARTICIPATING in this category of activities.**

Focus on: Setting SMART Goals (Part 4) to either build upon current engagement experiences or establish new ones to create more variety and better balance.

Threes — **You are INTERESTED in this category of activities.**

Focus on: Setting SMART Goals (Part 4) to help you take steps to move from being interested in this category to being actively engaged. Pick a few activities to pursue that will either complement one another or will help you to get a diverse range of experiences.

Twos — **You have SOME INTEREST in this category of activities.**

Focus on: Making sure that you have a strong understanding of what this category entails, and how it may relate to your future career goals. There is no need to be interested in everything! Just keep in mind that you might become more interested in this later on in college, so understanding the resources available may be helpful to you in the future.

Ones — **You have NO INTEREST in this category of activities.**

Focus on: Finding at least one or two other areas of interest that might not be of interest to you now but could potentially be opportunities in the future. Also, it is important to recognize that your interests may change.

Zeros — **You are UNFAMILIAR with this category of activities,**

Focus on the personal reflection questions in Part 3 to reflect on your interests and how to begin pursuing them. Take time to review opportunities found on the Beyond the Classroom Database through the USC Connect website and think about what you might want to learn more about. Meeting with an ACE Coach/advisor/instructor could also help you decide which opportunities might best serve your long-term goals.

Your Next Steps:

1) Do some personal reflection about engagement and discuss it with your ACE coach/advisor/instructor/class.

2) Learn more about high-impact practices and opportunities for engagement through a variety of campus resources.

3) Set SMART goals in an effort to find a good balance of engagement activities that will support your career and collegiate goals.

4) Use the mind mapping activity to understand the relationships between your activities in and out of the classroom and how they are tied to the Carolina Core and USC Connect.

SEP Part 3: Personal Reflection

It is helpful to reflect on your present and past experiences to better understand how they connect to your future involvement beyond the classroom. This reflection will help you to develop a clear plan for engagement at USC by tying in your interests and goals.

Please describe how you are currently involved beyond the classroom.

What's something you've accomplished that you are proud of?

What do you enjoy doing in your free time?

What opportunities are you looking for at the University of South Carolina?

What was a project or activity that you worked on for hours upon hours and lost track of time.

When was the last time you were really excited about something? What was exciting about it?

Once you have completed your reflection, discuss your discoveries with your ACE coach/advisor/instructor to continue planning how to become more engaged. Use Part 4 to help you design your personal engagement plan.

SEP Part 4: Knowing Campus Resources

The University of South Carolina offers several different areas in which students can participate and become engaged. Becoming familiar with offices and resources on campus can help you find ways to become more engaged while at USC. It will help to visit the websites and do a little information gathering in the areas of interest to you. You may also learn about new things that you had not even considered.

Engagement Category	Opportunity	Office
1. Interacting with professors	Out to Lunch	Student Success Center
	Mutual Expectations Workshops	Office of Student Engagement
	Last Lecture Series	Office of Fellowships & Scholar Programs
	Professors office hours	See professor or instructor
2. Practical experiences	Internships/Co-ops/Job Shadow	Career Center/ College or School of major
3. Research	Undergraduate research	Office of Undergraduate Research
	With professor	See professor
4. Residence learning community	Living & Learning Communities	University Housing
	Resident Mentors	University Housing
	Residence Hall Association (RHA)	University Housing
	National Residence Hall Honorary (NRHH)	University Housing
5. Student organizations	Fraternity and Sorority Life	The Office of Fraternity & Sorority Life
	Honor	Student Organizations
	Interest	Student Organizations
	International	Student Organizations, International Programs
	Political	Student Organizations
	Professional	Student Organizations
	Religious	Student Organizations, Carolina Campus Ministries
	Residence Hall Government	University Housing
	Service	Student Organizations
	Sport	Student Organizations, Campus Recreation
6. International Study Abroad/ Domestic Study Away	International study abroad	Study Abroad Office
	Domestic Study Away - National Student Exchange	Office of Student Engagement
	Domestic Study Away- Independent Programs	Office of Student Engagement
	Domestic Study Away Faculty-led courses	Office of Student Engagement
	Maxcy International House	University Housing & International Programs
	Conversation Partners	English Programs for Internationals
7. Arts on and off campus	USC Theatre and Dance performances	www.cas.sc.edu/THEA
	School of Music performances	www.music.sc.edu
	Longstreet Theatre	http://artsandsciences.sc.edu/THEA
	Koger Center events	http://koger.sc.edu
	Carolina Productions	www.cp.sc.edu
	McKissisk Museum	College of Arts and Sciences
	Columbia Museum of Art	www.columbiamuseum.org
	South Carolina Statehouse	http://www.scstatehouse.gov/visit.php
	SC Railroad Museum	http://www.scrm.org
	Town Theatre	http://www.towntheatre.com/index.html
	South Carolina State Museum	http://www.museum.state.sc.us

SEP Part 4: Knowing Campus Resources *continued*

Engagement Category	Opportunity	Office
8. Recreation	Outdoor adventure trips	Campus Recreation-Outdoor Recreation
	Intramurals	Campus Recreation
	Group Exercise classes	Campus Recreation
	Fitness Orientations	Campus Recreation
9. Health	Changing Carolina Peers	Campus Wellness
	Nutrition Consultation	Campus Wellness
	Fitness Assessment/Exercise Consulting	Campus Wellness
	Grocery Store Tours-Nutrition Knowledge	Campus Wellness
	Individual Stress Management Appointments	Campus Wellness
10. Peer leadership	See www.sc.edu/studentengagement for complete list of opportunities (over 50 groups)	Office of Student Engagement
11. Service	Service-Learning classes	Office of Student Engagement
	Service Saturdays	Community Service Programs
	Carolina Service Council	Community Service Programs
	Alternative Spring Break Trips	Community Service Programs
12. Employment	Student Leadership in the workplace	Student Life
	Work-study jobs	Office of Student Financial Aid & Scholarships
	On-and-off campus jobs	Career Center
13. Leadership	Emerging Leaders	Leadership Programs
	Leaders Engaging Across Perspectives	Leadership Programs
14. Diversity	Conversation Partners	English Programs for Internationals
	Maxcy International House	International Programs
	EMPOWER Diversity Peer Educators	Office of Multicultural Student Affairs
	Diversity Dialogues	Office of Multicultural Student Affairs
	Diversity Trainings	Office of Multicultural Student Affairs
	Safe Zone Allies Program	Office of Multicultural Student Affairs
	Student Leadership & Diversity Conference	OMSA, Leadership Programs
	Preston Residential College	University Housing
15. Sustainability	Eco-Reps – Peer Leaders	University Housing
	Green Quad Learning Community	www.housing.sc.edu/rsl/westquad.html
	SAGE: Students Advocating a Greener Environment	www.sageusc.org
16. Financial	Financial Literacy drop-in consultations	Student Success Center
	Financial Literacy seminars & workshops	Student Success Center
17. Faith	Campus ministry organizations	Carolina Campus Ministries
	Local churches	Carolina Campus Ministries
18. Student Media	*The Daily Gamecock*	Student Media
	Garnet & Black Magazine	Student Media
	SGTV (Student Gamecock Television)	Student Media
	WUSC-FM	Student Media

SEP Part 5: Creating Your Plan for Engagement

Consider the various interest areas you have explored and create goals to help guide your personal engagement at the University of South Carolina. Set SMART (Specific, Measurable, Attainable, Realistic, Timely) goals, list the available campus resources that will help you reach each goal, develop an action plan (specific steps you will take to reach the goal), and set deadlines for completing your action steps. Use this plan as a method to hold yourself accountable and to list the outcome of each action step.

As you work toward achieving your goals you may face challenges along the way. Therefore, it is important to be aware of the resources or alternatives that exist. Perhaps you will discover you need to adjust your goals to meet evolving interests, or once you complete a goal you'll realize it leads to another goal for that same interest area that will take you to the next level of engagement.

Engagement Goal Example

Participate in the National Student Exchange (NSE) Program to the University of Washington in the spring 2015 semester.

Available Campus Resources

Office of Student Engagement
My academic advisor

Action Steps	Deadline	Check when completed
1. Meet with a staff member in Student Engagement to discuss the program	10/16/2013	
2. Meet with my academic advisor to discuss my participation in NSE	10/30/2013	
3. Talk to my family about NSE over winter break	12/31/2013	
4. Apply to NSE by preferred application deadline	1/31/2014	
5. Interview with Student Engagement staff for NSE program	2/13/2014	

Possible obstacles I may face in trying to reach my goals:

Financial costs, and making sure it fits in my program of study.

Engagement Goal #1

Available Campus Resources

Action Steps	Deadline	Check when completed
1.		
2.		
3.		
4.		
5.		

Possible obstacles I may face in trying to reach my goals:

Engagement Goal #2

Available Campus Resources

Action Steps	Deadline	Check when completed
1.		
2.		
3.		
4.		
5.		

Possible obstacles I may face in trying to reach my goals:

SEP Part 5: Integrative Learning Reflection

Integrative learning is an understanding and a disposition that a student builds across the curriculum and co-curriculum, from making simple connection among ideas and experiences to synthesizing and transferring learning to new, complex situations within and beyond campus.

The University of South Carolina is committed to assisting you develop the skills needed to integrate your learning throughout your various experiences in and beyond the classroom.

After having participated in an engagement activity (e.g., job shadowing, service-learning course) it is useful to reflect on how your experience connects to what you're learning in the classroom and to your interests and future career goals. Take some time to reflect on:

Describe the beyond-the-classroom experience in which you participated. What was memorable?

After having participated in the experience, what have you learned about yourself that you didn't know beforehand?

Did you develop any skills or abilities as a result of your participation in this experience (e.g., teamwork, communication skills)? If so, what were they?

How has what you learned changed your perspective towards being engaged?

How can you apply what you learned during the experience to any of your classes or to other aspects of your life?

SEP Part 6: Mapping Your Academic and Beyond-the Classroom Experiences

Mind mapping allows you to see the relationship between the various activities in which you are currently engaging/have engaged and the concepts you are learning in the classroom. The following page includes an example of a mind map where the student linked his/her classes, beyond the classroom activities, and components of the Carolina Core (e.g., analytical reasoning and problem-solving; values, ethics, and social responsibility). As you complete this portion of the SEP, feel free to use this as an opportunity to create something that makes sense to you and communicates your experiences at USC.

Some questions to consider before creating your mind map

1. Pick 2-4 of your most significant classes

2. Pick 2-4 of your most significant beyond-the-classroom experiences

3. Think about how those various classroom and beyond-the-classroom experiences connect and are linked. Create a visual representation of those connections below.

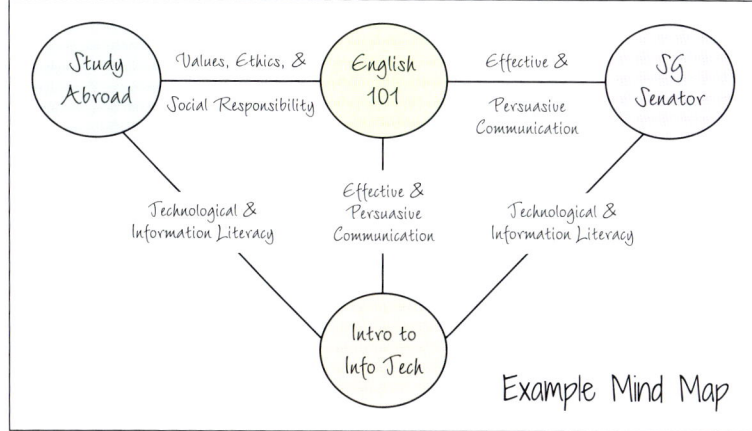

Your Mind Map:

Use this space to create your own mind map that shows the connections between you classroom and beyond-the-classroom experiences. Create something that makes sense to you!

SCENARIOS FROM COLLEGE LIFE

A Little Too Involved

Kevin was not very involved in high school so coming to college, he decided he wanted to change that. When the Organization Fair occurred during the second week of his first semester, Kevin joined three organizations. He also decided to rush a fraternity. Kevin called home shortly after the semester started to tell his parents about the exciting organizations he had joined. His parents were happy to hear that he was getting involved, but they cautioned him to be careful about balancing his time spent with the new organizations and his academic demands. Kevin assured his parents that he was not getting in over his head and promised that he would not get behind in his studies.

A few weeks went by and pledging started to take up more time than Kevin anticipated. Through one of the organizations he joined, Kevin met his girlfriend Annie. They began spending a lot of time together, and Kevin began neglecting his schoolwork and missing classes. Despite this, Kevin believed that he could still handle everything. He had become a recognizable face on campus due to his involvement in so many campus organizations, and his class absences and missed schoolwork did not seem to be a pressing concern, yet.

After midterms, Kevin learned that he had Ds in two of his major classes. Kevin decided to start getting serious about getting his grades back up, but he also planned to stay as involved he had been in his student organizations and continue his relationship with Annie.

A few weeks passed and Kevin found himself nearing initiation week for his fraternity—a week in which he knew he would probably get little to no sleep. He also had to help with community service projects for two of his organizations that require members to prepare for the upcoming holiday season. This left little time to spend with Annie, and to make matters worse, they were not getting along. Kevin had almost completely stopped studying, but he had been doing a better job of going to class the second half of the semester. He reasoned that being in class and making an effort to listen to professor meant he would not need to spend as much time studying on his own. Everything seemed to be happening at the same time. Finals week was approaching, as were the deadlines for all his other commitments.

Kevin decided to talk to a cross college advisor in the Student Success Center to get advice about his situation. After listening to Kevin, the advisor suggested that he quit two of the organizations in order to focus on school work and pull his grades up. Kevin went back to his room to think about what the advisor told him. Deep down he knew she was right; however, he was also afraid that if he quit some of his organizations, he would lose his status and jeopardize his desire to be involved in a leadership role the following semester. He didn't want to bring up what the advisor had suggested with Annie because she had already told him he was doing too much weeks before his advisor had. Kevin did not want to admit to Annie, let alone anyone, that he was not capable of handling all his commitments.

After a day or two of thinking things over, Kevin learned he could still get a decent grade in one of the classes he had been struggling in if he did well on the final exam. He knew that to prepare well for this exam, he would have to let go of two of the organizations or his fraternity involvement. He struggled to decide which to let go and worried what his peers and advisors would say about him. He hated the idea of being known as a "quitter." Sitting alone in his residence hall room, Kevin repeatedly thought, "What should I do?"

Processing Questions:

What organizations have you decided to get involved in at the University?

Can you relate to Kevin's situation of having too many things to do and not enough time?

What steps can you make to prevent being in Kevin's situation?

Have you had to make a decision you thought others might not agree with or understand? How did you come to your own conclusion on what to do?

How would you handle this situation if you were Kevin? What would you have done differently throughout this scenario?

RESOURCES

Opportunities on Campus

Campus Recreation
    Intramural Sports 576-9387
    Outdoor Recreation 576-9397
    Solomon Blatt Physical Education Center . . . 777-5261
    Strom Thurmond Wellness & Fitness Center . 576-9376
    http://campusrec.sc.edu

Carolina Productions 777-7130
    Campus Life Center, Russell House 227
    http://www.cp.sc.edu

Community Service Programs 777-7130
    Campus Life Center, Russell House 227
    http://www.sa.sc.edu/communityservice

Gamecock Athletics 777-4274
    http://gamecocksonline.cstv.com

Greek Life 777-3506
    Russell House 115
    http://www.sa.sc.edu/greeklife

The Koger Center for the Arts 777-7500
    1051 Greene Street, Columbia
    http://koger.sc.edu

Leadership Programs 777-7130
    Campus Life Center, Russell House 227
    http://www.sa.sc.edu/leaders

Office of Undergraduate Research 777-1141
    Legare College 223
    http://www.sc.edu/our

Peer Leadership/Education
    Complete list of opportunities available at:
    http://www.housing.sc.edu/
    studentengagement/pl.html

Residence Hall Involvement 777-4283
    http://www.housing.sc.edu

Student Government 777-2654
    Campus Life Center, Russell House 227
    http://www.sg.sc.edu

Student Media

Garnet & Black 777-1149
    Russell House 339
    http://gandbmagazine.com

Student Gamecock Television (SGTV) 777-3760
    Russell House 330
    http://www.sa.sc.edu/studentmedia/sgtv
    The Daily Gamecock 777-7726
    Russell House 333
    http://www.dailygamecock.com

Student Media Office 777-3888
    Russell House 343
    http://www.sa.sc.edu/studentmedia

WUSC-FM 777-5468
    Russell House 343
    http://wusc.sc.edu

Student Organizations 777-2654
    Campus Life Center, Russell House 227
    http://www.sa.sc.edu/studentorgs

Study Abroad 777-7557
    Legare College 321
    http://www.sa.sc.edu/sa

Opportunities in Columbia

Dance

Columbia City Ballet 799-7605
    1545 Main Street
    http://www.columbiacityballet.com

Columbia City Jazz 252-0252
    550 Rivermont Drive
    http://www.columbiacityjazz.com

Columbia Classical Ballet 252-9112
    2418 Devine Street
    http://www.columbiaclassicalballet.org

Festivals and Fairs

Columbia's Greek Festival 461-0248
    Sumter and Calhoun Streets
    http://www.columbiasgreekfestival.com

South Carolina Pride Movement 771-7713
    Findlay Park
    http://www.scpride.org

South Carolina State Fair 799-3387
    1200 Rosewood Drive
    http://www.scstatefair.org

Film

Nickelodeon Theatre 254-3433
    937 Main Street
    http://www.nickelodeon.org

Historical Sites

Historic Columbia Foundation 252-7742
    1601 Richland Street
    http://www.historiccolumbia.org

South Carolina Governor's Mansion 737-1710
    800 Richland Street
    http://www.scgovernorsmansion.org

South Carolina State Museum 898-4921
    301 Gervais Street
    http://www.museum.state.sc.us

Music

The Palmetto Mastersingers 765-0777
    http://www.palmettomastersingers.org

The South Carolina Philharmonic 771-7937
    721 Lady Street, Suite B
    http://www.scphilharmonic.com

University of South Carolina School of Music . . 777-4280
    http://www.music.sc.edu

RESOURCES CONTINUED

Other Opportunities for Fun

EdVenture 779-3100
   211 Gervais Street
   http://www.edventure.org

Riverbanks Zoo and Garden 779-8717
   500 Wildlife Parkway
   http://www.riverbanks.org

Theater

Columbia Marionette Theatre 252-7366
   401 Laurel Street
   http://www.columbiamarionettetheatre.org

Congaree National Park . . . . 776-4396, ext. 0
   100 National Park Road, Hopkins, SC
   http://www.nps.gov/cosw

Harbison State Forest 896-8890
   5600 Broad River Road
   http://www.state.sc.us/forest/refharb.htm

Sesquicentennial State Park 788-2706
   9564 Two Notch Road
   http://southcarolinaparks.com/park-finder/state-park/469.aspx

The South Carolina Shakespeare Company . . . 787-2273
   http://www.shakespearesc.org

Town Theatre 799-2510
   1012 Sumter Street
   http://www.towntheatre.com

Trustus Theatre 254-9732
   520 Lady Street
   http://www.trustus.org

University of South Carolina Theatre & Dance . 777-4288
   http://www.cas.sc.edu/thea

Workshop Theatre of South Carolina 799-4876
   1136 Bull Street
   http://www.workshoptheatre.com/info.html

Visual Arts

Columbia Museum of Art 799-2810
   1515 Main Street
   http://www.columbiamuseum.org

McKissick Museum 777-7251
   Horseshoe, 816 Bull Street
   http://www.cas.sc.edu/mcks

REFERENCES

Astin, A.W. (1993). *What matters in college? Four critical years revisited*. San Francisco, CA: Jossey-Bass.

Ender, S. C., & Kay, K. (2001). Peer leadership programs: A rationale and review of the literature. In S. L. Hamid (Ed.), *Peer leadership: A primer on program essentials* (Monograph No. 32, pp. 1-12). Columbia, SC: University of South Carolina, National Resource Center for The First-Year Experience and Students in Transition.

Kuh, G. D. (2003). *The National Survey of Student Engagement: Conceptual framework and overview of psychometric properties*. Bloomington, IN: Indiana University Center for Postsecondary Research and Planning.

Pascarella, E. T., & Terenzini, P.T. (1991). *How college affects students: Findings and insights from twenty years of research*. San Francisco, CA: Jossey-Bass.

Chapter Four

Managing Your Time

UNIVERSITY OF SOUTH CAROLINA

Dear First-Year Student,

Welcome to the University of South Carolina! As a faculty member in the English department, I spent years directing the university's English 101 and 102 classes, which thousands of first-year students complete each year. I notice that most successful students on our campus aren't always the most naturally gifted scholars or those with the best high-school preparation—but rather those who make productive use of their time.

Time management skills do not come naturally to most college students, though. With all the opportunities and obligations you need to juggle during your first semester on campus, it is normal to feel over-committed. Although no single strategy works for everyone, here are a few recommendations to consider as you plan for a successful first year:

- **Create a system.** Time management experts agree: keeping a calendar, whether it's a traditional agenda book or an app on your phone, helps you to chart out your obligations. Enter major deadlines and obligations first, so that you can plan around them.

- **Put academic obligations first.** You'll be pleased to find out that going to class and doing your work when assigned actually saves you time and stress! Plan to spend two hours outside of class for every hour you spend in class, and block this time into your calendar. Then show up—not only for class, but also for your appointed study time.

- **Make time for other activities.** No one can (or should) study all the time; time spent with friends or exploring non-academic interests is an important part of your college experience. You'll learn to strike a balance—and that starts with the word "no." This is your first semester. Give yourself some breathing room and don't try to do everything that interests you (save some things for later!).

- **Take care of your health.** Research on learning and the brain shows that exercise, getting enough sleep and eating right not only keeps you feeling well, it also helps you learn. So, when you're scheduling your time, you'll want to plan for sleep, exercise and healthy eating.

- **Expect the unexpected.** No plan is perfect, and emergencies happen. You might have two exams and a paper due on the same day, and then come down with the flu. Do the best you can and move if you need advice or support, don't hesitate to ask for help. Campus resources such as the Academic Centers for Excellence coaches in the Student Success Center specialize in helping students enhance their study and time management skills.

When you look at how you spend your time this academic year, remember to go after what you want most, not what seems most pressing this minute. That means you'll have to pass up some things from time to time—but don't worry. By keeping the truly important things a priority, you'll be better able to enjoy your friends and your university when you are free from the stress of undone work and overwhelming deadlines.

Best wishes for a great first year on campus.
Sincerely,

Christy Friend
Professor of English / Director, Center for Teaching Excellence

COLLEGE students report that one of the biggest challenges in their first year is managing their time. Approximately 91% of entering students at Carolina last year indicated that they frequently or occasionally felt overwhelmed by all they had to do. One of the first and most important steps in budgeting your time is learning when to say no. There may be times when you will need to postpone lunch with friends to study for an exam, and it is important to recognize your limits when it comes to managing your time. Whether you are spending time with new friends, assuming a leadership position in an organization, attending campus activities, or studying for an upcoming exam, your priorities will ultimately shape how you allocate your time. By postponing your lunch with friends in order to create time to study, you are demonstrating to yourself and others that your academic success is important to you.

In this chapter, you will identify where you spend your time, determine your values and priorities, and gain access to tools that will help you successfully manage your time. Students who are the most successful are those who use their values and priorities to guide their time management practices.

Time Management

Time management refers to your ability to balance responsibilities, manage priorities, and work toward your goals, while maintaining a lifestyle that is healthy and satisfying. Covey (1989) notes in his book *The 7 Habits of Highly Effective People* that the term *time management* is really a misnomer. The challenge is not to manage your time, but to learn to manage yourself. Thus, time management is really about motivation and discipline.

In high school, you may have followed the same schedule every day or were reminded by teachers and parents about deadlines and responsibilities. Your parents and teachers may have also helped to keep you on task and motivated. In college, you are responsible for setting your own schedule and determining how you will spend your time, which is both exciting and sometimes overwhelming!

Time can quickly get away from you, and it is important to stay organized so you are best able to identify where your time is going. Beyond academic success, another reason for managing your time is so that you will be able to participate in spontaneous gatherings with friends, campus activities and programming, and additional out-of-classroom opportunities.

According to Chickering and Gamson (1987), students who are most successful devote an appropriate amount of time to academic tasks. The only way to learn or develop new skills is to practice and spend time doing it. Allocating realistic amounts of time means effective learning for students. Time plus energy = learning! To effectively begin managing your time, you must first identify where you spend your time.

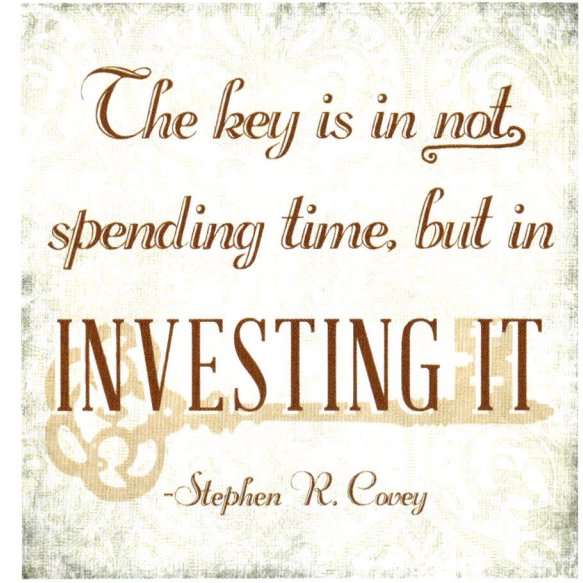

The key is in not spending time, but in INVESTING IT
—Stephen R. Covey

CONSIDER THIS

Think back to high school...
What activities and priorities did you have to balance?

How did you manage your time?

What techniques did you find most effective?

IT'S A MATTER OF TIME

A QUICK OVERVIEW OF COLLEGE STUDENTS AND TIME MANAGEMENT

THERE ARE 168 HOURS IN A WEEK...

Students Only Use 120 Hours Productively¹

- SLEEPING 56 HRS
- SOCIALIZING 15 HRS
- CLASS 15 HRS
- STUDYING/HOMEWORK 10 HRS
- JOB 10 HRS
- SOCIAL MEDIA 5 HRS
- EXERCISING 5 HRS
- TELEVISION 2 HRS
- CLUBS & ORGANIZATIONS 2 HRS

YET 75% OF COLLEGE STUDENTS PROCRASTINATE ON ACADEMIC TASKS:²

- READING
- STUDYING
- KEEPING APPOINTMENTS

Wasting Time

U101 STUDENTS REPORTED THEIR #1 TIME WASTER...

NETFLIX

DID YOU KNOW?

50%

50% OF STUDENTS REPORTED PROCRASTINATING REGULARLY AND CONSIDER IT A PROBLEM³

THE KEY TO TIME MANAGEMENT IS TO IDENTIFY:

- VALUES
- PRIORITIES
- GOALS

Aligning Your Goals and Values

How you spend your time is often determined by your goals and values. Everyone spends 168 hours each week devoting their time and energy to various tasks throughout the week; how are you spending your time? As a new student at Carolina, you will have to decide how to balance your time in order to be successful. Setting goals is a great first step in determining where you need to spend your time. Have you ever set goals for yourself only to find months later that you did not accomplish those goals? The key to effective goal setting is aligning your goals with your values. Unless you know why you want something, you are not likely to invest time discovering that particular goal. For example, you may be motivated to do well in organic chemistry because you know it will help you achieve your goal of getting in to medical school. Also, you might be motivated to maintain a 3.0 GPA because that is what you need in order to keep your scholarships.

Reflecting on what you value will help you recognize what is important in your life and act as a means of evaluating what decisions to make. Based on the results of your Values Inventory located at the end of the chapter, are your values supported by the way you spend your time? If not, it is time to realign your schedule to reflect what matters most to you. For example, if you rank *physical health* as a high priority, you should be sure to schedule time to exercise and take care of yourself. If you placed *love* highest, be sure to make time for the people and activities you love in your schedule. If *emotional health* is high on your values list, ensure you are making an effort to support your mental well-being. This could include making appointments with an ACE Coach or a counselor in the Counseling and Human Development Center to discuss ways to best support your success in this area. If you reflect back to this activity throughout the semester, you are more likely to ensure you are still supporting your values with your time.

Goal Setting

Most students believe that earning a high GPA is the key to having a successful college career, but what is even more important than the grades you earn are the goals you set and the plan you devise as well as the actions you take to attain those goals. Once you have identified what you value and where you want to invest time, you can set your goals (Owens & Pauk, 2008). Setting goals often provides a long-term goal with short-term motivation.

Major Versus Minor Goals

It is important to distinguish between minor and major goals.

Examples of minor goals are

- Completing a homework assignment
- Reading a chapter of your textbook before lunch
- E-mailing your professor about the topics on your midterm

Setting and fulfilling minor goals gives you a sense of accomplishment and the motivation to create and tackle major goals.

Examples of major goals are

- Earning a 3.6 GPA at the end of your first-year
- Being admitted to pharmacy school
- Securing a summer internship with a reputable organization or business

Did you know?

95% of your success in life and work will be determined by the kind of habits that you develop over time. (Tracy, 2005)

Did you know?

Gladwell (2008) reports that what separates one performer or athlete from another is not natural talent but time on task! For true expertise, 10,000 hours of practice is required to achieve a level of mastery.

Peer Leader Advice

Don't wait until last minute to study for a test. We have all done it, and I'm sure some of us have managed to slide by with a decent grade, but 99% of the time, it does not work. Start studying a week or even two weeks before the date of the test. You will have more time to absorb the information and be able to review the difficult concepts more than once.

- Leyna Antonucci
Oakland, NJ • Senior
Exercise Science

Consider This

Do you have trouble getting started on projects or regularly put off tasks?

What types of tasks do you avoid?

What are some reasons that you put off doing these tasks?

Do you consider yourself a procrastinator?

Major goals, often, are distant and future-focused. They are meant to motivate and inspire you to reach a target. For some students, setting major goals might come naturally, and for others, the process might seem scary and daunting. Even though goals will vary widely from student to student, all major goals come from same the place: the things you want and need. Choosing your goal might just seem like choosing an occupation, but in reality, it is about knowing yourself and what you value most in life (Owens & Pauk, 2008).

S M A R T Goals

When creating goals, it is important to move beyond the lofty dreams and wishes you may have had since you were a child. As a college student, you need to set goals that are specific (S), measurable (M), attainable (A), realistic (R), and timely (T). When creating goals, think of the destination and the process that will help you get there and use these criteria.

Specific – Goals that are too general are less likely to be accomplished. A specific goal answers these six questions: (a) Who is involved? (b) What do I want to accomplish? (c) Where is the location? (d) When will it happen? (e) Which requirements and restraints are needed? and (f) Why should I pursue this goal?

Measurable – For a goal to be measurable, you need to establish criteria for assessing your progress. By measuring your goal, you are more likely to stay on track, reach your target dates, and know the feeling of success after you have completed the steps along the way.

Attainable - Once you have identified your goals, it is time for you to plan your steps, develop a positive attitude, and identify the abilities and skills you need. By doing this, you will be able to accomplish almost any goal!

Realistic - A realistic goal is one that you are able to work toward. You are the only one who can decide whether or not your goal meets this standard.

Timely - Giving your goal a time frame provides you a clear target to work toward. Without a timeframe, there is no urgency or commitment to take action.

Procrastination

The reality is that everyone procrastinates about something at some point, but not everyone is a procrastinator. The term procrastination comes from Latin *procrastinare*, meaning to put off or postpone to another day (Ferrari et al, 1995). Generally, people put off the tasks that are harder and less enjoyable. Boice (1996) defined procrastination as "opting for short-term relief through acts that are easy and immediately rewarding, while generally avoiding even the thought (and its anxiety) of doing more difficult, delayable, important things" (p. XIX). Thus, many people occupy time by staying busy with easy and short tasks, which can lead to feelings of accomplishment because short-term items are getting checked off the to-do list. However, this can also mean that more important tasks are getting less attention.

Whether procrastination becomes a problem or not depends on how it impacts your life (Ferrari, 2010). It might be acceptable to procrastinate cleaning your room, but delaying on major academic projects, such as your papers or preparing for exams, could significantly impact your grades.

Research indicates that while about 20% of U.S. population are considered chronic procrastinators, about 75% of college students procrastinate on academic tasks such as studying, reading, and keeping appointments, and 50% reported doing it regularly and consider it a problem (Ferrari, 2010; Burka & Yuen, 2008). Piers Steel (2011), a leading scholar on procrastination, suggests that college students may be more prone to procrastination because academic tasks are viewed as unpleasant, the due date is generally far away, and there are lots exciting enticements on a college campus that provide alternatives to studying.

Procrastinators tend to be more impulsive, and are easily bored and distracted (Ferrari, 2010). They often believe that they do their best work under the pressure of last minute deadlines, which provides a rush of adrenaline to complete the task. The assumption is that procrastination stems from a need to increase excitement and reduce boredom. Thus, procrastinators begin to make excuses about deferring to the last minute and believe that they will perform better under those circumstances. However, research shows us that procrastinators do not do well under time limitations. They tend to make more mistakes and complete less of a task than non-procrastinators when there is a time limit (Ferrari, 2010).

So what can procrastinators do to break this habit? Get started! In their best-selling book *Switch: How to change things when change is hard,* Professors Chip and Dan Heath relayed a story about the 5-minute room rescue. As with most people, you have probably put off a tedious task such as cleaning your room. The idea of the 5-minute room rescue is that you set the timer for five minutes and try to get as much cleaning accomplished as possible. How much cleaning can you get done in five minutes? Probably not a lot. However, *starting* an unpleasant task can be worse than seeing it through, and once you get going you may not have to stop when the timer rings. Try this

Procrastinator's Clock

If you are you always running late to class or other meetings, try downloading a "procrastinator's clock." This computer program will display a digital clock that runs up to 15 minutes fast. The trick is the clock speeds up and slows down, assuring that you can't game the system.

CONSIDER THIS

What are the three biggest distractions you are currently facing?

1. _____

2. _____

3. _____

What are three things you can do to lessen these distractions?

1. _____

2. _____

3. _____

CONSIDER THIS

What items do you multitask with most often?

_____

_____

_____

How might your work suffer in one area because you are shifting your focus back and forth to the other tasks?

_____

_____

_____

What changes can you make to multitask less often?

_____

_____

_____

ACE Coaching

The Student Success Center offers Academic Engagement Coaching (ACE). This program provides one-on-one academic coaching with professional coaching staff. Time management is a commonly requested topic for ACE. Make an appointment today by calling 803-777-1000 or e-mail: ACE@sc.edu

---

with the academic tasks that you are inclined to put off. Set a timer for five minutes and tell yourself to work on that project until the buzzer rings. You may find that the initial step of getting started will give you the momentum you need to keep going.

It might also be helpful to set an action trigger for assignments and tasks. Alerts can be programmed into cell phones to grab your attention and remind you to start the task.

Ultimately college faculty members have much higher expectations for performance than high school teachers did, so waiting until the last minute to write a paper or study for an exam will not lead to the best results. Many procrastinators in college underestimate the amount of time it will take to successfully complete a project. Some students will figure this out the hard way and make adjustments, but the price can be a lower first-semester GPA. The bottom line is to recognize when you are procrastinating and find a way to motivate yourself to get started.

Multitasking

Many people in today's fast-paced and plugged-in world believe they can effectively multitask by focusing their attention on multiple stimuli at one time. For example, many students believe they can listen to a lecture or read their textbook while chatting via IM or texting their friends. However, the research (e.g., Cantor, 2011) is fairly clear that the belief in our ability to multitask is misguided. Simply stated: You cannot effectively multitask. Individuals can shift their focus from one priority to the next, but it is very difficult to do two things well at once. Paul Dux (n.d.), a neuroscientist at the University of Queensland, states that "Despite the immense processing power of the human brain, it is severely capacity limited: Humans can barely attend to more than one stimulus at a time and have extreme difficulty undertaking multiple tasks concurrently" (para. 1).

This reality is problematic when trying to learn new information. In a study by Junco and Cotton (2011), 93% of students admitted to using instant messenger or another chatting device while doing academic work. Of these students, more than 50% recognized that this habit had a detrimental effect on their schoolwork. Moreover, Junco and Cotton found that using Facebook and texting while doing schoolwork were negatively associated with overall college GPA, and Greenfield (2009) reported that multitasking decreases our ability to process and retain information. If you want to be your best in your academic work, take the time to focus on your studies and avoid multitasking.

Scheduling Tools

It is important to start managing your time to support your values, priorities, and goals. There are multiple scheduling tools to help you stay on track and achieve your goals, so you do not have to do it all by yourself.

Your Syllabus

One of the most important tools to help succeed in your academics and stay organized is the course syllabus. The syllabus provides a holistic understanding of the information to be covered in class and includes valuable information, such as

- Instructor(s)
- Course description
- Learning outcomes
- Required course materials
- Recommended course materials
- Grading scale
- Breakdown of course assignments
- Confidentiality and academic integrity information
- Classroom behavior expectations
- Attendance expectations
- Americans with Disabilities Act (ADA statement)
- Syllabus clause and contract
- Course calendar

Do not make the mistake of putting the syllabus in your binder (or trashcan) without looking at it. The course syllabus is considered a contract between you and your professor and outlines the expectations he or she has for the course. Be sure to review the syllabus to become familiar with all course expectations, exam and presentation due dates, workload, and policies. However, knowing is not the key to success; preparation is key! Use your syllabus as a preparation tool to stay abreast of assignments and exams.

This may be the first time you have ever used a course syllabus. A 10-15 page syllabus can, initially, appear daunting and present a challenge trying to navigate it. The Syllabus Mapping tool at the end of the chapter can help you break down a hefty syllabus into the most important parts. Take out all of your syllabi and start filling out the important information you find on a syllabus. This should include everything from weight of assignments and exams to types of projects and due dates. You may choose to fill out a syllabus map for every class so that

---

Peer Leader Advice

Planners and wall calendars are a life saver. Being able to physically see the dates in front of you makes it a lot easier to keep up with assignments, tests and other events you have planned throughout the semester. You don't have to worry about dates sneaking up on you, and you may be able to carve out some extra fun time for yourself.

- Adam Mayer
Avoca, WI • Junior
Exercise Science

A-B-C-D-E Method

(Adapted from *Eat That Frog* by Brian Tracy) After making your to-do list, place an A, B, C, D, or E before each item before you begin your first task.

A = very important, must do. If this task is not completed (e.g., finishing a research paper, completing a presentation), there are serious consequences involved. If you have more than one A on your list, prioritize them by using A-1, A-2, A-3, and so on.

B = important, should do. If this task is not completed (e.g., filling out an application for a travel grant, responding to an e-mail), there are only mild consequences. Someone may be unhappy or inconvenienced if you do not do it, but not as important as A. Never work on a B task when there is an A task left undone.

C = would be nice to do. There are no consequences for whether you complete this task (e.g., doing laundry, getting a haircut, having coffee with a friend) or not.

D = can delegate to someone else. Evaluate if you can delegate this task (e.g., buying groceries, picking up a prescription) to help you complete an A task.

E = can be eliminated altogether. This is often a task you continue to do out of habit or because you enjoy it.

you can have a quick reference sheet to all of the different expectations, assignments, and policies that your professors may hold you to.

Semester at a Glance

In the first few weeks of each semester, take all your syllabi and complete the Semester at a Glance Worksheet located at the end of the chapter. You can create your own document on your computer or spreadsheet if you prefer. This worksheet will help you compile all major due dates onto one document and display it where you will see your upcoming assignments often. Order your assignments by due date, and note the course and assignment description. Looking at your worksheet will help you prepare for the next project, test, or assignment. You may discover that certain weeks will be more demanding than others, so plan ahead to avoid becoming overwhelmed.

Planner

A planner can be valuable to keep track of classes, meetings, extracurricular activities, and guest speakers or special events on campus. You will want to set blocks of time for homework and studying and add any reoccurring meetings to your schedule (e.g., weekly student organization meetings or intramural practice). With all activities, be sure to schedule extra time to travel to and from each location.

A weekly schedule in your planner is helpful in breaking your semester into more manageable timelines. When using a weekly schedule, start by filling your schedule with your weekly commitments. Examples may include classes, work hours, and meal times. Create time in your schedule to study and work on assignments, and set aside specific times for each class. This will allow time to review your material even if nothing is due that particular week. Finally, make sure that you schedule time for yourself and your extracurricular activities.

Did you know?

Your student e-mail account has a calendar feature that can send reminders to your phone and/or laptop. Contact University Technology Services at 803-777-1800 for assistance in setting this up.

Digital Calendar

You may find that a mobile device or other digital calendar is more effective than a paper planner when getting organized. Your cell phone or e-mail calendar can be used to record meetings, appointments, or dinner with friends. There are also several applications designed to serve as a digital calendar that you can download on your iPad, Kindle, or Android tablet. Mobile devices can also be an effective tool in organizing your schedule, coursework, and extracurricular activities. Check out apps like iStudiez Pro or Erudio that are designed to help you manage your courses, keep track of your tasks and grades, provide a week by week timeline, and even syncs with your other devices. The key to using a digital calendar is to find a system or platform that works best for you.

To-Do-Lists

Making to-do lists can also be beneficial in managing and prioritizing your time. Consider breaking your list into categories of what you need to complete today and what you would like to complete within the week. This list can be on scratch paper, on your white board in your room, or in your planner. Choose a structuring system that works for you, such as deadline order, color-coded importance, number priority, A-B-C-D-E method, or your own design. It may take you 10 minutes a day to make your list, but it will save you hours in the long run.

Practice is necessary to become more effective in managing your time. Continue to manage your time in a manner that supports your values, priorities, and goals. Notice the changes you see as you make this shift and recognize when you are slipping from these habits.

CONSIDER THIS

What tools do you currently use to manage your time?

Are these tools effective?

What is one way you could use one of the tools listed in the chapter to become more efficient?

Check yourself

Academic Goal Setting Sheet

Class/Assignment	SMART Goal	Strategies	Deadline
Biology 101 midterm	To receive an A on my Biology 101 midterm	Attend all Supplemental Instruction sessions that are available for this course. Visit my professor's office hours whenever something is unclear. Visit ACE offices to learn new study strategies to help me study for my exam.	Before fall break

Check yourself

Where does my time go?

Estimate the amount of time you typically devote to each activity listed below in a full week. After entering your estimates, record the exact amount of time spent on each activity during one week. Then answer the questions posed at the end.

	Estimated Time (Hours/Minutes)	Actual Time (Hours/Minutes)
Attending classes		
Working a job		
Sleeping (include naps)		
Showering/bathing		
Traveling to and from work/class		
Eating (include snacks)		
Studying for test(s)		
Completing homework		
Socializing (include time just talking to friends)		
Organizational activities (band practice, fraternities/sororities, clubs, special groups, etc.)		
Time devoted to physical fitness		
Shopping (clothing, groceries, other)		
Religious/spiritual activities		
Time with family		
Time spent online (Facebook)		
Other (list) a. b. c. d.		
TOTALS		

What are you spending most of your time doing? What activities are you wasting time on?

Are there areas you could cut back on to better accomplish your goals? How many hours can you cut from each of these areas?

In what areas should you increase the amount of time you spend if you are going to accomplish your goals? How many hours will you increase each one by?

Which tasks do you most enjoy doing? Least enjoy doing? How can you adjust your schedule accordingly?

Check yourself

Values Inventory

Instructions: Each item contains a group of characteristics. In each grouping, rate the value you place on each characteristic. Rate the values according to how you really feel, not how you should feel. In front of each characteristic, place a number 1 for the characteristic you value most to 5 (the characteristic you value least). Be sure to place a number from 1 to 5 in front of each characteristic. You must give a different rating to each characteristic.

1. ____ Ambition
   ____ Broadmindedness
   ____ Competence
   ____ Popularity
   ____ Helpfulness

2. ____ Broadmindedness
   ____ Creativity
   ____ Self-sufficiency
   ____ Physical Health
   ____ Aesthetics

3. ____ Creativity
   ____ Security
   ____ Popularity
   ____ Appearance
   ____ Love

4. ____ Security
   ____ Success
   ____ Leadership
   ____ Ambition
   ____ Physical Health

5. ____ Success
   ____ Honesty
   ____ Appearance
   ____ Knowledge
   ____ Broadmindedness

6. ____ Honesty
   ____ Competence
   ____ Creativity
   ____ Leadership
   ____ Leisure

7. ____ Competence
   ____ Self-sufficiency
   ____ Knowledge
   ____ Emotional Health
   ____ Security

8. ____ Self-sufficiency
   ____ Popularity
   ____ Leisure
   ____ Religious Faith
   ____ Success

9. ____ Popularity
   ____ Physical Health
   ____ Emotional Health
   ____ Equality
   ____ Honesty

10. ____ Physical Health
    ____ Appearance
    ____ Religious Faith
    ____ Ethics
    ____ Competence

11. ____ Appearance
    ____ Leadership
    ____ Helpfulness
    ____ Self-sufficiency
    ____ Equality

12. ____ Leadership
    ____ Knowledge
    ____ Ethics
    ____ Aesthetics
    ____ Popularity

13. ____ Knowledge
    ____ Leisure
    ____ Physical Health
    ____ Helpfulness
    ____ Love

14. ____ Leisure
    ____ Emotional Health
    ____ Aesthetics
    ____ Ambition
    ____ Appearance

15. ____ Emotional Health
    ____ Religious Faith
    ____ Love
    ____ Broadmindedness
    ____ Leadership

16. ____ Religious Faith
    ____ Equality
    ____ Ambition
    ____ Creativity
    ____ Knowledge

17. ____ Equality
    ____ Ethics
    ____ Broadmindedness
    ____ Security
    ____ Leisure

18. ____ Ethics
    ____ Helpfulness
    ____ Success
    ____ Emotional Health
    ____ Creativity

19. ____ Helpfulness
    ____ Aesthetics
    ____ Security
    ____ Honesty
    ____ Religious Faith

20. ____ Aesthetics
    ____ Love
    ____ Equality
    ____ Success
    ____ Competence

21. ____ Love
    ____ Ambition
    ____ Honesty
    ____ Self-sufficiency
    ____ Ethics

Scoring

Check yourself

Values Inventory

Scoring: Each value appeared in a different grouping five times on the preceding page. After each value on the scoring chart below, place the numbers you assigned to each value for each time that value appeared. Then add the total numbers across. Below the tabulating chart, list the values starting with the lowest totals and so on for all 12 values. This list will show the values of most importance to you.

Value (group numbers where listed)	1	2	3	4	5	Total
Aesthetics (2, 12, 14, 19, 20)						
Ambition (1, 4, 14, 16, 21)						
Appearance (3, 5, 10, 11, 14)						
Broadmindedness (1, 2, 5, 15, 17)						
Competence (1, 6, 7, 10, 20)						
Creativity (2, 3, 6, 16, 18)						
Emotional Health (7, 9, 14, 15, 18)						
Equality (9, 11, 16, 17, 20)						
Ethics (10, 12, 17, 18, 21)						
Helpfulness (1, 11, 13, 18, 19)						
Honesty (5, 6, 9, 19, 21)						
Knowledge (5, 7, 12, 13, 16)						
Leadership (4, 6, 11, 12, 15)						
Leisure (6, 8, 13, 14, 17)						
Love (3, 13, 15, 20, 21)						
Physical Health (2, 4, 9, 10, 13)						
Popularity (1, 3, 8, 9, 12)						
Religious Faith (8, 10, 15, 16, 19)						
Security (3, 4, 7, 17, 19)						
Self-sufficiency (2, 7, 8, 11, 21)						
Success (4, 5, 8, 18, 20)						

Values in order of importance:

1.	8.	15.
2.	9.	16.
3.	10.	17.
4.	11.	18.
5.	12.	19.
6.	13.	20.
7.	14.	21.

Variations of this inventory appear on multiple institutional websites. Original source unknown.

Check yourself

Syllabus Mapping

Use the following prompts to better understand the syllabus/syllabi in your class(es):

Student Name: _____ Date: _____

Class: _____ Class Location: _____

Professor's Name: _____

Office Location: _____ Phone #: _____ Office Hours: _____

Based on the syllabus for this class, which of the following areas are most important in determining your final grade (check all the apply and list the percentage, if given):

- ☐ Exams _____ %   ☐ Quizzes _____ %   ☐ Final Exam _____ %
- ☐ Papers _____ %   ☐ Homework _____ %   ☐ Class Participation _____ %
- ☐ Lab Work _____ % ☐ Presentations _____ % ☐ Field Activities _____ %
- ☐ Other _____ %   ☐ Other _____ %   ☐ Other _____ %

What is the professor's attendance policy? _____
_____

What is the professor's homework/quiz/test make-up policy? _____
_____

Final Exam Date & Time: _____

Plan regular times during which you will study for this class. Also, it is a good idea to know the names and phone numbers of one or two people in the class for study partners and/or someone to call when you have questions.

Study Times:
_____

Classmate:
_____

Classmate:
_____

Check yourself

Write down key due dates for papers, tests, etc.

Type of Project	Due Date
Example: Short Essay (1 - 3 pgs)	Monday, Aug 30

Use this chart to list all the grades you receive in your class.

	Date	Grade	Date	Grade	Date	Grade	Date	Grade
Homework								
Quizzes								
Exams								
Presentations								
Field Activities								
Other:								
Other:								
Other:								

Chapter 4: Managing Your Time

Check yourself

Semester at a Glance

Use this form to help you visualize and organize chronologically when your assignments are due. List all of your assignments, according to due date, for the entire semester.

Due Date	Class	Assignment

Check yourself

Weekly Schedule

TIME	MON	TUES	WED	THURS	FRI	SAT	SUN
6:00 AM							
7:00 AM							
8:00 AM							
9:00 AM							
10:00 AM							
11:00 AM							
12:00 PM							
1:00 PM							
2:00 PM							
3:00 PM							
4:00 PM							
5:00 PM							
6:00 PM							
7:00 PM							
8:00 PM							
9:00 PM							
10:00 PM							
11:00 PM							
12:00 AM							

Chapter 4: Managing Your Time

RESOURCES

Academic Success Resources

Academic Coaching & Engagement 777-1000
Bates House, Columbia Hall, Sims,
Thomas Cooper Library
http://www.sa.sc.edu/ssc/acecoaching/
student.success@sc.edu

REFERENCES

Boice, R. (1996). *Procrastination and blocking: A novel, practical approach*. Westport, CT: Praeger.

Cantor, J. (2011). Getting students to turn off digital distractions and tune into lectures and learning. *E-Source for College Transitions, 9*(1), 7.

Chickering, A., & Gamson, Z. (1987, March). Seven principles for good practice in undergraduate education. *AAHE Bulletin, 39*(7), 3-7.

Covey, S. R. (1989). *The 7 habits of highly effective people*. New York, NY: Simon and Schuster.

Dux, P. (n.d.). *About Queensland Attention and Control Lab*. Retrieved from http://www.paulduxlab.org/

Ferrari, J. R., Johnson J. L., & McCown, W. G. (1995). *Procrastination and task avoidance: Theory, research, and treatment*. New York, NY: Plenum Press.

Gladwell, M. (2008). *Outliers: The story of success*. New York, NY: Little, Brown and Co.

Greenfield P. M. (2009). Technology and informal education: What is taught, what is learned. *Science, 323*, 69-71.

Heath, C., & Heath, D. (2010). *Switch: How to change things when change is hard*. New York, NY: Broadway Books.

Junco, R., & Cotten, S. (2011). Perceived academic effects of instant messaging use. *Computers & Education, 56*(2), 370-378.

Owens, R. J. Q., & Pauk, W. (2008). *How to study in college*. Boston, MA: Houghton Mifflin Company.

Steel, P. (2011). *The procrastination equation: How to stop putting things off and start getting stuff done*. New York, NY: Harper Collins.

Tracy, B. (2007). *Eat that frog!* (2nd ed.). San Francisco, CA: Berrett-Koehler Publishers.

Time Management Infographic

Burka, J. B., & Yuen, L. M. (2008). *Procrastination: Why you do it, what to do about it now*. Cambridge, MA: Da Capo Life Long.

Ferrari, J. R. (2010). *Still procrastinating: The no-regrets guide to getting it done*. Hoboken, NJ: Wiley.

Ruiz, S., Sharkness, J., Kelly, K., DeAngelo, L., & Pryor, J. (2009). Findings from the 2009 Administration of the Your First College Year (YFCY): National Aggregates. Retrieved from http://www.heri.ucla.edu/PDFs/pubs/Reports/YFCY2009Final_January.pdf http://bls.gov/tus/charts/students.htm

UNIVERSITY OF SOUTH CAROLINA

Dear First-Year Student,

Welcome to the University of South Carolina! Your decision to be a Gamecock is the just first of many important decisions you will make on your path to success. As the director of the Student Success Center, I am often asked, "What is the key to being a successful student?" My response consists of the things you might expect: attend every class meeting; get to know your instructors; carefully manage your time; and take care of your body with plenty of exercise, healthy food, and rest. However, I also explain that true academic success comes from understanding yourself as a learner.

Learning is a process. It takes time and has multiple steps. As learners, we are all different, progressing at different rates with different styles. The sooner we come to understand how we learn best, the more quickly we are able to adapt to the new college learning environment. Understanding your learning preferences can be helpful in saving you time and frustration when you study. Remember, when you are challenged by course material and are having trouble learning it, try something new. Different material can call for different study methods.

Unlike high school, courses at USC will require you to comprehend the big picture. Developing a conceptual understanding of complex material can be frustrating if in the past you were only required to memorize facts about a topic. Recognizing the different levels of knowledge you are being asked to demonstrate can help you study more efficiently and be properly prepared for the questions on your exams. Learn to look for clues in your text, lectures, and the feedback you receive on your graded work.

Developing personal strategies for note-taking, reading your texts, and taking exams will help you to process new information in ways that are meaningful to you. Pay attention to what works for you, and be willing to explore new methods. Build an arsenal of skills, and you will always be prepared. There are many people on campus who want to help you do this. Your professors can provide insight on how to learn in their classes. The Student Success Center provides a variety of resources and services that can help you build that arsenal of study skills. Your University 101 instructor can guide you as you begin to explore college resources. Pay attention to your learning. It is an investment that pays off in time—time that you can spend taking advantage of all the exciting opportunities you will encounter as a Gamecock!

Best of luck,

Eric J. Moschella
Director, Student Success Center

ACADEMIC success is connected with many elements of your college experience. The ability to perform well, academically, at the University of South Carolina is contingent on your ability to manage class responsibilities. Your academic success in college requires new techniques that are different from the skills you may have developed in high school. As mentioned in chapter 4, the ability to prioritize and manage your time effectively will contribute to your success. While allocating time to study certainly supports success, there are other skills necessary to make the time you block for your academics productive and effective. These skills include

- Note-taking
- Listening
- Reading comprehension
- Test preparation
- Test taking

> ### Peer Leader Advice
>
> Until I graduate from college, my main job is to be a good student. In order to maintain a high GPA, I treat the days I have class exactly like a work day--I wake up early and begin a day full of studying that ends at around five or six in the evening when I'm off "work". This method has worked really well as it also allows me to take time during the evenings to relax and do whatever I want, whether it be watching a free movie at the Russell House Theatre or playing board games with my roommates.
>
> - Claire Maeda
> Tokyo, Japan • Senior
> International Business and Management

You may have noticed there is a big difference in the amount of time you spent studying in high school versus now. In the 2013 Cooperative Institutional Research Program (CIRP) Freshman Survey, 53.6% of first-year students reported studying less than five hours a week in high school. In college, it is recommended that students study two hours for every one hour they are in class to be successful in their courses. This means if you are enrolled in 15 hours, you should be studying at least 30 hours a week!

In addition, there can be significant differences in college-versus-high-school classroom expectations and requirements, such as now needing to prepare for quizzes, having test scores or a paper comprise a major part of your grade, and requiring supplemental reading to understand a lecture. In this chapter, the focus is on making your study time efficient and productive by developing and implementing critical study skills into your academic work load.

Staying on Top of Your Academic Work Load

If you maintain your coursework throughout the semester, you will find that studying for tests and preparing for exams will be less stressful. You can stay on top of your academics by incorporating some of the following best practices.

Before Class

Read the required or recommended readings before class. This allows you to understand the big picture for the lecture content and helps you ask knowledgeable questions of your professor. Sometimes an instructor will choose to only highlight major parts of the text in a lecture but will test your knowledge on the lecture and readings. Ask your professors what they expect you to gain from the readings; whether big picture, definitions, key issues, or supplemental understanding.

Review your notes from the previous class. This will remind you of the topics currently being covered and prime your mind for new material.

Ask your instructor or classmates any questions you have from your previous reading or notes. If you have questions about content, swing by your professor's office during office hours or call a classmate.

It may be appropriate to ask the instructor a quick, clarifying question before class to confirm your understanding of previous information.

Attend office hours. Professors often indicate specific office hours in their syllabus to meet with students and answer any questions about assignments and class content. Take advantage of valuable one-on-one time with faculty, especially for your larger lecture courses.

Dos and Don'ts of Faculty Office Hours

The Dos

- Ask questions about the week's readings and lectures – This is a perfect time to ask for clarification on topics you have read in your assigned text or that you heard in the classroom.
- Ask questions about academic skills and how to improve them – Bring your notes from class and ask for your professor's feedback. They can help you fill in any gaps you might have!
- Ask questions about upcoming exams and assignments – This is an opportunity to ask your professor the format or you exams (are the essay or multiple choice?), the scope of the exams (is it cumulative?), and ask for any clarification you need on a project or paper that you have due in class.
- Ask questions about past performance so that you can improve in the future – It's important to bring old exams and papers with specific questions on the areas you lost points or got wrong. It is also important to know that you should not use this time to solely argue for a higher grade.
- Ask questions about future classes, majors, and future careers or graduate school – Your professors are experts in their field and will know about the resources available to students on campus. Inquire about possible majors and what resources there are on campus to help you explore. Furthermore, they might be able to help you pinpoint careers or graduate schools that meet your interests.

The Don'ts

- Don't ask your professor for copies of their lecture notes – It is now your responsibility to take notes during class. If for some reason you missed class, you need to make the appropriate arrangements with one of your peers in the class for a copy of his or her class notes.
- Don't ask offensive questions like - "Will we need to know this?" or "Did I miss anything important?" Asking questions like these infer that you only want to do the bare minimum to receive a good grade and that you are not dedicated to you studies.
- Don't solely attend Faculty offices for the purpose of arguing for a higher grade – Faculty do make mistakes, but it is important to be mindful of the tone you use for you do not want to offend them. Additionally, telling them that you always get A's is not an excuse for a higher grade.

*Adapted from: Andreatte, B. (2009). *Navigating the research university: A guide for first-year students.* Boston, MA: Wardsworth Cengage Learning.

During Class

Attend class. This is imperative to your success as a student at the University of South Carolina. If you hope to build on your current understanding in the course, you need to attend the class. While your instructor may not notice your absence in a large lecture, when you skip a class, you miss out on critical information not covered in the text or key class discussion points that you will be tested on. Attending class helps you stay on top of your academic workload. Further, research studies have found a strong negative correlation between absences and final grades (e.g., Gump, 2005).

Demonstrate academic etiquette. Professors have expectations of you that your high school teachers may or may not have had. Faculty expect a certain level of maturity in the classroom that includes

- Arriving on-time to every class
- Bringing all materials
- Participating actively in discussion
- Remaining fully engaged for the entire class period
- Refraining from distractions, including cell phones
- Sharing any academic problems or personal issues with the instructor that could impact class attendance and/or performance
- Notifying the instructor ahead of time if you have to miss class

Complete assignments. It is important to turn in assignments at or before the deadline. Your hard work, and pride in that work, can be demonstrated through a thoroughly completed assignment.

Incorporate active learning. Become a contributing and active member in the classroom. Participate in class and make connections with the instructor and your peers. Practice active listening; ask questions to yourself that will help you maintain interest in the topic. Nod your head as you listen to the instructor. Sit straight in your chair and keep a writing instrument in your hand. Keep yourself focused on the course by avoiding distractions and searching for the main ideas and key phrases within the lecture.

Take notes. Do not solely depend on a copy or print out of an instructor's PowerPoint or slides. These are meant to provide the class with an overview of the broad themes that will be discussed. Most times, professors will expand upon the themes in their PowerPoint and add new information to the class discussion; therefore, it is vital that you still take notes so you receive all of the relevant information that is discussed.

Make connections between old and new material. Incorporate new information into your knowledge of the concepts previously discussed in class. Ask yourself how the material you learned relates to something you already know or an experience you have had. Constantly apply newly acquired information to your framework of understanding. If you struggle to make the connections, ask your professor, teaching assistant, and/or study group to help you understand where this new material fits.

Ask questions. Whether you ask questions out loud to the professor, to yourself, or in the margins of your notes, this process can be very beneficial. Asking questions gets your mind prepared to learn sometime new, keeps your interest in the topic, and helps you become more engaged with the material in class. Be sure to ask informed questions in class. For example, instead of

Memory Curve

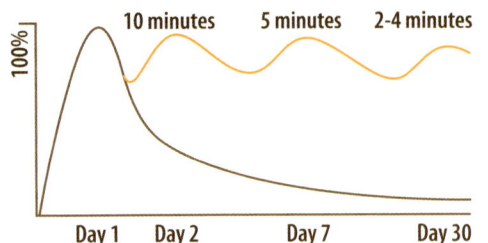

The figure above represents the amount of information you forget in a 30-day period, depending on the amount of time you spend reviewing the information from your notes.

On Day 1, you begin with little to no knowledge of the subject, but after the lecture you know 100% of the information instructors have shared with you (or relatively close to 100% considering a few questions are expected). However, if you do not review your notes and other materials for just a few minutes within the first 24 hours following the lecture, you will forget 50%-80% of the information by Day 2. Rather, if you spent just 10 minutes on Day 2 reviewing your notes, you would retain closer to 90% of the information you learned the day before.

Source: The University of Waterloo, Counseling Services.

simply inquiring what a term means, ask how the definition can be applied. Or, preface a question with what you know, demonstrating your understanding, and then ask what you do not grasp (e.g., state that you comprehend a theory definition but are struggling to see how the theory applies in a particular setting).

Sit where you can see the instructor and where the instructor can see you. You will find that sitting near the instructor will benefit you significantly. You can see and hear all material and notice where he or she places emphasis within the subject matter. An added perk is that your professor may begin to recognize your face, creating the opportunity for you to develop a strong student/faculty relationship that can pay dividends in the future. Faculty also benefit from your seating placement in that they can gain an understanding of whether you are learning the material by your facial expressions and visual cues.

Avoid distractions. Do not distract yourself with any updates or texts received on a mobile device. Using electronics can have a negative effect on your grades (Jacobsen & Forste, 2011). Instead, focus on taking notes and listening in class. Also, try not to sit next to friends who want to chat with you during class or classmates who are attempting to multitask with their electronic devices. Find a location in class that allows you to concentrate on the instructor and the course material, exclusively. Avoid the distractions that may interrupt you from the course topic.

After Class

Reread your notes. At the end of class, most students leave the classroom within seconds of the instructor's dismissal. Avoid this tendency, stay in your seat, and take a few minutes to recall what you have listened to in class and written in your notes. Draw a line across your paper below your notes. Under this line, write a summary of the key points and terms you learned in class. Include anything you found particularly challenging to understand from the class in your summary, but also list the concepts you were able to easily understand. This summary will help you prioritize what to study when you prepare for your exam later in the semester. If the instructor remains in the room after class, consider asking a question about a concept you found particularly challenging or discuss a topic you found interesting.

Do a weekly review of your notes. Reread your notes at the end of each week. Store them in a temporary folder, and make it a habit to reread the notes before filing them in your permanent binder(s).

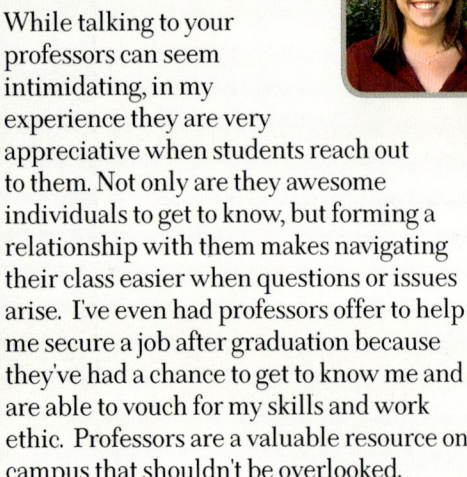

Peer Leader Advice

While talking to your professors can seem intimidating, in my experience they are very appreciative when students reach out to them. Not only are they awesome individuals to get to know, but forming a relationship with them makes navigating their class easier when questions or issues arise. I've even had professors offer to help me secure a job after graduation because they've had a chance to get to know me and are able to vouch for my skills and work ethic. Professors are a valuable resource on campus that shouldn't be overlooked.

- Cassandra Staton
Columbia, SC • Senior
Management and Finance

Build relationships with professors. In the transition from high school to college, you are not only switching from having the same schedule each day, but from having teachers to professors. In high school, most teachers took the initiative to build relationships with you; however, in college, professors look to *you* to initiate relationships. Developing relationships with faculty members is valuable for many reasons—most importantly—they can serve as excellent resources and even become mentors. When faculty recognize you by name and are aware that you are trying your best, that you are engaged in class and prepared, they will be much more willing to help you on your academic journey.

Communicating With Your Professors

The Dos

- Get in the habit of checking your university e-mail daily. Your professors will use this e-mail address when contacting you.
- Be aware that you may not always get an instant reply from your instructors, so plan in advance if you are letting them know about a class absence or asking about an assignment.
- When e-mailing your professor, make sure you include:
    - A subject line for the e-mail
    - A respectful greeting that addresses the instructor by the proper title. (i.e. Dear Dr. Sewell)
    - Your full name
    - The course name/section you are enrolled in
    - A closing signature (i.e. Thanks, Adrienne Moody)
- Be mindful in your message to avoid:
    - Text message style communication
    - Grammatical errors
    - Disrespectful language/tone

The Don'ts

- Don't use "one-liners" in an e-mail (i.e. I need help in your class). Make sure you provide enough detail about what it is you are e-mailing the instructor about.
- Don't e-mail your instructor to ask them information that might be on the syllabus. Make sure you take time to review the syllabus for important homework/test information.
- Don't forget to include your name and course information on any assignments you are e-mailing your instructor as an attachment.
- Don't forget to check your spelling and use your words carefully. Asking an instructor if you missed anything important after a class absence could send the wrong message. Take the extra minute to review your e-mail before sending.

Out-to-Lunch Program

Another great way to meet your professors in a more casual setting is through the Student Success Center (SSC) Out-to-Lunch Program. With this program, you are given a voucher that will cover a professor's meal at any dining location on campus. All you have to do is invite them to lunch. If this intimidates you, consider asking another classmate to come along as well. You can pick up an Out-to-Lunch ticket at any SSC office and the campus offices for University Housing, including

- Patterson Hall SSC satellite office
- Columbia Hall SSC satellite office
- Bates House SSC satellite office
- Student Success Center, Thomas Cooper Library
- Capstone Scholars Office (behind Gibbs)

There is no limit to the number of times you can use the Out-to-Lunch program!

Get to know your classmates. It is important to form relationships with your peers in each class. Not only will this make going to class more enjoyable, but if you miss class, you will have someone you can contact to copy notes from and find out what you missed. At the beginning of each semester, consider exchanging e-mail addresses and phone numbers with at least three peers in each class.

These suggestions are useful strategies to keep up-to-date with your academic coursework. Engaging in these practices will better prepare you for tests and exams and facilitate a deeper understanding of course material. Academic skills are important to develop and refine to become a more effective and efficient student.

Consider This

Who were the teachers that you had the best relationships with in high school? Why?

How can connecting with your professors outside of the classroom enrich your experience at Carolina?

What are some benefits of reaching out to professors?

What can you do in the next week to become more connected to at least one of your professors?

Note-Taking

You may find that your high school note-taking style is insufficient for college-level work. Taking notes assists you in staying focused on the course material, allows you opportunities to recognize where the instructors' priorities are, and may add to your knowledge base with information not found in the textbook. It is a necessary skill for college success. Using the Note-Taking Skills Inventory, assess your current note-taking practices.

Check yourself

Assessing Your Note-Taking Skills

Check Yes or No for each item that describes your note-taking habits.

	Yes	No
I check my course syllabus before each class to make sure I'm ready for each assignment.		
I read the text chapter(s) before class to make sure the lecture material will be familiar.		
I use a three-ring binder and loose-leaf paper for note-taking.		
I pay attention in class even if the instructor wanders from the point or makes remarks with which I don't agree.		
I ask questions if I don't understand the material presented in class.		
I identify introductory and concluding statements and recognize transition words and phrases when the instructor is lecturing.		
I pick out the main ideas and supporting details without difficulty.		
I understand my notes when I look them over several days or weeks later.		
I take notes in my words rather than trying to write down everything the instructor says.		
I use abbreviations and symbols so that I can note all of the important information.		
I make sure to include examples and all key information the instructor puts on the board.		
I leave enough space to fill in or add to my notes later.		
I review and edit my notes on a daily basis.		
I use my notes to think of possible test questions.		

What can you do to improve upon the skills you indicated that you do not currently practice?

Have your note-taking habits changed since high school? If so, how?

ACADEMIC SUCCESS
The Key to being Successful at USC

AT SOUTH CAROLINA

being academically successful is based on your ability to manage a variety of responsibilities. As past Carolina students have experienced, your actions, thoughts, and habits can have an impact on your success.

- **74.3%** found gaining a general education and appreciation of ideas a very important deciding factor in going to college.
- **95.6%** frequently or occasionally seek feedback on their academic work before coming to college.
- **89.4%** believe they have a very good chance of making at least a "B" average at USC.

Yet...

- Only **28.3%** of students frequently asked a teacher for advice in high school.
- **34.6%** Frequently and **60.7%** Occasionally of students were bored in class before coming to USC.
- **92.3%**  were frequently or occasionally overwhelmed by all the work they had to do prior to college.

Developing Good Habits

Study with other students
89.2% of students frequently or occasionally studied with another peer before their first-year at Carolina.

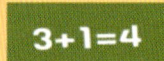
Attend Class
Only 1.4% of students have frequently skipped school and/or class before starting their college career.

Study 2 Hours
It is recommended that students study 2 hours for every hour of class while in college.

Complete HW
Only 3% of students have frequently failed to complete homework on time prior to coming to Carolina.

Source: Eagan, K., Lozano, J. B., Hurtado, S., & Case, M. H. (2013). The American freshman: National norms fall 2013. Los Angeles: Higher Education Research Institute, UCLA

Note-Taking Strategies

Some of you may have professors that will not repeat information or may move at a faster pace during a class lecture. It is important to develop note-taking strategies that will help you spend more time in the classroom listening so you can process information rather than trying to write down everything you hear.

Adapting to Fast Paced Instructors

In order to keep up with the material covered in class, Ellis (2006) suggests several ways that will help you be successful:

- **Prepare for class.** Take time to review the material that will be covered in class before you attend. Write down major headings or bolded words in your course readings. Familiarity with a subject will help you identify the key points and also allow for greater understanding.
- **Identify key words.** Focus on key words to write down and revise your notes immediately after class. Use the textbook or other materials to fill in the gaps of information that you might have missed.
- **Keep moving with the pace.** If you miss something, leave a space or use a symbol so that you can remember to return to it later. If you spend time trying to catch what you missed, you will miss the next concept as well. Work with a classmate to get what you may have missed or utilize your professor's office hours.
- **Use your technology.** Ask your professor if you can use your phone or laptop to record the lecture. Free apps like Super Note or TapNotes can help assure you do not miss anything and gives you a chance to hear it again.
- **Learn to abbreviate.** It is not realistic to try and write down every word your professor says and you do not need to. Make up abbreviations that work for you. Invent one or two letter symbols for common words and phrases. Always review or rewrite your notes soon after though so you do not forget what your abbreviations stand for!
- **Don't be afraid to ask questions.** It is ok to ask the instructor if he or she will repeat something or ask for clarity. Chances are a question you have is one that your classmates have as well.
- **Attend a Supplemental Instruction or peer tutoring session if offered.** Refer to the schedule on the Student Success Center website for more information regarding these opportunities.
    - http://www.sa.sc.edu/ssc/supplementalinstruction/
    - http://www.sa.sc.edu/ssc/peertutoring/

Key Phrases & Words to Listen For

- In addition to
- On the other hand
- Most important
- In comparison to
- Finally
- The main concept is
- For example
- Most important
- As stated earlier
- The key steps are

Peer Leader Advice

I always try to find a couple of friends in each of my classes and form a study group with them throughout the semester. Sometimes it is hard to catch everything in class so if you have other people that you can compare your notes with, you will be much more prepared when it comes time to study for tests. Also, structure the notes in whatever way works best for you; for example, use colors or draw charts!

- Katie Strickland
Charlotte, NC • Junior
Spanish and Education

Note-Taking Methods

When taking notes, there are several methods you can use. Many of you may have used a version of the outline method to take notes in high school. You may find that you have to find a new method that works for you or polish an old one in your lecture courses.

Outline Method. This method tends to be the most popular form of note-taking. Using an outline format (i.e., main topics, subtopics, and supporting information) is useful for organizing information and showing the relationship between points. Outlining also makes it easier to review information and create study guides by removing key words from your notes to memorize.

The Outlining Method

Extrasensory perception
- Definition: means of perceiving without use of sense organs
- 3 kinds -
    - Telepathy: sending messages
    - Clairvoyance: forecasting the future
    - Psychokinesis: perceiving events external to situation
- Current status
- Few psychologists say impossible
- Door open to future

Sentence Method. This method could be helpful during lectures that are well organized but there is a lot of content and it is being delivered quickly. Using the sentence method, you would write down a new topic or fact on a separate line, numbering as you move forward.

The Sentence Method

Example: (The teacher would say this in lecture)

> A REVOLUTION IS ANY OCCURRENCE THAT AFFECTS OTHER ASPECTS OF LIFE, SUCH AS ECONOMIC LIFE, SOCIAL LIFE, AND SO FORTH. THEREFORE REVOLUTIONS CAUSE CHANGE. SEE PAGE 29 TO 30 IN YOUR TEXT ABOUT THIS.

(what you would write down)

Revolution— occurrence that affects other aspects of life: e.g. econ. social, etc. see text pp. 29-30.

Reading and Lecture Notes Method. Best used in courses that require heavy reading in addition to the lectures, this method can be valuable if your reading directly supports the lectures. Before class, take notes from your reading on the front side of the paper. Then, in class, take notes from the lecture on the back side of the paper. By incorporating both your reading and lecture notes, you are able to tie in material from both sources and prepare effectively for your exam.

Note-Taking Shortcuts

Word or Term	Abbreviation or Symbol
About	~
Amount	Amt.
And	&
Chapter	Ch.
Company	Co.
Continued	Cont'd.
Decrease	Decr.
Definition	Def.
Economic	Econ.
Example	Ex. or X or e.g.
General	Gen.
Government	Gov.
Hour/hourly	Hr., hrly.
Illustrate	Illus. or e.g.
Important	Imp.
Increase	Inc.
Information	Info.
Introduction	Intro.
Months	Mo(s.)
Number or Pound	#
Organization	Org.
Page(s)	Pg., p., pp.
Psychology	Psyc.
Principal	Princ.
Significant	Sig.
Social or sociology	Soc.
Summary/summarize	Sum.
Versus	Vs.
Volume	Vol.
Year	Yr.
Equal/Not Equal	= and ≠
Less than/more than	< and >
Positive/negative	+ and −
With/without	w/ and w/o

Additional Note-Taking Tips

- Label and date all of your notes with the course title, number, and lecture topic.

- Rewrite (or type) your notes to better understand and remember the content.

- Highlight and underline important parts within your notes. Be careful of overhighlighting as the quality of highlighting is crucial in helping students learn (Wollen, Cone, Britcher, & Mindemann, 1985).

- Have materials ready to take notes (e.g., pen or pencil, binder, textbook, handouts from web).

- Review, review, review! Review your notes from previous lectures or the assigned reading before class. Take 10 minutes after class to glance over your notes and clarify any unclear points (e.g., abbreviations or shorthand symbols).

CONSIDER THIS

What nonverbal cues have you noticed your professors use while they are teaching?

_____
_____
_____
_____

What verbal cues have you noticed?

_____
_____
_____
_____
_____

Additional Tips for Reading Comprehension

- Stop occasionally to ensure you are invested in the reading.
- Take notes while you read especially if you are struggling to stay focused.
- Take breaks to ensure your eyes are rested and you are still curious about the material.
- Write summaries after reading a chunk of material for better understanding.
- Read…then reread!
- Highlight and underline where appropriate—but not too much.
- Discuss the reading with a friend in class or develop a study guide based on your reading.

Listening Skills

Selecting a note-taking method is important; however, knowing what is most relevant to write down is also critical. When listening to a lecture, watch for nonverbal and verbal cues from your professor in order to evaluate information to include in your notes. Examples of nonverbal (N) and verbal (V) cues are

- Pauses in a lecture—Professors will sometimes pause before introducing a major concept to the class. (N)
- Repeated words or themes—If a word or a theme is repeated multiple times, it is most likely relevant to the course material. (V)
- Illustrations—Material written on the board (e.g., words or diagrams) is certainly relevant to the lecture and is worth writing in your notes. (N)
- Hand gestures—Instructors may use hand motions (e.g., pointing to the board or illustrating a list with their hands) to signal an important piece of information. (N)
- Examples—When an instructor provides examples, these are often note-worthy. (V)

Reading Comprehension

In college, you will be required to read more than you did in high school. Your reading requirements will be listed in the syllabus, and there may be limited time in class dedicated to discussion and explanation. The reading could directly relate to the lecture or only provide background content. Developing good reading comprehension skills will help you understand lectures, improve the quality of your class participation, assist in exam preparation, and expand your knowledge base.

A reading strategy that can help you read faster and retain more is the SQ3R Method. The letters refer to the five steps, which Hirsch (2001) describes as

1. **(S) Survey** — Look at the content you are preparing to read. Examine how many pages the text includes and look at what the pages look like. Are there graphs? Charts? Look at the headings and subheadings and note anything that is boldface or italics.

2. **(Q) Question** — Have you ever zoned out when talking to a friend, only to snap back to reality after hearing your friend ask a question? Questions are useful because they make you alert and get your mind prepared for an answer.

Ask yourself questions to get yourself interested in the material. For example, take a heading you see and turn the heading into a question. Simply add "what is" to the beginning of the heading, or ask yourself how this heading connects with past content. You will want specific and interesting questions in order to best incorporate this new material into your understanding.

3. **(R) Read** — Read the material under each boldface heading. Recall the questions you asked yourself and find the answers. You may want to ask additional questions as you move forward through this process.

4. **(R) Recite** — Ask yourself the answers to the questions you prepared. If you cannot remember the answer to your question, go back and search for the answer in the text.

5. **(R) Review** — After moving through the entire section of readings, go back and review your questions. Do you know the answers? Can you recall the answers? Review the material to keep it fresh in your mind.

Practice the SQ3R method often. Once you have made the SQ3R a habit, you will realize you automatically use it without having to review the model!

Test Preparation and Test Taking

Test preparation is an ongoing process that will help you become successful in your coursework. Professors use tests to measure your understanding of the course material. Preparation does not simply begin a couple of days before the test but is the cumulative result of all your semester's work. The first steps in becoming successful are (a) attending class, (b) participating in class discussion, and (c) taking notes (Carter, Bishop, & Kravits, 2008).

Test Preparation

Throughout the semester you should be rereading your notes, reviewing major themes and concepts, and connecting the lectures to the text. If the syllabus does not describe the type of exams in the course (e.g., multiple choice, matching, fill-in-the-blank, true-false, essay), you should ask your instructor. Study groups may also be helpful as you prepare for your exams. Ultimately, you want to avoid cramming for a test, as you will not be able to retain the information as well as if you pace yourself throughout the semester.

> **Practice Testing**
>
> Practice testing as a learning technique has higher benefits than highlighting and re-reading for learners of all ages and abilities.
>
> *Source: Dunlosky, Rawson, Marsh, Nathan, & Willingham, 2013.*

Study Groups

A study group is a wonderful environment for reviewing material and preparing for exams. Study groups not only help you learn the material and make your large lecture feel smaller, they can also aid in your transition into the University by gaining new perspectives, friendships, and teamwork experience. This study strategy can provide you strength and motivation, offer camaraderie, and firm your resolve to study on days when you would rather be outside or you lack inspiration. Groups also create a sense of accountability. No one knows if you skip a solo study session, but if you decide to study with others, your group members are depending on your input, information, and motivation. If you skip a study group session, you are not only letting yourself down, but the members of your group as well (Ellis, 2006).

Form a Successful Study Group

To form a successful study group, these are the important rules to follow.

1. Choose a clear focus for your group. Establishing a plan early on for why you are meeting will help you stay on track.

2. Look for dedicated students. You not only want to find people you are comfortable with, but you also want to study with dedicated students who share some of your similar academic goals. Looking for students who pay attention in class, ask questions, and take detailed notes are likely to be good study group members.

3. Find students who will compliment and counterbalance your strengths and weaknesses. By choosing people with different methods of learning each of you will gain new perspectives on the material and it will enhance your ability to learn and adapt to different learning styles.

4. Limit your group to 4-6 members. Having a study group larger than six people could potentially become unruly and prove to be highly ineffective. Having a group smaller than four would defeat the purpose of a study group and might not allow for an equal distribution of responsibilities to all of its members.

5. Create a contract. Before you even begin studying you will want to create a contract that specifically outlines everyone's responsibilities to the group and identifies a time and location that everyone can attend.

Once in a study group, there are several ways to review content material. You may

- Test each other by asking group members questions that pertain to the material you are studying.
- Take time to teach each other. By taking the time to teach others you can further reinforce difficult concepts and ideas.
- Compare notes.

Adapted from Ellis (2006)

The most successful of study groups focus on the content of the course and use their time wisely. When meeting with classmates (a) discuss your notes and overall understanding of the class concepts, (b) review material from the unit, (c) share study tips, and (d) compare notes to ensure you have all the information. Utilize the time you have with your study group and work together to create review materials or practice tests for your next exam.

In addition to a study group, consider attending a Supplemental Instruction (SI) session at the Student Success Center in the Thomas Cooper Library. SI sessions are similar to study groups, but these review sessions are facilitated by a SI leader, an upper-level student who excelled in the challenging course. SI leaders use active learning strategies to review the material and maintain communication with the instructor to ensure the sessions are relevant to the material the instructor wants you to learn and understand.

Most of you will use study groups to prepare for tests or exams, but this is not the only type of study group. Cuseo (n.d.) identifies other groups that focus on

- Note-taking—The group meets directly after class to compare class notes.
- Reading—Students compare notes that they have either written down in the margins, on paper, or highlighted in the textbooks after they have completed a reading assignment.
- Library research—Classmates conduct research and combat library anxiety.
- Test-results review—These groups meet after they have received their results on an exam to help each other identify the source of their errors.

Test Taking

There are several test-taking techniques that can help you during an exam. Listed below are strategies for the most common test administrations.

True-False. If your test incorporates true-false questions, be sure to read the question in its entirety. True-false questions can become tricky when they incorporate a negative word (i.e., not or no) or omit a negative from the statement (Carter, Bishop, & Kravits, 2008). With true-false, be sure to confirm that the entire sentence is true. If one word departs from the truth, the statement becomes false. With true-false questions it is important to remember you have a 50-50 chance of answering correctly. Words such as *always, all,* or *only* should alert you to a potentially false statement while *usually, sometimes,* and *mostly* are often associated with true statements (Carter, Bishop, & Kravits).

Test Taking Strategies

- Start preparing for the exam on the first day the topic is assigned, the first time you read the text, and the first time the material is covered in class. The night before the exam then becomes a final review session instead of a last minute cram session.

- Get a good night's rest. Before going to sleep, relax and visualize yourself remaining calm in the test situation and performing well on the exam.

- Be organized. Take all the necessary materials to class. Do you need #2 pencils? Take a couple. Do you need an erasable pen for possible essay questions? Do you need to take paper or a blue book? Getting to a class and realizing that you are not prepared simply increases anxiety and interferes with performance.

- Be on time! If you are commuting, leave early enough to deal with potential traffic delays. This is one more way to keep anxiety under control.

- Sit in a quiet spot. Talking a great deal with other students right before the exam about the material on which you will be tested can interfere with your prior learning. You may want to glance over key terms or mnemonic devices one last time, but do not try to learn any new information at this time.

- When the test is handed out, pay particular attention to any last-minute verbal instructions or instructions written on the board.

- Skim over the entire test, making sure that you understand all directions. Check to see if different amounts of credit are given for different questions. Jot down any key words or mnemonics that go with particular questions right away. Then you can come back later and complete these questions.

- Make sure you know whether you have to answer all questions or only a certain number of questions. Also, determine if you get credit for all correct answers (thus making it worth your while to guess if you are unsure of an answer), or if a certain percentage will be counted against you for incorrect answers. This is particularly important information if the test is standardized.

- Budget your time! Wear a watch or make sure there is a clock in the room, and monitor how much time you are spending on different sections of the test.

- If you allowed to write notes on the test, take a moment at the beginning of the exam to write down key words or phrases. Use that to your advantage.

Multiple Choice. For this test style, consider reading the question and asking yourself what the answer should be before looking at the possible answers. This may assist you in feeling more confident in your answer. With multiple choice, it is important to pay attention to the directions. You may find that your instructor gives a variety of directions that could include circling the correct option, the incorrect option, or multiple answers (Pauk, 2001). Be sure to read these directions as you take the test so you know what the professor expects from you. Another important strategy is to first answer all the questions you know immediately, then the questions that you can eliminate down to two answers, and finally the remaining questions. Choose the best answer you can. Answers to previous questions may help you answer questions later in the exam. Do not get hung up on the tough questions. Circle the ones you are unsure of and then guess. Return if time permits. Other helpful tips are

- Read each choice carefully. Read words such as *often, sometimes,* and *always* very carefully so that you do not miss out on their meaning. Select the answer that is most correct.
- Read all choices. Even if the first answer seems correct, another choice may be better, or all of the above may be the correct response.
- Mark off each answer that you know you can eliminate as a possible answer. If you can eliminate just one answer, your chances of choosing the correct answer increase significantly.
- Pay attention to opposite statements appearing in a question; one of them is often correct.

Matching. As with multiple choice exams, when answering matching questions, you want to complete the questions you are confident in first. Be sure to read the directions to confirm that matches cannot be used multiple times. Also, reading the definitions may trigger your mind to recall the answer and correctly match the word (Carter, Bishop, & Kravits, 2008).

Fill-in-the-Blank. With fill-in-the blank questions, determine what answers are most appropriate for the missing section. Eliminate anything that seems too outlandish or does not connect with the content. If you are struggling to narrow your answer to one word, consider writing both answers down on the test or ask your professor a specific question that shows both your knowledge of the subject and your confusion on how the sentence needs to be completed. This demonstrates you are thinking about the problem and may result in partial credit if you are not confident in a particular answer (Carter, Bishop, & Kravits, 2008).

Essay. It is important to pace yourself with all tests but especially with essay questions. Give yourself plenty of time to complete the essays. First, carefully read the directions to determine what the question is asking of you and that you are responding appropriately. For example, if the question asks for an explanation, you will want to detail the reasons an event happened and its effects. For questions that solicit an interpretation, you should incorporate your own personal opinions. In an essay test, creating an outline will help organize your thoughts into well-defined areas. Make sure you allow time to go back and reread what you have written, make edits, and correct any errors (Carter, Bishop, & Kravits, 2008).

Test Anxiety

(Adapted from the Missouri University of Science and Technology Counseling Center http://counsel.mst.edu/selfhelp/vpl/testanxiety.html. Used with permission.)

Poor test performance is most often a direct result of a lack of preparedness; however, it can also be a product of classic test anxiety, a true mental, physical, and/or emotional state not influenced by the level of preparedness. Common test anxiety symptoms can included mental block, panic, and physical discomfort (e.g., nausea, perspiration, muscle tension).

To combat and cope with test anxiety, it is important to first identify why you have anxious feelings and understand how you are affected by stress. Strategies to avoid test anxiety include

- Arriving to class early on test day
- Sitting in your regular seat to instill a sense of familiarity
- Reading all test directions first
- Using positive self-talk for encouragement
- Moving forward when you come to an answer you do not know and returning to the blank questions at the end of the test
- Skipping difficult sections (to avoid being overwhelmed) and returning later

If you begin to feel test anxiety symptoms, sit up, look forward, and breathe. Take a minute to clear your head. If permitted, you may want to walk outside, get a drink of water, or take a quick walk up and down the hall to clear your head. Focus on budgeting your time, pacing yourself to allow time to review your answers.

This chapter has presented you with various ideas on how to best support your academic coursework and further develop skills that will help you become successful both in your college career and beyond the classroom (e.g., in student organization meetings, networking, relationships, employment). Recognize and use the resources available at the University of South Carolina to help you refine and master these skills as you move forward.

Did you know?

There are many resources on campus that are available to help you with test anxiety or learning strategies.

Student Success Center (SSC)

At the Student Success Center, an ACE Coach can help you identify the academic barriers that are making you anxious and find methods to ensure your success. Barriers may include the lack of preparation for the test, negative self-talk, or worrying about past test performance.

Counseling Center

If you find that your test anxiety is impacting your academic success, the Counseling Center, located on the 7th floor of the Byrnes Building, may be a helpful resource. The Counseling Center provides individual and group sessions that can assist you in developing skills to cope with anxiety.

Check yourself

Identifying Your Academic Strengths

Check the appropriate column for each item to identify your academic strengths.

	I do this	I need to do this
I arrive on time for all of my classes. Class attendance is a high priority for me.		
I sit in the front or middle of the class. I can easily see and hear and will not be distracted.		
I pay attention in class. I do not disrupt others by talking, nor do I space out and miss important information.		
I come prepared for class. I have read the chapter and my homework is done. I bring my book, notepaper, and pens to class so I am ready to listen and take notes.		
I participate in class discussions. I know I will learn more if I am involved, plus I am contributing to the learning process.		
I ask questions in class. If I don't understand or if I want to know more, I seek additional information.		
I give the instructor and others positive feedback in class. I make eye contact when someone is talking, and I express appropriate body language.		
I get to know other students in class. I have at least one other person I can ask for help or with whom I can compare notes. I don't feel like a stranger.		
I contact the instructor if I know I must miss class. I get any hand-outs and information that I missed prior to the next class session whenever possible.		
I develop and use my own, personalized learning tools. I mark my textbooks to suit my needs. I have what I need (e.g., calculator, pocket dictionary, planner) to do my assignment.		
I turn in all assignments on time. I don't lose unnecessary points by turning in late or incomplete work.		
I follow directions. When I'm doing an assignment, I make sure it is what I'm supposed to do.		
I seek help when I need it. I use the support services USC provides (e.g., tutoring, counseling). I don't let pride keep me from getting tutoring. I would rather pass than fail.		

GPA Calculator

Your grade point average (GPA) is computed on the basis of all semester hours attempted for credit, except for credit hours carried under the Pass-Fail or audit options. The grade points earned in any course carried with a passing grade (A, B+, B, C+, C, D+, D) are computed by multiplying the number of semester hour credits assigned to the course by a factor determined by the grade.

A = 4; **B+** = 3.5; **B** = 3; **C+** = 2.5; **C** = 2; **D+** = 1.5; **D** = 1

No grade points are assigned to the symbols F, S, U, WF, W, I, AUD, T, or NR.

The grade point average is determined by dividing the total number of semester grade points earned by the total number of semester hours attempted for credit.

Course	Grade and (grade points)	x	Credit hours	=	Total grade points
English 101	B (3 pts)	x	3	=	9
History 111	C (2 pts)	x	3	=	6
Geology 103	B+ (3.5 pts)	x	4	=	14
Mathematics 111	D (1 pt)	x	3	=	3
University 101	A (4 pts)	x	3	=	12
TOTAL			16 hours		44 pts

GPA TOTAL	44 pts	÷	16 hours	=	2.75 GPA

(Adapted from http://www.sc.edu/bulletin/ugrad/acadregs.html#course%20credit)

Calculate your GPA

Course	Grade and (grade points)	x	Credit hours	=	Total grade points
		x		=	
		x		=	
		x		=	
		x		=	
		x		=	
TOTAL					

GPA TOTAL		÷		=	

Chapter 5: Academic Skills

Check yourself

Test Anxiety Inventory

Directions: Read each statement below to see if it reflects your experience in test taking. If it does, place a check mark on the line next to the number of the statement. Check any item that seems to fit your experience. Be honest with yourself.

____ 1. I wish there were some way to succeed without taking tests.

____ 2. Getting a good score on one test does not seem to increase my confidence on other tests.

____ 3. People (family, friends, etc.) are counting on me to do well.

____ 4. During a test, I sometimes find myself thinking about things that have nothing to do with the test.

____ 5. I do not enjoy eating before or after an important test.

____ 6. I have always dreaded courses in which the teacher has the habit of giving pop quizzes.

____ 7. It seems to me that test sessions should not be made the formal, tense situations they are.

____ 8. People who do well on tests generally end up in better positions in life.

____ 9. Before or during an important exam, I find myself thinking about how much brighter some of the other test-takers are.

____ 10. Event though I don't always think about it, I am concerned about how others will view me if I do poorly.

____ 11. Worrying about how well I will do interferes with my preparation and performance on tests.

____ 12. Having to face an important test disturbs my sleep.

____ 13. I cannot stand to have people walking around watching me while I take a test.

____ 14. If exams could be done away with, I think I would actually learn more from my courses.

____ 15. Knowing that my future depends in part on doing well on tests upsets me.

____ 16. I know I could outscore most people if I could just get myself together.

____ 17. People will question my ability if I do poorly.

____ 18. I never seem to be fully prepared to take tests.

____ 19. I cannot relax physically before a test.

____ 20. I mentally freeze up on important tests.

____ 21. Room noises (from lights, heating/cooling systems, other test-takers) bother me.

____ 22. I have a hollow, uneasy feeling before taking a test.

____ 23. Tests make me wonder if I will ever reach my goals.

____ 24. Tests do not really show how much a person knows.

____ 25. If I score low, I am not going to tell anyone exactly what my score was.

____ 26. I often feel the need to cram before a test.

____ 27. My stomach becomes upset before important tests.

____ 28. I sometimes seem to defeat myself (think negative thoughts) while working on an important test.

____ 29. I start feeling very anxious or uneasy just before getting test results.

____ 30. I wish I could get into a vocation that does not require tests for entrance.

____ 31. If I do not do well on a test, I guess it will mean I am not as smart as I thought I was.

____ 32. If my score is low, my parents will be very disappointed.

____ 33. My anxiety about tests makes me want to avoid preparing fully, and this just makes me more anxious.

____ 34. I often find my fingers tapping or my legs jiggling while taking a test.

____ 35. After taking a test, I often feel I could have done better than I actually did.

____ 36. When taking a test, my emotional feelings interfere with my concentration.

____ 37. The harder I work on some test items, the more confused I get.

____ 38. Aside from what others may think of me, I am concerned about my own opinion of myself if I do poorly.

____ 39. My muscles tense up in certain areas of my body when I take a test.

____ 40. I do not feel confident and mentally relaxed before a test.

____ 41. My friends will be disappointed in me if my score is low.

____ 42. One of my problems is not knowing exactly when I am prepared for a test.

____ 43. I often feel physically panicky when I have to take a really important test.

____ 44. I wish teachers understood that some people are more nervous than others when taking tests, and that this could be taken into account when test answers are evaluated.

____ 45. I would rather write a paper than take a test for a grade.

____ 46. I am going to find out how others did before I announce my score.

____ 47. Some people I know will be amused if I score low, and this bothers me.

____ 48. I think I could do much better on tests if I could take them alone and/or not feel pressured by a time limit.

____ 49. My test performance is directly connected to my future success and security.

____ 50. During tests, I sometimes get so nervous that I forget facts I really know.

Analysis

Check yourself

Test Anxiety Inventory

Circle the numbers to the statements that you checked in the inventory. The areas you have answered "yes" to the most will help you identify the causes of your text anxiety.

4 Main Sources of Test Anxiety

1. Concerns about how others will view you if you do poorly

Statement
- 3
- 10
- 17
- 25
- 32
- 41
- 46
- 47

2. Concerns about your own self-image

Statement
- 2
- 9
- 16
- 24
- 31
- 38
- 40

3. Concerns about your future security

Statement
- 1
- 8
- 15
- 23
- 30
- 49

4. Concerns about not being prepared for a test

Statement
- 6
- 11
- 18
- 26
- 33
- 42

3 Main Expressions of Test Anxiety

1. Bodily reaction

Statements
- 5
- 12
- 19
- 27
- 34
- 39
- 43

2. Thought disruptions

Statement
- 4
- 13
- 20
- 21
- 28
- 35
- 36
- 37
- 48
- 50

3. General test-taking anxiety

Statement
- 7
- 14
- 22
- 29
- 44
- 45

How strong is each of these sources of test anxiety for you?

How would you summarize your reactions to each of the sources of anxiety?

E-mail Etiquette

Read the following e-mails and provide feedback on what the student did well and what they could improve upon. Look at page 105 for best practices in communicating with your professors.

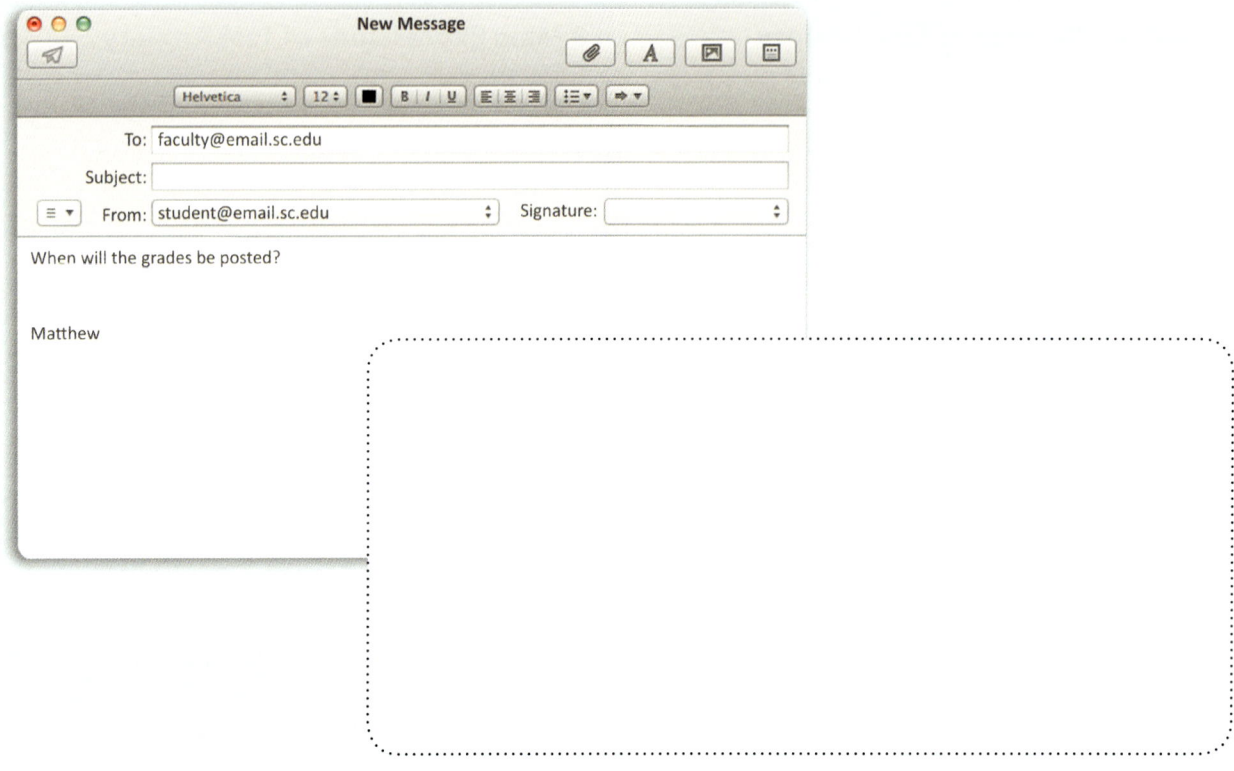

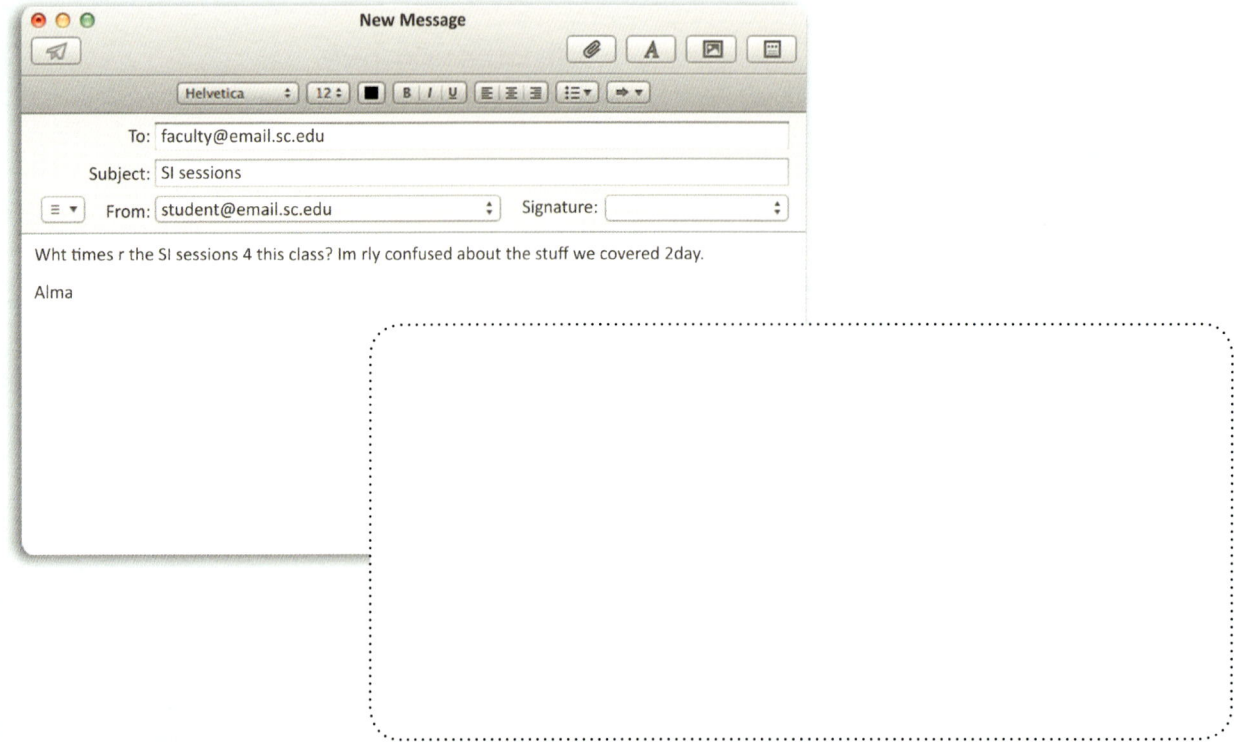

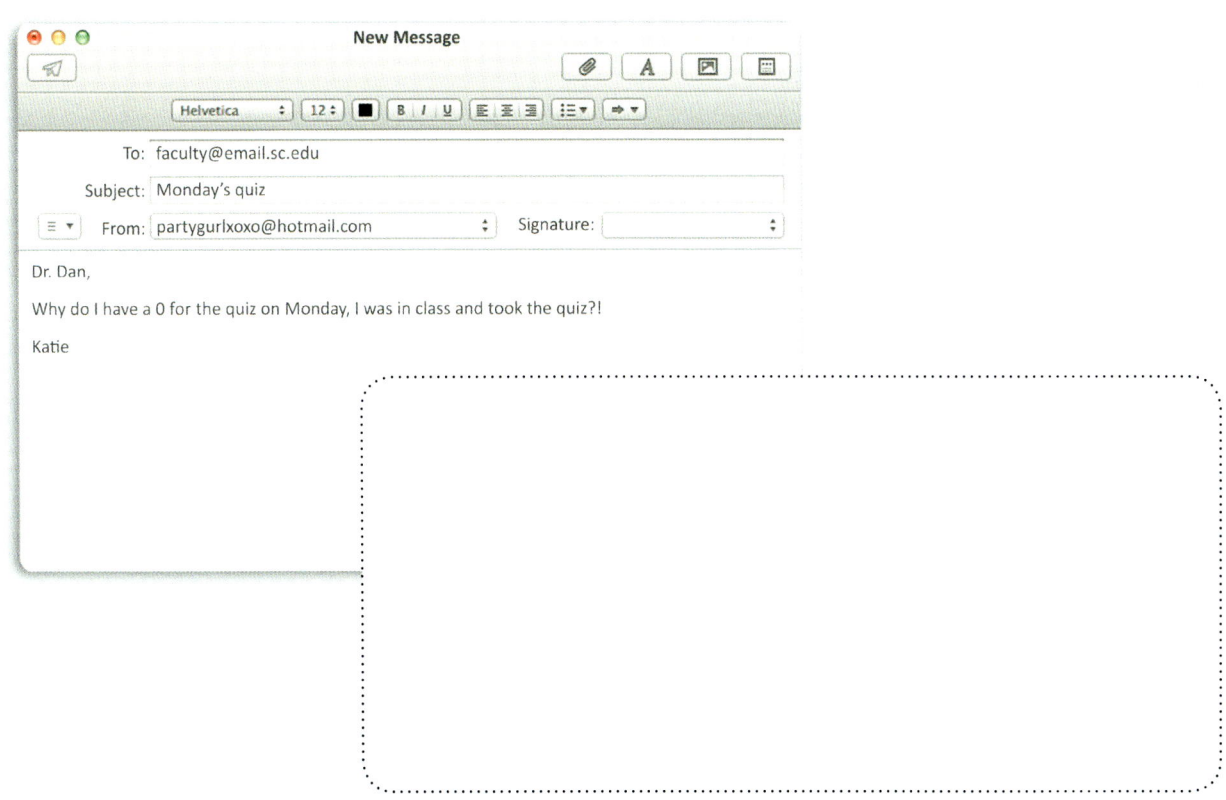

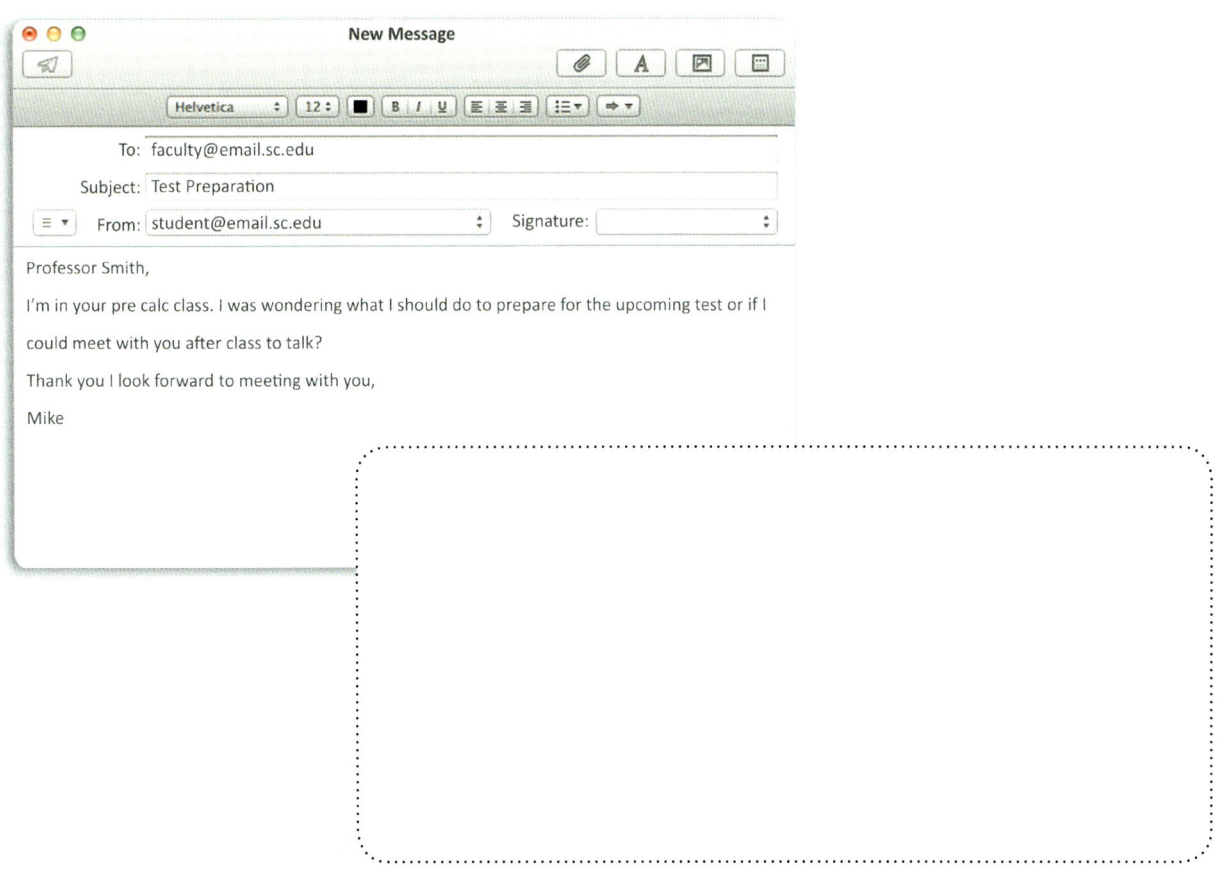

RESOURCES

Academic Assistance

Academic Coaching and Engagement 777-5430
Bates House, Columbia Hall, Sims,
Thomas Cooper Library
http://www.sa.sc.edu/ssc/
student.success@sc.edu

Math Tutoring Center
LeConte College, Room 105
http://www.math.sc.edu/mathlab.html

Student Disability Services 777-6142
LeConte College, Room 112A
http://www.sa.sc.edu/sds/

Student Success Center. 777-0684
Thomas Cooper Library-- Mezzanine Level
Services include: Supplemental Instruction,
Tutoring, and Creating Academic Responsibility
student.success@sc.edu
http://www.sa.sc.edu/ssc/

Writing Center. 777-2078
Humanities Classroom Building, Room 014
http://www.cas.sc.edu/write/

Writers' Hotline 777-7020

REFERENCES

Carter, C., Bishop, J., & Kravits, S. L. (2008). *Keys to effective learning: Developing powerful habits of mind.* Upper Saddle River, NJ: Pearson Prentice Hall.

Cuseo, J. (n.d.). *Academic-support strategies for promoting student retention and achievement during the first-year of college.* Retrieved March 19, 2011, from http://www.ulster.ac.uk/star/resources/acdemic_support_strat_first_years.pdf

Dunlosky, J., Rawson, K. A., Marsh, E. J., Nathan, M. J., & Willingham, D. T. (2013) Improving students' learning with effective learning techniques: Promising directions from cognitive and educational psychology. *Psychological Science in the Public Interest, 14*(1), 4-58.

Ellis, D. (2006). *Becoming a master student.* St. Charles, IL: Houghton Mifflin Company

Gump, S. E. (2005). The cost of cutting a class: Attendance as a predictor of success. *College Teaching , 53*(1), 21-26.

Hirsch, G. (2001). *Helping college students succeed: A model for effective intervention.* Ann Arbor, MI: Sheridan Books.

Jacobsen, W., & Forste, R. (2011). The wired generation: Academic and social outcomes of electronic media use among university students. *Cyberpsychology, Behavior, and Social Networking, 14*(5),275-280.

Pauk, W. (2001). *How to study in college.* Boston, MA: Houghton-Mifflin.

Wollen, K. A., Cone, R. S., Britcher, J. C., & Mindemann, K. M. (1985). The effect of instructional sets upon the apportionment of study time to individual lines of text. *Human Learning, 4*, 89-103.

Chapter Six

Charting Your Path

UNIVERSITY OF SOUTH CAROLINA

Dear First-Year Student,

Many students find that one of their favorite parts of college is having the chance to make important choices for themselves -- choices about how to spend their time, what to major in, what to do outside of class, and eventually what to do for a career. What you do in the short-term and in the long-term is up to you! This chapter, "Charting Your Path," provides some valuable information about resources at Carolina – and responsibilities, too – that are yours as a college student at USC.

The first step is exploring your interests as well as what opportunities are available to you. You will begin this exploration the first semester in U101. In "Charting Your Path" you will reflect on who you are, what you like to do, and career options that might be a good fit for you. This will help you with choosing a major, finding great classes and great professors, and discovering beyond-the-class activities such as internships, service-learning courses, research projects, global study programs, or leadership opportunities. "Charting Your Path" provides a framework, some tools, and some good company – your classmates, peer leader, and instructor – for developing your own plan.

You likely have already done some career exploration, but most of our students want to do a lot more before they settle on one pathway. Go to the Career Center this semester and see what free resources they have for you. You will find helpful information, friendly peer leaders and counselors, and online references that can really make a difference in "Charting Your Path." At USC there are amazing people and programs in place to help you succeed on your journey.

Your academic advisor is your advocate. Find out who your advisor is and how to make the most of your time together. Do your part to make that relationship a big plus in your college years. Also familiarize yourself with the academic policies covered in "Charting Your Path." Know how many credits you need each semester, how to drop classes without long-term penalties, what "grade forgiveness" is, and how best to stay in good standing for on-time graduation. Working closely with your advisor and knowing Carolina's academic policies help ensure your success.

Finding your path in college and custom-designing your lifetime career is up to you. As members of the Carolina family we walk a path of discovery together, offering each other lots of help and information to make sure all of us are successful. Enjoy "Charting Your Path," and I look forward to watching your own "custom story" unfold!

Best wishes,

Helen Doerpinghaus
Vice Provost and Dean of Undergraduate Studies

AS an undergraduate student at the University of South Carolina you may be facing challenges associated with living and learning in a new environment. You might feel there is too much to learn and that it is virtually impossible to figure out everything you need to know. At Carolina, individual colleges and schools (e.g., the College of Arts and Sciences, the Moore School of Business) set college-specific academic policies and procedures that can often be confusing to students. In University 101, the aim is to foster academic success by helping you and your classmates identify relevant academic policies, processes, and procedures related to advising, course planning, and major exploration. This chapter will address the interconnected topics of career planning, major exploration, academic advising, and University academic policies, as well as suggest strategies that you can use to chart your academic and career path.

While you will not be expected to know or interpret the policies for all undergraduate units, you will be expected to understand policies related to your chosen academic college and the general rules that apply to all students, regardless of class level. Your academic advisor is a key person to get to know and can provide valuable assistance in guiding you through the maze of choices, policies, and procedures you encounter as a new student. Make establishing a working relationship with your advisor a priority this semester, and the dividends will continue throughout your college career. While your advisor is key to navigating your academic path, other staff and faculty can also provide valuable assistance. Do not hesitate to share any advising concerns or questions you have with your U101 instructor, other faculty, staff, or your peer or graduate leader; if they do not have the direct answer, they will be able to guide you to the right resource. Asking questions now can save you time and avoid potential headaches and hassles later.

Equally important to becoming familiar with the policies and procedures defining the undergraduate experience is to recognize the connection between your academic coursework and career aspirations. As a first-year student, you may not be concerned about finding a job upon graduation; however, it *is* important for you to begin to understand the career planning process and engage in a course of action that will enhance your self-understanding, which is the first step in choosing, or confirming, a major. A solid understanding of self will also help you determine an appropriate career path based on your interests, abilities, values, and personality as well as

- See the relevance of the courses you will take
- Wisely choose your elective courses
- Develop a cohesive undergraduate program of study that will lead you toward your initial career goal

CONSIDER THIS

Have you chosen your major yet? If so, what is your current major?

How did you decide on your current major?

What career path do you plan to take with the degree you are pursuing?

> **Did you know?**
> - Approximately 75% of first-year students do not have a major chosen when they enter college (Cuseo, 2005).
> - More than 50% of students who declare a major will change their major at least once during college (Orndorff & Herr, 1996).

> **ON THE WEB**
> You can find helpful resources as well as more information about the Career Center by visiting:
> **sc.edu/career**

Major Exploration and Career Planning

Imagine working full time for the 50 years following graduation. It may sound unbelievable, but this is exactly what is happening in the world of work today; people are working longer for a variety of reasons, chief among them is the fact that people are living longer. Therefore, it is crucial to choose a major that you enjoy and one that will give you essential and multiple marketable skills within a larger field of work.

If you have decided upon a major or career, you can explore your choice further through career-related work experiences. The Career Center resources can help you locate internships, job-shadowing opportunities, and part-time or summer work. You can also investigate cooperative education programs (i.e., full-time student status alternated with full-time work) available in some majors. Additionally, the Career Center website offers resources to assist you in researching broad career fields as well as specific employers.

If you are still unsure about a major or career, schedule a visit to the Career Center. They offer a variety of assessment tools to identify your career interests, personality type, personal values, and skills/abilities. Information from these tools can be coupled with workshops and one-on-one appointments to help you make informed and intentional career decisions. These assessment tools are not designed to tell you what to be or what major to choose; instead, they indicate how your interests, personality, or values relate to various occupations.

Whatever your needs regarding career exploration, the Career Center is available to help you. They are prepared to assist students from the time they are admitted to the University until after they graduate.

Career Decision Making: Four-Step Model

The process of deciding on a career is complex and comprehensive. It is not something you can do in one sitting or in a short period of time. In order to make an informed career decision, it is helpful to follow this four-step process.

Step 1: Develop Self-Awareness and Understanding: Who Am I?

Answering this question involves a thorough investigation of your background, interests, values, feelings, abilities, needs, ambitions, achievements, and lifestyle. The better you can articulate who you are and what you want, the more likely it is that the decisions you make will be informed choices that lead to success and happiness in your future career.

Each new experience provides you with a unique opportunity to deepen your self-awareness, which develops over time as you engage in significant reflection and think about your interactions with others and the world. Sustained effort and attention to making meaning out of your experiences is what leads to enhanced self-awareness. Staff members at the Career Center can use assessments, interviews, and interactive group workshops to help you gather information about yourself and integrate what you learn into a meaningful whole. There are also several assessments (e.g., FOCUS, Strong Interest Inventory, Myers-Briggs Type Indicator) available to guide you through many aspects of this process.

CONSIDER THIS

Use the following questions to guide you on your self-awareness discovery:
What interests and activities do I like and enjoy?

In what types of activities and school subjects have I had the most success?

What skill areas do I need to strengthen?

What job or career characteristics (e.g., salary, location, advancement) will be important to me after college? List three to five.

What types of work activities do I prefer (e.g., working with people, organizing or analyzing data, creating ideas, doing hands-on or practical activities)? Are there any specific examples from my previous work experiences that I enjoyed doing?

How have my family members or other significant people influenced my potential career direction?

Step 2: Acquire Knowledge of Fields of Study and Careers: What Is Out There?

The answer to this question requires extensive investigation and research. Becoming aware of the career options available to you will also help you select a major and determine an initial career path. The University of South Carolina offers more than 160 majors and additional minors from which to choose. Talking with professors, upper-level students majoring in fields of your interest, and academic advisors can all be good sources of information about majors and minors.

The world of work is vast and ever-changing, and the job or field you will be entering after graduation may not even exist today! Investigating the possibilities in the work world can be very helpful as you chart your path and can be gathered through activities such as researching career literature, informational interviews, job-shadowing experiences, visiting the workplace, and viewing media presentations regarding careers.

CONSIDER THIS

Use the following questions as you begin your research process:

What majors or minors are offered at the University of South Carolina, and how could they help me reach my occupational goals?

What career fields will offer the most work opportunities in the next 5-10 years?

Who are the major employers and what types of work opportunities are there in the areas I would prefer to live after graduation?

Where can I find good information about the occupations or career fields that interest me?

What types of internships, job-shadowing experiences, and cooperative education positions will help me explore career options?

Step 3: Synthesize Information and Make Choices: How Do I Fit?

Arriving at this answer will require you to synthesize all accumulated information to determine a good fit in a potential career. Once you have engaged in significant and intentional self-awareness and have investigated the career options available, you are ready to begin processing and choosing a major and career direction. Making choices can be a difficult process, so it is usually helpful to test out your thoughts with others. Staff members at the Career Center, as well as your academic advisor, can assist you in collecting information that will be helpful in your career exploration. Others who are close to you and who have known you for many years can be helpful as well. Friends and family members can serve as sounding boards as you synthesize information and tentatively test out possibilities.

JobMate

JobMate is an online integrated job search resource center that allows students and alumni to search job postings, view and apply for on-campus interviewing opportunities, and access employer and Career Center events. All students and alumni have free access to JobMate and should take advantage of this great tool! Visit the Career Center for full access to your JobMate account.

CONSIDER THIS

Use the following guiding questions as you consider possibilities:
What occupations or career fields interest me? List 3-5.

How do my interests, skills, values, and personality fit occupations that interest me?

How will I explain my career choice to others, especially if they are not supportive of my decision?

Step 4: Develop an Effective Plan for Achieving Goals: What Is My Plan of Action?

Once you have made a decision, developing a plan can be energizing and exciting. Answering this important question involves the creation of a plan or strategy to achieve desired career goals and an awareness of options. Your plan of action will vary depending on your goals. Aspects that you should consider in your action plan, in addition to careful academic course choices, include part-time and summer work options, internships, involvement in clubs and organizations, community service and volunteer opportunities, and leadership development experiences.

Beyond the campus, there are countless avenues for achieving your goals. Professional networking is helpful in learning more about your desired career path and connecting with people who are already working in the field. Participating in a variety of these beyond-the-classroom activities is critical to your plan, as prospective employers are increasingly interested in students whose time in college includes a balance of on- and off-campus involvement.

Effective job search skills will be necessary to assist you in achieving your goals. Workshops at the Career Center and sessions with staff members can help you develop a résumé, refine your interviewing style and technique, identify key people to serve as references, search for a job, and learn how to put your best foot forward.

CONSIDER THIS

Use the following questions as you develop a plan to meet your goals:

What major and/or minor do I need to pursue occupations that interest me?

What are the academic requirements for my potential major and/or minor?

What is a realistic goal for my GPA?

What additional education or training beyond a bachelor's degree will be required?

What student organizations or other cocurricular activities will assist me in reaching my career goals?

How will I develop leadership skills and assume leadership roles during my undergraduate experience?

What types of career-related work experiences (e.g., internships, part-time or summer jobs, cooperative education experiences) will best assist me in reaching my career goals?

What is my timeline for getting career-related work experience?

Suggested Career Planning Timeline

Although graduation is several years away, now is the perfect time to begin thinking about potential career paths and your post-graduation goals. Focusing on this now will allow you to best use your time and the services at the University in preparing for your future career.

First Year

- Develop relationships with USC faculty and staff and identify at least one person by the end of your 1st semester that could serve as a positive influence for you.
- Attend USC's Student Organization Fair and get involved on campus. Employers seek students who are active on campus and in the community.
- Visit USC Connect's website and search the database for opportunities within the Leadership pathways.
- Explore options and decide on a major or confirm your selected major.
- Write a résumé based on your current experiences. Visit the Career Center for a résumé review.
- Investigate part-time and/or summer jobs using JobMate.
- Review the experiences you have had so far and consider opportunities for future development, such as job shadowing, study abroad, career-related student organizations, part-time work, internships, and externships.
- Reflect on and identify personal traits to develop self-awareness of your strengths, weaknesses, work values, and interests.

Sophomore Year

- Continue to stay involved on campus and enhancing relationships with your professors and advisors.
- Participate in Sophomore September programming sponsored by the Office of Student Engagement.
- Upgrade your JobMate account to full access and post your résumé and cover letter. JobMate can be used to search for internships, job-shadowing opportunities, part-time, and summer jobs. Full access is required for Spur Connections, mock interviews, and for interviewing for several peer leadership positions on campus.

Spur Connections

Spur Connections is a new mentor program designed to assist USC students and alumni in learning more about various positions and industries. USC students and alumni will be able to search the Spur Connections database and contact mentors about opportunities such as networking, information interviewing, and job shadowing. Spur Connections is a part of USC's JobMate database.

Did you know?

The U.S. Department of Labor has developed *The Occupational Outlook Handbook*, which includes the following information on hundreds of different types of jobs:

- Training and education needed
- Earnings
- Expected job prospects
- Job duties
- Working conditions

In addition, the *Handbook* offers job search tips, links to information about the job market in each state, and more. For more information, visit http://www.bls.gov/ooh

---

Did you know?

Employers initially spend 10-30 seconds reviewing your résumé!

(Source: University of South Carolina Career Center)

Did you know?

- 76.6% of employers prefer to hire new college graduates who have gained relevant work experience.
- 75% of employers screen job candidates on their GPA; 63% use a 3.0 GPA as a cutoff.

(Source: NACE, 2010)

ON THE WEB

The Career Center has several sample résumés and cover letters for students to view online. Check out this resource at:

sc.edu/career/resume.html

Did you know?

According to a survey of employers by Peter D. Hart Research Associates, the top skills employers are looking for in college graduates are:

- The ability to work well in teams—especially with people different from yourself
- The ability to write and speak well
- The ability to think clearly about complex problems
- The ability to analyze a problem to develop workable solutions
- An understanding of global context in which work is now done
- The ability to be creative and innovative in solving problems
- The ability to apply knowledge and skills in new settings
- The ability to understand numbers and statistics, as well as science and technology
- A strong sense of ethics and integrity

(Source: AAC&U, 2007)

- Partner with faculty to pursue research or scholarly experiences in your chosen field.
- Identify volunteer opportunities through the Office of Community Service Programs.
- Revise your résumé to reflect the additional experience you have using OptimalResume.

Junior Year

- Pursue leadership roles in order to enhance your "marketability" to employers.
- Sharpen your interviewing skills through a mock interview in the Career Center.
- Find another internship, add a co-op, or, if possible, consider studying abroad or participating in the National Student Exchange program.
- Revise your résumé again, adding in your career-related work and academic experiences.
- If attending graduate or professional school is critical to your career plan, start searching possible institutions and programs and begin preparing for any specific application requirements, such as personal statements, essays, specific work experience, and entrance exams.
- Attend fall and spring job fairs and begin networking for your senior year job search.

Senior Year

- Select professors or advisors to serve as your references, discuss your plans with them, and give them a copy of your updated résumé and/or personal statements.
- Start at least nine months before graduation with your job search or the graduate school application process.
- Finalize your résumé and cover letter, making sure they are tailored to each application you submit during your job search.
- Use the Career Center, which has specialized tools to help you with your transition from your college experience to life after college.
- Participate in job fairs and information sessions held on campus.

Check yourself

What's right for you?

Review the table below to determine which experience may be right for you. ✓ = Yes

	Information Interviewing	Job Shadowing	Part-time Job	Internship	Co-op
I would like to get a sneak peek of a career in order to confirm the type of work experience I would eventually like to obtain	✓	✓			
I need to earn extra income while in school			✓	✓	✓
I would like to be able to work somewhere other than locally during the fall or spring semester without losing my student status			✓ (Summer only)	✓ (Summer only)	✓ (Summer only)
I would like to increase my odds of obtaining a full-time offer after graduation from the company that employs me as a student			✓	✓	✓
This type of experience would look most favorable by the profession I'm considering				✓	✓
I am willing/able to defer graduation for a semester					✓
I am willing to commit 2 - 3 semesters of work for the same employer					✓
I would like to have an official notation of my experience appear on my University transcript					✓

Check yourself

Gathering More Information

At this point, you may be decided on a career path, or maybe you are still exploring. A great external resource is the *Occupational Outlook Handbook* (bls.gov/ooh/) published by the United States Department of Labor. You can search hundreds of occupations and discover what they do, the work environment, educational requirements, job outlook, salary, and more! Take a moment to look up the following information for the career/careers you may be interested in:

What is the entry-level education requirement?

Is work experience in a related occupation required?

What is the job outlook for 2012-2020?

What is the 2012 median pay?

Are there similar occupations of interest to you?

first-year student résumé

Tricia Kennedy
123-456-7890
tkennedy@email.sc.edu

Current Address
321 College Street
Columbia, SC 29208

Permanent Address
123 Kennedy Lane
Waunakee, WI 53597

Education

University of South Carolina, Columbia SC
Bachelor of Arts May 2018
Major: Comparative Literature
Minor: English and Spanish

Waunakee Community High School May 2014
Enrolled in honors and advanced placement courses
Graduated with 3.67/4.0 GPA

Coursework
Current courses fulfill School's General Education Requirements. Highlights include: Critical Reading and Composition, Calculus for Business Administration and Social Sciences, and Introduction to Logic

Experience

University of South Carolina Career Center, Columbia, SC August 2014 – Present
Student Worker
- Utilize organizational skills to assist with administrative duties as assigned

Waunakee Youth Day Camp, Waunakee, WI June 2013 – August 2013
Camp Counselor June 2014 – August 2014
- Organized and supervised activities for children's day camp
- Provided safe and fun environment for kids ages 5-10

Computer Skills
Proficient in Adobe InDesign and Photoshop

Activities
Writer, Waunakee Community High School Yearbook August 2010 – May 2014
Member, Waunakee Community High School Chorus August 2010 – May 2014

Volunteer Work
Community service participant, Unity Temple Baptist Church
- Participated in various outreach programs through church involvement

senior résumé

ELISE PORTER
123 Glenbrook ▪ Columbia, SC 29208 ▪ (123) 456-7890 ▪ portere@gmail.com

EDUCATION
Bachelor of Science in Computer Science May 2018
University of South Carolina, Columbia, SC

PROFESSIONAL EXPERIENCE
Severien, LLC, Columbia, SC
Computing and Web Design Intern October 2015 – Present
- Maintain, update and design multiple websites
- Migrate multiple SQL databases to one database
- Maintain multiple SQL databases and corresponding websites
- Create documentation for multiple client types, including political, fitness, non-profit, and retail

Walt Disney World Resort, Lake Buena Vista, FL
Design and Engineering Intern May 2015 – August 2015
- Managed and developed solutions for data collection and reporting for department wide metrics
- Developed solutions, tools, and documentation for improved business management
- Designed and built SharePoint test site as template for SharePoint site migration
- Troubleshooted and maintained department's SharePoint sites
- Created department wide documentation and various software training

IBM, Durham, NC
Pre-Professional Programmer and Technical Writer June 2014 – December 2014
- Edited and published documents and web content for internal and external customers
- Developed documentation standards for particular technologies
- Migrated documents between internal and external websites
- Researched and assisted in the development of various support tools

Gap and Old Navy, Columbia, SC and Cary, NC
Brand Experience Associate, Customer Service Associate May 2013 – June 2014
- Followed and enhanced marketing guidelines for store displays and sales floor
- Reached daily and monthly sales and credit card goals

LEADERSHIP EXPERIENCE
STARS Outreach (Computing Student Recruitment and Outreach), Columbia, SC
Outreach Leader January 2014 – Present
- Organize and participate in outreach events, including high school visits, university tours, and student luncheons
- Call accepted students to discuss computing opportunities, answer questions, and provide information

Dance Marathon Executive Board, Columbia, SC
Technology Chair September 2017 – May 2018
- Designed, built, and maintained website
- Edited and maintained media and graphics
- Edited content, documentation, and other publications

LANGUAGE AND TECHNICAL SKILLS
Operating Systems: Windows 7, Windows Vista and Windows XP; Mac OS X; Linux/Unix
Programming and Web Design: Java; C and C++; Object Oriented Programming; CSS, HTML, and basic Javascript; basic SQL
Software and Solutions: Microsoft SharePoint; Microsoft Office suite; Microsoft InfoPath; Microsoft SQL Server and SQL Server Management; Netbeans IDE, Visual Paradigm, and Junit; Adobe Creative Suite and Lotus suite
Hardware and Networking: Network architecture and maintenance; Personal Computer builds, upgrades and repairs; component replacements

Developing your CAREER PATH

First Stop: Academic Advising

12 minimum hours per semester to be considered full time

REGISTRATION is the date and time when you can schedule your courses for next semester

ADVISEMENT is when you meet with your current advisor and discuss courses for next semester

MY.SC.EDU is where you can find out who your advisor is.

Follow-Up with: Career Exploration

50% of students who declare a major will change it at least once

IN YOUR FIRST YEAR:

- Explore your options and decide on a major or confirm your selected major.

- Write a resume based on your current experiences.

- Review your experiences and consider opportunities for future development.

- Reflect & identify personal strengths, weaknesses, work values, and interests.

Top 6 Qualities Employers Look For
1. Communication Skills
2. Strong Work Ethic
3. Initiative
4. Interpersonal Skills
5. Problem-solving Skills
6. Teamwork Skills

Ask for Help: Campus Resources

76.6% of employers prefer to hire new college graduates who have gained relevant work experience

Meet with a Cross College Advising (CCA) staff member who will help you navigate the process of changing a major.

The Career Center has several sample resumes and cover letters that you can view online. You can also meet with a staff member and get your resume reviewed.

The Undergraduate Bulletin contains useful and important information regarding policies and procedures that apply to all students and individual colleges. Visit www.bulletin.sc.edu

Academic Advising

The primary goal of academic advising is to help you achieve your educational, career, and personal goals. You will note that the objectives of academic advising and the steps in the career development process are, in many ways, two approaches to interconnected educational goals.

Academic advising involves developing a positive working relationship between you and a faculty or staff member at the University. You will meet with your advisor at least once a semester, either individually or in a group setting. Your advisor can provide you with information, insight, and direction related to your academic, personal, and social situations.

In an early model of academic advising, author Terry O'Banion (1972) suggested that the key elements in academic advising include

1. An exploration of life goals
2. An exploration of career goals
3. Consideration of options available in program (major) choice
4. Choosing courses to fulfill curricular requirements
5. Consideration of the options available to you concerning the scheduling of courses

Note the order of the actions outlined. Students sometimes view advisement as simply scheduling classes. O'Banion asserted many years ago, and many academic advisors today believe, that in meeting its potential, academic advising is far more than just scheduling classes for the upcoming term. When students make the most of academic advising, choosing classes is merely an outgrowth of the career and life planning process.

> **Check yourself**
>
> My Academic Advisor is:
>
> _____
>
> My Academic Advisor's Office is located in
>
> building: _____
>
> room #: _____

> **Peer Leader Advice**
>
> As a U101 peer leader and resident mentor, I can tell you that one of the most frustrating topics for first-year students is advisement. Don't let the hype scare you. It can certainly be confusing if you go it alone, but there are plenty of resources available to you to tackle advisement with confidence. Cross-Campus Advising, the Student Success Center, upperclassmen in your major, your RM, and your U101 professor are all present to help you prepare for advisement and registering for classes. Take advantage of those resources, *Transitions* textbook, and you'll be more than prepared.
>
> - Brewer Eberly
> Greenville, SC • Senior
> Biology

Academic Planning Strategies

The primary outcome of your experience at the University of South Carolina is earning a baccalaureate degree. This requires an investment of time, energy, and focus over the next four years. During your time at Carolina, you will actively engage in academic planning. Components involved with successful academic planning include knowing and understanding yourself, the University academic environment, and the requirements of your chosen college or school. The more knowledgeable you are as you plan your undergraduate academic path, the more likely you are to make decisions that will ultimately keep you progressing toward a timely graduation. Successful academic planning strategies include:

Know yourself. Reflect on how and why you chose to attend the University of South Carolina and where you are in the process of selecting an academic major. If you have already made a decision about a major, think about what led you to that decision. If you are undecided, identify what information you still need to make a good decision. Meanwhile, do not worry about your uncertainty; the Cross College Advising Program in the Student Success Center was created to help students from every major make informed academic decisions, particularly when you are considering changing your major. Cross College

> **Did you know?**
>
> Cross College Advising can assist you with a variety of your advising needs including:
>
> - Determining how classes you have taken would fit into a different major before switching
> - Comparing various majors and college/program requirements side by side
> - Creating a plan to graduate with more than one major and/or experiential learning opportunity
> - Preparing for or clarifying information from your departmental advisement appointment
> - Helping you find the campus resources and offices that can answer your specific questions
>
> For more information, or to schedule an appointment, call 803.777.1000 or go online to sc.edu/success. The Student Success Center is located on the Mezzanine level of the Thomas Cooper Library. Cross College Advising is offered in the Student Success Center as well as in Bates House and Columbia Hall.

Advising cannot advise students changing majors within their current college/school. Students should see their departmental advisor for advisement. CCA will advise students who are changing majors between schools/colleges at the Columbia Campus. CCA also provides general supplemental advising help for any student.

Know and understand the University academic environment. By reviewing the *Undergraduate Studies Bulletin*, you will learn about the many options for academic majors, minors, and elective courses, as well as the University's academic policies and regulations. Understanding your options will also make the time you spend with your advisor more productive and fulfilling.

Be aware that the central elements of advising will change as you progress through your college career. Advising for first-year students typically emphasizes Carolina Core requirements and choice of an academic major, whereas advising for sophomores, juniors, and seniors places greater emphasis on the academic major, minor, or cognate requirements and career or graduate school plans. You should discuss possible internship, graduate school, and career plans with your advisor as you advance toward graduation.

Familiarize yourself with other campus resources. The University has numerous offices that support student success and achievement, and it is your responsibility to take advantage of all that it has to offer. Offices such as the Career Center, Writing Center, Math Lab, Student Success Center, Office of Fellowships and Scholar Programs, Office of Pre-Professional Advising, and the Counseling Center are staffed with well-trained students and professional staff ready to help you as you navigate your academic journey.

Remember the final responsibility for a successful college career is yours! Your advisor, academic major department office, dean's office, and other campus offices are resources who can provide additional information, help prevent and resolve difficulties, give insight into possible alternatives, and suggest new opportunities. However, YOU are ultimately responsible for making appropriate and informed decisions about your educational plans, career goals, and meeting the requirements for your degree.

> **Did you know?**
>
> - Every student must meet with an advisor before registering for the upcoming semester's classes.
> - A full-time academic load is 12-18 credit hours per semester. Note: A student must maintain a full-time academic load (minimum of 12 credit hours) to continue eligibility for most scholarships, financial aid, and health insurance under their parents' policies.
> - If you plan to take courses during the summer at a different institution, you must have an advisor approve the courses in advance.

Being a Good Advisee

Developing an academic advising relationship is a shared responsibility between you and your advisor—someone who can be a mentor, confidante, and aid in assisting you in major and career planning. To make the most of this opportunity, you should cultivate and develop a significant bond with your advisor by:

- *Taking the initiative to get to know your advisor.* All too frequently, students visit their advisor only when they need something like a signature on a form. It is unrealistic to expect advisors to remember every detail about each student's entire academic situation, but advisors do remember more about students they see frequently. Advisors will also be more helpful to students who take the time to develop a relationship before they need something. The better your advisor knows you, and the more prepared you are for your advising appointment, the more productive your time together will be.

- *Preparing diligently for appointments.* If you initiated the meeting, be sure to have questions ready. A mental or written agenda will help you structure your meeting and remember the questions and discussion points. If your appointment is for a specific purpose, such as scheduling courses for an upcoming term, be sure to have possibilities and alternatives ready for discussion. Prior to your meeting, review the curriculum for your major and learn how to access relevant information online. Be sure you understand the significance of course numbers, section numbers, schedule codes, and session codes. The Advising Preparation Sheet located at the end of this chapter is a great tool to help you plan ahead for your advising appointment!

Advisee/Advisor Responsibilities

Student Responsibilities

As an advisee, you are expected to:

- Make contact with your advisor each semester. Although you are required to meet with your advisor during your assigned appointment time before registration, you are strongly encouraged to meet with your advisor other times throughout the semester to form a relationship.
- Come to each appointment with questions or materials you want to discuss.
- Be proactive in the advising experience and be willing to learn.
- Ask questions if you do not understand something.
- Become knowledgeable about your college's programs, degree requirements, policies, and procedures.
- Refer to the academic success web site at http://www.sc.edu/academicsuccess/ to gain information about the advising process.
- Complete all assignments or recommendations from your advisor.
- Clarify personal values and goals and provide advisor with accurate and truthful information regarding your interests and abilities.
- Accept responsibility for your decisions and your actions that affect your educational progress and goals.

Advisor Responsibilities

Advisors should:

- Provide you with information about campus resources and services.
- Treat you with respect and as an adult.
- Uphold the integrity of the South Carolina degree by enforcing all University and departmental policies.
- Understand and effectively communicate the curriculum, requirements, and academic procedures. If they don't know the answer to a question, they will find the answer or direct you to the appropriate resource in a timely manner.
- Assist you with choices, such as courses to take in the upcoming semester.
- Encourage you to develop and continually refine your academic and career goals.
- Monitor and accurately document your educational progress.
- Be accessible during office hours, by appointment, and via telephone and e-mail.
- Assist you in gaining decision-making skills and in assuming responsibility for your educational decisions and goals.
- Maintain confidentiality.

USC ADVISING QUICK FACTS

WHAT IS DIFFERENCE BETWEEN ADVISEMENT AND REGISTRATION?

Advisement is when you meet with your current advisor (either one-on-one or in a group setting) and discuss what courses you should take for the upcoming semester, as well as any questions you may have regarding your major or schedule. You do not actually register for any classes during this time.

Registration is the specific date and time you are assigned to log into Self Service Carolina and schedule your classes for the upcoming semester. You can find your registration appointment time under Registration Status tab on Self Service. Remember, you don't have to actually register at this exact time; you can actually register at any point after it as well.

HOW DO I FIND MY ADVISOR?

The department/advisor may send you a post card and/or email with advisement information.

You may also be able to find out your advisor information through Self Service Carolina.

Remember, all departments have different methods of advising, so when in doubt, call the Dean's office for your academic department.

WHAT IS GRADE FORGIVENESS?

Every current, fully admitted, degree-seeking undergraduate student at USC earning a D+, D, F, or WF in a University course may take up to two courses for a second time for grade forgiveness.

Both the first and second grades will appear on the student's permanent record, but only the second grade will be used in computing the USC cumulative grade point average.

Once grade forgiveness is applied to a repeated course it may not be revoked.

Students may apply grade forgiveness to a course at any time during their undergraduate enrollment, but not after the degree is awarded.

Grade forgiveness can only be applied once per course for a maximum for two courses. The course must be repeated at the same USC campus.

Necessary documentation must be filled out and submitted by the student. Information can be found at http://registrar.sc.edu/html/grade_forgiv.stm.

Where can I find the forms I need for grade forgiveness, transient credit, and change of major forms?

You will be able to locate all of these forms on the Registrar's website: http://www.registrar.sc.edu.

Can I transfer courses from another school while enrolled at USC Columbia?

In some programs, and with permission of the academic dean, students may take up to 18 credit hours in transient status provided they have a 2.00 USC grade point average.

The last 30 hours of a student's work must be completed at USC, and at least half of the hours in a student's major courses and minor courses must be taken at the University.

How do I change majors within my current college/school?

If you want to switch your major within your current department, you should consult with your advisor or with the Dean's Office.

How do I change majors outside of my current college/school?

You should make an appointment with Cross College Advising to discuss your options, determine how classes you've taken would fit into a different major, and identify necessary campus resources.

Once you've determined your new major, you need to fill out the Change of Major form to be signed by the college of your new major (provided you meet all of the entrance requirements).

What is the difference between a "W" and a "WF"?

If a student withdraws from a course before the last day to add/drop a course, a "W" will not be recorded on a student's permanent record.

During the first seven weeks of a semester, the grade of a "W" will be recorded on the transcript, but the semester hours will not be added into the hours attempted, grade point average, or any other totals.

Students dropping a course, or withdrawing from the University, after the first seven weeks of the semester will receive a "WF." This grade is treated as an "F" in the hours attempted, grade point average, etc.

Where can I go if I'm thinking about doing pre-med, pre-law, pre-dental, or pre-vet.

The Office of Pre-Professional Advising can help students locate information on courses, applications, and test information for these professional areas of interest.

They are located in Sumwalt 208, and their phone number is 803.777.5581

Course Planning

With careful planning, most students can graduate in four years. It is recommended that you average 15 hours per semester to stay on track for the 120 hours required for graduation for most majors. Changing your major, experiencing academic difficulties, or pursuing a double major may require you to take summer classes or more than 15 hours each semester.

As you meet with your advisor to discuss course scheduling for future, the complexities of course planning come into play. Planning a four-year degree program is in some ways like cooking a multicourse dinner with complicated recipes that you have never used before. There are many different aspects that must be executed well and coordinated to produce the desired outcome—a delightful, delicious, and on-time dinner. In planning your schedule you must consider many different aspects of the undergraduate academic experience. All your selected courses should apply toward your degree in one of the following categories:

- **Carolina Core courses.** Each degree program has a group of courses that will fulfill this requirement. These courses usually comprise approximately 30-40 credit hours of coursework. Courses are drawn from many different departments in order to produce graduates who are academically well-rounded.
- **Major courses.** The second block of courses constitutes the major. Majors vary in the number of required courses and credits in the discipline (e.g., some majors require as few as 18 credits while music majors take as many as 60 credits of required courses).
- **Minors and cognates.** In some colleges, a minor is available or even required. Minors usually consist of 18 hours (six 3-credit courses) chosen from a predetermined list of courses. The colleges publish materials outlining the available minors and program course requirements. A cognate is 12 hours of upper-level course work related to your major and approved by your major advisor. When choosing courses for a cognate, advisor approval is key.
- **Electives.** These courses may or may not meet graduation requirements and do not fulfill Carolina Core, major, minor, or cognate requirements. Electives can be a great way to explore other interest areas and possible majors. Even though the course may not count towards graduation, it will still appear on your transcript and may factor into your GPA. For this reason, it is important to check with your advisor about any courses you want to take as electives.

Course Planning & Study Abroad

If you are planning to study abroad in the coming years, you may want to save some of your Carolina Core classes for your semester or year abroad to stay on track in meeting your graduation requirements and timeline. Many foreign institutions may not have your major courses available, but, most likely, will have courses that can be used to meet Carolina Core requirements. Whenever possible, it is beneficial to take a few major courses overseas in order to get a different perspective on your major field of study and potential careers. Sometimes this can be achieved by taking major elective courses overseas, or by choosing a study abroad program that has been designed specifically for your major.

Course Sequencing and Balancing

After you determine how each of your selected courses fit into your degree requirements, you can get ready for the upcoming semester. Planning a set of courses that will enable you to be successful in a given semester is an important step in schedule preparation. Both course sequencing and course balancing need to be considered.

Course sequencing means taking courses in the proper order. Many courses require a prerequisite course that must be completed before enrolling (e.g., PSYC 101 before PSYC 226). Knowledge acquired in a lower-level or prerequisite class is frequently needed to understand advanced material and be successful in higher-level courses.

Course balancing means selecting a group of courses for a given semester by evaluating the course content, the professor's teaching style, and course type (e.g., reading intensive, product intensive, homework intensive). For example, you would not want to take five art studio

All general education requirements leading to baccalaureate degrees in colleges and departments at the University of South Carolina Columbia include as a minimum:

Carolina Core components	Carolina Core learning outcomes	Credit hours in Carolina Core
I. Lower division: Core courses	**Learning outcomes to be met at foundational level of mastery**	**28-34 hours**
Aesthetic and interpretive Understanding	Create or interpret literary, visual or performing arts.	3
Analytical reasoning and problem solving	Apply the methods of mathematical, statistical, or analytical reasoning to critically evaluate data, solve problems, and effectively communicate findings verbally and graphically.	6
Effective, engaged, and persuasive communication: Writing	Identify and analyze issues, develop logical and persuasive arguments, and communicate ideas clearly for a variety of audiences and purposes through writing and speaking.	6 Written component
Global citizenship and multicultural understanding	Use the principles of the social sciences to explore diverse cultural identities and to analyze political and environmental issues.	3
Global citizenship and multicultural understanding	Use the principles of historical thinking to assess the relationships between modern societies and their historical roots.	3
Global citizenship and multicultural understanding	Communicate effectively in more than one language.	0-6 (depending on placement test)
Scientific literacy	Apply the principles and language of the natural sciences and associated technologies to historical and contemporary issues.	7
II. Lower division: Stand-alone or overlay-eligible courses	**Up to two of these three core requirements may be met in overlay courses.**	**3-9 hours (depending whether these 3 outcomes are met with stand-alone or up to two overlay courses)**
Effective, engaged, and persuasive communication: Speech (S)	Identify and analyze issues, develop logical and persuasive arguments, and communicate ideas clearly for a variety of audiences and purposes through writing and speaking.	0-3 Spoken component
Information literacy (IL)	Collect, manage and evaluate information using technology, and communicate findings.	0-3
Values, ethics, and social responsibility (VESR)	Examine different kinds of social and personal values, analyzing the ways in which these are manifested in communities as well as individual lives.	0-3
III. Upper Division: Integrative Course in the Major	**Required upper-division course in the major program of study; includes learning outcomes from the Carolina Core chosen by the program area.**	N/A
TOTAL hours in *Carolina Core*		**31 – 43 hours** (depending on language placement tests and use of at most two overlay courses)

ON THE WEB

For a list of Carolina Core courses visit:
sc.edu/carolinacore/courses.php

Peer Leader Advice

Take time to prepare for your advisement appointments. Understand what courses you need to take next, think of any questions or concerns you have, and be familiar with the opportunities Carolina offers specifically for your major or college. Make the best of your four years at Carolina by fully taking part in outlining your courses and overall college career!

- Dane O'Neill
Roswell, SC • Senior
Visual Communications

Did you know?

The Advisement Policies section of the Undergraduate Studies Bulletin states,

"Information, advice, and interpretations of University policies offered by advisors do not supersede the official statement of policies and academic regulations described in the Undergraduate Studies Bulletin. Exceptions to University regulations cannot be made by academic advisors."

This means that you are expected to be familiar with the rules, and YOU are responsible for following them! If you have questions about any of these policies, contact the academic dean's office of your major for clarification.

View the Undergraduate Studies Bulletin online at http://bulletin.sc.edu .

---

classes in one semester because you would have too many production projects to complete. Likewise, you would not want to take five literature and history classes in one semester because all of the classes would require a significant amount of reading.

The Four-Year Curriculum Planner Worksheet at the end of the chapter will help you map out your coursework so you can properly sequence and balance your undergraduate studies. After you have carefully considered all the courses needed for your degree and when to take them, you can begin thinking about your schedule for the upcoming term.

Academic Policies and Procedures

The University has a number of policies and procedures related to undergraduate education that are important for you to know. The *Undergraduate Studies Bulletin* is an indispensable reference since it contains useful and important information regarding policies and procedures that apply to all students, as well as those for individual colleges. Each academic unit (e.g., College of Nursing, School of Music) lists their faculty, degree and progression requirements, and brief descriptions of their courses.

The extensive set of policies and procedures found in the *Bulletin* includes critical information on class attendance, final exams, the grading system, dropping a class, repetition of course work, academic probation, academic honors, and other campus issues. To avoid costly mistakes (due to being unaware) that could delay your degree progress and graduation, make it a point to become familiar with the *Bulletin*.

Your success at the University of South Carolina is up to you! Balancing your social life with your academic life is indeed possible and should be one of your college goals. Engaging in career exploration from the start, developing a positive relationship with your academic advisor, and familiarizing yourself with the University's academic policies and procedures will position you for an outstanding undergraduate experience and a bright and promising future!

Four-Year Curriculum Planner

First Year	Fall Classes	Spring Classes	Summer Classes

Second Year	Fall Classes	Spring Classes	Summer Classes

Third Year	Fall Classes	Spring Classes	Summer Classes

Fourth Year	Fall Classes	Spring Classes	Summer Classes

Academic Policies

Using the Undergraduate Studies Bulletin (bulletin.sc.edu), locate the answers to important questions regarding academic policies and procedures.

1. What is the difference between a "W" and a "WF" on your transcript?

2. What number of credits signifies you are a sophomore?

3. How does the bulletin define "excessive absences?"

4. How many classes may you take for a second time through course grade forgiveness?

5. What is the minimum GPA you can receive before being put on academic probation?

6. What must a student's GPA be in order to graduate with honors (summa cum laude, magna cum laude, and cum laude)?

7. At what times can you add/drop during the semester?

8. What is the minimum number of hours needed for your college or school per semester to graduate in a normal period of time?

Advising Preparation Sheet

My name:		Date:
Current major:	Other majors I am considering:	
My advisor's name:	Advisor's phone number:	Advisor's e-mail address:
Advisor's office building and room number:	Office hours:	Is an appointment required?
Courses I am currently taking and estimated final grade for each:	Classes I would like to take next semester:	

Topics and questions I would like to discuss with my advisor:

Registration Worksheet

Instructions: Use the Master Schedule to pick out SEVEN courses you would like to register for. For each course, pick three different sections you would be interested in taking, and record the schedule code as well as days/times for each section.

Course Option #1	Requirement	Section Number	Schedule Code	Days/Times

Course Option #2	Requirement	Section Number	Schedule Code	Days/Times

Course Option #3	Requirement	Section Number	Schedule Code	Days/Times

Course Option #4	Requirement	Section Number	Schedule Code	Days/Times

Course Option #5	Requirement	Section Number	Schedule Code	Days/Times

Course Option #6	Requirement	Section Number	Schedule Code	Days/Times

Course Option #7	Requirement	Section Number	Schedule Code	Days/Times

Schedule Worksheet

Instructions: As you plan for next semester, use the Schedule Worksheet to map out your weekly academic calendar.

Monday	Tuesday	Wednesday	Thursday	Friday
8:30am-9:20am	8:30am-9:45am	8:30am-9:20am	8:30am-9:45am	8:30am-9:20am
9:40am-10:30am	10:05am-11:20am	9:40am-10:30am	10:05am-11:20am	9:40am-10:30am
10:50am-11:40am	11:40am-12:55pm	10:50am-11:40am	11:40am-12:55pm	10:50am-11:40am
12:00pm-12:50pm		12:00pm-12:50pm		12:00pm-12:50pm
1:10pm-2:00pm	1:15pm-2:30pm	1:10pm-2:00pm	1:15pm-2:30pm	1:10pm-2:00pm
2:20pm-3:35pm	2:50pm-4:05pm	2:20pm-3:35pm	2:50pm-4:05pm	
3:55pm-5:10pm	4:25pm-5:40pm	3:55pm-5:10pm	4:25pm-5:40pm	
5:30pm-6:45pm	6:00pm-7:15pm	5:30pm-6:45pm	6:00pm-7:15pm	
7:05pm-8:20pm		7:05pm-8:20pm		

SCENARIOS FROM COLLEGE LIFE

It's Your Choice

Matthew grew up in a family of doctors. His mother was a pediatrician; his father was a dermatologist, and his older sister—a senior in college—was studying to work in physical therapy. It was always assumed that Matthew would follow in the family footsteps and study to be a physician. Matthew always excelled in the sciences, receiving an A in advanced biology and chemistry in high school, but he also really enjoyed his English courses and reading literature. When applying to colleges, his parents encouraged him to apply to schools with notable medical programs and urged him to pursue pre-med as his major. When he decided to attend the University of South Carolina, his parents were thrilled. This meant Matthew would be remaining in-state and close to home. When Matthew and his parents attended summer orientation, they explored the USC campus and Columbia. They took a tour of the science buildings, located the nearest hospitals to consider for internship possibilities, and talked with his advisor about the best course schedule for his first semester as a pre-med student. His entire orientation visit seemed to center on his parents' career goal for him.

Once Matthew arrived on campus and started classes, he took the typical first-year courses, such as English, chemistry, and psychology. He also decided to take University 101 because his orientation leader told him that the course would help him form strong study habits as well as identify resources on campus. He really enjoyed all of his classes and was doing well in them.

Matthew's University 101 class was scheduled to visit the Career Center for a presentation. In order to prepare for the class period, the students were asked to complete an interest inventory. The presenter asked each student what their academic focus or major was and why. When she got to Matthew, he said his reason for choosing a pre-med path was because of his parents. As Matthew reviewed his interest inventory results, he noticed most of his interests aligned with literature and English. He liked reading and writing and was excited about learning more in these subject areas. The more Matthew thought, the more he realized he wasn't interested in going to medical school or becoming a doctor. He recognized that his parents and sister had rewarding careers; however, deep down inside he knew that he wanted study something that interested him. Matthew was concerned that his parents would be disappointed by his decision.

Processing Questions:

Why do you think it took Matthew so long to realize his true academic interests?

How would you advise Matthew to talk to his family about his interests?

Matthew discovered he was passionate about studying literature and English. What are your passions and how did you know this to be true?

Have you ever made compromises to please others? How do you feel when you compromise something for the sake of others' goals? What have you done or can you do in these kinds of situations?

How can you ensure you are working toward your own goals throughout your college experience?

RESOURCES

Important Academic Information and Websites

Academic Calendars
http://registrar.sc.edu/html/calendar/

Academic Success at South Carolina
http://www.housing.sc.edu/academicsuccess/

Master Schedule of Classes
http://registrar.sc.edu/html/Course_Listings/

Office of the University Registrar 777-5555
516 S. Main St.
http://registrar.sc.edu/

Undergraduate Bulletin
http://bulletin.sc.edu/

VIP
http://vip.sc.edu/

Academic Advising and Career Planning

Career Center 777-7280
BA Building, 6th floor
http://www.sc.edu/career/
career@sc.edu

Cross Campus Academic Advising 777-0684
General academic advising and planning
Student Success Center
Thomas Cooper Library, Mezzanine Level
http://www.sa.sc.edu/ssc/ccaa/

Office of Pre-Professional Advising 777-5581
Sumwalt College, Room 208
http://www.sa.sc.edu/oppa/

REFERENCES

Association of American Colleges and Universities (AAC&U). (2007). *How Should Colleges Prepare Students to Succeed in Today's Global Economy?* Results of a national poll by Peter D. Hart Research Associates. Retrieved from http://www.aacu.org/leap/students/employerstopten.cfm

Collegiate Employment Research Institute (CERI). (2009-2010). *Annual report: Collegiate Employment Research Institute 2009-2010*. Retrieved from http://www.ceri.msu.edu/wp-content/uploads/2010/01/CERI-Annual-Report.pdf

Cuseo, J. (2005). Decided, undecided, and in transition: Implications for academic advisement, career counseling, and student retention. In R. S. Feldman (Ed.), Improving *the first year of college: Research and practice* (pp. 27-50). Mahwah, NJ: Lawrence Erlbaum.

National Association of Colleges and Employers (NACE). (2010). *Job outlook 2010*. Retrieved from http://www.naceweb.org/Research/Job_Outlook/Job_Outlook.aspx

O'Banion, T. (1972). An academic advising model. *Junior College Journal, 42*(6), 62-69.

Orndorff, R. M., & Herr, E. L. (1996). A comparative study of declared and undeclared college students on career uncertainty and involvement in career development activities. *Journal of Counseling and Development, 74*, 634.

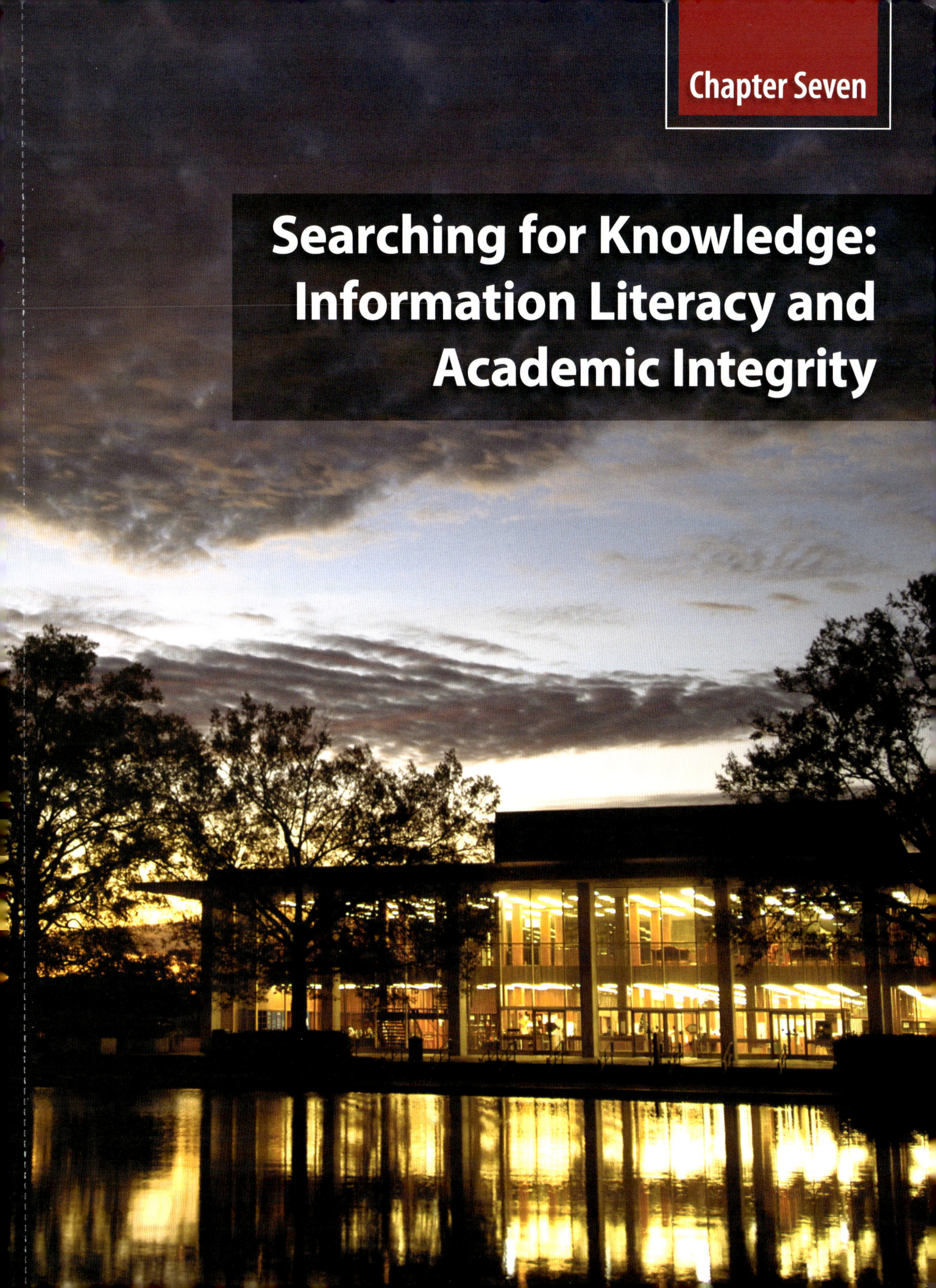

Chapter Seven

Searching for Knowledge: Information Literacy and Academic Integrity

Dear First-Year Student,

Welcome to USC! The University of South Carolina Libraries is an extensive library system consisting of the Thomas Cooper Library (where I work!), which is the main library on campus; the Hollings Special Collections Libraries; the Springs Business Library; the Moving Image Research Collections (MIRC); the Music Library; and the South Caroliniana Library. During your time at USC, please let us help you find all of the information and materials you will need to be a successful student.

As a student, you will be asked to complete assignments and write papers for your various classes. Finding the right information for your specific needs can often be a difficult task. At the Thomas Cooper Library, we can help you learn how to access information effectively and efficiently, and how to choose the best sources for your given assignments. Key concepts you will learn during your four years at Carolina are how to make informed decisions and solve problems, both in your schoolwork and personal life. These are skills that you will continue to hone throughout your life. The library can aid you in enhancing and practicing these skills by helping you become information literate, which includes knowing when information is needed, evaluating information sources, and using information ethically and legally.

Whether it's finding sources for your ENGL 102 paper or finding a book that your professor has put on reserve, please don't hesitate in asking the staff of the libraries for help! We are happy to aid you in all of your academic endeavors. You can schedule one-on-one sessions with a librarian, chat with us online, or just come in and ask your questions at the Research, Instruction, and Reference desk at Thomas Cooper. The library is open 24 hours a day during fall and spring semesters. Simply put, we are here to help you find the information you need for all of your classes and achieve your scholastic goals!

Come see us at the library!

Sincerely,

Timothy Simmons
First-Year Experience Librarian

THE digital age has created an unprecedented explosion of information. Almost everywhere we turn, we are confronted with facts, data, and opinions, and the rate at which these are being delivered is increasing at a dizzying pace. The overabundance of information can easily cause a "menacing cloud of data smog" (Shenk, 1997, p. 16)—a term used to describe the surplus of information in our lives. As a student, you might find that being surrounded with so much information is challenging, especially as you are trying to gather and sift through evidence for papers, projects, and other class assignments.

The Internet has changed the way in which information is created, disseminated, and incorporated into new knowledge. Prior to the Internet, information was filtered through intermediaries or gatekeepers (e.g., journalists, editors, trained resource professionals) who proofread and checked for inaccuracies before material was formally published. Now, anyone can develop content and publish a web page, blog, video, etc. Many open-source sites, such as Wikipedia, allow all users to edit or add content. There are benefits to having an open exchange of information that allows for many individuals to contribute. However, this shifts the burden on the information user to check for inaccuracies and determine reliability. Students must now become more critical consumers of information than ever before

This chapter will (a) define information literacy, (b) introduce you to the research process, (c) acquaint you with resources and services available from the University Libraries, and (d) provide you with a set of criteria that can be used to evaluate an information source.

Information Literacy

At this point you may have heard the term information literacy, but may still be unclear as to what it means. According to the American Library Association (ALA), information literacy is a set of abilities requiring individuals to "recognize when information is needed and have the ability to locate, evaluate, and use effectively the needed information" (ALA, 1989, para. 3). One of the learning outcomes of University 101 is for students to be able to effectively evaluate information sources and use the University Libraries and information systems for academic inquiry. Information literacy will be useful for success in all of your college classes, and forms the basis for lifelong learning. An information literate individual is able to

- Assess and define what information is needed to better understand a topic
- Utilize a library catalog, article databases, and search engines to find information
- Evaluate the credibility, reliability, bias, and currency of information sources
- Practice the ethical use and citation of sources
- Synthesize information for class assignments such as papers, presentations, and/or debates

On the following page, you will find the Information Literacy Framework, which further explains the five components of information literacy and the questions you may need to consider when seeking information.

Adapted from ALA Information Literacy Standards

Information Literacy Framework

DEFINE — Broaden or narrow topic to refine research question

ACCESS — Use databases, catalogs & search engines to retrieve information

EVALUATE — Determine quality and usefulness of sources

USE — Synthesize information with own ideas

DOCUMENT — Use and cite information properly & ethically

DEFINE
- What do you want to know?
- What kind of information is needed?
- How will you frame your research question?

ACCESS
- How and where do you find necessary information?
- What tools are offered by the library? How do you use them effectively?
- How do you design a search strategy?
- Which search terms are most effective?

EVALUATE
- Is the information/source authentic, valid, reliable, relevant, valuable, accurate, timely, and/or biased?
- Is the source scholarly?
- Is the source useful for your needs?
- Do you have enough information? Are there gaps? What additional information is needed?

USE
- How do you compare and contrast concepts found in the research process to create an argument?
- How do you effectively incorporate research into assignments using quotes, paraphrasing, or synthesizing information with your own ideas?
- What does the final product look like? How is it organized?

DOCUMENT
- What is academic integrity and how does the Honor Code affect your work?
- What is the ethical use of information?
- What is plagiarism? How do you separate your ideas from others?
- How do you cite sources in-text and in a works cited? Which documentation style should you use?

Adapted from *Information Literacy Competency Standards for Higher Education*, The Association of College Research Libraries, Chicago, IL, 2000

University Libraries

The University is home to six libraries: The Thomas Cooper Library, the Hollings Special Collections Library, the Business Library, the Moving Image Research Collections, the Music Library, and the South Caroliniana Library. The University Libraries hold more than 3 million volumes; 1 million government documents; 400,000 maps and aerial photographs; rare books; and manuscripts. They also provide access to a variety of online, subscription-based content including more than 300 databases and thousands of online journals.

With all of these resources available, where do you start your research? The faculty and staff employed by the University Libraries are here to help and can assist you in a variety of ways, including (a) locating information needed for papers and projects, (b) demonstrating how to select and use article databases, (c) obtaining books and articles not available from the University Libraries, and (d) providing procedures for checking out a key to an individual or group study room. University Libraries has access to a vast amount of resources and librarians are willing to assist you at any time; all you have to do is ask!

Developing a Research Strategy

Your academic responsibilities at the University of South Carolina will require you to complete a number of papers, projects, and other assignments that include accurate and reliable information. Searching for reliable information at times can be difficult, but no matter how simple or complex your question, having a research strategy will help you navigate your way through the data smog.

What Is Your Topic?

The first and most important part of the information research process is defining your topic. You may be given a topic or a list to choose from, or you may pick a topic on your own. No matter how the topic is selected, it is imperative to know what it is that you are looking for, as this will predicate future steps of the information-seeking process. Once your topic is decided upon, it may still need tweaking. A topic that is too broad, too narrow, or not well-defined can lead to a frustrating research experience. Think about your topic and try to determine its breadth and depth as well as strategies to refine it. For example, if your theme is too broad, consider narrowing it by time period, location, or genre. Also, consulting a general or subject-specific encyclopedia article on your topic can be helpful to hone your research by presenting background information and various aspects.

How Do I Contact the Libraries?

Thomas Cooper Library,
Reference Department............ 803-777-4866
South Caroliniana Library....... 803-777-3132
Business Library 803-777-6032
Music Library............................. 803-777-5139
Hollings Special
Collections Library 803-777-3847
Moving Image
Research Collections 803-777-6841

Facts About the University of South Carolina Libraries

- The libraries rank in the top 50 among public research libraries in the United States, according to the Association of Research Libraries.
- The University had the first freestanding college library in the United States. The original building still serves as a library—the South Caroliniana Library on the historic Horseshoe.
- There are more than 300 databases from which to choose; many are full-text and can be accessed both on and off campus.
- The library has world-renowned collections, including the F. Scott Fitzgerald collection.

Peer Leader Advice

It's really important to get acquainted with the library early on. The books are not your only resource. The librarians are really helpful and are always open to questions. I would definitely find out how to rent a study room before exam week. These are awesome for group projects and give you a place to collaborate as students.

- Cari Moore
Summerville, SC • Senior
Early Childhood Education

Developing a research question once you have developed a specific topic will help you determine what exactly you want to know, and how much information you need to answer the question. At this point, you will be able to develop a research strategy to find information.

Reference librarians are available to help you test your topic for the availability of resources and appropriateness for your timeframe as well as locate sources. Defining and testing your topic early in the research process will save you from the last-minute panic that can result when you learn that your topic is not manageable or that all the required books are checked out, and there is not enough time to borrow from another library. Stop by the Thomas Cooper Library Research and Reference Help desk or use the Ask a Librarian service (on the library website) to test your topic with a librarian.

Check yourself

Beginning Research – Breaking Down a Topic

1. What is your topic?:

2. What do you know about your topic? For example:
   - Where? Does this topic have local, regional, national or global setting? Is there a particular physical environment for this topic?
   - When? Do you want to research a current or historical view of this topic? What is the time period?
   - Who? Are there specific names or groups of people involved? Consider gender, ethnicity, age groups, occupations, etc. Who does this topic effect?

3. Narrowed Topic:

4. For your narrowed topic develop some keywords and synonyms that best describe your topic.

Concept 1	Concept 2	Concept 3
OR	OR	OR
OR	OR	OR

5. What disciplines or subject areas might be interested in your topic?

Source: Karen Brown, University Libraries, University of South Carolina

Check yourself

Evaluate Your Own Research Question

Ask the following 8 questions to evaluate the quality of your research question and the ease with which you should be able to answer it:

1. Does the question deal with a topic or issue that interests you enough to spark your own thoughts and opinions?

2. Is the question easily and fully researchable? (e.g. is there information to be found?)

3. What type of information do I need to answer the research question?
   (e.g., The research question, "What impact has deregulation had on commercial airline safety?," will obviously require certain types of information: statistics on airline crashes before and after, statistics on other safety problems before and after, information about maintenance practices before and after, & information about government safety requirements before and after)

4. Is the scope of this information reasonable?
   (e.g., can I really research 30 online writing programs developed over a span of 10 years?)

5. Given the type and scope of the information that I need, is my question too broad, too narrow, or okay?

6. What sources will have the type of information that I need to answer the research question (e.g., journals, books, Internet resources, government documents, people)?

7. Can I access these sources? From where?

8. Given my answers to the above questions, do I have a good quality research question that I actually will be able to answer by doing research?

How Much Information?

Before you begin to conduct research, think about the information that you will need to locate. The amount of information required to complete an honors thesis will vary greatly from what is needed to write a 12-page research paper or to conduct a three-minute persuasive speech. Your professor may define the information necessary to complete an assignment, but generally, you will be expected to use your own judgment to determine an acceptable amount. You often need to consult many different sources including books and articles to find ones that are most applicable to your research question.

What Type of Information?

Just as there are a variety of sources of information, there are also many different types (e.g., current events, historical background, statistics, general overview, detailed or expert analysis), and you will need to determine what is appropriate for your project. A 100-level English class may accept very general information about the Great Depression, but a 400-level history class will most likely expect more detailed evidence written by an expert.

Information can also differ by other factors, such as audience, style, purpose, and review process, and it is important to understand these differences to use them effectively and appropriately. For example, you may have a professor who requires you to use scholarly articles rather than popular magazine pieces in your research paper. Scholarly articles, most often, appear in journals that are peer-reviewed or refereed, which means the articles have been examined by a number of experts (i.e., scholars or peers in the field) before being accepted for publication. The peer-reviewed or refereed process provides a higher level of scrutiny to ensure that articles reflect solid scholarship.

Comparing Magazines and Journals
How can you tell the difference between a scholarly article and a popular magazine?

	Popular Media	Scholarly Journal
Audience	General public	Academic disciplines
Purpose	Inform or entertain	Communicate new findings & theories
Style	Language is accessible Strong visual appeal Lots of advertisements with broad appeal Articles rarely have bibliography	Assumes previous knowledge and includes specialized terminology Front cover is often plain Few ads Articles include abstract & bibliography
Authors	Reporters or freelance writers	Researchers, scholars, or professionals in the field
Examples	*Newsweek* *Entertainment Weekly* *Bon Appétit* *Blogger*	*Journal of Popular Film and Television* *Journal of Hospitality and Tourism Research*
Level of Scrutiny	Articles are often under strict deadlines with quick turn-around times; content may or may not be reviewed by anyone other than the author	Articles can take months to get published and undergo greater scrutiny to ensure they reflect solid scholarship

Listed below are some of the most frequently used types of information and when they are usually published.

Types of Sources

Type of information	Tools to find information	Author	Timeline
Current events	World Wide Web Newspapers Transcripts (radio or TV)	Journalists Freelance writers	Day of the event or several days after the event
Magazine articles	Article databases	Typically journalists	Week(s) later
Scholarly articles/ Reports on original research	Article databases	Experts and scholars in the field	Months or year(s) later
Books	Library catalog	Varies	Typically one year to years later

ON THE WEB

The UNIV 101 LibGuide is specially designed for U101 students. The guide provides information about library resources and services of interest to first year students.
To explore the guide, visit:
guides.library.sc.edu/u101

Did you know?

The Thomas Cooper Library Ask a Librarian service provides reference by online chat, e-mail, and telephone. For more information on how to access these services go to http://library.sc.edu/ask.html

Did you know?

If you cannot locate materials in the stacks of the Thomas Cooper Library or have a security concern, pick up a phone located near the elevators. You will automatically be connected to someone who can help.

As you exit a library, the attendant needs to make sure all library materials are checked out. So, if you have library books, please hand them to the attendant rather than packing them.

The Thomas Cooper Library has individual and group study rooms available for study sessions. These rooms must be checked out with a valid USC ID at the Circulation Desk. To check out a group study room, at least two group members must be present at the time of check out; both must have valid USC ID.

Searching for Information

Once you have identified your topic and established how much and what type of information is required, it is time to search for information. This is sometimes the most daunting part of the research project as you are typically inundated with information from a wide variety of sources. Knowing where to find information is the next step.

Library Catalog

The University of South Carolina libraries catalog contains a list of all the books, hardcopy journals, magazines, newspapers, government documents, videos, sound recordings, CDs, DVDs, maps, and manuscripts held by the libraries. The catalog will indicate where items are located and whether they are available for checkout. You may search a single library, such as Thomas Cooper, or all the University of South Carolina libraries, including the regional campus libraries. Access to the library catalog is made available through the University Libraries home page and the UNIV 101 LibGuide, a library research guide created especially for UNIV 101 students.

When using the catalog, make note of the location, call number, and availability of an item. If the book you want is checked out or not available from the University Libraries, it may be possible to request it from another South Carolina academic library using PASCAL Delivers or an out-of-state or foreign library using Interlibrary Loan.

Article Databases

Article databases are a great way to find information on a certain topic, especially when you're not entirely sure what you're looking for. The article databases provide targeted searching on a given topic. At a minimum, article databases list the citation information for an article, including author; title; the publishing journal, magazine, or newspaper; volume; issue; date; and page numbers. Many article databases include a short summary of the article (i.e., abstract), and some provide the full text.

An article database differs from a web search engine in that it is a collection of articles from newspapers, magazines, and journals which are often also available in print, whereas a search engine typically only searches web pages. Article databases search subscription based content, meaning content that is paid for by the University Libraries, and this content is often not freely available through a web search engine. An article database provides opportunities for subject, author, and title searches and can provide more narrowly tailored results. Search engines often provide the most popular results, or those with similar keywords, which may or may not provide accurate information.

You may choose to start your research with an article database entitled Academic Search Complete, which offers citations, abstracts, and, in many cases, the full-text of articles from journals, magazines, and newspapers. It covers a wide variety of disciplines and is a great starting point for almost any topic. You may also want to explore one of the many subject-specific article databases that provide in-depth coverage of a subject area (e.g., MathSciNet for current mathematical publications; America History and Life for U.S. and Canadian historical and cultural publications).

Academic Search Complete, subject-specific article databases, and other resources can be accessed from the University Libraries homepage or from the UNIV 101 LibGuide.

Search Tips - Library Catalog and Article Databases

There are a variety of ways to search the library catalog and article databases. You can search by a specific author or title, or if this information is not available, a keyword search is best.

Once you have decided on your topic, take a few moments to identify the critical points of your question and write down a list of keywords and synonyms describing those points. These synonyms will be the keywords you will use when searching for information on your topic. For example, the table below shows the topic *narcotics trafficking*. Are there other words you could use to describe this topic? Broader (large overarching) or narrower (specific) terms? Different endings to your terms (e.g., dealer / dealing)? Jot down some ideas and use these as search terms. On the next page is a list of possible keywords that could be used as search terms.

Be Proactive

- Orient yourself to the library or libraries you expect to use.
- Talk to the librarians. Do not be bashful. Ask them questions. They are knowledgeable professionals trained to help you.
- Do not wait until the last minute to do your research. Chances are you are not the only person researching the topic.
- Come prepared. Bring a copy of your assignment. Have your CarolinaCard to check out books, print, or make photocopies. You also may want to bring a flash drive so you can save information.
- Make note of the databases you are searching and the search terms you use. If you have to repeat a search, you will need this information.

Possible search terms for "narcotics trafficking"		
	Key Concept: Narcotics	**Key Concept: Trafficking**
Alternate Terms	Drugs	Dealing (dealer)
Alternate Terms	Cocaine	Selling
Alternate Terms	Marijuana	Distributing (distributor)
Alternate Terms	Illegal substance(s)	Cartel(s)

Boolean operators tell the computer how to search for the words you enter. The most common operators include **AND**, **OR**, **( )**, and **wildcard** (usually * or ?):

AND	both words must be present	narcotics **and** trafficking	Less results, specialized results
OR	either word may be present	narcotics **or** drugs	More results, wider net
( )	group words	(Note: this example searches for narcotics trafficking **OR** drug trafficking)	More results
wildcard	finds multiple endings of a word	**deal*** finds dealing, dealer, deals	More results

Use this technique with a topic you have recently been assigned to research.
To help you brainstorm, use the boxes below.

	Key Concept:	**Key Concept:**	**Key Concept:**
Alternate Terms			
Alternate Terms			
Alternate Terms			

Evaluating Information Sources

Once you have located a few sources, it is important to critically evaluate the information to determine if it is appropriate for your research. Every day, thousands of sites are added to the Internet by individuals, companies, researchers, organizations, and the government, and there are no standards in place to ensure the accuracy and authority of the content. Anyone anywhere can develop a website and put anything on the Internet. Books and articles are important information sources, but not all books and articles are valid or reliable. The criteria below can be used as a checklist to help you determine if an information source is suitable for your research needs or personal use.

Authority

Be skeptical and use good judgment. Authors who are proud of their work will provide contact information and tell you who they are and why they are experts on a particular topic. Ask yourself the following questions:

- Is biographical or background information on the author(s) provided?
- Is an institutional or organizational affiliation provided? If so, what can I find out about that institution or organization?
- What are the basic values or goals of the organization or institution?
- What are the possible biases of the author or organization?
- Has the author written anything else?
    - Use the biographical information located in the publication itself to help determine the author's affiliation and credentials.
    - You can also use biography databases and resources available from the University Libraries.
- Is there a way of verifying the legitimacy of the content creator? Did the author(s) provide full contact information (e.g., phone number or postal address)? Only an e-mail address is not enough, since they are easily obtained and difficult to verify.
- If the source is an Internet site, what is the domain?
    - .gov indicates a government site
    - .edu indicates an educational site
    - .org indicates a nonprofit, advocacy, or public interest site
    - .com indicates a commercial site such as news, business, or marketing

Accuracy and Reliability

As a general rule of thumb, never quote from an unknown source, and do not use information that you cannot verify. Use the points below to help you determine the accuracy and reliability of your information.

- Are the sources for any factual information clearly listed so they can be verified in another source?
- Is there documentation provided in the form of a bibliography or citations in the text, and is it enough to verify the information?
- Is the information free of errors (e.g., grammatical, spelling, typographical)? If the information source is an Internet source, does the source have a sponsor?
    - What is the purpose of the content (e.g., to instruct, entertain, inform, persuade, sell)?
- Is the author's name familiar (e.g., mentioned by your instructor or cited in other sources)? Respected authors are cited frequently by other scholars. For this reason, always note those names that appear in many different sources.

Google Scholar

The number of times a source is cited in the literature is usually a good indicator of its validity and reliability. You can often use Google Scholar to find this information for scholarly articles, papers, and books. Here is how:

1. Go to: http://scholar.google.com/ and type in the author, journal, or title of the article you are looking for.

2. Search for your topic, article, book, etc. You can search by keyword, author, publication, or title.

3. Use the search results to find what you are looking for, and determine the value of the source. If a large number of individuals cited that work, it is most likely a good source.

The illustration below shows that Astin's source was cited by 2271 other works, a good indication that this would be a quality source

Very Important: Google Scholar often links to content from commercial publishers, and you may be asked to pay to access an article. Do not pay for an article! The University Libraries may already provide access to the article. If not, you can request a copy of the article through the University Libraries Interlibrary Loan service at no cost to you. Questions? Ask a Librarian.

The number of sources that are cited is usually a good indicator of how reliable the source is. 2271 other works cited this source by Astin.

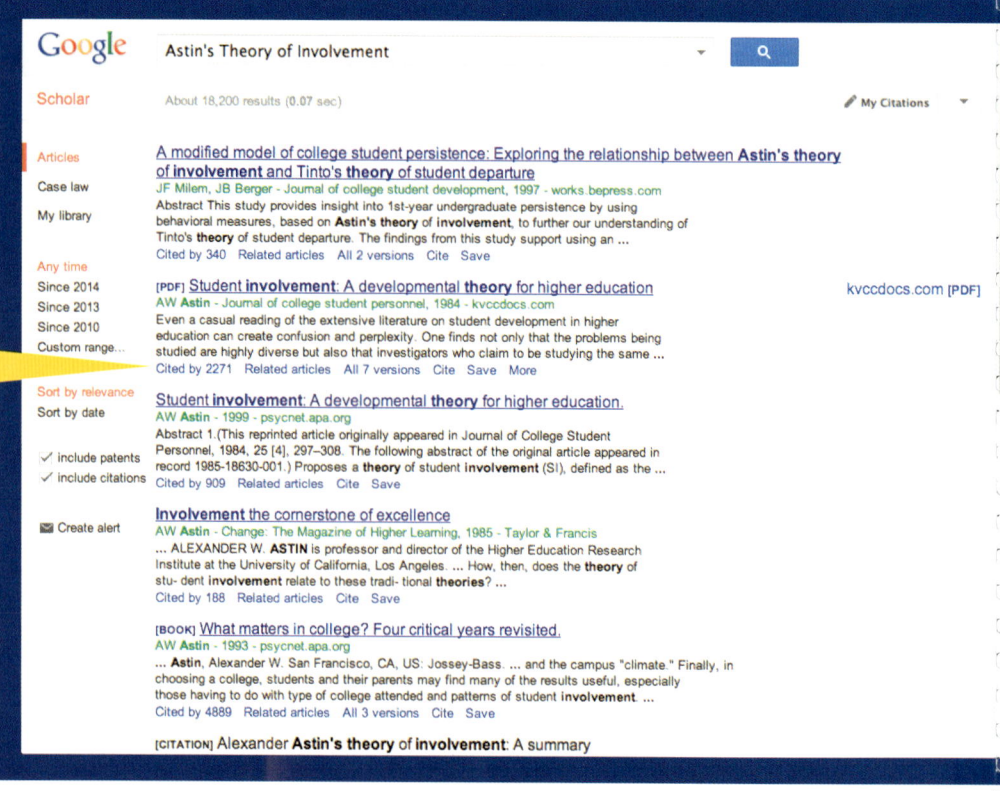

168 Chapter 7: Searching for Knowledge: Information Literacy and Academic Integrity

Relevancy

It may often seem easier to adopt a grab-and-go method of research, for example using the first five articles you find, however you may find yourself overwhelmed with information since your results may have very different information or may not relate directly to your specific research question. Your results may be too broad or too narrow to adequately answer your questions. Therefore, while reviewing a wide breadth of articles, think about what you specifically need by asking

- Is there adequate information?
- Is the content written in understandable language?
- Does it add to what I have retrieved elsewhere?
- Is my topic covered or does the information source just happen to contain some of the same keywords or phrases?

Currency

Depending on your topic, when an information source was published may or may not have an impact on the validity of the information. For example, the data from current research studies may contradict conclusions from an older study (even one held to be a classic in the field) because of newly discovered information or methods that are now accepted as the new industry or field standard.

To determine the currency of an information source, ask yourself the following questions:

- Can I tell when the information was published?
- For websites, do I see a date that lets me know that someone is monitoring the site? Are the sources listed current, do the links work, or are there other clues that indicate the information is current?
- Is this a first edition of this publication? Multiple editions indicate a source has been revised and updated to reflect changes in knowledge, include omissions, and harmonize with its intended reader's needs. Also, many printings or editions may indicate that the work has become a standard source in the area and is reliable.

Objectivity

Many information sources are produced by people or organizations with a particular agenda, for a specific group, or with a political or religious message. Therefore you need to be aware of bias when selecting information to use. Ask yourself these questions when considering a resource:

- Does the content present scholarly information or personal opinion?
- Is the content fact or opinion?
- Is the coverage balanced—presenting multiple sides of an issue?
- From whose viewpoint or perspective is the content presented? Bias is not necessarily negative, especially if you are seeking a strong viewpoint. What is important is whether the author hides a bias.
- Is advertising, sponsorship, or funding evident? For example, if the information source is a scholarly article reporting the results of a study, is there a statement about how the study was funded?
- Are ads clearly delineated and separated from the informational content?
- If the information source is a website, does the organization or business posting the information have a financial interest in the information posted? For instance, a car company may state

safety test results in a format that is advantageous for sales. However, you need to compare the results with those posted by the government or consumer agency that performed the tests.

- Who is the publisher, and what other types of work have they distributed? If the source is published by a university press, it is likely to be scholarly. Although the fact that the publisher is reputable does not necessarily guarantee quality, it does show that the publisher may have high regard for the source being published.

Useful Terms

These are words you would find mostly associated with catalogs and databases:

Boolean Operator - (logical operators). Terms such as "and", "or" and "not" used to express the relationship of one term to another when searching an index/database or catalog.

Call Number - A notation used to identify the placement and location of particular publications in the stacks (both circulating and non-circulating collections). The call number is found on the spine of the book.

Catalog - A list of library materials contained in a collection.

Keyword Search - A search method that allows the search for the occurrence of a word anywhere in a record.

Title Search - A search method that allows searching by the title of the item.

Truncation - In a keyword search, a word root followed by a truncation symbol to retrieve variant endings. Example: psycholog* can bring up psychology, psychologist, and psychological.

Subject Search - A search method which requires using the databases' or catalogs own exact predetermined vocabulary.

Author Search - A search method that allows searching by the author's name. Tip: most catalogs will search the author's name using the last name first and the first name last.

These are words you would find mostly associated with articles, citations, and journals:

Abstract - A brief summary that gives the essential points of a book, article, or pamphlet. Abstracts can help give you an idea of what the document is about without reading the whole document.

Academic or Scholarly Journal - A periodical issued by an institution, or professional or scholarly society containing current news and/or reports of research activities and work.

Annotated Bibliography - A bibliography that includes a brief description of each article or book listed. The description should help the reader evaluate the content and usefulness of each item.

Bibliography - A list of citations to journal articles, books, and other materials on a particular subject or by a particular author. It is also a list of references given at the end of research reports, journal articles, and books.

Citation - Information that identifies a book, article, web site, video or map. It typically includes: author, title, volume, publication information, page numbers, and sometimes an abstract.

Database - An organized collection of information, data, or citations stored in electronic format that can be searched for specific information.

Magazine - A periodical published primarily for the general public.

Peer - Reviewed or Refereed Journal - A journal where articles are reviewed and selected by professional colleagues for publication.

Periodical - A publication with a unique title that is issued at established intervals (weekly, monthly, and quarterly).

INFORMATION LITERACY & ACADEMIC INTEGRITY

HONESTY **RESEARCH**
CAROLINIAN CREED

WHAT EXACTLY IS IT?

Information Literacy is "recognizing when information is needed and having the ability to locate, evaluate, and use effectively the needed information."[1]

Academic Integrity "is the responsibility of every student at the University of South Carolina Columbia to adhere steadfastly to truthfulness and to avoid dishonesty, fraud, or deceit of any type in connection with any academic program."[2]

THERE ARE 6 UNIVERSITY LIBRARIES:

1. The Thomas Cooper Library
2. The Hollings Special Collections Library
3. The Business Library
4. The Moving Image Research Collections
5. The Music Library
6. South Caroliniana Library

Carolina Library Fast Facts
- More than 3 million volumes
- 1 million government documents
- 400,000 maps and aerial photographs

DID YOU KNOW...

84.4% of students frequently used the internet for research or homework.[3]

85.7% of students frequently or often looked up scientific research articles and resources.[3]

35.7% of college students believe they have above average computer skills when compared with the average person their age.[3]

...AND IN REGARDS TO ACADEMIC INTEGRITY:

MORE THAN 1/2 of all students surveyed acknowledge at least one incident of serious cheating in the past academic year.[4]

75% of high school students engaged in serious cheating.[5]

50% of high school students don't think copying the questions from a test is considered cheating.[5]

Sources:
1 American Library Association (ALA). (1989). American Library Association Presidential committee on information literacy: Final report. Retrieved from the Association of College and Research Libraries website at http://www.ala.org/ala/mgrps/divs/acrl/publications/whitepapers/presidential.cfm
2 Office of Academic Integrity (2010). University of South Carolina. Retrieved from http://www.housing.sc.edu/academicintegrity/
3 Eagan, K., Lozano, J. B., Hurtado, S., & Case, M. H. (2013). The American freshman: National norms fall 2013. Los Angeles: Higher Education Research Institute. UCLA
4 McCabe, D. (2005.summer/fall). It takes a village: Academic dishonesty and educational opportunity. Liberal Education, v.91(3),26-31.
5 Slobogin, K. (2002). Survey: Many students say cheating is okay. retrieved from http://edition.cnn.com/2002/fyi/teachers.ednews/04/05/highschool.cheating/.

> Today's digital culture has blurred the lines of originality and authorship. It is imperative that within this culture, writers, academics, and students have a clear sense of what constitutes plagiarism.
>
> (Turnitin, p. 8, 2012)

A Note About "Self-Plagiarism"

Acts of "self-plagiarism", like when a student recycles or resubmits materials they have previously used for another class or assignment, actually falls under the "Lying" policy of the University of South Carolina's Honor Code. While you might have been the original author, unless you clear it with your professor first, avoid reusing old assignments.

Professors typically expect original work that fulfills the criteria for that assignment… not one you did years ago. If your professor does give you permission to use your previous work, make sure you properly cite yourself. If you are not sure how to do this, just ask your professor.

SafeAssign

You may submit assignments and papers on your course Blackboard site using SafeAssign, a plagiarism prevention tool. SafeAssign will review your assignment and identify any areas of possible plagiarism.

Academic Attribution and Plagiarism

Once you have found reliable and relevant information for your paper or presentation, you will need to ensure that you provide the proper attribution. In other words, you will need to appropriately cite your sources. Providing appropriate citations is a cornerstone of academic work. Citing sources (a) helps establish context for material, (b) allows the reader to identify and locate additional information, and (c) gives the reader an idea as to the legitimacy of your claims. It also acknowledges authors that have made previous contributions to your topic. Research and scholarly inquiry involve ongoing conversations with the academic community, whereby ideas and knowledge are advanced and developed. Citing the relevant previous research on your topic gives credit to those that came before you and demonstrates how your contribution adds to the body of knowledge. For all these reasons, academic honesty is essential in ensuring the integrity of information and protecting scholarly inquiry.

What Is Plagiarism?

The failure to properly cite your sources is considered plagiarism. The Office of Academic Integrity at the University of South Carolina defines plagiarism as the act of taking another's ideas, writings, or work and presenting it as your own in part or in whole. Plagiarism includes the following:

- Copying and pasting words, sentences, ideas, conclusions, and/or examples from any source (e.g., book, article, website, or even another student) and submitting as your own work, without properly acknowledging the source
- "Sloppy" or improper paraphrasing- only changing a few words here and there in an otherwise directly copied passage so that the passage still retains the same thought as intended by the original author
- Patch-writing words, sentences, and/or examples from a source without proper acknowledgement
- Submission of another person's completed assignment, term paper, and/or exam as your own
- Knowingly aiding another student in any of the actions listed above

Why Do Students Plagiarize?

There are many reasons why students plagiarize. Some students run out of time while working on a project; some are uninspired by the assignment; some are driven by intense competition; while still others may not understand the material they are working with. The predominant reason, though, is that many students do not *fully* understand *what* they must cite nor *when to do so*. It is important for you to know the general guidelines for when to cite, as well as strategies for avoiding this form of academic dishonesty.

When and What to Cite

A common concern among new scholars is determining when and what to cite. You should cite in text when

You provide statistics, data, or other factual information taken from a source. This is important so your reader knows how to find this information. The source can be a clue as to the validity of the data. Readers may also want to be able to see the context of the study that provided the data to ensure that the statistics are being used appropriately.

> Between 1971 and 2000, the average price at public four-year institutions rose by 121 percent (Baum, 2001).

You use a direct quotation from someone else. Anytime you use someone else's words, you must put them in quotation marks (or a block quote for long passages) and cite the original source along with the page number so the reader can easily find the original text.

> Morphew (2002) found that "since 1990, more than 120 public and private four-year colleges have changed their names and became universities" (p. 207).

> **Tips for Managing Your Citations**
>
> **Use proper citations when citing material.** Review the Reference Department online citation guides at http://guides.library.sc.edu/citationguides. There are also many software programs available that make citing your sources quick, easy, and accurate. Tools like Endnote or Zotero (a free plug in for the Mozilla web browser) allow you to create a database of the sources you use for your papers and will automatically format your in-text citations and works cited or bibliography. The newer versions of Microsoft Word also have a built-in citations manager that will automatically format your in-text citations and reference page.
>
> **Keep track of citations when writing your rough draft.** When writing, highlight your citations in a different font color. This gives you a visual cue to help you keep track of where your citations are, what sources you are using, and how much of the current work is actually your own. This also helps when making your reference page!

You summarize or paraphrase someone else's words, ideas, or concepts. When paraphrasing, you do not need to use quotation marks, but you must cite the author(s).

> Massy (1999) argued that prestige is viewed as a surrogate for higher education's contribution to society.

Citing information or text you found quoted or cited by another work that you have not read. In this case, you need to give attribution to both sources.

> These trends created what Pat Callan of the National Center for Public Policy in Higher Education referred to as the "perfect storm" (as cited in Ehrenberg, 2006).

You do not need to cite in text when

The information is commonly known (either by the general population, or within the particular discipline). While there is no absolute list of criteria to make this determination, generally, common knowledge includes information that

- Is familiar (e.g., South Carolina is a coastal state)
- Is easily available in various sources, such as encyclopedias (e.g., Abraham Lincoln was the 16th president of the United States)
- Is not arguable or in question (e.g., smoking is hazardous to your health)

Remember that what *you* may think is common knowledge may *not* be as common as you think!

Citation Styles

There are many different styles and formats for citing work, and depending on the class you take, you may be asked to use APA, MLA, Chicago, or some other style. The various styles reflect the differing needs of diverse academic disciplines for how information is organized, explained, and attributed. Once you get into your major, you will generally use one citation style. In the meantime, you may be required to become familiar with several styles. The four main styles of documenting sources are

APA (American Psychological Association)—generally used by disciplines such as psychology, social sciences, nursing, and education

MLA (Modern Language Association) — used by English departments and other humanities

Chicago Manual of Style—used by history departments and other humanities

CSE (Council of Science Editors) —generally used by the sciences

To learn more about a specific style, including how to format your citations, please visit the Thomas Cooper Library's webpage at http://guides.library.sc.edu/citation-guides and check out the Style Guide at the end of the chapter.

ON THE WEB

Another free online resource is known as the "OWL at Purdue". This site has a number of examples of proper citation formats and can be found at
owl.english.purdue.edu/

It is your own original thought or opinion.

When in doubt, cite! You will not be accused of plagiarism for too much citing. Keep in mind, however, that you want to find your own voice in your writing rather than over-relying on other people's words.

How to Avoid Plagiarism

Hunt and Birks (2008) offer some practical solutions for making sure you do not inadvertently plagiarize. Here are their suggestions:

1. Have varied and quality sources to work from.
2. Take good notes from your sources.

    Write down keywords, not whole phrases.

    Include the page number and source if you write down a whole phrase so you can cite it later if you use it verbatim. Be sure to put the phrase in quotation marks to remind yourself that the wording is identical to the original source.

    Write notes from each different source on separate sheets of paper, with the citation for the source at the top. It is much easier to remember where you got the information if you do it this way.

3. Write from your notes, not the sources you have used.
    a) It is less tempting and not as easy to plagiarize if you are writing from your notes. However, your notes must be well-written and organized.

4) Write in your own words.
    a) Many students are concerned about grammar or vocabulary, and they lift whole sentences from other people's writing because they are afraid of making mistakes.
    b) Write simple sentences; short is okay.
    c) Concentrate on getting your meaning across in the simplest way.

5) Give yourself plenty of time to complete the paper. Do not try to research and write all at the same time.

What Is Academic Integrity and Why Is It important?

Plagiarism is one component of the broader issue of academic integrity, which is a cornerstone of scholarly inquiry and academic work. Academic integrity is central to the community of scholars at the University of South Carolina.

The first tenant of the Carolinian Creed states that the South Carolina academic community of students, faculty, and staff "will practice personal and academic integrity." The Office of Academic Integrity notes that, "it is the responsibility of every student at the University of South Carolina Columbia to adhere steadfastly to truthfulness and to avoid dishonesty, fraud, or deceit of any type in connection with any academic program (Office of Academic Integrity, 2010, para. 2)."

Integrity, honesty, and cheating are not concerns exclusive to higher education. Colleges and universities exist within the larger society and student and faculty conduct are reflections of larger societal beliefs and attitudes. Recently, there has been considerable attention paid to the perceived decline of personal integrity in today's world. It is difficult to open the paper each morning without reading tales of CEOs that have acted unethically, athletes that have gained an unfair advantage by using performance-enhancing drugs, or other acts of dishonesty or cheating. And while acts of academic dishonesty are as old as colleges themselves, there has been increased attention in recent years to rising incidents of cheating on college campuses. McCabe (2005) has found that more than half of all students surveyed acknowledge at least one incident of serious cheating in the past academic year and more than two-thirds admit to one or more questionable behaviors, such as collaborating on assignments when specifically asked for individual work.

To Cheat or Not to Cheat

When students are asked to discuss why they should act with integrity when it comes to academics, many respond that they would be cheating themselves. This is certainly a valid point. If you are not learning the material, you will not be gaining the knowledge of what you need to learn to be successful. In addition, having a mark on your transcript that indicates you violated the academic integrity code will cast a shadow on your character and make it much harder for you to find a job or get into graduate school. You may also receive a failing grade for the course.

Cheating also impacts more than just the cheater. The entire academic community at the University of South Carolina will suffer if cheating is rampant. Cheating impacts students who are honestly working to make good grades and it provides an unfair advantage in competition for jobs, scholarships, or admission to graduate school. Also, if an institution gets pegged with a reputation for cheating, the prestige of that institution and value of the degrees of current students and the thousands of alumni who came before you will be damaged, thus diminishing the value of everyone's degree. Cheating is unjust, because it undermines the good faith efforts of those acting with integrity, and it violates student rights that arise from the implicit (if not explicit) social contract created when they voluntarily become a member of the university community. According to Daniel Wueste (2008), "Cheating thwarts the aspirations for genuine excellence of individual students and the university" (p.21).

> **Did you know?**
>
> According to a 2008 survey of South Carolina first-year students, 35% of the incoming cohort reported that they cheated on an exam or assignment during their last year of high school.

Common sense indicates that cheating is not ethical, though many rationalize it as appropriate behavior. In his book *The Cheating Culture*, David Callahan (2004) suggests four reasons why people are likely to cheat in today's society:

- Increased pressures to set oneself apart (more competition for spots in elite colleges, entry into graduate school, promotions at work, etc)
- Bigger rewards for winning (CEOs inflating earning's reports, athletes looking for a bigger contract or even just trying to stay in the pros)
- Greater temptation as it becomes easier to cheat and not get caught
- Trickle down corruption that leads people to mistakenly believe that everybody is doing it

But why should you have integrity? Why should you not cheat? Do people follow the rules because it is the right thing to do, or do they follow the rules because they are afraid to get caught? The renowned theorist of moral development, Lawrence Kohlberg, posited three developmental levels that explain why people follow the rules or do the right thing. The first level, characterized by most young children, is the avoidance of punishment. These individuals are motivated to follow the rules to avoid getting in trouble, but often believe that the action is not wrong if you do not get caught. The second level explains individuals who try to do the right things in order to live up to the expectations of others, to gain approval, and to maintain an image of being a good person. The highest level is where individuals do what is right based on the extent to which they promote fundamental values. Acting with integrity is thus a social contract (Evans, Forney, & Guido-DiBrito, 1998). It is this higher-order thinking that Carolina students should use when making the decision to do their academic work honestly.

The University of South Carolina Honor Code

The Honor Code serves two purposes:

1. To educate the Carolina community about academic integrity and its importance in our scholarship.
2. To hold students accountable in a consistent and fair manner when they violate the Honor Code.

Through education, the Honor Code seeks to reduce cheating and plagiarism on campus and create an environment that does not tolerate those behaviors. The Honor Code is intended to prohibit all forms of academic dishonesty and should be interpreted broadly to carry out that purpose. Conduct that violates the Honor Code includes, but is not limited to:

a. Giving or receiving unauthorized assistance, or attempting to give or receive such assistance, in connection with the performance of any academic work.

b. Unauthorized use of materials or information of any type or the unauthorized use of any electronic or mechanical device in connection with the completion of any academic work.

c. Unauthorized access to the contents of any test or examination or the purchase, sale, or theft of any test or examination prior to its administration.

d. Use of another person's work or ideas without proper acknowledgment of source.

e. Intentional misrepresentation by word or action of any situation of fact, or intentional omission of material fact, so as to mislead any person in connection with any academic work (including, without limitation, the scheduling, completion, performance, or submission of any such work).

f. Offering or giving any favor or thing of value for the purpose of influencing improperly a grade or other evaluation of a student in an academic program.

g. Conduct intended to interfere with an instructor's ability to accurately evaluate a student's competency or performance in an academic program.

Whenever a student is uncertain as to whether conduct would violate this Honor Code, it is the responsibility of the student to seek clarification from the appropriate faculty member or instructor of record prior to engaging in such conduct.

What Happens if You Violate the Honor Code?

How are violations reported? Reports of possible violations of the honor code are made online at http://www.sc.edu/academicintegrity/report.html, or by phone at 803-777-4333. Anyone within the Carolina Community has the right to make reports. Both students and faculty are encouraged to report incidents as they arise.

> **ON THE WEB**
>
> For more information on the University of South Carolina Honor Code, please visit the Office of Academic Integrity website:
> **sc.edu/academicintegrity**
> or read the full Honor Code:
> **sc.edu/policies/staf625.pdf**

What happens after violations are reported? Students who are suspected of violating the honor code will receive an e-mail from the Office of Academic Integrity about an appointment that has been made to discuss the incident. The student and hearing officer will meet and a decision will be made regarding responsibility.

If I am found responsible, what will I have to do? There are many options that the hearing officer has in regards to sanctioning. Sanctions range from attending an academic integrity workshop to suspension or expulsion from the university. Other options such as a notation on the student's transcript are possible. Sanctions are designed to educate students about the consequences of academic dishonesty and are not purely punitive.

Conclusion

Information literacy is the cornerstone of lifelong learning. The ability to find information and evaluate it effectively is a skill that will enhance your academic success in college and your ability to think critically. Practice will make perfect, and librarians are a fantastic resource to utilize as your learn to find, evaluate, and use information.

In addition, navigating your way successfully through your academics can be challenging, particularly in the area of academic integrity. If you are ever in doubt as to whether some action may be considered cheating (e.g., group work or collaboration) or constitute plagiarism, ask your professor for clarification! Professors are required to report suspected instances of cheating or plagiarism, so it is important that your work is honest. Use the resources on campus and in this book to help you learn and effectively use the research process.

Check yourself

To Cite or Not to Cite

Look at the following statements and decide whether you would need to provide a citation.

1. A recent study showed that students who attended Supplemental Instruction for Biology earned significantly higher grades than students who did not attend.

    Citation needed? _____

    Why or why not? _____

2. Many studies indicate that college graduates earn higher salaries than those with only a high school degree.

    Citation needed? _____

    Why or why not? _____

3. The University of South Carolina, founded in 1801, is the flagship institution of our state.

    Citation needed? _____

    Why or why not? _____

4. Alcohol abuse is a serious problem among college students.

    Citation needed? _____

    Why or why not? _____

5. Sixty percent of college students will graduate within five years.

    Citation needed? _____

    Why or why not? _____

6. Chlamydia is a treatable bacterial infection that can affect a woman's ability to have children.

    Citation needed? _____

    Why or why not? _____

7. Chlamydia is the most common sexually-transmitted infection among college students.

    Citation needed? _____

    Why or why not? _____

8. College students trying to eat healthy on campus should eat plenty of fruits and vegetables and stay away from high-fat foods like brownie bites.

    Citation needed? _____

    Why or why not? _____

Check yourself

Is This a Violation of the Honor Code?

Read the prompt and in the blank write Yes or No in answer to the question,
"Is this a violation of the Honor Code?"

1. _____ Tyrone is given an assignment from his instructor that states the assignment must be completed without the help of an outside source. He works with another student to figure out the homework problem but does his own work.

2. _____ Jenny turns in a paper where chunks of material were copied and pasted directly from the original work. She cites the information correctly within the paper and her work cited.

3. _____ Devin is approached by Laura, who has obtained a test that will be administered in the upcoming weeks. Laura offers to tell Devin what is on the test if he pays her $20.

4. _____ Molly's best friend Olivia skipped class and has Molly sign her in on the roll.

5. _____ Jane is in CHEM 111, which has three sections taught by the same instructor. She has a friend in another section who is taking a test in that class before her. After the test, Jane's friend tells her what to study based on of the questions on her test.

6. _____ Megan writes a paper for her English 101 class, and on her works cited there are sources listed that were not referenced within the paper.

7. _____ Lauren took a class with Dr. Fowler where she wrote a paper on the topic of political campaigns in relation to the influence on voter turnout. The next semester she enrolls in a marketing class where she received an assignment to write about any kind of marketing and its effects on a consumer. Lauren decides to turn in the paper she wrote for Dr. Fowler to her marketing class.

8. _____ Simon is in his CHEM 341 lab and is doing an experiment to find the specific gravity of the compounds that make up the drug aspirin. During his experiment his sand bath stops working, and he cannot get an accurate reading of the compounds' boiling point. He has a rough idea of what the results should be, so he documents that and makes it look like the experiment was successful.

9. _____ Carlos is writing a research paper and sends his paper to his mom to proofread.

10. _____ Tim has a friend who took MATH 141 last semester with the same instructor. Tim's friend offers him his old tests to study from for his upcoming exam.

11. _____ Ashley and Tameka are both writing papers on the topic of civil liberties. Ashley shows Tameka her outline and asks for feedback on how to improve it.

Comparison of APA, Chicago, MLA, and CSE styles

Book

APA Eggins, S., & Slade, D. (1997). *Analyzing casual conversation*. London, England: Cassell.

Chicago Chicago Humanities/Turabian
Eggins, Suzanne, and Diana Slade. *Analyzing Casual Conversation*. London: Cassell, 1997.

Author-Date
Eggins, Suzanne, and Diana Slade. 1997. *Analyzing casual conversation*. London: Cassell.

MLA Eggins, Suzanne, and Diana Slade. *Analyzing Casual Conversation*. London: Cassell, 1997. Print.

CSE Citation Sequence
Kelly, EB. Stem cells. Westport (CT): Greenwood Press; 2007.

Name-year
Kelly, EB. 2007. Stem cells. Westport (CT): Greenwood Press.

Chapter in an Edited Book

APA McCrae, R. R, &Weiss, A. (2007). Observer ratings of personality. In R. W. Robins, R. C. Fraley, & R. F. Krueger (Eds.), *Handbook of research methods in personality* (pp. 259-272). New York, NY: Guilford Press.

Chicago Chicago Humanities/Turabian
McCreae, Robert, and Alexander Weiss. "Observer Ratings of Personality." In *Handbook of Research Methods in Personality*, edited by Richard W. Robins, R. Chris Fraley and Robert F. Krueger, 259-272. New York: Guilford Press, 2007.

Author-Date
McCreae, Robert, and Alexander Weiss. 2007. Observer ratings of personality. In *Handbook of research methods in personality*, ed. Richard W. Robins, R. Chris Fraley and Robert F. Krueger, 259-272. New York: Guilford Press.

MLA McCrae, Robert R., and Alexander Weiss. "Observer Ratings of Personality." *Handbook of Research Methods in Personality Psychology*. Eds. Richard W. Robins, R. Chris Fraley and Robert F. Krueger. New York: Guilford Press, 2007. 259-272. Print.

CSE Citation Sequence
Bayliss MK, Skett P. Isolation and culture of human hepatocytes. In: Jones GE, editor. Human cell culture protocols. Totowa (NJ): Humana Press; 1996. p. 369-391.

Name-year
Bayliss MK, Skett P. 1996. Isolation and culture of human hepatocytes. In: Jones GE, editor. Human cell culture protocols. Totowa (NJ): Humana Press. p. 369-391.

Journal Article (print and electronic)

APA Kohl, D. (2007, July). Peer review and the academic twelfth man. *Journal of Academic Librarianship, 33*, 437-438.

Moore, R.S., Ames, G. M. & Cunradi, C. B. (2007, June 30). Physical and social availability of alcohol for young enlisted naval personnel in and around home port. *Substance Abuse Treatment, Prevention, and Policy, 2*. Retrieved from http://www.pubmedcentral.nih.gov/articlerender.fcgi?artid=1934352

Comparison of APA, Chicago, MLA, and CSE styles

Chicago Chicago Humanities/Turabian
Kohl, David F. "Peer Review and the Academic "Twelfth Man"." *Journal of Academic Librarianship* 33, no. 4 (July 2007): 437-438.

Author-Date
Kohl, David F. 2007. "Peer review and the academic "Twelfth Man"." *Journal of Academic Librarianship* 33, no. 4: 437-438.

Chicago Humanities/Turabian
Jones, Julia C., M. R. Myerscough, S. Graham, and B. P. Oldroyd. "Honey Bee Nest Thermoregulation: Diversity Promotes Stability." *Science* 305, no. 5682 (July 16, 2004): 402-404. http://web.ebscohost.com/(accessed July 24, 2007).

Author-Date
Jones, Julia C., M. R. Myerscough, S. Graham, and B. P. Oldroyd. 2004. "Honey bee nest thermoregulation: Diversity promotes stability." *Science* 305, no. 5682: 402-404. http://web.ebscohost.com/ (accessed July 24, 2007).

MLA Kohl, David F. "Peer Review and the Academic 'Twelfth Man'." *Journal of Academic Librarianship* 33 (July 2007): 437-438. Print.

Moore, Roland S., Genevieve M. Ames, and Carol B. Cunradi. "Physical and Social Availability of Alcohol for Young Enlisted Naval Personnel In and Around Home Port." *Substance Abuse Treatment, Prevention, and Policy* 2.17 (2007): n. pag. Web. 2 Jun. 2009.

CSE Citation Sequence
Levin Y. The real lessons of stem cells. Newsweek. 2009 Mar;153(13):47.

Name-year
Levin Y. 2009 Mar. The real lessons of stem cells. Newsweek. 153(13):47.

Citation Sequence
Shahid SA. Transition from 2D to 3D in-situ soil information. Eur J Sci Res [Internet]. 2009 [cited 2009 Apr 01]; 27(3): 349-357. Available from: http://www.eurojournals.com/ejsr_27_3_05.pdf.

Name-year
Shahid SA. 2009. Transition from 2D to 3D in-situ soil information. Eur J Sci Res [Internet]. [cited 2009 Apr 01]; 27(3): 349-357. Available from: http://www.eurojournals.com/ejsr_27_3_05.pdf.

Web Page

APA The Library of Congress, American memory, born in slavery: Slave narratives from the Federal Writers Project 1936-1938. (2001, March 23). *Voices and faces from the collection "Sarah Gudger, Age 121."* Retrieved from http://memory.loc.gov/ammem/snhtml/snvoices03.html

Chicago American Memory, Born in Slavery: Slave Narratives from the Federal Writers Project 1936-1938. Voices and Faces from the Collection "Sarah Gudger, Age 121." Library of Congress, http://memory.loc.gov/ammem/snhtml/snvoices03.html (accessed May 12, 2008).

MLA "Josephine Baker." *Encyclopaedia Britannica Online*. Encyclopaedia Britannica, 2009. Web. 3 June 2009.

CSE Citation Sequence
Farrelly B. Careers in the biological sciences [Internet]. American Institute of Biological Sciences; c2009 [cited 2009 Apr 17]. Available from: http://www.aibs.org/careers/.

Name-year
Farlley B. c2009. Careers in the biological sciences [Internet]. American Institute of Biological Sciences. [cited 2009 Apr 17]. Available from: http://www.aibs.org/careers/.

Adapted from *University Libraries Citation Formats* at http://guides.library.sc.edu/citationguides

SCENARIOS FROM COLLEGE LIFE

Friend or Foe

Stuart, an 18-year-old first-year student at the University of South Carolina, was from Greenville, SC. She had many friends at the university and roomed with her best friend of 10 years, Molly. Molly and Stuart were both exceptional students throughout high school, and neither of them ever really had to study for the grades they received. At Carolina, Stuart and Molly had multiple classes together including Anthropology 201. At the beginning of the semester they learned that the top 30% of students in this course would receive an "A" regardless of their raw score.

As the semester began to wind down Stuart and Molly began to prepare for their final exams. Both were on scholarship and needed to maintain a cumulative 3.0 to keep them. Stuart had been studying and succeeding all semester long. She understood that her success in class was not only important for her to be able to remain at the university, but could also enhance her future endeavors. Molly, on the other hand, struggled somewhat and was at risk of losing her scholarship. Her parents made it perfectly clear that if she lost her scholarship she would have to come home and go to the local community college.

Molly's problems were mostly self-inflicted. All semester long she neglected her studies, and instead went to a lot of parties, even the night before an exam. Stuart tried to remind Molly that since most of her final exams were cumulative, if she didn't take time to prepare she wouldn't be able to cram all of the material in the night before the test. Molly continued to believe that she would be fine, and she did not plan to study until the night before.

When exam week arrived, Stuart was completely prepared, and her grades reflected this. Molly was in a panic and struggled through her first few exams. She then realized that if she didn't get an "A" on her final in Anthropology that she would drop below the required GPA to maintain her scholarship. She asked Stuart for advice. Stuart suggested that she speak with their professor to see if there was anything she could do to possibly boost her grade. Molly went to her professor the day before the exam, but the professor was firm and said there is nothing more she could do at this late point in the semester. While she was in the office the professor received a phone call and was forced to leave the room. While Molly waited for the professor to return she noticed that on the desk there were copies of the exam. Right next to the exam was a copy of the answer key. Molly took the opportunity to copy down the answers.

Later that evening Stuart returned to her room and noticed that Molly was not in. She looked on her desk to see if she left a note, but instead found what appeared to be the answer key for the final exam.

Processing Questions:

What are the major issues with both Stuart's and Molly's situations?

What options does Stuart have in this scenario?

What would you do if you discovered your friend was behaving similar to Molly?

What are resources could Molly have utilized throughout the semester to avoid the need of cheating on her exam?

RESOURCES

Academic Integrity

Carolina Community
http://www.sa.sc.edu/carolinacommunity/

The *Carolinian Creed*
http://www.sa.sc.edu/creed/

Office of Academic Integrity 777-4333
Byrnes Building, Suite 201
http://www.sc.edu/academicintegrity/

Office of Student Conduct. 777-4333
Byrnes Building, Suite 201
http://www.sc.edu/osjp

University Libraries

Ask a Librarian Services. 777-4866
http://www.sc.edu/library/ask.html

Business Library 777-6032
Business Administration Building, 2nd floor

Computer Lab 777-0244
Thomas Cooper Library, 5th floor

Educational Films 777-2858
Thomas Cooper Library, 3rd floor

Electronic Resources
http://www.sc.edu/library/er/

E-mail Renewal
http://www.sc.edu/library/pubserv/erenew.html

Interlibrary Loan
http://ill2.tcl.sc.edu/default.html

Law Library. 777-5942
Law Center

Math Library. 777-4741
LeConte Hall, 3rd floor

Music Library 777-5139
Music Building, 2nd and 3rd floors

Reference Department. 777-4866
Thomas Cooper Library, main floor

Science Library 777-3151
Thomas Cooper Library, 4th floor

South Caroliniana Library. 777-3131
Horseshoe

University Libraries
http://www.sc.edu/library

REFERENCES

American Library Association (ALA). (1989). *American Library Association Presidential committee on information literacy: Final report*. Retrieved from the Association of College and Research Libraries website at http://www.ala.org/ala/mgrps/divs/acrl/publications/whitepapers/presidential.cfm

American Library Association (ALA). (2000). *Information literacy competency standards for higher education*. Retrieved from the Association of College and Research Libraries website at http://www.ala.org/ala/mgrps/divs/acrl/standards/informationliteracycompetency.cfm#ilassess

Callahan, David (2004). *The cheating culture*. Orlando, FL: Harcourt, Inc.

Evans, N. J., Forney, D. S., & Guido-DiBrito, F. (1998). *Student development in college: Theory, research, and practice*. San Francisco, CA: Jossey-Bass Publishers.

Hunt, F. & Birks, J. (2008). *More hands-on information literacy activities*. New York, NY: Neal-Schuman Publishers.

McCabe, D. (2005, summer/fall). It takes a village: Academic dishonesty and educational opportunity. *Liberal Education*, v.91 (3), 26-31.

Morse, A. (2006). Cheaters ever prosper. *On Campus*. Retrieved March 27, 2006, from http://www.boundless.org/2000/departments/campus_culture/a0000242.html

Office of Academic Integrity (2010). *University of South Carolina*. Retrieved from http://www.housing.sc.edu/academicintegrity/

Shenk, D. (1997). *Data smog: Surviving the information glut*. San Francisco, CA: HarperEdge.

Turnitin. (2012). White Paper: The Plagiarism Spectrum: Instructor insights into the 10 types of plagiarism. Oakland, CA: Turnitin.

University of South Carolina (2009). *Characteristics, experiences and expectations of University of South Carolina freshmen: Results of the fall 2009 CIRP Freshman Survey*. Columbia, SC: Division of Student Affairs and Department of Academic Support.

Wueste, D. (2008). Unintended consequences and responsibility. *Teaching Ethics*. Fall 2008, 13-24.

Chapter Eight

Making Healthy Decisions

Dear First-Year Student,

Welcome to the University of South Carolina! I am glad you have chosen Carolina to be your home for the next few years. It is my alma mater, and, while here, I developed many healthy habits that continue to this day.

One of the great things about being in college is independence. Without parents to tell you when to get up, what to eat, or how to manage your time, the first few months on your own can be a challenge. However, this time is also an opportunity to cultivate healthy behaviors and routines that will last a lifetime. Fortunately, the University of South Carolina has a variety of resources available for you to attain and maintain wellness in body, mind, and spirit during your collegiate career.

At the full-service Thomson Student Health Center, you can see a physician if you are not feeling well, but the Center provides so much more. Students may fill prescriptions, meet with a registered dietitian, and get flu or allergy shots. In addition, the Campus Wellness office provides blood pressure, body composition, and fitness assessments; exercise consultations; and a variety of programs related to nutrition, physical activity, sexual health, stress management, and disease prevention. Finally, the Counseling and Human Development Center (CHDC) is here whenever you feel the need to talk with a professional about personal challenges.

This campus provides many opportunities for physical activity. From walking the beautiful Horseshoe to playing intramural sports, there is something for everyone. The Strom Thurmond Wellness and Fitness Center is a state-of-the-art fitness facility where students can take group exercise classes, climb a rock wall, swim, learn to kayak, and work out in the weight room.

Carolina Dining provides ample places to eat on campus and offers many healthy choices. Campus Wellness registered dietitians can help you learn how to eat nutritious meals and snacks while navigating your busy days.

Another aspect of college life may involve engaging in risky behaviors, including using alcohol or other drugs, developing sexual relationships, and walking alone at night from popular hangouts like Five Points. There are a range of University services from free taxis to tattooing personal items to campus emergency alert boxes to help you stay safe. Campus offices, such as Sexual Assault and Violence Intervention and Prevention, Substance Abuse Prevention and Education, and Student Conduct, can also help you deal with risky situations. In addition, Campus Wellness has sexual health educators to answer your questions about developing relationships.

Another aspect of the wellness wheel depicted in this chapter is spirituality. The University is rich with faith-based groups and places to worship. You are sure to find your spiritual home.

I wish you all the best as you embark upon your Carolina journey!

To your health,

Marguerite O'Brien
Marguerite O'Brien
Director, Campus Wellness

OFTEN, when students are asked to describe their personal wellness, they automatically talk about their physical activity and nutritional habits. While these are two very important health components, wellness is far more comprehensive than what you eat and how much you exercise. The University of South Carolina defines wellness as a holistic, well-balanced approach to living that involves the mind, body, and spirit. Carolina cares about you and your personal wellness because it has a direct impact on your academic success as well as your quality of life.

Healthy Carolina is an institution-wide initiative to create a campus environment that makes it easy for students, faculty, and staff to make healthy choices. With an understanding that wellness means more than being free of illness or disease, Healthy Carolina is adapted from the seven dimensions of wellness:

1. **Physical Wellness** - Respecting and caring for your body. Applying knowledge, motivation and skills toward enhancing personal fitness and health

2. **Social Wellness** - Contributing to your human and physical environment for the common welfare of and social justice within your community

3. **Emotional Wellness** - Striving to meet your emotional needs constructively, responding resiliently to emotional states and the flow of life events. Taking responsibility for your own behavior and having the ability to form interdependent relationships based on mutual commitment, honesty, and respect

4. **Intellectual Wellness** - Having a curiosity and strong desire to learn. A lifelong process of creating and reflecting upon experience, staying stimulated with new ideas and sharing

5. **Spiritual Wellness** - Searching for meaning, value, and purpose resulting in hope, joy, courage, and gratitude. Encourages one to develop a personal faith and to seek the divine in all things

6. **Occupational Wellness** - Combining who you are called to be and what you are called to do. Finding the place where your deep desires and gifts meet the needs of the community

7. **Environmental Wellness** - Being aware of the state of the earth and the effects of daily habits on the physical environment. Respecting all of creation and the beauty and balance of nature

This content is modified from Montague, J., Piazza, W., Peters, K., Eippert, G., & Poggiali, T. (2002,March-April). The wellness solution. The Journal on Active Aging, 17-20. Retrieved from http://www.aahf.info/sec_news/section/pdf/thewellnesssolution2.pdf

CONSIDER THIS

What is wellness?

What does it mean to be well?

If you eat healthy and exercise, does that mean you are healthy?

ON THE WEB

To learn about the resources available for each area of your wellness wheel, visit the Healthy Carolina website at:

sc.edu/healthycarolina/

 facebook.com/HealthyCarolina

 @MyHlthyCarolina

The illustration below highlights these seven components as equal parts of a complete wellness wheel. It is important to try to maintain a balance between all areas on the wellness wheel. Where do you stand now? The wellness wheel assessment at the end of the chapter will provide you with an understanding of the status of your current personal wellness as well as areas that need improvement.

Top Ten Impediments to Academic Success

Top impediments in rank order to academic success according to the 2013 National College Health Assessment at USC:

1) Stress

2) Anxiety

3) Sleep Difficulties

4) Cold/Flu/Sore Throat

5) Work

6) Depression

7) Internet/Game Use

8) Concern for Troubled Friend/Family

9) Extracurricular Activities

10) Relationship Difficulties

Physical Wellness

As a student, you have likely made decisions regarding issues affecting your physical well-being including your nutrition, physical activity, sexuality, sleep, the use of alcohol and other drugs, self-care, and the use of healthcare resources. The ability to recognize that your behaviors have a significant impact on your wellness and adopting healthful habits will lead to optimal physical wellness.

Healthy Eating

Nutrition and healthy eating are two of the most talked about health topics in mainstream media. It can be difficult at times to determine what information is accurate. A great place to start is with the four main food groups. Foods in each of the four main food groups individually offer different nutrients, so in order to maintain your body's overall health, it is important to incorporate a variety of foods from *all* the food groups.

When planning each meal, be sure to consume whole grain carbohydrates, lean protein, and a colorful array of fruits and vegetables. In a healthy diet, there are no forbidden foods, just foods that you should choose more often than others. Consume refined carbohydrates, such as soda and candy, and saturated fats, trans fat, and cholesterol in moderation while focusing on incorporating whole grains, fruits and vegetables and healthy fats, found in fish and nuts, to help reduce your risk of many diseases. Suggested foods to keep in your dorm room are: Greek yogurt, fruits, nuts, pretzels, string cheese, and hummus.

> **Did you know?**
>
> Eating breakfast can raise metabolism by as much as 10%! People who eat breakfast also have a better quality of diet overall and report less overeating and cravings later in the day, and an increase in energy and concentration. *(Source: Min et al., 2011)*

Are You Nutrition Savvy?   **Check yourself**

Select true or false for each item below. The answers are on the following page.

#			
1	True	False	A fat-free diet is a healthy diet.
2	True	False	A healthy diet includes some junk food.
3	True	False	Eating well affects how you feel.
4	True	False	It is impossible for college students to eat well.
5	True	False	College students should take vitamins to stay healthy.
6	True	False	Milk, yogurt, peanut butter, and fish are all good sources of protein.
7	True	False	Drinking 2-3 cups of coffee per day is perfectly healthy.
8	True	False	Foods high in cholesterol are high in calories.
9	True	False	If you have a bakery bagel for breakfast, you have just eaten about four servings of grain foods.
10	True	False	Eating well today is important in preventing heart disease, cancer, osteoporosis, and diabetes.

Check yourself

Are You Nutrition Savvy?

Answers

1.		**A fat-free diet is a healthy diet.**
	False	A healthy diet contains some fat. Dietary fat performs many functions in your body. On a practical level, since fat is a nutrient that makes the diet satisfying, a fat-free diet will leave you hungry and always wanting more. The goal is low fat, not no fat.
2.		**A healthy diet includes some junk food.**
	True	Eating well is about balance. Choose foods from the grain group, fruit and vegetable group, dairy group, protein group… and then some that do not fit in anywhere, but you eat them because they taste good, not because they are good for you. There are no good foods or bad foods, just good diets and poor diets.
3.		**Eating well affects how you feel.**
	True	You are, quite literally, what you eat. A well-balanced diet will give you more energy, protect you from illness, and probably make you look better.
4.		**It is impossible for college students to eat well.**
	False	Although college students can easily eat a poor diet, they can just as easily eat a healthy diet.
5.		**College students should take vitamins to stay healthy.**
	False	In certain situations, vitamin supplements are necessary, and chances are that taking a daily supplement will not be harmful. But, a poor diet is not corrected by taking a supplement.
6.		**Milk, yogurt, peanut butter, and fish are all good sources of protein.**
	True	Protein is found in all animal foods, including meat, fish, poultry, and dairy products, and in many vegetable foods, including legumes, peanut butter, and tofu.
7.		**Drinking 2-3 cups of coffee is perfectly healthy.**
	True	For most people, 200-300 milligrams of caffeine per day (2-3 cups of coffee) won't cause negative effects, but for some, overconsumption can cause anxiety, nervousness, and digestive problems. Drinking "half-cafs", herbal teas, and limiting your soda intake can help lower the negative symptoms of caffeine overload.
8.		**Foods high in cholesterol are high in calories.**
	False	Cholesterol is a fat-like substance that does not contain calories. An egg, which is a relatively rich source of cholesterol, is not a high-calorie food.
9.		**If you have a bakery bagel for breakfast, you have just eaten about four servings of grain foods.**
	True	Bakery bagels are quite large and generally contain between 250 and 330 calories per serving, which translates into four to five servings of grains.
10.		**Eating well today is important in preventing heart disease, cancer, osteoporosis, and diabetes.**
	True	Many of the chronic diseases affecting adults are diet-related. Eating a healthy diet can prevent or delay the onset of some of these conditions.

(Source: Selkowitz, 2000)

Monitoring Food Intake

Monitoring intake has been shown to help individuals become more aware of what and how much they eat and drink. A "food diary" is a useful tool to evaluate your diet. You may find that in order to eat healthy, you will need to adjust your food intake and learn the correct portion sizes and how to read the nutrition labels.

Sample label for Macaroni & Cheese

Nutrition Facts
Serving Size 1 cup (228g)
Servings Per Container 2

① **Start Here**

② **Check Calories**

③ **Limit these Nutrients**

④ **Get Enough of these Nutrients**

⑤ **Footnote**

Amount Per Serving	
Calories 250	Calories from Fat 110
	% Daily Value*
Total Fat 12g	18%
Saturated Fat 3g	15%
Trans Fat 3g	
Cholesterol 30mg	10%
Sodium 470mg	20%
Total Carbohydrate 31g	10%
Dietary Fiber 0g	0%
Sugars 5g	
Protein 5g	
Vitamin A	4%
Vitamin C	2%
Calcium	20%
Iron	4%

* Percent Daily Values are based on a 2,000 calorie diet. Your Daily Values may be higher or lower depending on your calorie needs.

	Calories	2,000	2,500
Total Fat	Less than	65g	80g
Sat Fat	Less than	20g	25g
Cholesterol	Less than	300mg	300mg
Sodium	Less than	2,400mg	2,400mg
Total Carbohydrate		300g	375g
Dietary Fiber		25g	30g

⑥ **Quick Guide to % DV**

- 5% or less is Low
- 20% or more is High

Printed with permission from United States Department of Agriculture.

The best resource to gain useful and accurate information about healthy eating is the United States Department of Agriculture's website, www.choosemyplate.gov, which allows you to personalize a plate for your age, gender, and level of activity. The dietary guidelines describe a healthy diet as one that:

- Emphasizes fruits, vegetables, whole grains, and fat-free/low-fat milk and milk products
- Includes lean meats, poultry, fish, beans, eggs, and nuts
- Is low in saturated fats, trans fats, cholesterol, salt (sodium), and added sugars

If you do not eat meat, you will need to consume foods such as nuts, beans, and soy for your daily protein needs. It is healthier to choose whole-wheat bread rather than a croissant and to select brown rice instead of white rice. These foods have more fiber, less fat, and more of the daily required nutrients. It is unhealthy to completely eliminate fat from your diet. Our bodies need fat to maintain healthy skin and hair, to cushion our organs, and to store fat-soluble vitamins. It is also unhealthy to

---

Did you know?

33% of college students describe themselves as overweight or very overweight. *(ACHA, 2013)*

CONSIDER THIS

Why do you think that obesity is such a problem in the United States?

What causes students to gain weight during college? Is it preventable?

Do you think America is the most image-conscious nation? Why or why not?

What are the differences in body image perceptions between males and females?

Are these perceptions realistic and how are relationships affected by them?

Healthy Carolina Farmer's Market and On-Campus Produce Delivery

The Healthy Carolina Farmers Market is a convenient way for Carolina students, faculty, and staff to shop for fresh, healthy, locally grown products.

Location:	Greene Street in front of the Russell House University Union
Day:	Selected Tuesdays in the fall, spring, and summer
Time:	10 a.m.-2 p.m.

On-campus produce delivery is also available. Visit www.sc.edu/healthycarolina for details on this service.

ON THE WEB

Carolina Dining offers weekly menus of all the dining options on campus so you can plan your meals based upon the campus menu.
sc.edu/dining

eliminate carbohydrates from your diet. Our brain and bodies need carbohydrates for energy. Whole grains, fruits, and vegetables are healthy sources of carbohydrates as compared to soda and candy.

Eating Healthy on Campus

The goal of maintaining a healthy weight while eating on campus is achievable. Carolina Dining Services offers a number of healthy food options on campus. Try to balance your weekly choices by dining at Plan-It Healthy in the Grand Market Place, or look for the Healthy Choice (HC) icon at dining halls around campus to identify the balanced and nutritious meal and vending machine options on campus.

If you are trying to lose weight, remember that healthy weight loss is 1-2 pounds per week. Any supplement or diet that promises fast weight loss is not healthy for you and will most likely cause you to overeat. This type of approach to weight loss and dieting can be dangerous to your health and has been shown to hinder weight control. Everyone needs a baseline amount of energy each day, but this amount is unique to every individual and every situation. When it comes to balancing a healthy lifestyle, it is important to think about life-long habits that are maintainable compared to "quick fix" solutions. If you would like assistance with weight management or weight loss, contact Student Health Services Campus Wellness to sign up for their next weight management program or meet with the registered dietitian. http://www.sa.sc.edu/shs/cw/nutrition/

Sodexo offers many choices to make your dining experience great. Look for these icons to help you identify menu items that meet your needs:

- **HC** Balanced
- **GF** Gluten Free
- **L** Local
- **O** Organic
- **VG** Vegan
- **V** Vegetarian

Healthy Choice Icon

Making **healthy, nutritious** selections at USC has never been easier. Just look for the HC icon when selecting food items to create a **balanced**, healthy meal!

HC Healthy vending options
< 35% calories from fat
< 10% calories from sat. fat
< 35% total weight from sugar
(Nuts and seeds excluded)

HC Balanced Plates
< 600 calories
< 30% calories from fat
< 800mg of sodium
≥ 3g of fiber

Healthy Carolina
UNIVERSITY OF SOUTH CAROLINA

Physical Activity

Physical activity has many benefits, including managing stress and preventing injury, illness, and disease. Chances are that when you were in high school, you had physical activity planned into your day through gym class or a sports team. Now that you are in college, you will need to make a conscious effort to get the recommended 30 or more minutes of physical activity on most days or a total of 150 minutes per week.

There are numerous resources on campus to help you meet your physical activity goals. Full-time students have access to the Strom Thurmond Wellness and Fitness Center as well as the Blatt PE Center. Both facilities are equipped with state-of-the-art strength and conditioning equipment as well as pools, basketball courts, and group exercise classes. The Strom Thurmond Wellness and Fitness Center also offers students the opportunity to use the climbing wall, indoor track, outdoor pool, and sand volleyball courts. In addition, Campus Wellness offers fitness assessments and one-on-one exercise consultations for individuals that are new to the workout scene or are looking to change their regular workout routine!

Many students talk about knowing the importance of exercise, but they often struggle to make physical activity a habit or are unsure of how to get started. The following tips may be helpful as you learn to make physical activity a normal part of your daily routine:

- Find a workout partner or take a group exercise class. Exercising with others is always more fun and it allows you to hold each other accountable!
- Put physical activity in your planner just as you would your class assignments. Try to spend 2 hours and 30 minutes a week exercising for moderate benefits, or increase it to 5 hours per week for additional health benefits. Join an intramural team or a sport club as mentioned in chapter 3.
- Keep track of what you have done, and reward yourself when you reach your goals.
- Fit physical activity into your day by taking the stairs instead of the elevator or parking in the Coliseum lot and walking to class.
- Take a walk on one of the FitWalk paths on the campus. Visit http://www.sa.sc.edu/shs/paths/

> **Peer Leader Advice**
>
> Stress relief is such an important part of wellness, and USC offers so many services to help us navigate that. One of my favorite ways to relieve stress, though, is to just go for a run. Luckily, our beautiful campus, city of Columbia, and facilities like Strom make it easy to let go of pent up energy and get fit at the same time!
>
> - Jacqueline Chiari
> Cranford, NJ • Junior
> Marketing

Regardless of how you incorporate physical activity into your busy schedule, it is important to stick with it, especially during stressful times like midterms and finals.

Health Care

As an enrolled student, you are provided affordable, convenient access to primary healthcare through Student Health Services. This campus service supports student success by offering primary care, wellness education, mental health counseling, and sexual assault violence prevention services to the Gamecock community.

Most services are covered by the student health fee included in tuition. The student health fee pays for:

- Healthcare provider visits at the Thomson Student Health Center's General Medicine Center and Women's Care
- Access to wellness care and education, including nutrition consults, stress management services, and exercise consultations
- Twelve one-on-one annual individual visits with trained psychologists, family/marriage therapists, and social workers at the Counseling & Human Development Center
- Urgent care response to campus medical emergencies through our EMT First Responders program
- Access to 24/7 sexual assault advocates

You have access to board-certified physicians with a wide range of specialties (e.g., internal medicine, emergency medicine, family medicine, pediatrics, obstetrics and gynecology, psychiatry), nurse practitioners, registered nurses, and other health professionals. Additional fees apply if you need lab work, x-rays, psychiatric services, physical therapy, sports medicine or pharmaceutical products at the health center.

ON THE WEB

For more information about Student Health Services, visit:

sa.sc.edu/shs

 Facebook: University of South Carolina Student Health Services

 @UofSCshs

Did you know?

The pharmacy at the Thomson Student Health Center can provide you with prescriptions, over-the-counter medications, and various medical supplies for a lower cost than off-campus pharmacies. Download the app! South Carolina PocketRx is an easy way to order and refill prescriptions on campus.

Table 1. Health and Well-Being Offices on Campus

Office	Services	Contact information
Campus Recreation	Aquatics Group exercise classes Intramurals Outdoor recreation Sport clubs	(803) 576-9375 campusrec.sc.edu/
Campus Wellness	Blood pressure screenings Body fat estimations Cancer prevention Chronic disease prevention Cooking classes Nutrition consultations Grocery store tours Sexual health information STI/STD information Stress management Tobacco cessation assistance Physical activity programs Weight management programs	(803) 576-9393 www.sa.sc.edu/shs/cw/students (803) 777-3175 (Nutrition Appointments)
Counseling & Human Development Center	Individual therapy Group therapy Self-hypnosis	(803) 777-5223 www.sa.sc.edu/shs/chdc
Division of Law Enforcement & Safety	Engraving personal property Registering bicycles	(803) 777-8400 www.les.sc.edu
Healthy Carolina	Healthy Carolina Farmers Market On-Campus Produce Delivery Program Lactation Support Initiative Tobacco Free USC Initiative Healthy Carolina Wellness Community (Living/Learning Community) Fitness Buddies Healthy Dining Initiative Fit Walk Paths University of South Carolina Health Assessments	(803) 777-1650 www.sc.edu/healthycarolina

Sexual Assault and Violence Intervention & Prevention	24-Hour on-call services
	Services provided:
	    Academic assistance
	    Medical accompaniment
	    Safety planning
	    Temporary alternative housing and/
	      or permanent relocation
	    Legal advocacy
	    Referral assistance
	    Support groups
	    Peer and staff led outreach presentations
		(803) 777-8248
		www.sa.sc.edu/shs/savip/
		After 5:00 pm an advocate can be reached by calling USC PD at (803) 777-4215

Substance Abuse & Prevention Education	AlcoholEDU Alcohol and Drug Resource Center Outreach Presentations Alcohol Policy Workshops Peers Impact 803	(803) 777-3933 www.sa.sc.edu/sape
Thomson Student Health Center	General Medicine Clinic Immunizations/Allergy Clinic Lab Nutrition Pharmacy Physical Therapy Psychiatry Sports Medicine Women's Care X-ray	(803) 777-3175 www.sa.sc.edu/shs

Core Institute Survey

The University of South Carolina Office of Substance Abuse Prevention and Education administers the Core Alcohol and Drug Survey (Core Institute, 2012), which was developed to measure alcohol and other drug usage, attitudes, and perceptions among college students at two- and four-year institutions. Annually, our campus surveys more than 1,100 undergraduate students ages 18-22.

The following statistics were compiled from the 2012 Core Survey:

- 46.5% of students reported binge drinking in the previous two weeks
- 73.5% of underage students consumed alcohol in the past 30 days
- 92% of students believe the average student on campus uses alcohol once a week or more
- 36% experience peer pressure to drink or use drugs
- 34% of students reported having used marijuana in the past year

ON THE WEB

A complete list of South Carolina state laws related to alcohol and the University's Alcohol Policy can be found on the Office of Substance Abuse Prevention and Education website at:
sa.sc.edu/sape
State laws are subject to change.

Did you know?

Binge drinking is defined as four or more drinks in a two-hour sitting for women; five or more drinks in a two-hour sitting for men. *(Source: CORE Institute 2011)*

Alcohol, Tobacco and Other Drugs

As a first-year student, you are going to have freedom and choices that you may not have had in the past. New freedom also brings new responsibilities and consequences for actions. A major component of the physical dimension on the wellness wheel is healthy lifestyle habits, which includes making smart decisions regarding alcohol and drugs.

Alcohol. This is ranked as the most widely used and abused drug in the United States and on college campuses. Alcohol misuse in college can lead to other difficulties such as poor academic performance, unintended sexual activity, health problems, and legal implications. While alcohol use is prevalent on the USC campus, not all Carolina students are frequent drinkers. The latest Core Institute and NCHA data show that nearly one fourth of University of South Carolina college students did not drink alcohol in the last 30 days.

Legal Implications. The consequences of irresponsible drinking behavior can include jail time, fines, loss of scholarship funding, and suspension of your driver's license. All alcohol offenses are misdemeanors, except a felony DUI (driving under the influence) conviction, and are placed on your permanent criminal record. Students caught breaking the law regarding alcohol and drug use can face state and/or local repercussions, as well as, University sanctions.

In addition to underage drinking laws, alcohol offenses can be stacked. In other words, a person charged with and convicted of three separate offenses can receive all three fines or jail terms, not just the largest of the three. Any alcohol-related conviction will result in the revocation of a LIFE Scholarship.

In South Carolina, you must be 21 to consume alcoholic beverages legally, except when you are in your home with your parent or as part of a religious ceremony. Underage possession of alcohol and the use of false ID cards are serious legal offenses. Even if you are of legal age, there are stiff penalties for giving alcoholic beverages to an underage person.

Blood Alcohol Content. Various types of alcohol beverages have differing amounts of alcohol, and many exotic or mixed drinks (e.g., Long Island Iced Tea, PJ) can contain more than the standard drink alcohol levels. Understanding the amount and type of alcohol you are drinking will dramatically increase your ability to make healthy and safe decisions about alcohol.

A standard drink is:

1 oz. of
100-proof liquor
(considered 50% alcohol by volume)

1 1/2 oz. of
80-proof liquor
(considered 40% alcohol by volume)

one 12 oz. beer

one 5 oz. glass of wine

The following factors directly impact an individual's blood alcohol content (BAC) and the rate of intoxication:

- **Number of drinks consumed**—Your body can only metabolize one standard drink per hour so the speed at which you drink directly impacts your level of intoxication. Instead of participating in drinking games, alternate each alcoholic drink with a nonalcoholic, non-caffeinated drink, such as water or a sports drink.
- **The speed at which you drink and the time spent drinking**—Your body metabolizes alcohol more effectively when consumption is spaced over longer periods of time.
- **Your body weight**—The more an individual weighs the more water they have within their system to dilute the alcohol.
- **Your body composition**—Men and women have different body compositions and, therefore, metabolize alcohol differently. Women are more likely to have higher BAC levels than men after drinking the same quantity of alcohol.
- **Eating before drinking**—Consuming a full or heavy meal (bread, protein) before drinking will slow down the rate of alcohol absorption in your system.
- **Types of drinks consumed**—Alcoholic drinks that contain carbonation cause an individual to become intoxicated more rapidly.

FREE Evening Taxi Service

Sponsored by Student Government, Thursday through Sunday from 10 p.m. – 3 a.m., Checker Yellow taxi cabs pick up from the Five Points fountain and return students home within a five-mile radius. Cabs are clearly identified with the Carolina Cab insignia and Carolina students just need to present their Carolina Card to the cab driver for a free ride.

Did you know?

A person's blood alcohol concentration (BAC) can continue to rise even while he or she is passed out. Even after a person stops drinking, alcohol in the stomach and intestine continues to enter the bloodstream and circulate throughout the body. It is dangerous to assume the person will be fine by sleeping it off.

As a student at the University of South Carolina you are a member of a larger family often referred to as the Carolina or Gamecock Community. As a member of this community you are expected to follow the guidelines set forth by the *Carolinian Creed*. As stated in the *Creed*, all members of the Carolina family have a responsibility to care for each other.

If you suspect that someone is suffering from the consumption of too much alcohol, it is important to get this student help as quickly as possible. An intoxicated person should never be left alone! For anyone exhibiting signs of alcohol poisoning, seek medical attention immediately by dialing 911. The acronym "CUSP" is a memorable way to identify symptoms of those experiencing alcohol poisoning:

Cold, clammy, pale, or bluish skin

Unconscious or unable to be roused

Slow or irregular breathing

Puking repeatedly or uncontrollably

If someone has passed out from too much drinking, try to keep the individual sitting up (back against a wall). If the person must lie down, keep the individual on his or her side with the head turned to the side (fetal position, if possible). Prevent the person from rolling onto his or her back, and watch for choking. The number one reason an intoxicated person dies is because they aspirate or choke on their own vomit.

If you live on campus in a residence hall, you will want to inform your resident mentor (RM) or any other on-duty University Housing staff if someone has been drinking too much. When unhealthy decisions are made about alcohol, it is important that help is received as quickly as possible. As a member of the Carolina community, taking care of each other is a top priority.

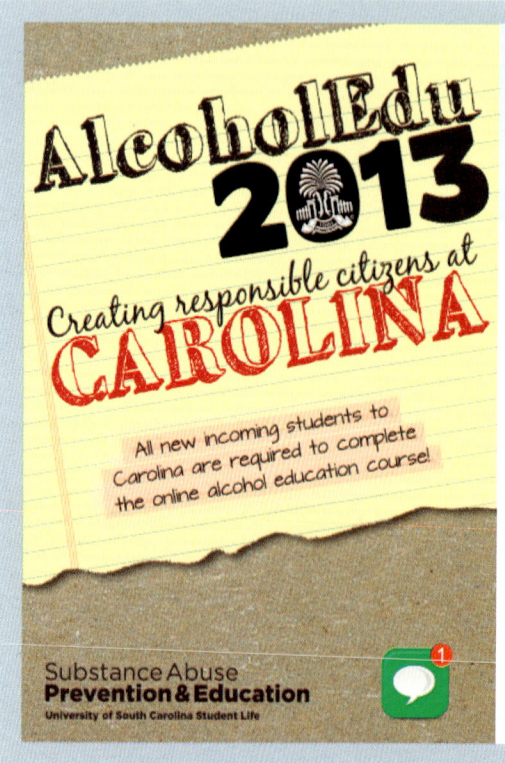

AlcoholEdu for College is an online prevention program that helps students make decisions about alcohol and deal with the behaviors of peers.

Students reported that AlcoholEdu prepared them:

- 85% can identify when someone has consumed too much alcohol
- 89% can prevent an alcohol overdose
- 89% can identify the signs of alcohol poisoning
- 81% can plan ahead of time to make responsible decisions about alcohol
- 86% can intervene when a friend is drinking too much

http://www.sa.sc.edu/alcoholedu/

USC Alcohol & Drug Consequences

	Alcohol	**Drugs**
First Offense	- $250 fine - CAAPS and Evaluations or STIR screening (based on age) - Parental notification call - Written statement of future consequences	- $350 fine - CHDC assessment and six weeks of group counseling - Parental notification phone call - "If I was suspended" essay - Random drug testing for one academic year ($35 each)
Second Offense	- $350 fine - Assessment for STIR screening or group counseling - Probation/loss of privileges - Another phone call and letter to parents - "If I was suspended" essay	- Minimum of one semester of suspension (immediately)
Third Offense	- Minimum of one semester of suspension (immediately)	- Minimum of one year of suspension (immediately)

(Source: Office of Student Conduct, University of South Carolina)

Tobacco. Nicotine is the addictive ingredient in all tobacco products. Tobacco use is the single most preventable cause of death, disability and disease. Secondhand smoke also causes premature death. If you are exposed to secondhand smoke at home or work your chances for lung cancer increases 20-30% (U.S. Department of Health and Human Services, 2006). It is not uncommon to hear college students refer to themselves as social smokers (e.g., I only smoke when I drink). All smoking, social or otherwise, is addictive and quitting is not an easy process. Student Health Services Campus Wellness offers tobacco cessation resources for all University students, faculty, and staff.

Recreational and Prescription Drugs. While alcohol is the most widely abused drug on college campuses, it is not the only one. Marijuana use has been closely linked to depression and anxiety among regular users (Deykin, Levy, & Wells, 1987; Musty & Kaback, 1995). Research shows that marijuana negatively impacts memory and decreases motivation. Also, the use of prescription drugs for nonmedical use is on the rise on college campuses. Amphetamines (Adderall) are being used by college students to help them study or just to get high. The health

Did you know?

87% of Carolina students don't smoke.

94% of Carolina faculty & staff don't smoke.

American College Health Association (ACHA). (2013, spring). National College Health Assessment (ACHA-NCHA) University of South Carolina reference group report.

ON THE WEB

For more information about the smoking cessation resources, visit:
sa.sc.edu/shs/cw/students/tobacco

risks associated with these drugs are serious. Health risks are varied and include loss of appetite, tremors, paranoia, delusions, formication (the sensation of bugs or worms crawling under the skin), and even death. Mixing any drug with alcohol can have deadly adverse effects. If you suspect a drug addiction in either yourself or a friend, Student Health Services has counselors available that are trained and experienced in dealing with addictions.

In addition to the health risks associated with the misuse of prescription drugs, possession of a drug that has not been prescribed for you is a federal offense, as is sharing your prescription drugs with other students.

USC Definitions

Illegal Drug: any drug or controlled substance that was not obtained legally.

Controlled Substance: any drug declared by federal or state law to be illegal for sale or use, but may be dispensed under a physician's prescription.

Improper Use: utilization of a drug for something other than what it was prescribed and issued for by a licensed medical practitioner.

Paraphernalia: any instrument, device, article, or contrivance used, designed for use, or intended for use in ingesting, smoking, administering, manufacturing, or preparing a controlled substance.

Table 2. Signs of Drug Misuse

This table provides a list of physical and behavioral signs that may indicate drug misuse. If you or a friend exhibit any of these signs, consider seeking medical advice at the Student Health Center.

Physical Signs

- Loss of appetite, increase in appetite, any changes in eating habits, unexplained weight loss or gain
- Inability to sleep, awake at unusual times
- Red, watery eyes; pupils larger or smaller than usual; blank stare
- Cold, sweaty palms; shaking hands
- Puffy face, blushing or paleness
- Smell of substance on breath, body or clothes
- Extreme hyperactivity; excessive talkativeness
- Runny nose; hacking cough
- Needle marks on lower arm, leg or bottom of feet
- Nausea, vomiting or excessive sweating
- Tremors or shakes of hands, feet or head
- Irregular heartbeat

Behavioral Signs

- Change in overall attitude/personality with no other identifiable cause
- Changes in friends; new hang-outs; sudden avoidance of old crowd; doesn't want to talk about new friends; friends are known drug users
- Drop in grades at school or performance at work
- Change in habits at home; loss of interest in family and family activities
- Difficulty in paying attention; forgetfulness
- General Lack of motivation, energy, self-esteem, "I Don't Care" attitude
- Sudden oversensitivity, temper tantrums, or resentful behavior
- Moodiness, irritability, or nervousness
- Paranoia
- Excessive need for privacy; unreachable
- Chronic dishonesty
- Unexplained need for money, stealing money or items

Source: American Council for Drug Education (n.d.).

Sexual Health

There is a misperception among college students that your peers are having lots of sex with numerous sexual partners. The most recent University of South Carolina student data determined that 73% of Carolina students had one or zero sexual partners in the last academic year (American College Health Association, 2013). While abstinence (refraining from sexual activities) is the safest way to protect yourself and your partner from unplanned pregnancy and sexually transmitted infections (STIs), there are other precautionary measures you can take if you make the decision to engage in sexual activity.

Sexually Transmitted Infections (STI)

STIs are infections transmitted through sexual contact. A person with an STI can potentially infect others without showing signs of disease or infection. Many signs and symptoms of STIs are mild and can be easily overlooked, so testing is crucial. The most common infections that can be passed through sexual activity include:

- Chlamydia
- Gonorrhea
- Herpes
- Syphilis
- Yeast infections
- Jock itch
- Human Papillomavirus (HPV)
- Human Immunodeficiency Virus (HIV)
- Hepatitis B
- Trichomoniasis

Even though many students take all the necessary precautions to practice safer sex, things can still go wrong. Having a basic understanding of the most common sexually transmitted infections and diseases and their corresponding symptoms can alert you to problems at an early stage. This may help you avoid complications that could arise from treatment delays.

Did you know?

It is estimated that 20 million people contract an STI each year.

(Source: Centers for Disease Control and Prevention, 2013)

Chlamydia and Gonorrhea

Chlamydial and gonorrheal infections in women are usually asymptomatic and often go undiagnosed. In 2011, South Carolina ranked 4th among 50 states in chlamydial infections and ranked 5th in Gonorrheal infections. (CDC, 2011a)

CONSIDER THIS

Why do you think so many people make unhealthy decisions regarding sexual health and sexual behavior when they are drinking?

How do you plan on communicating with your partner or potential partners about safe sexual practices?

Table 3. Sexually Transmitted Infections and Their Symptoms

Sexually Transmitted Infection	Female Symptoms	Male Symptoms	Curable or Treatable
Chlamydia	Abdominal pain; abnormal vaginal discharge; bleeding between menstrual periods; low grade fever; painful intercourse; painful urination; swelling inside the vagina or anus; more than usual urination; vaginal bleeding after intercourse	Pus or water or milky discharge from the penis; swollen or tender testicles; swelling around the anus	Curable
Gonorrhea	Abdominal pain; bleeding between menstrual periods; fever; menstrual irregularities; painful intercourse; swelling or tenderness of the vulva; urge to urinate more than usual; throwing up; yellowish or yellow-green vaginal discharge	Pus-like discharge from the penis; pain or burning feeling while urinating; more frequent urination than usual	Curable
Hepatitis B	Extreme tiredness; tenderness and pain in the lower abdomen; loss of appetite; nausea and vomiting; pain in the joints; headache; fever; hives	Extreme tiredness; tenderness and pain in the lower abdomen; loss of appetite; nausea and vomiting; pain in the joints; headache; fever; hives	Treatable
Hepatitis C	Newly acquired infections have no symptoms; chronic infection leads to jaundice, fatigue, loss of appetite, or nausea	Newly acquired infections have no symptoms; chronic infection leads to jaundice, fatigue, loss of appetite, or nausea	Treatable
Herpes	Blisters; burning feeling if urine flows over sores; inability to urinate if severe swelling of sores blocks the urethra; itching; open sores; pain in the infected area	Blisters; burning feeling if urine flows over sores; inability to urinate if severe swelling of sores blocks the urethra; itching; open sores; pain in the infected area	Treatable
HIV/AIDS	Thrush; severe or recurring yeast infections; chronic pelvic inflammatory disease; periods of unexplained tiredness; long periods of frequent diarrhea; swelling or hardening of glands located in the throat, armpit or groin; periods of persistent deep, dry coughing; increasing shortness of breath; frequent or unusual skin rashes; confusion, personality change, or decreased mental abilities	Thrush; chronic pelvic inflammatory disease; periods of unexplained tiredness; long periods of frequent diarrhea; swelling or hardening of glands located in the throat, armpit or groin; periods of persistent deep, dry coughing; increasing shortness of breath; frequent or unusual skin rashes; confusion, personality change, or decreased mental abilities	Treatable
HPV Human Papillomavirus (also known as genital warts)	Depends on type of HPV virus. Symptoms may include visible warts or no symptoms at all	Depends on type of HPV virus. Symptoms may include visible warts or no symptoms at all	Treatable
Pubic Lice	Intense itching in the genitals or anus; mild fever; feeling run-down; irritability; the presence of lice or small egg sacs in the pubic hair	Intense itching in the genitals or anus; mild fever; feeling run-down; irritability; the presence of lice or small egg sacs in the pubic hair	Curable
Syphilis	A painless sore or open, wet ulcer; chancres appearing on genital, in the vagina, on the cervix, lips, mouth, breasts or anus; swollen glands; mild fever; fatigue; sore throat; hair loss; weight loss; headache; muscle pain	A painless sore or open, wet ulcer; chancres appearing on genitals, lips, mouth, breasts or anus; swollen glands; mild fever; fatigue; sore throat; hair loss; weight loss; headache; muscle pain	Curable in early stages
Trichomoniasis	Frothy, often unpleasant-smelling discharge; blood spotting in the discharge; itching in and around the vagina; the urge to urinate frequently-often with pain and burning	Discharge from the urethra; the urge to urinate frequently-often with pain and burning	Curable

Source: Planned Parenthood.

Communication

If you are currently sexually active or plan to become sexually active in the future, the most important part of a sexual relationship is open communication with your partner. Healthy sexual relationships include trust as well as an ability to express your needs and wants to others. Prior to becoming sexually involved with a new partner, it is important to have an open and honest conversation regarding past sexual partners and sexually transmitted infections. Definitions of common sexual terms (abstinence, intercourse, foreplay, STIs) may differ from person to person; therefore, open communication is essential. On the next page, you will find helpful tips for communicating with your partner about sex.

The two most common concerns students have when engaging in a sexual relationship are pregnancy and sexually transmitted infections. Abstinence and condoms are the only two methods of contraception that protect against both pregnancy and STIs. Also, using both a hormonal and barrier method is recommended. The chart below provides an illustration of the numerous types of contraception available.

Table 4. Types of Contraception

Method	Does it provide protection against STI/HIV?	Do I need a prescription	Effectiveness (Based on correct and consistent usage)
Abstinence	Yes	No	100%
Cervical Cap	No	Yes	86% effective for women who have never been pregnant 71% effective for women who have given birth vaginally
Contraceptive Injection (Shot)	No	Yes	99%
Diaphragm	No	Yes	94%
Female Condom	Yes	No	95%
Implant	No	Yes	99%
IUD (intrauterine device)	No	Yes	99%
Male Condom	Yes	No	98%
Vaginal Ring	No	Yes	99%
Patch	No	Yes	99%
Oral Contraceptive (the pill)	No	Yes	99%
Spermicide	No	No	85%

Source: Planned Parenthood.

Tips for Communicating With Your Partner About Sex

- To reach mutual understanding and agreement on sexual health issues, choose a convenient time when you will both be free of distractions.

- Do not use alcohol/drugs to reduce your inhibitions.

- Use "I" statements when talking. For example, "I feel that abstinence is right for me at this time." Or, "I would feel more comfortable if we used a condom."

- Be assertive! Do not let fear of how your partner might react stop you from talking with him/her.

- Be a good listener. Let your partner know that you hear, understand, and care about what she/he is saying and feeling.

- Be patient with your partner, and remain firm in your decision that talking is important.

- Understand that success in talking does not mean one person getting the other person to do something. It means that you both have said what you think and feel, respectfully and honestly, and that you have both listened respectfully to each other.

- Avoid making assumptions. Ask open-ended questions to discuss relationship expectations, past and present sexual relationships, contraceptive use, and testing for STIs, including HIV, among other issues.

- Avoid judging, labeling, blaming, threatening, or bribing your partner. Don't let your partner judge, label, blame, threaten, or bribe you.

- Do not wait until you become sexually intimate to discuss safer sex with your partner. In the heat of the moment, you and your partner may be unable to talk effectively.

- Stick by your decision. Don't be swayed by lines like, "If you loved me, you would have sex with me." Or, "If you loved me, you would trust me and not use a condom."

Most methods of contraception do not protect against sexually transmitted infections or diseases. Contraception is not a one-size-fits-all type of decision; you need to determine which method of contraception is optimal for you and your current lifestyle. What works well for your friend may not be the best option for you. There are several questions to consider when selecting a birth control method:

- Are you comfortable with you or your partner being solely responsible for contraception?
- Will you be able to remember to take a pill at the same time each day?
- Are you afraid of needles?
- Are you allergic to latex?
- Are you comfortable enough with your body (or your partner's body) to insert and remove contraception daily or monthly?

Answering these questions will help determine the best method of contraception for you and your partner. Student Health Services (SHS) has healthcare providers able to answer questions you may have. Within the Thomson Student Health Center, the Sexual Health office provides various types of barrier methods of protection (male and female condoms) free to students. The SHS Pharmacy carries a variety of birth control options and can fill your prescriptions. You may even have prescriptions transferred from home. If you have been sexually active or think you have been exposed to an STI, the Student Health Services has a variety of resources to help you.

As you review the components of physical wellness, take a moment to reflect on what you are already doing to support this component of the wellness wheel and what changes you can make using the Wellness Wheel Check Yourself at the end of the chapter.

Did you know?

Emergency contraception (EC, also known as the morning-after pill) is available at the Thomson Student Health Center Pharmacy. Emergency contraception can be used after unprotected sex or when contraception fails (e.g., a condom breaks) to prevent an unplanned pregnancy. EC can be used up to 120 hours after unprotected intercourse, but it is not intended to be a regular form of birth control. It should only be used in the cases of emergencies since it can have side effects, such as nausea, vomiting, and cramping. Using emergency contraception will not abort a baby. If you think you are pregnant, please make an appointment with a healthcare provider.

Consider This

Are you engaged in the process of physical wellness?
Are you aware of important health numbers, such as cholesterol, weight, blood pressure, and blood sugar levels?

How are you planning to eat healthy on campus?

How often do you avoid using tobacco products or excessively consuming alcohol?

Are you practicing safe sexual habits and communicating with sexual partners?

How often do you exercise?

Social Wellness

The second dimension of wellness is social wellness. Social wellness refers to one's ability to interact with people around them. It involves using good communications skills, having meaningful relationships, respecting yourself and others, and creating a support system that includes family members and friends. It also consists of recognizing the need for leisure and recreation and budgeting time for those activities.

The importance of student engagement cannot be understated. USC is committed to facilitating students' integrative learning and encouraging participation in a variety of experiences. In chapter 3, we focused on the importance of finding your place here at Carolina and setting goals for your campus engagement. It is not simply about getting involved; engagement goes beyond joining student groups. Developing and cultivating relationships with other students, faculty and staff, and individuals in the Columbia community will make a significant impact on your overall wellness. It is equally as important to recognize the need to allot time for activities beyond your academics. In chapter 4, we touched on managing your time and learning how to become engaged on campus without being overwhelmed. Take a look at your Student Engagement Plan in chapter 3 and use the "Consider This" questions to reflect on your current social wellness and what you could be doing to enhance this dimension.

Interpersonal Violence: Staying Safe and Standing Up

In college, you will grow and build many new relationships with friends, roommates, peers, and faculty and staff. It's important to determine your personal boundaries early on in this growth period, because if someone crosses them, it puts you at an increased risk for interpersonal violence.

It is a fact that college communities—similar to all communities around the country—experience interpersonal violence. Interpersonal violence includes sexual harassment, sexual assault, attempted sexual assault, drug-facilitated sexual assault, stalking, cyber stalking, bullying, rape, dating and relationship violence, domestic violence, and hate crimes.

No one is completely immune to interpersonal violence, but there are things you can do to keep yourself safe. First, learn the facts about types of violence and what to do if you or a friend is assaulted, injured or are fearful of someone's behavior toward you. Then, learn what you can to do stand up for yourself and your peers and prevent interpersonal violence within our campus community.

Did you know?

Sense of belonging is the #1 predictor of persisting through college.

University of South Carolina Definitions of Interpersonal Violence

Sexual Assault and Harassment is the unwelcome sexual advances, request for sexual favors, and other verbal or physical conduct of a sexual nature.

Stalking is a pattern of words or conduct intended to cause or that does cause a person to have fear. Stalking behaviors include any persistent unwanted contact such as telephone calls and emails.

Relationship Violence describes any harsh physical behavior (e.g., slapping, pulling hair, punching), threats of abuse, and emotional abuse directed toward a current or former partner or spouse.

Types of Interpersonal Violence

Sexual Assault & Harassment

One in five college-age women report experiencing sexual assault or attempted sexual assault since age 14. One in six men report the same before age 25 (Warsaw, 1994).

Sexual assault is any sexual act without consent including:

- Rape
- Fondling
- Grabbing sexually
- Having sex with someone who is intoxicated
- Having sex with someone who does not explicitly consent
- Sexual harassment (unwanted sexual advances, requests for sexual favors and other verbal or physical conduct of a sexual nature)

If you have been sexually assaulted:

- Call the police: USC Police Department (803) 777-4215.
- Report the assault: Reporting the assault is not the same as prosecuting. If the assault occurred on campus, University Police should be notified, if the assault took place off-campus, local law enforcement will handle the case. You can even report anonymously to SAVIP at http://www.sa.sc.edu/shs/savip/asarf/.

If you choose not to Report the Assault, you can still get medical assistance and assistance from a SAVIP advocate. An advocate can be reached by contacting the SAVIP office at (803) 777-8248 during normal business hours. Afterhours please call the USC Police Department at (803) 777-4215 and request the advocate on call.

- Seek medical attention: If the assault occurred within 72-hours, go to Palmetto Richland Emergency Room (803) 434-7000 for the most appropriate care. You don't have to go alone; an advocate can accompany you to the exam.

If the assault occurred more than 72-hours all of the same procedures apply with the EXCEPTION of the necessity to go to the hospital for evidence collection (sexual assault exam.) You should still report the assault to the police, applicable on campus offices and go to a medical center to check for internal injuries, sexually transmitted infections, and pregnancy.

- Seek emotional support and legal assistance: Advocates from the office for SAVIP are available 24-hours a day to provide support, information, advocacy, and referrals. Call (803) 777-8248 and (follow the emergency prompt system after business hours) to contact an advocate. Students may also receive free and confidential counseling at the USC Counseling & Human Development Center (803) 777-5223.

ON THE WEB

View the University of South Carolina's Equal Opportunity Policy regarding sexual harassment at **sc.edu/eop/policies.shtml**

Did you know?

Student Health Services offers advocacy services 24-hours a day for times when relationships become unsafe. The office is staffed with trained professionals in areas of sexual assault, sexual harassment, stalking, and relationship violence. If you or one of your friends is in an unhealthy relationship, it is important to seek help. Contact Student Health Services Sexual Assault and Violence Intervention and Prevention (SAVIP) at 803-777-8248.

Stalking

The majority of stalking victims are stalked by someone they know. Sixty-six percent of female victims and 41% of male victims of stalking are stalked by a current or former intimate partner. Stalking occurs most frequently after an abusive relationship ends, but it also can occur between friends, acquaintances, dating partners, or strangers. Stalking behaviors include any persistent, unwanted contact such as phone calls; text or e-mail harassment; persistent following; Facebook, Twitter, or Instagram posts; destroying property; and receiving unwanted gifts.

Some behaviors may be normal under certain circumstances, such as calling someone repeatedly after a relationship is over to "talk things out." However, stalking occurs when one person feels threatened or fearful due to unwanted contact. It is important to trust your instincts if you are uncomfortable with the repeated contacts attempts or behaviors of another person. Never assume someone is harmless or that you are overreacting.

If someone is stalking you:

- Contact the police.
- Document every incident of contact and record dates, times, locations and witnesses to each incident including phone calls, emails, notes, and visual sightings.
- Vary your schedule and the routes you take to class and/or work.
- Save all evidence including voicemails, emails, letters, and gifts.
- Tell your friends, neighbors, resident mentor, coworkers, or anyone else you see on a regular basis.
- Have roommates and coworkers screen your phone calls.
- Block the person from your social media pages.
- Never post personal information such as your address or location.

Relationship Violence

As many as one third of high school and college students experience violence in an intimate or dating relationship (Davis, 2008). Relationship violence has extreme consequences including physical and sexual abuse, long-lasting emotional trauma, diminished self-esteem, fear, and even death.

Relationship violence includes:

- Physical abuse
- Sexual abuse
- Emotional abuse
- Psychological abuse

If you or someone you know feels threatened by a current or former partner, it is best to have a safety plan in place. Leaving an unhealthy or violent situation can be a very precarious time and the safety of the threatened individual is important.

During an explosive incident:

- Call 911 for emergency assistance.
- If an argument is unavoidable, try to position yourself where you can easily get away. Avoid areas where weapons maybe available. Know the locations of all exits.
- Identify a friend, roommate, or other person with whom you have established a code word that alerts them to call for help in a potentially harmful situation.
- Familiarize yourself with the locations of the emergency blue light stations on campus.
- Contact SAVIP at 803 777-8248 to assist you with seeking emergency "alternative housing."

As a bystander during an explosive incident:

- Call 911.
- Distract the partners.
- Gather a group to assist in intervening.
- If you feel safe enough, directly intervene and take one partner away from the incident.

Standing Up to Interpersonal Violence

You can help prevent interpersonal violence in many ways at USC. In addition to being on the lookout for harmful situations, you can help generate awareness of issues and become an accountable bystander to help foster the expansion of our campus culture that doesn't accept violence or harassment. Sexual Assault and Violence Intervention & Prevention, a department within Student Health Services, offers students, faculty, and staff resources to overcome and prevent interpersonal violence. In addition to offering advocacy, support and crisis intervention services 24/7 for survivors, it offers the campus community these programs.

Stand Up Carolina

Offering resources to help people identify and safely intervene in potentially harmful situations, Stand Up Carolina is a campus-wide movement that empowers and encourages people to become accountable bystanders. An accountable bystander can be a peer, friend, teammate, classmate, coworker, teacher, family member, or even a complete stranger who observes harmful actions being committed and does something about it. These harmful situations can include sexual harassment, sexual assault, fighting, bullying, intimidation or coercion. If you witness one of these situations, you can intervene by simply asking someone if they are okay, offering to drive or walk someone home, or even calling the police if you suspect something is not quite right. You can learn all about Stand Up Carolina and how you can safely intervene at www.sa.sc.edu/shs/savip/stand-up.

Men's Groups

True Strength is an organization formed by SAVIP that invites men to become actively engaged in ending interpersonal violence. Members discuss personal experiences, develop strategies to keep the women and girls in their lives safe, and actively speak out against behaviors and attitudes that perpetuate interpersonal violence.

GRIT (Gentlemen Representing Interacting & Trusting) is an organization comprised of male students at USC dedicated to ending interpersonal violence. They educate the campus community about interpersonal violence, teaching men to make a difference.

Consent

USC's parameters of consent indicate that both people are:

- equally free to act
- fully conscious
- positive and sincere in their desires
- clear about their intent

ON THE WEB

For more information about Stand Up Carolina, find them on:

 **facebook.com/USCStandUp**

 **@StandUpSAVIP**

 **standup-carolina.blogspot.com**

 **@standupcarolina**

UofSC Stand Up Carolina

Check yourself

Personal Relationship Quiz

Answer the following questions about your current partner or past relationships.

1 = Never   2 = Sometimes   3 = Often

Does your partner:

1.	Criticize you for your appearance (weight, dress, hair, etc.)?	1	2	3
2.	Embarrass you in front of others by putting you down?	1	2	3
3.	Blame you or others for his or her mistakes?	1	2	3
4.	Curse at you, say mean things, or mock you?	1	2	3
5.	Demonstrate uncontrollable anger?	1	2	3
6.	Criticize your friends, family or others who are close to you?	1	2	3
7.	Threaten to leave you if you don't behave in a certain way?	1	2	3
8.	Manipulate you to prevent you from spending time with friends or family?	1	2	3
9.	Express jealousy, distrust, and anger when you spend time with other people?	1	2	3
10.	Tell you that you are crazy, irrational, or paranoid?	1	2	3
11.	Call you names to make you lose confidence in yourself?	1	2	3
12.	Make all the significant decisions in your relationship?	1	2	3
13.	Intimidate or threaten you, making you fearful or anxious?	1	2	3
14.	Make threats to harm others you care about?	1	2	3
15.	Prevent you from going out by taking your car keys?	1	2	3
16.	Control your telephone calls, listen in on your messages, or read your email?	1	2	3
17.	Punch, hit, slap, or kick you?	1	2	3
18.	Gossip about you to turn others against you or make them think bad things about you?	1	2	3
19.	Make you feel guilty about something?	1	2	3
20.	Use money or possessions to control you?	1	2	3
21.	Force you to have sex or perform sexual acts that make you uncomfortable?	1	2	3
22.	Threaten to kill himself or herself if you leave?	1	2	3
23.	Control your money and make you ask for what you need?	1	2	3
24.	Set many rules that you must abide by?	1	2	3
25.	Follow you, call to check on you, or demonstrate a constant obsession with what you are doing?	1	2	3

Scoring:

Now look at your responses to the above questions. If you answered "sometimes" to one or more of these questions, you may be at risk for emotional or physical abuse. If you answered "often," to any question, you may need to talk with someone about immediate threats to your emotional or physical health.

Source: Donatelle, R. J. (2006). Access to health (9th ed). San Francisco: Benjamin Cummings.

Safety

The University of South Carolina campus is a community, and as in any community, crime happens; the University is not immune to its effects. The majority of crimes that occur on campus are crimes against property. Use the components of the formula C=O/D (Crime equals Opportunity over Desire) when taking precautions to guard your personal property and safety. You have no control over someone's desire to commit a crime, but you certainly can take steps to reduce the opportunity. University officials have taken many proactive measures to minimize the occurrence of criminal activity on campus, but we all share responsibility for our safety and the safety of others in our community. Heed the following advice to help minimize your chances of becoming a victim of crime.

Protecting Yourself

Avoid jogging or walking alone at night or during the early morning hours. During evening hours, always walk with a group or with at least one other person in well-lit areas. Avoid alleys, short cuts, and vacant lots. Walk quickly with confidence and purpose. Use the University shuttle service. Make use of campus escort services, and if you are returning late from Five Points, make use of the taxi stands. Taking a taxi back to campus is inexpensive and much safer than walking.

Be aware of your surroundings, particularly when traveling or shopping in an unfamiliar place. Remember where you parked your car. Change direction or cross the street if you feel that you are being followed. Keep in mind that talking on your cell phone or listening to music can limit your awareness of your surroundings.

Report suspicious people or incidents to the appropriate authority (e.g., your resident mentor, campus police, and municipal police). Do not be afraid to call. If you sense something may be wrong, let someone know. Most calls can be placed anonymously.

Be alert when approached by a stranger. Avoid carrying large sums of cash or wearing excessive jewelry. Walk in well-lit and populated areas. Locate a building or safe area to run to in the event of a suspicious person approaching you. Look for a way to escape. If you are attacked, try to stay calm and do what is in your ability to protect yourself. Get a good look at your attacker, so you can give an accurate description to the police.

Be aware of the amount of information that you share on the Internet. change to Websites and blogs as well as online social communities (e.g., Facebook, Twitter) provide an easy, alluring and efficient means to express yourself and meet people. However, providing too much information (e.g., your room number, class schedule, home address or phone number) makes it easy for predators to find you on campus, in the residence hall, or even at home.

Campus Safety Tips

- Secure your belongings and do not leave them unattended.
- Do not display cash openly, especially if leaving an ATM at night.
- If you are followed, find a well-lit area where there are other people around.
- Read body language and pay attention to clues that indicate things are not right.
- Take a self-defense class. Women can register for an on-campus class at: http://www.sa.sc.edu/shs/savip/self-defense/.
- Put important emergency numbers in your cell phone.
- Avoid being alone with people you do not know well.
- Leave notes for a roommate or friend about where you are going and what time you will be back.
- If you do not know someone, do not let him or her walk you home, especially if you have just met the person.
- Never approach an unfamiliar vehicle to answer a stranger's questions.
- Never give your phone number or address to a stranger.

 For more info on Campus Safety

Locate emergency call boxes around campus. These emergency call boxes were installed through the efforts of Student Government and the University Safety Committee. The call boxes provide community members with a means of instant communication with the University police department. Pushing the call button activates the system. The campus police desk officer knows instantly the location of the box and will dispatch officers to the scene. Additionally, the box provides for two-way communication between the individual and the police. These boxes are for EMERGENCY use only.

shuttle cock

The Evening Shuttle consists of two vans running from 5:30pm to 12:30am, Mon-Fri, when classes are in session.

Stops are at the Coliseum, Russell House, Nursing, BA/Capstone, Maxcy, Byrnes Center, CLS/Honors Res. Hall, Swearingen, Academic Enrichment Center, the Roost, Bates, the PE Center/South & East Quad area, and the Greek Village. A white strobe light and a color scheme related to the Carolina Shuttle System will identify the Evening Shuttle.

Students, Faculty, and Staff can wait inside residence halls or academic college lobbies and see the shuttle from a secure area.

The Late Night Shuttle operates from 12:30 am to 6:30 am, Mon-Fri, when classes are in session.

The shuttle is stationed at the Russell House, and will pick up riders at their location and deliver them to any campus destination. Its white strobe light and color scheme related to the Carolina Shuttle System makes the shuttle easily recognizable. It can be dispatched by calling 777-3351. Students, Faculty, and Staff can wait inside their secure area until the shuttle arrives.

APO Escort service is sponsored by the Iota Mu Chapter of Alpha Phi Omega National Service Fraternity.

As a service to the University community, APO provides escort transportation anywhere on campus. APO helps make night travel safer by operating a van which picks up and drops off people during the late night hours. All students, faculty, and staff are encouraged to take advantage of this free service.

This service is available from Sunday through Thursday, 8pm to12am, when classes are in session. To arrange a pickup, just call 777-DUCK (3825). On occasions when APO is not available, please call 777-3351.

Visit the Vehicle Management & Parking Services (VMPS) website www.sc.edu/vmps/shuttle.html for more details about these services.

Protecting Your Property

Protecting Your Books

Book theft continues to be a serious problem on college and university campuses. Individuals who steal textbooks generally do so for the primary purpose of converting them into ready cash at the local campus bookstore. Take a few easy steps to minimize opportunity.

Never leave your books unattended. Once you purchase your books and are certain that they are the correct books for your courses, write your name in each book along with an additional identifying characteristic only you know. Do this in a couple of places within the book. Should your books be lost or stolen and turn up at the local bookstore, you then can identify them as yours. Remember all new books for a particular course look the same. By placing your name and an additional identifying characteristic somewhere in the book, you personalize the item in a manner that will assist, if necessary, with future identification.

Protecting Your Bicycle

Many University students choose to avoid the parking crunch and use alternate forms of transportation. One popular alternative is the bicycle. It is important to take steps to secure your bike with an adequate locking device manufactured specifically for the security of bicycles.

A U-lock type bicycle lock is recommended to properly secure your bicycle. Registration is required for all bicycles on campus and is provided free to all students. Parking Services will assist you with this process. You will be provided with a decal as well as the opportunity to engrave a personal mark somewhere on your bicycle. This office will also help you locate your bicycle serial number and provide you with a card so you can maintain a record of this information. Moped registration is also required. Contact VPMS at 803-777-5160 for more information or visit their website at www.sc.edu/vmps/

Did you know?

To register your bicycles please visit http://www.sc.edu/vmps/bike.html, the University Parking Service office, or the University Division of Law Enforcement and Safety.

Protecting Your Residence Hall Room and Personal Items

Many students live on campus, particularly during their first year. If you are one of these students, take time to become familiar with security policies and procedures that pertain to your particular residence hall. Remember to get in the habit of locking your room (a practice that you probably did not follow while living at home) even if you are going down the hall for a few minutes. It takes less than a minute to remove items from an unlocked room. If you see suspicious activity in or around your

ON THE WEB

To access the Project ID database and register your property, follow the steps below:

1. Visit: **webapps.csg.sc.edu/lespips/**
2. Log in with your USC network username and password
3. Complete the form with all of your personal information and submit
4. At this point you will return to the log in screen; log in again
5. Clink the link for "My Personal Property"
6. Select "Add New" to register any of your personal belongings

Chapter 8: Making Healthy Decisions

CONSIDER THIS

Are you engaged in the process of social wellness?
How often do you plan time to be with family and friends?

_____
_____
_____

Are you enjoying the time you spend with others?

_____
_____
_____

What are you doing to ensure your relationships with others are positive and rewarding?

_____
_____
_____

In what ways do you explore diversity by interacting with people of other cultures, backgrounds, and beliefs?

_____
_____
_____

What steps are you taking to ensure your personal safety?

_____
_____
_____

---

residence hall, report it to your resident mentor or the campus police. Reduce your risk of theft of laptops and other personal items by purchasing STOP security tags from the information desk at Russell House. These tags contain a unique bar code, making your item personally identifiable and are attached with adhesive that makes the tag virtually impossible to remove if stolen. Underneath the tag is a stolen property tattoo that cannot be removed without defacing the item.

Take Part in Project ID

An excellent way to reduce the opportunity for theft is to take the time to mark your valuables. One method to do this on campus is to participate in the University Project ID program, which was developed through a joint effort between the University Police Department and the Residence Hall Association. This program is designed to discourage theft of personal property from your residence hall. You will be provided with the necessary tools to engrave your stereos, refrigerators, television sets, and other items of value. You also will be given a coded number to engrave on your property that will aid in its identification and recovery if stolen. Remember, some people will steal anything, so it is best to take a proactive approach and work toward reducing their opportunity to do so. The property is then registered with the USC Police Department and stored on a database in the event the item is stolen. Visit http://www.les.sc.edu/CPCR/property.asp for more details.

Emotional Wellness

Emotional wellness is striving to meet emotional needs constructively, responding resiliently to emotional states and the flow of life events. It requires you to *deal* with a variety of situations realistically, and *learn* how your behaviors, thoughts, and feelings affect one another and your decisions. The ability to acknowledge and share feelings of anger, fear, sadness or stress as well as hope, love, joy and happiness in a productive manner contributes to emotional wellness. An emotionally well person is self-aware and self-accepting, while continuing to develop as a person.

Stress

During your first year of college you may experience levels of stress that are well beyond what you have dealt with in the past. This increased level of stress could be directly related to your increased level of responsibility. This may be the first time in your life you are solely responsible for your academic decisions (e.g., what classes to take, what time to take classes, whether to attend class), health-related decisions (e.g., what to eat, when to exercise) as well as financial and personal decisions. All of these added responsibilities can make life rather hectic, so equipping yourself with good time management skills is extremely important.

There are two main types of stress: eustress and distress. *Eustress* refers to the positive events in our life that produce stress, such as going off to college or getting married. Even though the event is positive, it causes physical stress to our bodies. *Distress* refers to negative stress and encompasses negative events such as financial troubles or a death in the family.

Individuals that have high levels of stress for long periods of time are more likely to have problems with high blood pressure, excess weight gain, heart disease, and other physical disorders. To better manage your stress, you must first recognize your stressors (i.e., things that cause you stress) and learn to manage the stress. The Student Stress Scale located at the end of the chapter will help you identify the various life events that may be currently causing you stress. On the next two pages you will find some of the top strategies for managing and responding to stress. The challenge lies in recognizing when you need to use them and having the ability to actually do so in spite of your stress.

There are many departments on campus that offer services and programs for stress management. Which service do you think you would find most beneficial?

Did you know?

According to the National College Health Assessment (2013) conducted with Carolina students *stress* was the main reason why students did not perform as well as they had hoped in their classes.

CONSIDER THIS

What are the majors stressors (e.g., classes, work, relationships) in your life?

What do you do to relieve stress?

Common Physical and Emotional Signs of Distress

- Headache
- Dry mouth
- Cough
- Muscle tension or pain
- Hypertension or chest pain
- Loss of appetite
- Heartburn or indigestion
- Insomnia
- Depression
- Fatigue
- Suicidal thoughts
- Agitation
- Difficulty making decisions
- Relationship problems
- Negative feelings about yourself

TOP 10 STRATEGIES SUCCESSFUL PEOPLE EMPLOY WHEN EXPERIENCING STRESS

1 THEY APPRECIATE WHAT THEY HAVE

Taking time to contemplate what you're grateful for actually improves your mood. Reflection on what you are thankful for reduces the stress hormone cortisol by 23%. Research conducted at the University of California, Davis found that people who worked daily to cultivate an attitude of gratitude experienced improved mood, energy, and physical well-being.

2 THEY AVOID ASKING "WHAT IF?"

"What if?" statements only add to a pile of stress and worry. Things can go in a million different directions, and the more time you spend worrying about the possibilities, the less time you'll spend focusing on taking action that will calm you down and keep your stress under control. Calm people know that asking "what if?" will only take them to a place they don't want—or need—to go.

3 THEY STAY POSITIVE

Positive thoughts help make stress intermittent by focusing your brain's attention onto something that is completely stress-free. Think about your day and identify one positive thing that happened, no matter how small. If you can't think of something from the current day, reflect on the previous day or even the previous week. Or perhaps you're looking forward to an exciting event that you can focus your attention on. The point here is that you must have something positive that you're ready to shift your attention to when your thoughts turn negative.

4 THEY DISCONNECT

Technology enables constant communication and the expectation that you should be available 24/7. Given the importance of keeping stress intermittent, it's easy to see how taking regular time off the grid can help keep your stress under control. Forcing yourself offline and even—gulp!—turning off your phone gives your body a break from a constant source of stress.

5 THEY LIMIT THEIR CAFFEINE INTAKE

Drinking caffeine triggers the release of adrenaline. Adrenaline is the source of the "fight-or-flight" response. The fight-or-flight mechanism sidesteps rational thinking in favor of a faster response. When caffeine puts your brain and body into this hyper aroused state of stress, your emotions overrun your behavior. The stress that caffeine creates is far from intermittent, as its long half-life ensures that it takes its sweet time working its way out of your body.

6 THEY SLEEP

Not enough can be said about the importance of sleep to increasing your emotional intelligence and managing your stress levels. When you sleep, your brain literally recharges, shuffling through the day's memories and storing or discarding them (which causes dreams), so that you wake up alert and clear-headed. Your self-control, attention, and memory are all reduced when you don't get enough—or the right kind—of sleep. Sleep deprivation raises stress hormone levels on its own, even without a stressor present. Stressful projects often make you feel as if you have no time to sleep, but taking the time to get a decent night's sleep is key to helping to get things under control.

7 THEY SQUASH NEGATIVE SELF-TALK

A big step in managing stress involves stopping negative self-talk in its tracks. The more you focus on negative thoughts, the more power you give them. Most of our negative thoughts are just thoughts, not facts. You can bet that your statements are not true any time you use words like "never," "worst," "ever," etc. When you find yourself believing the negative and pessimistic things, your inner voice says, stop what you're doing and write down what you're thinking. Once you've taken a moment to slow down the negative momentum of your thoughts, you will be more rational and clear-headed in evaluating their authenticity. Identifying and labeling your thoughts as thoughts by separating them from the facts will help you escape the cycle of negativity and move toward a positive new outlook.

8 THEY REFRAME THEIR PERSPECTIVE

Stress and worry are fueled by our own skewed perception of events. You cannot control your circumstances, but you can control how you respond to them. So before you spend too much time dwelling on something, take a minute to put the situation in perspective. A great way to correct this unproductive thought pattern is to list the specific things that actually are going wrong or not working out. Most likely you will come up with just some things—not everything—and the scope of these stressors will look much more limited than it initially appeared.

9 THEY BREATHE

The easiest way to make stress intermittent lies in something that you have to do every day anyway: breathing. When you're feeling stressed, take a couple of minutes to focus on your breathing. Close the door, put away all other distractions, and just sit in a chair and breathe. The goal is to spend the entire time focused only on your breathing, which will prevent your mind from wandering. Think about how it feels to breathe in and out. If staying focused on your breathing proves to be a real struggle, try counting each breath in and out until you get to 20, and then start again from 1. You will be surprised by how calm you feel afterward and how much easier it is to let go of distracting thoughts that otherwise seem to have lodged permanently inside your brain.

10 THEY USE THEIR SUPPORT SYSTEM

It's tempting to attempt tackling everything by yourself. To be calm and productive, you need to recognize your weaknesses and ask for help when you need it. This means tapping into your support system when a situation is challenging enough for you to feel overwhelmed. Everyone has someone who is on their team, rooting for them, and ready to help make the most of a difficult situation. Identify these individuals in your life and make an effort to seek their insight and assistance when you need it. Asking for help will alleviate your stress and strengthen your relationships with those you rely upon.

Reprinted with permission: "How Successful People Stay Calm" from Forbes.com, 2/6/2014 Retrieved 3/14/14. http://www.forbes.com/sites/travisbradberry/2014/02/06/how-successful-people-stay-calm/

Anxiety

Students report that anxiety is the number two factor negatively impacting their academic performance. Anxiety disorders are one of the most common disorders on college campuses, with 13% of Gamecocks reporting that they were diagnosed or treated for an anxiety disorder in 2013. It is important to be able to recognize what may be "common" worries versus an anxiety disorder.

Symptoms of anxiety include:

- Excessive anxiety and worry that occurs more days than not
- Difficulty controlling the worry
- Trouble making decisions or putting off decisions
- Feeling restless or "on edge"
- Difficulty concentrating or mind going blank
- Feeling tired or fatigued
- Frequent irritability
- Muscle tension
- Difficulty falling or staying asleep, or unsatisfying, restless sleep
- Experiencing moments of sudden terror or fright which can feel paralyzing
- Having frequent thoughts of bad things happening that are unwarranted or baseless
- Removing oneself from situations or engaging minimally due to worries/fears

Anxiety disorders are often treated with therapy (both individual and group), medication, mindfulness strategies, or a combination of these. Even though anxiety disorders are highly treatable, only about one-third of people suffering from an anxiety disorder receive treatment. If you think it is interfering with your daily living or you are not feeling like yourself, you probably would benefit from talking to a counselor.

Depression

Many people experience the first symptoms of depression during their college years. Unfortunately, college students who have depression are not often getting the help they need. They may not know where to go for help, or they may believe that treatment won't help. Others don't get help because they think their symptoms are just part of the typical stress of college, or they worry about being judged if they seek mental health care. Depression is a medical illness and treatments can be very effective. Early diagnosis and treatment of depression can relieve depression symptoms, prevent depression from returning, and help students succeed in college and after graduation. The University of South Carolina's Student Health Services, specifically the Counseling & Human Development Center (CHDC), offers mental health services to students. In 2013, the American College Health Association–National College Health Assessment (NCHA) of University of South Carolina students found 25% of students reported feeling "so depressed that it was difficult to function" at some time in the past year.

> **Did you know?**
> At least 48% of Carolina students reported feeling overwhelming anxiety in the course of a year. (ACHA 2013)

> **Did you know?**
> CHDC offers much more than individual, couples, and group therapy services. Other services include mindfulness, guided relaxation, biofeedback, "Let's Talk" sites, consultation services, and mental health screening. To find out more about the services, visit www.sa.sc.edu/shs/chdc.

The symptoms of depression vary. If you are depressed, you may feel:

- Sad
- Empty
- Hopeless
- Worthless
- Restless
- Anxious
- Helpless
- Guilty
- Irritable
- Tired

You may also experience one or more of the following:

- Loss of interest in activities you used to enjoy
- Aches, pains, headaches, cramps, or digestive problems that do not go away
- Lack of energy
- Loss of appetite or eating too much
- Problems concentrating, remembering information, or making decisions
- Problems falling sleep, staying asleep, or sleeping too much

As you can see, these symptoms can significantly impact your academics, social life, dating relationships, physical health, or daily functioning.

Suicidal Ideation

Suicide is the third leading cause of death for young adults ages 15 to 24 (CDC, 2014). Each year, caring students recognize and respond to signs of mental health issues and suicide risk by connecting students in crisis with the appropriate resources. Being there for your friends and peers could help save a life. Therefore, it is important to know the signs of a suicidal person, the resources, and how to respond.

The warning signs of suicide include:

- Ideation: Threatening to hurt or talking of wanting to hurt or kill him/herself
- Increased alcohol or drug use
- Expressing no reason for living or no sense of purpose in life
- Anxiety, agitation, inability to sleep or sleeping all the time
- Feeling trapped like there is no way out
- Hopelessness, feelings of despair
- Withdrawal from family, friends, and society
- Uncontrolled rage and anger
- Acting reckless or engaging in risky activities
- Dramatic mood swings

If you observe any of these warning signs, you can help by:

- Being actively involved in getting the person connected with treatment, assisting him or her in making an appointment or walking with them to the appointment if needed
- Talking to your friend about your concerns. Be direct, but gentle and non-judgmental
- Asking if they are thinking about suicide
- Listening and be available
- Offering support and hope
- Taking action, such as informing housing staff, parents, police or a university official

ON THE WEB

The CHDC offers suicide prevention training for students. Register at **sa.sc.edu/shs/chdc/training**

CONSIDER THIS

What is one thing you can do daily to help take care of your mental health?

What would you say to a friend who is struggling with depression or anxiety? How would you approach them?

Sleep Resources

If your sleep has been seriously disrupted for more than one month and is affecting your ability to function, contact the Counseling & Human Development Center at 803-777-5223. Staff can evaluate your sleep problems and help you find effective solutions that don't involve using medications. You can also make an appointment with a provider in the General Medicine Center at the Thomson Student Health Center to evaluate your condition and make recommendations: www.sc.edu/myhealthspace or 803-777-3175.

CONSIDER THIS

Are you engaged in the process of emotional wellness?
Are you able to maintain a balance of work, family, friends, and other obligations?

How are you reducing stress in your life?

How much sleep are you getting a night?

If a student is talking about suicide or is at immediate risk for harming themself, call 911, University Law Enforcement & Safety at 803-777-4215, or CHDC at 803-777-5223. You can also inform your resident mentor, housing staff, and file a Behavioral Intervention Team report at www.sc.edu/bit. Stay with the person until help arrives. Never ignore comments about suicide or be sworn to secrecy.

Sleep

Lack of sleep affects us mentally, physically and emotionally. A lack of sleep can lead to anxiety, depression, and academic difficulties. Poor sleep habits—also referred to as **poor sleep hygiene**—are among the most common health problems people report today.

According to the 2013 National College Health Assessment conducted at USC, sleep was ranked number three among the top health issues affecting academic performance. Approximately 50% of students reported daytime sleepiness three to five days a week and 16.9% of students reported sleep difficulties affect their academic success.

Sleep is essential to maintaining a healthy immune system. It also balances our appetites by regulating hormones that play a role in our feelings of hunger and fullness. Therefore, when you are sleep deprived, you may feel the need to eat more, which can lead to weight gain.

Healthy Sleep Habits

- **Stick to a sleep schedule.** Go to bed and wake up at the same time each day.
- **Exercise is great, but not too late in the day.** Try to exercise at least 30 minutes most days, but not later than two to three hours before your bedtime.
- **Avoid caffeine and nicotine.** Caffeine and nicotine are stimulants. Caffeine's effects can take as long as 8 hours to wear off fully. Nicotine often causes smokers to sleep very lightly.
- **Avoid alcoholic drinks before bed.** Consuming alcoholic beverages before sleep can rob you of deep sleep and REM sleep.
- **Avoid large meals and beverages late at night.** A light snack is okay.
- **Don't take naps after 3 p.m.** Naps can help make up for lost sleep, but late afternoon naps can make it harder to fall asleep at night.
- **Relax before bed.** Don't overschedule your day so that no time is left for unwinding.
- **Have a good sleeping environment.** Have a comfortable mattress and pillow, get rid of distractions such as noises, bright lights or warm temperatures and turn the clock's face out of view so you don't worry about the time while trying to fall asleep.
- **Don't lie in bed awake.** If you find yourself awake after staying in bed for more than 20 minutes, or if you are starting to feel anxious or worried, get up and do something relaxing until you feel sleepy.

Making Healthy Choices

In the Carolina Community...

#1

In 2010, stress was the number one academic impediment for Carolina students

73%

of Carolina students had one or zero sexual partners in the last academic year

FREE

Thursday through Sunday, Checker Yellow taxi cabs pick up from Five Points & return students home within a 5 mile radius

41%

of students experience peer pressure to drink or use drugs

11

free 1-on-1 sessions at the Counseling & Human Development Center

Students & Alcohol

1563 total reported alcohol violations in 2012-2013

Of those total reported alcohol violations

637 involved first-year students.

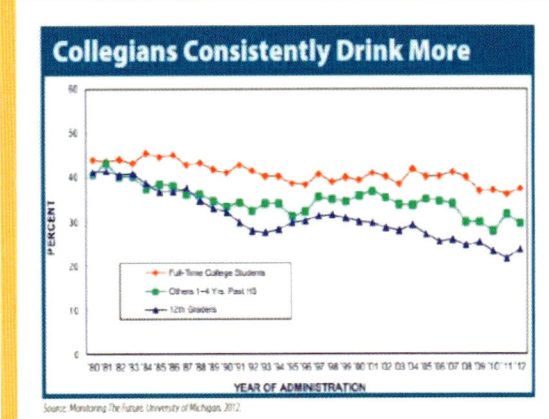

Nearly 1/4 of all Carolina students did not drink alcohol in the last 30 days

Data has shown that college students consistently drink more than their peers in the same age group and 12th graders

Chapter 8: Making Healthy Decisions

Did you know?

The Daily Gamecock has a puzzle in each edition! Great opportunity to exercise your brain!

1		2						
		3						
								4
	4			5				
	6			7				
						2		
	8							
					8			

http://commons.wikimedia.org/wiki/File:Oceans_SudokuDG11_Puzzle.svg

Consider This

Are you engaged in the process of intellectual wellness?
Are you open to new ideas?

What skills have you developed recently?

What new learning opportunities and stimulating mental activities have you participated in recently?

In what ways have you been able to use your creativity?

Intellectual Wellness

The fourth dimension of wellness is intellectual wellness. As a college student, you are being exposed to new ideas and information daily. Intellectual wellness involves having a curiosity and strong desire to learn. It is a lifelong process of creating and reflecting upon experiences and staying stimulated with new ideas. Your mind needs to be exercised just as your body does. In chapter 3, you were introduced to the importance of integrative learning and opportunities for growth through experiences inside and beyond the classroom. We also listed opportunities that would contribute to your overall intellectual area such as working with a faculty member to conduct research or serving as a leader in one of the may peer leadership programs on campus. Other ways to enhance this dimension of wellness include:

- **Teach someone.** By sharing what you have learned with others, you increase your brain function. Consider becoming a mentor, tutor, or supplemental instruction leader.

- **Exercise your brain.** Trying activities such as taking a new route to class, brushing your teeth using your non-dominant hand, or working on puzzles will stretch your mind. Remember, your brain needs exercise too!

- **Learn a foreign language.** Language uses many parts of the brain and learning a new one will help to form new connections.

- **Take time to read.** Keeping current on the news, reading a biography, non-fiction, poetry, or classic literature all promote cognitive growth.

- **Attend cultural events.** Consider going to museums, plays, concerts, and art galleries. You can also study abroad or take part in a domestic study away experience to immerse yourself in a new culture.

- **Take on a new creative pursuit.** Learn to play an instrument, paint, write poetry, or dance. Do what appeals to you, but do something different from what you have done in the past. This will stretch you and use different parts of your brain.

Spiritual Wellness

College is a time of transition, of exploring the boundaries between late adolescence and adulthood and learning to live independently. It's a time of exploration, decision-making and reinventing oneself. Often, students begin to ask themselves big questions such as "Who am I?" "What is my purpose?" "How do I fit in?" These questions are a natural part of becoming an adult and it's common for students to question what they've believed or thought as they are exposed to new people and ideas.

Students arrive at college with a set of values and beliefs that stem from their families. Meeting people from different parts of the country and world can open one's mind to different ways of being, believing and behaving. Sometimes these new experiences conflict with what we've known. Sometimes they cause us to re-think patterns of thought and behavior and bring about changes.

Many students have grown up in a community of faith with a structured set of worship rituals, beliefs, holidays and practices. Many have grown up with a less formal structure of worship, but with a strong connection to a higher power. Many, too, have grown up with a less formal structure of ritual and doctrine, but with a strong sense of purpose and connection to others. For all of these reasons and others, it is a normal and necessary part of human growth and development to question our purpose in life.

To find that purpose, many consider their spirituality, which can manifest in many ways. Some look to an organized community of faith. Others may find their connection to purpose through meditation, interacting with nature, solitary prayer, or devotional readings. No matter what your choice will be, know that spiritual wellness is just as important as all the other dimensions of wellness to one's overall wellbeing.

In order to thrive as students and as human beings, it's important to grapple with these big questions – and to seek guidance in ways that make sense to you. Ultimately, your decisions about how you explore and express your spirituality are up to you. Carolina offers many options for you to talk about, explore, and engage in spiritual practice.

CONSIDER THIS

Are your current spiritual or faith beliefs inherited or are they beliefs that you have carefully considered and claimed as your own?

How are you living an authentic life – are your attitudes and behaviors consistent with your deepest held values?

QUOTES TO PONDER

You are what you do, not what you say you'll do. - C.G. Jung (Psychologist)

Those who live for one another learn that love is the bond of perfect unity. - Fools Crow (Native American)

The wise man does not lay up his own treasures. The more he gives to others, the more he has for his own. - Lao Tzu

Generosity is the most natural outward expression of an inner attitude of compassion and loving-kindness. - Dalai Lama XIV

Thousands of candles can be lighted from a single candle, and the life of the candle will not be shortened. - Buddha

To be able to practice five things everywhere under heaven constitutes perfect virtue...[They are] gravity, generosity of soul, sincerity, earnestness, and kindness. -Confucius

CONSIDER THIS

Are you engaged in the process of spiritual wellness?
In what ways do you build in relaxation time during your day?

_____

Do you make time for meditation and/or prayer?

_____

How do your values guide your decisions and actions?

_____

In what ways are you accepting of the views of others?

_____

ON THE WEB

For a list of the Religious Organizations at Carolina visit:
sc.edu/sos/organizations.php

Did you know?

Ninety-one percent of people born between 1977-1997 expect to stay in a job for less than three years, according to the Future Workplace survey. This means they could have 15 – 20 jobs over the course of their working lives!

Values

Values are tightly connected to your spirituality. Values evolve and mature as people have new experiences. Individuals are capable of arriving at values through an intelligent process. For something to be an authentic value for you, it must meet the following test:

It has been chosen by you

- Freely
- From alternatives
- After thoughtful considerations of the consequences of each alternative

It is something you prize

- That you cherish and are happy with the choice
- That you are willing to affirm publicly

It is something that you act upon

- That you do something with (or as a result of) the choice
- Repeatedly in some life pattern

(Sources: Raths, Harmin, & Simon, 1966; Simon, Howe, & Kirschenbaum, 1972)

Becoming Engaged in Spiritual Wellness

Opportunities to practice mindfulness include:

- Finding a quiet space on campus (the Horseshoe has gardens and alcoves) and practice deep breathing surrounded by nature.
- Taking 5-10 deep breaths each hour you are awake throughout the day.
- Taking a warm shower or bath using scented soap.
- Admiring the trees, plants, flowers, and wildlife as you walk across campus.
- Noticing the faces of those you pass as you walk across campus.
- Pausing before eating to reflect and mindfully savor each bite.
- When you're on the phone, giving the person your undivided attention.
- Turning off social media at least an hour before bedtime and spending time writing in a journal, relaxing, meditating, or praying.

Occupational Wellness

Occupational wellness is arguably the most important wellness dimension. If you do not have the opportunity to do something that you regularly enjoy, the odds of having high wellbeing in the other dimensions diminishes rapidly. Occupational wellness is a balance between who you are called to be and what you are called to do. It is finding the place where your deep desires and gifts meet the needs of the community. A "vocationally well" person expresses his or her values through paid and volunteer activities that are personally rewarding and that make a contribution to the well-being of the community. Vocational wellness involves continually learning new skills and seeking challenges that lead to personal growth and a better world. Listening for and following your vocational following is a lifelong process.

According to Hettler (1976), occupational wellness follows these tenets:

It is better to choose a career which is consistent with our personal values, interests, and beliefs than to select one that is unrewarding to us.

It is better to develop functional, transferable skills through structured involvement opportunities than to remain inactive and uninvolved.

In chapter 6, you explored the four-step process for career decision making. The first step was taking time to develop self-awareness and understand who you are, which includes identifying your values and matching what you value with what your career goals are. As you work through your first semester at Carolina, take advantage of opportunities to help ensure you find your vocational calling. Be aware of pressures you may be experiencing in regards to a career such as choosing a major your parents want or because you think you will make a lot of money. You'll know when you're on the correct path for career wellness when your work and hobbies become exciting. People who have a high occupational wellness take more time to enjoy life, have better relationships, and do not take things for granted.

Environmental Wellness

Environmental wellness is an awareness of the precarious state of the earth and the effects of your daily habits on the physical environment. Environmental wellness involves maintaining a way of life that maximizes harmony with the earth and minimizes harm to the environment. It includes being involved in socially responsible activities to protect the environment. People very often understand and want to live on and in the earth in a manner that will

CONSIDER THIS

Are you engaged in the process of occupational wellness?
Have you job shadowed someone in a profession you are considering?

What research have you done on your future career?

Have you met with someone in the career center to discuss internships?

ON THE WEB

What is your ecological footprint?
To take the quiz, visit:
earthday.org/footprint-calculator

Did you know?

Green Quad was one of the first Leadership in Energy & Environmental Design (LEED) certified buildings in South Carolina and was the first certified residence hall in the Southeast.

Quick tips for energy and water savings

1. Swap your incandescent light bulbs for CFLs (compact fluorescent light bulbs). CLFs use 75% less energy and last 10 times longer.
2. Plug all appliances and electronics into a power strip and turn off the power strip whenever you leave your room.
3. Unplug your cell phone chargers when finished charging; they continue to draw electricity even if they're not plugged into your phone.
4. Take a shorter shower! Five minutes less will save up to 20 gallons of water.
5. Always turn off the faucet while brushing your teeth. This can help you save up to 5 gallons of water.

Consider This

Are you engaged in the process of environmental wellness?
Are you using resources in a way to allow future generations to also enjoy a comparable lifestyle?

_____

Do you recycle? How do you conserve energy in your residence hall?

_____

How are you involved and making change on campus?

_____

allow them to use the resources they need, but still leave sufficient resources for future generations. These concepts are at the center of sustainability and are encompassed in many of the daily experiences here on campus; from residential living to dining experiences, unique in and out of the classroom experiences, and access to USC community gardens.

Part of learning about the environment is the recognition that a "well environment" requires moral consideration from human beings. We all have a moral obligation to treat nature with respect and to protect the many benefits that nature offers. We depend on natural resources for so many fundamental things: energy, clean water, clean air, aesthetic pleasures, personal inspiration, and many other valuable gifts.

To deal with increasing pressures on our environmental resources, citizens and government are realizing the need for new technological and behavioral approaches for sustaining resources for future generations. Faculty and students engage in environmental research at Carolina to develop new mechanisms and innovations to meet our future energy needs, minimize our wastes and improve sustainability. Research and scholarship also provide new insights and approaches to environmental law and regulation and business strategies, while spatial studies and data analysis promote improved land use and resource planning.

It is up to all of us to accept and share the challenges of living sustainably with the opportunities of a well environment. Looking for ways to incorporate environmental ethics into the scope of your daily activities and your long-term goals should be an important focus.

The University offers an abundant variety of sources related to environmental issues. The more you learn about the environment, the more you can see that your wellness and environmental wellness are interconnected. It is up to you to find a way to integrate that knowledge into meaningful, ethically-based paths of action.

Conclusion

Wellness is a lifelong pursuit of continued growth and balance in the seven dimensions of wellness. Each dimension contributes to your own sense of wellness or quality of life, and each affects and overlaps the others. At times one may be more prominent than others, but neglect of any one dimension for any length of time has adverse effects on overall health. Utilize the vast resources at Carolina to continue your pursuit of a balanced life.

carolina recycling guide

Recycling will take only a few minutes but will have a profound impact on the environment.

MIXED PAPER

White and colored paper
Notebook paper
Magazines
Newspapers
Junk mail and envelopes
Post-it® Notes
Manila folders and paper binder dividers
Remove paper clips and tape if possible

NO: Paper towels, napkins, tissues, transparencies, cardboard, food

Did you know? One ton of recycled paper can save 17 trees.

CORRUGATED CARDBOARD

Flattened corrugated cardboard (thick with ridges and grooves) and flattened paperboard (ex: cereal box)
Stack next to recycling center

NO: Pizza boxes with food on them, waxy paperboard

Did you know? USC makes $100 per ton of recycled cardboard; we would have to pay to put it in a landfill.

BATTERIES

Dry cell battery collection stations are located in the lobby of your residence halls!
*except the Horseshoe Apartments

CFL COLLECTION

COMING SOON

Look out for CFL collection centers in residence hall lobbies!

ALUMINUM/PLASTIC

Aluminum cans and steel food cans
#1 – 7 plastic jugs and bottles
Clean aluminum foil
Please empty and rinse

NO: aerosol cans, plastic bags, plastic cups or tubs

Did you know? Recycling an aluminum can uses only 5% as much energy as it does to make one from raw materials.

GLASS

Clear and colored glass

Glass can only be recycled in the trash rooms of the West Quad, at the Green Quad Learning Center, and at outdoor multi-sort receptacles at Woodroow, Maxcy, and West Quad.

Did you know? Because it doesn't degrade during recycling, glass is considered infinitely recyclable.

FAQs About Recycling

What is a Waste Warrior?
Waste Warriors are multi-sort recycling stations that collect office paper, aluminum cans, plastic bottles, and newspaper. They are located around campus and in the lobbies of almost all residence halls.

Where can I recycle plastic grocery bags?
Plastic grocery bags are collected in the Green Quad Learning Center, and at many retail and grocery stores including Publix, Piggly Wiggly, and Target. They are also collected during our Give It Up event in the Spring Semester.

What else can I recycle?
Almost everything! You can donate many unwanted items to the Take It or Leave It program. Most carriers will collect used cell phones and batteries in their stores, or provide you with a postage label for shipping. Printer cartridges can be taken to stores like Best Buy, Kinkos FedEx, and Stapes. Staples also collects personal electronics like digital cameras, PDAs, and chargers. Ask your hall Sustainability Rep for more ideas!

Wellness Wheel Inventory

Read each statement below and check the box that most accurately describes you at this point in your life.	Seldom or never 1	Sometimes 2	Usually or often 3	Always 4	Totals
I engage in physical activity at least three times per week.					
I eat a healthy, well balanced diet.					
I avoid tobacco, drugs, and excessive alcohol consumption.					
I seek appropriate medical care when necessary.					
I eat five servings of fresh fruits and vegetables each day.					
I avoid eating foods high in simple sugars, salts, and fat.					
Physical Wellness Total	+	+	+		=
I have healthy, supportive friendship and family relationships.					
I communicate effectively with friends, family, and coworkers.					
When I have a conflict with another person, I try to resolve it in an honest, assertive manner.					
I respect lifestyles and cultures different than my own.					
It is important to me to contribute to the well-being of others in my family and social network.					
I can say No to someone without feeling guilty.					
Social Wellness Total	+	+	+		=
I am aware of a wide range of feelings in myself.					
I recognize my personal limitations and accept help when necessary.					
I have the skills to cope with daily challenges and stressors.					
I feel positive about myself and my life.					
I am autonomous but able to create meaningful and satisfying relationships with others.					
I avoid people who are "down" all the time and who bring those around them down.					
Emotional Wellness Total	+	+	+		=
I challenge myself mentally with stimulating ideas and activities on a regular basis.					
I am able to solve problems and think independently.					
I have the opportunity to learn new concepts in my personal or professional life.					
I pursue interests that are important to me.					
I enjoy spending time learning new things.					
I take time to read for enjoyment and relaxation.					
Intellectual Wellness Total	+	+	+		=
My actions align with my personal values and beliefs.					
I feel a sense of inner peace and strength.					
I feel my life has purpose and meaning.					
I have faith in something greater than myself.					
I look for and work towards balance.					
Morals, ethics, and principles guide my actions.					
Spiritual Wellness Total	+	+	+		=
I am satisfied with my work (e.g., volunteer, part-time).					
I am satisfied with my current major.					
I am comfortable with my current professional goals.					
I am able to contribute unique talents and skills to my work.					
My major and studies align with my needs and strengths.					
I feel comfortable making short- and long-term goals.					
Occupational Wellness Total	+	+	+		=
I try and reduce the amount of pollution I generate.					
I regularly reuse containers, bags and batteries when possible.					
I recycle paper, glass, aluminum and plastic.					
If I see a safety hazard, I take the steps to fix the problem.[3]					
I am aware of my surroundings at all times.[3]					
I am involved in socially responsible activities to protect the environment.[3]					
Environmental Wellness Total	+	+	+		=

Check yourself

Personal Wellness Wheel

After you have completed your inventory, take a moment to color in your wheel. Use your score from each Wellness Total to shade in the corresponding portion of your Personal Wellness Wheel.

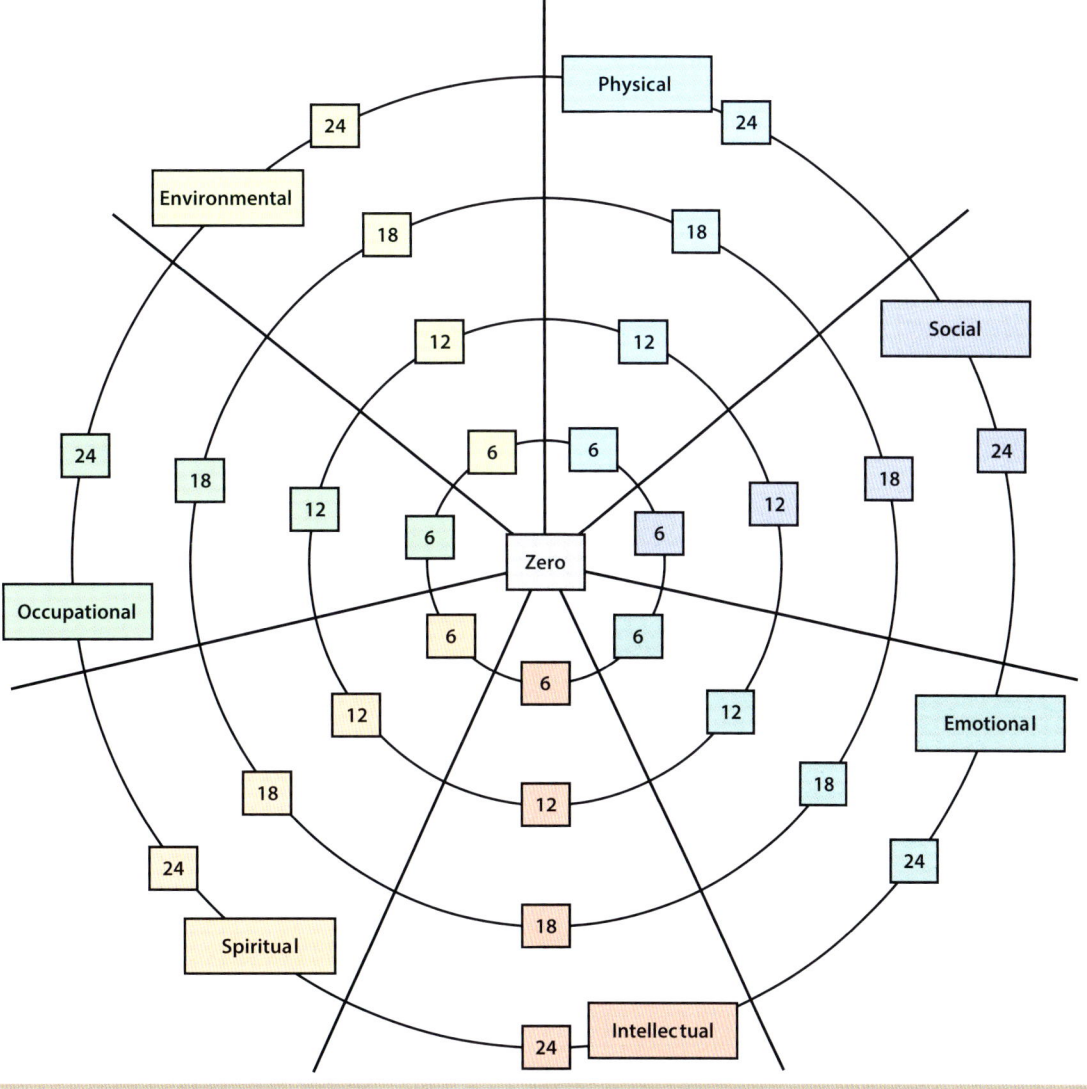

Wellness Wheel Processing Questions

Read and answer the questions below after completing your personal Wellness Wheel.

In which dimensions of life are you most well?

In which dimensions are you least well?

Comment on the pattern you see in your inventory. Is your wheel round (would it roll)?

How do you feel about what you see?

What improvements, if any, would you like to see in your wheel profile?

List two or three immediate steps you could take to make these improvements and make your wheel more round.

Chapter 8: Making Healthy Decisions

The Seven Dimensions of Wellness

Category	Components
PHYSICAL: promotes increased knowledge for achieving healthy lifestyle habits and encourages participation in activities contributing to high-level wellness	• Fitness • Nutrition and weight control • Healthy lifestyle habits • Health screenings • Appropriate use of the medical system
SOCIAL: emphasizes the creation and maintenance of healthy relationships and encourages positive contributions to the welfare of the community	• Respect for self and others • Interaction with others and environment • Creation and maintenance of relationships • Improvement of self-concept
EMOTIONAL: involves the capacity to manage feelings and behaviors and accept yourself unconditionally	• Express and recognize feelings • Control stress • Solve problems • Manage success and failure • Recognize self worth and personal expectations
INTELLECTUAL: encourages individuals to expand their knowledge and skill base through a variety of resources and cultural activities.	• Engage in lifetime learning • Use your mind • Learn and think creatively • Explore new areas
SPIRITUAL: the process of seeking meaning and purpose in human existence	• Discovering meaning and purpose in life • Determining/exploring morals, values and ethics • Self-determined, not always religiously based • Seeking feelings of love, hope, abundance
OCCUPATIONAL: the process of setting and achieving personal and occupational interests and goals through meaningful activities	• Recognize abilities • Identify personal mission and goals • Learn new skills, develop new interests
ENVIRONMENTAL: involves maintaining a way of life that maximizes harmony with the Earth and minimizes harm to the environment. It includes being involved in socially responsible activities to protect the environment	• Reduce the amount of pollution you generate • Reuse containers, bags and batteries • Awareness of one's surroundings at all times • Recycling paper, glass, aluminum and plastic • Participation in socially responsible activities to protect the environment

This bulleted outline of the dimensions was developed by Jan Montague, Montague, Eippert & Associates.

Check yourself

How do you personally address each dimension of your health?

Dimension	Existing Efforts	Ideas for Change	Immediate Action Step
PHYSICAL			
SOCIAL			
EMOTIONAL			
INTELLECTUAL			
SPIRITUAL			
OCCUPATIONAL			
ENVIRONMENTAL			

Check yourself

The Student Stress Scale

For each event that occurred in your life within the past year, record the corresponding score. If an event occurred more than once, multiply the score for that event by the number of times the event occurred, and record that score. Total all the scores.

Life Event	Value	x Occurrence	= Score
Death of a close family member	100	x	=
Death of a close friend	73	x	=
Divorce of parents	65	x	=
Jail term	63	x	=
Major personal injury or illness	63	x	=
Marriage	58	x	=
Getting fired from a job	50	x	=
Failing an important course	47	x	=
Change in the health of a family member	45	x	=
Pregnancy	45	x	=
Sex problems	44	x	=
Serious argument with a close friend	40	x	=
Change in financial status	39	x	=
Change of academic major	39	x	=
Trouble with parents	39	x	=
New girlfriend or boyfriend	37	x	=
Increase in workload at school	37	x	=
Outstanding personal achievement	36	x	=
First quarter/semester in college	36	x	=
Change in living conditions	31	x	=
Serious argument with an instructor	30	x	=
Getting lower grades than expected	29	x	=
Change in sleeping habits	29	x	=
Change in social activities	29	x	=
Change in eating habits	28	x	=
Chronic car trouble	26	x	=
Change in number of family get-togethers	26	x	=
Too many missed classes	25	x	=
Changing colleges	24	x	=
Dropping more than one class	23	x	=
Minor traffic violations	20	x	=
		Total Stress Score	=

Score Interpretation: The SSS represents an adaptation of Holmes and Rahe's SRRS. Each event is given a score that represents the amount of readjustment a person has to make in life as a result of the change. People with scores of 300 and higher have a high health risk.
People scoring between 150 and 300 points have about a 50-50 chance of serious health change within two years.
People scoring below 150 have a 1 in 3 chance of serious health change.

Source: Mullen, K., & Costellow, G. (1981). Health awareness through discovery. Minneapolis, MN: Burgess Publishing Company.

SCENARIOS FROM COLLEGE LIFE

A Roommate with a Secret

Catherine, a student from Ohio, was thrilled to be attending the University of South Carolina and anxious to start her new adventures at Carolina. She connected with her roommate, Jeni, on Facebook over the summer and was excited to meet her on move-in day. Catherine knew that she and Jeni would have a lot in common because both she and Jeni were from out of state and neither of them had any high school friends attending USC.

Catherine and Jeni got to know each other very well as the semester began. They were both from the north, which worked out great for them so they could get accustomed to the southern living styles together. They also both liked to party. They realized they had been matched perfectly and were a great pair.

Weeks went on and settling into their new home away from home was quite easy because Catherine and Jeni loved not having anyone to tell them what to do. They got along great and were pretty much inseparable. They spent their time in between classes together and they went out with each other quite frequently. The only problem Catherine found was that Jeni would never eat meals with her because she said she had already eaten. The first few weeks of this didn't really phase Catherine, and she didn't really think anything was wrong with the situation.

One day Catherine finally realized Jeni had a major problem. She heard Jeni violently coughing and realized that she was throwing up in one of the bathroom stalls. Jeni walked out wiping her mouth and went back into their room to grab her toothbrush. Catherine asked if she was alright, and Jeni just replied that she didn't feel well. The next few days Catherine paid closer attention to what Jeni was eating and also to the amount of time she spent in the bathroom after meals. She also started to become aware that Jeni would go to the gym for hours every day.

Catherine just didn't get it. She and Jeni had become close friends over the past few weeks and she didn't understand why she would ever want to keep anything from her. Jeni seemed like a completely normal and happy girl, doing things that most normal college students do like going out and going shopping. She didn't seem depressed or self-conscious about her appearance.

Catherine was concerned about her friend. She wondered if Jeni was felt pressured by all of the women who lived on their floor who were attractive. Jeni was already a pretty thin girl, and Catherine worried about her losing any weight. Catherine was sad about the situation and knew something drastic needed to be done, but she also didn't want to compromise their friendship by pressuring Jeni to talk about something that she obviously had worked hard to hide all this time.

Processing Questions:

What are the major problems in this scenario?

What options are there for Catherine in this scenario?

Are there resources available at the University for both Catherine and Jeni?

Have you been aware of an issue with a family member or friend that you were nervous to point out? How did you deal with this issue?

SCENARIOS FROM COLLEGE LIFE

A Night of Letting Loose

Kathy, a student from Northern Virginia, chose to attend Carolina because she had aspirations to be a doctor and was impressed with the university's academic reputation. Kathy was a very focused student, and was serious about her schoolwork. She didn't go out on weeknights and believed that her commitment to her academics would pay off in the long run.

The fall semester was almost over and the Friday night before finals her suitemates invited her to go to a party at a nearby house. All semester, Kathy tried to spend more time working on school than partying, but this particular Friday, Kathy was ready to have a good time. She thought that it would be good for her to stop stressing out so much and have a good time. She decided that she could return to her studying on Saturday.

Kathy and her suitemates, Allie and Heather, walked to the party from their residence hall. On the way the girls talked about the fun they expected to have that night and also agreed on a system for sticking together at the party. They all agreed that if one of the girls felt uncomfortable that they would all leave together, no matter how much fun they were having. They all turned their cell phones on so that they can get in touch with one another at the party if they got separated. Kathy tried to remember how they got to the party, in case she needed to find her own way home. Allie had the number for a cab and recommended they all program it into their phone. Kathy did even though she doesn't have any cash on her and didn't really want to go home without her friends.

As soon as the girls got to the party, Allie and Heather went straight for the keg. Kathy felt a little uncomfortable, because she hardly ever attended parties like this. Kathy wasn't sure what to do, so when a very cute senior came up to her and offered to get her a drink, she accepted happily. He came back with the drink and he took her to an empty couch and put his arm around her. He asked her questions about her first semester at school and seemed really interested in what she had to say. Kathy sipped on her drink hardly believing that this guy was paying so much attention to her. He told her how pretty she was and how much fun he was having talking to her. Kathy began to feel really drunk, even though she couldn't remember drinking very much. The boy told Kathy that she looked tired and offered to let her sleep over in his room.

Kathy felt dizzy but she knew this didn't seem right. She tried calling her friends but neither of them answered. Kathy tried not to seem worried and wanted to look for her friends but she didn't feel very well. She didn't know what to do. This boy seemed really nice and she couldn't find her friends but she didn't think she was ready to spend the night with a stranger. She knew that her friends were probably off having a great time and she didn't want to ruin their night, but she really wanted to go home. She didn't know anyone else at the party and didn't really know anyone on campus that she felt comfortable calling. The boy was trying to get her to stand up and walk to his room but Kathy wanted to stay out in the open space of the party. She was starting to feel sick and drowsy. She knew she couldn't call her parents, because they were in Virginia but Kathy really wanted to call someone she trusted. The boy was being very persuasive and pushy. Kathy's thinking was cloudy but she began to realize that she might be in trouble.

Processing Questions:

What precautions did Kathy make to ensure her safety at the party?

Were there things that Kathy could have done differently to further ensure her safety? What would you have done differently?

Kathy worried she would ruin her friends' nights if she asked to leave the party. Have you ever felt pressured to ignore your own feelings for the sake of others? What is one way you can work through this?

Who are the people you can trust to help you when you need it?

What is your responsibility as a friend or bystander?

RESOURCES

Alcohol & Drugs

Quit for Keeps Program . . . . (800) QUIT-NOW
    http://www.scdhec.gov/health/chcdp/
    tobacco/quitforkeeps.htm
Substance Abuse Prevention & Education (803) 777-5781
    Russell House
    http://www.sa.sc.edu/sape

General Wellness Resources on Campus

Allergy Clinic. . . . . (803) 777-7026
American Social Health Association . . . . (919) 361-8400
**Counseling & Human Development
    Center** . . . . (803) 777-5223
    Byrnes Building, 7th Floor
    http://www.sa.sc.edu/shs/chdc
Emergencies. 911
    General Medicine Center/Laboratory
    Radiology . . . . (803) 777-3175
Immunizations/Travel Clinic . . . . (803) 777-9511
Pharmacy. . . . . (803) 777-4890
STI Resource Center Hotline . . . . (800) 227-8922
    www.ashastd.org
Student Health Services
    Thomson Student Health Center
    http://www.sa.sc.edu/shs
Student Wellness Promotion . . . . (803) 576-9393
    Strom Thurmond Wellness & Fitness Center, 1st fl
    http://www.sa.sc.edu/shs/cwp/swp
Women's Care . . . . (803) 777-6816

Healthy Carolina

Healthy Carolina . . . . (803) 777-4752
    http://www.sc.edu/healthycarolina

Hospitals

Palmetto Baptist Medical Center . . . . . . (803) 296-5010
Palmetto Health Richland Hospital. . . . . (803) 434-6350

Physical Fitness & Nutrition

Carolina Dining. . . . . (803) 777-6339
    http://www.sc.edu/dining/main.html
Outdoor Recreation . . . . (803) 576-9397
    http://campusrec.sc.edu/orec
Registered Dietitian. . . . . (803) 777-3175
    Thomson Student Health Center
Solomon Blatt Physical Education Center (803) 777-5261
    http://campusrec.sc.edu/PEC
**Strom Thurmond Wellness & Fitness
    Center** . . . . (803) 576-9376
    http://campusrec.sc.edu/WFC
USDA Food Pyramid
    http://MyPyramid.gov

Safety & Transport

APO Escort Service . . . . (803) 777-DUCK(3825)
    Sunday-Thursday, 8 p.m. – midnight
Blue Ribbon Taxi Cab Corporation . . . . . (803) 754-8163
Checker Yellow Cab Company . . . . (803) 799-3311
Emergency. 911
Shuttlecock (Campus Shuttles) . . . . (803) 777-1080
    http://www.sc.edu/vmps/shuttle.html
Suicide Prevention Lifeline . . . . (800) 273-TALK
USC Police Department . . . . (803) 777-4215
Victim/Witness Coordinator . . . . (803) 777-7786

Sexual Assault & Violence Intervention Prevention (SAVIP)

**24-Hour Crisis Assistance
    (USC Police Department)**. . . . . (803) 777-4215
National Center for Victims of Crime . . . (202) 467-8700
National Sexual Violence Resource Center (877) 739-3895
Rape, Abuse & Incest National Network .(800) 656-HOPE
SC Victim Assistance Network . . . . (803) 750-1200
**Sexual Assault & Violence Intervention
    Prevention** . . . . (803) 777-8428
    Thomson Student Health Center
    http://www.sa.sc.edu/shs/shvp/
**Sexual Trauma Services of the
    Midlands Hotline** . . . . (803) 771-RAPE(7273)
    http://www.stsm.org/
Sister Care Crisis Line . . . . (803) 926-0505
    http://www.sistercare.com/index.html
**South Carolina Coalition Against Domestic
    Violence and Sexual Assault** . . . . . . (803) 256-2900

Stress Reduction

Biofeedback Appointments. . . . . (803) 777-5223
Massage Therapy Appointments . . . . . . (803) 576-9393

REFERENCES

American College Health Association (ACHA). (2013, spring). *National College Health Assessment (ACHA-NCHA) University of South Carolina reference group report.*

American Council for Drug Education. Facts for health professionals. Signs and symptoms of youth substance use and abuse. (n.d.) Retrieved from http://www.phoenixhouse.org/prevention/signs-and-symptoms-of-substance-abuse/

American Psychiatric Association. (2013). *Diagnostic and statistical manual of mental disorders* (5th ed.) Washington, DC: Author.

American Psychiatric Association. (2000). *Diagnostic and statistical manual of mental disorders* (4th ed.). Washington, DC: Author.

Anxiety Disorders Association of America. (2010-2013). *Understanding anxiety.* Retrieved from http://www.adaa.org/understanding-anxiety

American Association of Suicidology. (n.d.). *Know the warning signs.* Available online at: http://www.suicidology.org/stats-and-tools/suicide-warning-signs

Centers for Disease Control and Prevention. (2013). Incidence, prevalence, and cost of sexually transmitted infections in the United States: CDC fact sheet. Retrieved from http://www.cdc.gov/std/stats/STI-Estimates-Fact-Sheet-Feb-2013.pdf

Centers for Disease Control and Prevention. (2011a). Chlamydia-reported cases and rates by state, ranked by state, United States. Retrieved from http://www.cdc.gov/std/stats11/tables/2.htm.

Centers for Disease Control and Prevention. (2011b). Gonorrhea-reported cases and rates per 1,000 population, ranked by state, United States. Retrieved from http://www.cdc.gov/std/stats11/tables/2.htm.

Core Institute. (2011). *Core Alcohol and Drug Survey.* University of South Carolina, unpublished raw data.

Davis, Antoinette, MPH. 2008. Interpersonal and Physical Dating Violence among Teens. The National Council on Crime and Delinquency Focus. Available at http://www.nccdrc.org/nccd/pubs/Dating%20Violence%20Among%20Teens.pdf.

Deykin, E. Y., Levy, J. C., & Wells, V. (1987). Adolescent depression, alcohol, and drug abuse. *American Journal of Public Health, 77*(2), 178-182.

Donatelle, RJ. (2006). Access to health (9th ed) San Francisco: Benjamin Cummings.

Eisenberg, D., Golberstein, E., & Gollust, S. E. (2007, July). Help-seeking and access to mental health care in a university student population. *Med Care, 45*(7), 594–601. PubMed PMID: 17571007

Evert, Alison, MS, RD, CDE, Nutritionist, University of Washington Medical Center Diabetes Care Center, Seattle, Washington. Also reviewed by David Zieve, MD, MHA, Medical Director, A.D.A.M., Inc.

Garlow, S. J., Rosenberg, J., Moore, J.D., Haas, A.P., Koestner, B., Hendin, H., & Nemeroff, C.B. (2008). Depression, desperation, and suicidal ideation in college students: Results from the American Foundation for Suicide Prevention College Screening Project at Emory University. *Depress Anxiety, 25*(6), 482–488. PubMed PMID: 17559087

Healthy Carolina. (2013, spring). *Faculty and Staff Health Assessment.*

Smith, M., & Segal, J. (2013, April). Signs of abuse and abusive relationships. Retrieved from http://www.helpguide.org/mental/domestic_violence_abuse_types_signs_causes_effects.htm

Hettler, B. (1976). The six dimensions of wellness model. Retrieved from http://c.ymcdn.com/sites/www.nationalwellness.org/resource/resmgr/docs/sixdimensionsfactsheet.pdf

Higgins, J., Tuttle, T., & Higgins, C. (2010). Energy beverages: Content and safety. *Mayo Clinic Proceedings, 85*(11), 1033-1041.

Hysenbegasi, A., Hass, S. L., & Rowland, C.R. (2005, September). The impact of depression on the academic productivity of university students. *Journal of Mental Health Policy and Economics, 8*(3), 145-151.

Johnston, L. D., O'Malley, P. M., Bachman, J. G., and Schulenberg, J. E., (2013). Monitoring the Future national survey results on drug use, 1975–2012: Volume 2, College students and adults ages 19–50. Ann Arbor: Institute for Social Research, The University of Michigan.

Kentucky Higher Education Assistance Authority (KHEAA). (2011, April). *Protect yourself against identity theft.* Retrieved from http://www.kheaa.com/website/kheaa/pressroom?PDFPath=/pdf/press/ky042011mtcs.pdf

Meister, J. (2012, August 14). *Job hopping is the 'new normal' for Millennials: Three ways to prevent a human resource nightmare.* Retrieved from http://www.forbes.com/sites/jeannemeister/2012/08/14/job-hopping-is-the-new-normal-for-millennials-three-ways-to-prevent-a-human-resource-nightmare/2/

Min C., Noh, H., Kang, Y. S., Sim, H.J., Baik, H.W., Song, W.O., Yoon, J., Park, Y.H., & Joung, H. (2011). Skipping breakfast is associated with diet quality and metabolic syndrome risk factors of adults. *Nutrition Research in Practice, 5*(5), 455-463.

Montague, J., Piazza, W., Peters, K., Eippert, G., & Poggiali, T. (2002, March-April). The wellness solution. *The Journal on Active Aging,* 17-20. Retrieved from http://www.aahf.info/sec_news/section/pdf/thewellnesssolution2.pdf

Mullen, K. & Costellow, G. (1981). Health awareness through discovery. Minneapolis, MN: Burgess Publishing Company.

Musty, R. E., & Kaback, L. (1995). Relationship between motivation and depression in chronic marijuana users. *Life Science, 56*(23-24), 2151-2158.

National Institute of Mental Health (2013). *Depression and college students.* Available online at: http://www.nimh.nih.gov/health/publications/depression-and-college-students/index.shtml

Planned Parenthood. Birth Control Effectiveness Chart. (n.d.) Retrieved from http://www.plannedparenthood.org/health-topics/birth-control/birth-control-effectiveness-chart-22710.htm

Rape Abuse and Incest National Network, 2013. *Stalking.* Retrieved from http://www.rainn.org/news-room/sexual-assault-issues/stalking

Rath, T., & Harter, J. (2010). *Well Being: The five essential elements.* (1st ed.). New York, NY: Gallup Press.

Raths, L. E., Harmin, M., & Simon, S. B. (1966). *Values and teaching.* Columbus, OH: Merrill Publishing Co.

Santana, A. E. (1997). Healthwatch: Eat breakfast for energy. Retrieved from http://www.navy.mil/navydata/news/mednews/med97/med97018.txt

Selkowitz, A., (2000/2007). *The college student's guide to eating well on campus.* Bethesda, MD: Tulip Hill Press.

Simon, S. B., Howe, L.W., & Kirschenbaum, H. (1972). *Values clarification: A handbook of practical strategies for teachers and students.* New York, NY: Hart Publishing Co.

"Suicide Prevention." Centers for Disease Control and Prevention. Centers for Disease Control and Prevention, 09 Jan. 2014. Web. 18 Mar. 2014.

The Jed Foundation. (2008, October 29). Press release: mtvU and the Jed Foundation ask students "How are you a friend?" Retrieved from http://www.jedfoundation.org/press-room/press-releases/_how_are_you_release

Warsaw, R. *I Never Called it Rape.* New York: HarperCollins Publishers, 1994.

Wengreen, H. J., & Moncur, C. (2009, July). Change in diet, physical activity, and body weight among young-adults during the transition from high school to college. *Nutrition Journal, 8,* 32. doi: 10.1186/1475-2891-8-32.

U.S. Department of Health and Human Services. (2008). Physical Activity Guidelines for Americans. Washington, DC: U.S. Department of Health and Human Services, ODPHP Publication No. U0036. Retrieved from http://www.health.gov/paguidelines

U.S. Department of Health and Human Services. The Health Consequences of Involuntary Exposure to Tobacco Smoke: A Report of the Surgeon General. Atlanta: U.S. Department of Health and Human Services, Centers for Disease Control and Prevention, Coordinating Center for Health Promotion, National Center for Chronic Disease Prevention and Health Promotion, Office on Smoking and Health, 2006 [accessed 2013 June 10].

Chapter Nine

Value of Diversity

Dear First-Year Student,

By now you have read and/or heard of our *Carolinian Creed*. This pledge profoundly and poignantly states the values that we uphold as members of the Carolina community. As Carolinians, the *Creed* guides our discourse and treatment of each other. The *Creed* does not suggest that we suspend our personal beliefs and values. Rather, it requires that we bring our beliefs and values to the university as a means of learning from one another while respecting and honoring our individual differences.

To that end, your learning is not confined to the interactions that take place in the classroom. Your success at Carolina and beyond is also derived from your interactions with, understanding of and respect for all of the diverse groups of students, faculty and staff that are represented at our university. My hope for you is that you don't waste these four years by remaining in your comfort zone and failing to make friends or develop relationships with people who may at first seem very different from you. Rather, I hope that you take every opportunity to explore all that the university has to offer. I hope that you explore all of the organizations that support the diversity of our students' interests and commit yourself to learning from and about all of your classmates, their cultures, viewpoints and motivations.

Using the *Carolinian Creed* as our beacon, The University of South Carolina will continue to encourage and support an environment that is both diverse and inclusive. However you define yourself, you are a welcome member of our university community.

Best wishes for a productive and engaging freshman year!

John H. Dozier, Ed.D.
Chief Diversity Officer

DURING your lifetime, the general population of America has diversified significantly, a trend that is expected to continue into the future. Individuals that are identified as minorities in the United States are already numerical majorities in the world (U.S. Census Bureau, 2009). With increased access to higher education, colleges are now populated with a greater diversity of individuals than at any point in history (American Council on Education, 2005; Crissman Ishler, 2005; Pryor, Hurtado, Saenz, Santos, & Korn, 2007).

Each year, thousands of students enter the University of South Carolina for the first time. The size of the University and the national and international draw of its programs attract a wide variety of people to the campus. Each student has his or her own unique personal history, characteristics, beliefs, and pathway to the University. Research suggests that students benefit from studying at a college or university that has a significant number of students from different backgrounds than their own (Gurin, Nagda & Lopez, 2003), and for many students, attending Carolina is the first opportunity they have had to be exposed to diversity. For some of you, your high school may have been more racially diverse, but the array of diversity is much richer at University of South Carolina.

You have probably already met many people at the University of South Carolina who are different from you, your family, and your friends at home in a number of ways, such as ethnicity, religion, sexual orientation, gender, culture, age, physical ability, income, social class, hometown, native language, learning style, family status, or major. The variety in the student population of the Carolina community is one of the things that will make your college years such a rewarding learning experience.

Educational Value of Diversity

Research has pinpointed three good practices that promote students learning: (a) academic challenge and high expectations, (b) good teaching and high quality interactions with educators, and (c) diversity experiences (Goodman, Magolda, Seifert & King, 2011). The individuals you are surrounded by in your learning environment are just as important as where you receive your education (Gurin, Nagda & Lopez, 2003). Interactions with a diverse range of people provide opportunities to develop skills related to learning effective communication and fostering mutual respect and teamwork—skills that will enhance your employability. Major corporations have stated that the skills needed in today's global market can only be obtained through exposure to widely diverse people, ideas, and cultures. The qualities that you can develop through contact with diversity require a conscious effort on your part to be open and willing to explore the differences you may experience in your interactions.

CONSIDER THIS

What words do you associate with diversity?

Do you believe your high school was diverse? Why or why not?

What are some examples of diversity that you see at Carolina?

Tomorrow's Population

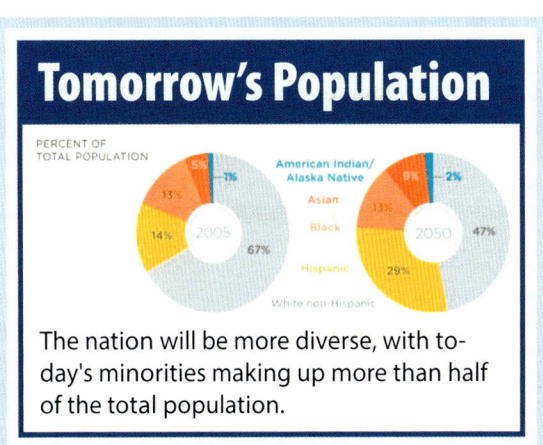

The nation will be more diverse, with today's minorities making up more than half of the total population.

Did you know?

In the National Survey of Student Engagement (2011), 11% of incoming Carolina students stated that they had *never* had serious conversations with students of a different race or ethnicity.

It is important to remember when interacting with and "learning from people with different backgrounds, college offers a fundamentally different opportunity from most other environments, [which] arises precisely because all incoming students are likely to share certain values" (Light, 2001, p. 132) that drew them to South Carolina.

Carolina Community

Communities are often born out of similarities between individuals rather than in ways that celebrate differences. Your high school was most likely comprised of students who were from the same geographic area and/or who shared a similar religious or personal history. If you are from a small town or rural region, you might have been in classes with many of the same people since elementary school. Your closest friends are probably from your neighborhood and share similar characteristics and personal histories.

Learning about, accepting, and valuing diversity is an ongoing process toward intercultural competence and maturity. The more you interact with and talk with people from a variety of backgrounds, the easier it will become to accept and respond appropriately to differences and the more you will gain from your college experience. Ultimately, knowledge you gain from diverse experiences will help build communities where members are judged by the quality of their character and contributions, not by their external appearance or other stereotypical attributes.

At this point, all of you have been introduced to and agreed to live by the tenants of the *Carolinian Creed*. The *Creed* establishes a set of shared values, including personal and academic integrity, respect, concern for others, and regard for human dignity. The tenant of the *Creed* pertaining to diversity states that we "will respect the dignity of all persons (and) discourage bigotry, while striving to learn from differences in people." Students who adhere to this principle recognize that differences among students present positive learning opportunities.

Ongoing internal reflection on your own personal identity and values is important to many college experiences and critical to your understanding of diversity. However, an appreciation of diversity is impossible without placing yourself within a community. A full appreciation of diversity comes with the ability for an individual to interact effectively and meaningfully with others. Diversity is ultimately about relationships and communities.

Fellow students are not the only members of the campus community. Professors, academic administrators, instructors, student affairs staff, and administrative support staff are also community members that you will have many opportunities to interact with throughout your time at Carolina. These faculty and staff, like your peers, represent a broad spectrum of backgrounds, cultures, interests, experiences, and personal characteristics that can add to your understanding of others. For example, you may be in a class taught by an instructor who has lived or studied in a country outside of the United States and offers a different perspective on course content based on his or her life experience.

> The tenant of the *Creed* pertaining to diversity states that we "will respect the dignity of all persons (and) discourage bigotry, while striving to learn from differences in people."

As you engage in discussions in your University 101 class, in other classes, in your living environment, and with friends, consider the commonalities that you share with your peers and how these similarities and differences will affect your understanding of one another.

> **Did you know?**
> University of South Carolina is home to students who represent more than 18 different religions. *Source: CIRP (2013)*

Chapter 9: Value of Diversity

Check yourself

Diversity Quiz

Select the appropriate answer to each item below.

1. The percentage of out-of-state students represented in the incoming cohorts of first-year students at the University of South Carolina is

    (a) less than 10%   (b) 18%
    (c) 32%   (d) over 40%

2. According to survey data collected from first-year students at this campus, the percentage of entering students at the University of South Carolina who frequently socialized with someone of another racial or ethnic group during their senior year of high school is higher than the national average for first-year students at four-year colleges.

    True or False

3. Based on fall 2012 data, what percentage of Carolina students are male?

    (a) 35%   (b) 44%
    (c) 53%   (d) 62%

4. Which of the following disability categories represents the largest proportion of students registered with the Office of Student Disability Services?

    (a) Audio/Visual   (b) Learning Disability/AD(H)D
    (c) Physical   (d) Psychiatric

5. What percent of entering Carolina first-year students agreed with the statement: Same-sex couples should have the right to legal marital status?

    (a) less than 20%   (b) 30%
    (c) 40%   (d) greater than 50%

6. What percent of University of South Carolina first-year students frequently interact with peers having different social, political, or religious views from their own?

    (a) 35%   (b) 50%
    (c) 60%   (d) 80%

7. Based on fall 2012 data, how many students in the first-year class are from a foreign country?

    (a) 38   (b) 45
    (c) 57   (d) 62

8. How many countries were represented by the fall 2012 first-year class?

    (a) 10   (b) 15
    (c) 19   (d) 24

9. Which of the following labels did the largest proportion of Carolina first-year students use to characterize their sociopolitical views?

    (a) Liberal   (b) Middle-of-the-road
    (c) Conservative   (d) Far Right

10. According to 2012 institutional data, approximately what percent of first-year students at Carolina received some form of financial aid?

    (a) 20%   (b) 40%
    (c) 60%   (d) 80%

*Answers on page 221

CONSIDER THIS

What words would you use to describe yourself to someone who has never met you?

What characteristics are present in that description?

As you listen to others describe themselves, what identity elements are present in their descriptions that you did not include in your own? Why did you choose not to use those same descriptors for yourself?

How would the description of yourself change if you were communicating it to a new roommate, a blind date, or as part of a job interview?

Which elements were consistent across all of those situations, and which changed?

Why did you choose to change the descriptors you used based upon the person and context?

CONSIDER THIS

Who are you?

List 2-3 cultural groups with which you identify. (e.g., race, spirituality, gender)

_____
_____
_____
_____

List 3-5 values that you associate with the group with which you identify.

_____
_____
_____
_____

Write down the names of 5-8 people who you spend the most time with during the week. Next to their name, write down the ways that they differ from you and the similarities you share.

_____
_____
_____
_____
_____
_____
_____

Have you met someone who has expressed different values from you? Explain.

_____
_____
_____
_____

Have your values been challenged as a student at Carolina? If so, explain.

_____
_____
_____
_____

Diversity and Self-Awareness

Often, our first reaction to the notion of diversity is to immediately look at others. Who are my fellow students? How do they look, act, and behave? What do their decisions and actions represent about their identity, beliefs, and background? Although this curiosity is natural and an important part of embracing and incorporating difference into a meaningful learning experience, it overlooks a critical aspect of the process of intercultural competence: self- awareness. To appreciate what someone else brings to an interaction, offers to a relationship, or contributes to the community, it is important to understand what you bring to those situations. At the core of self-awareness are the concepts of identity and values.

Identity

Identity is the combination of personal elements that create your understanding of who you are as a person and, within the context of the University, who you are as a student. Identity elements are the characteristics you use to understand and articulate your individuality and include both *internal* dimensions and *external* dimensions.

Internal dimensions are aspects over which you have no control or are not easily altered. Examples include: race, age, and physical abilities.

External dimensions are aspects of our identity "which we have some control over, which might change over time, and which usually form the basis for" life decisions. (Amelio,2008, pp. 6-7). Examples include gender, relationship status, income, work experience, appearance, personal habits, and hobbies.

Throughout your college experience and in your life, your sense of identity will shift and adapt. At certain points or in certain situations, aspects of your identity may become more or less important. For instance, if you are transitioning from a religiously affiliated high school to Carolina, you may find that your religion is a particularly critical aspect of your identity as a first-year college student. Similarly, if you are one of only a few women in a course or a major, your gender may be the primary element of your identity in that environment. Further, you may find that your connection to particular ethnic traditions may strengthen or lessen as you separate from your family and cultural community and become part of new communities on campus.

Regardless of the identity elements that are important to you, the building blocks of identity are also typically the elements of diversity. For example, internal elements are often used to describe ourselves as well as to identify aspects of similarity or difference with other individuals or groups. Similarly, external dimensions are also used to describe who we are as well as to identify diversity in a student population.

Identity elements generally do not exist in a vacuum. It is rare that people describe themselves using only one term or considering only one aspect. People generally combine multiple aspects of identity into their awareness (e.g., Italian-Catholic, Black man, urban youth). As such, it is helpful to have a firm understanding of the identity elements that are important to you because they represent the viewpoint from which you perceive the similar and different identity elements in others. Your ability to understand and embrace a multifaceted sense of self is a valuable skill both with respect to your own development as well as for your ability to accept and embrace the complex identities of the people with whom you interact.

Values

Values represent another important aspect of self-awareness and, thus, another foundational piece of our understanding of diversity. They are defined as the attitudes and beliefs that determine what is important to us. While similar to identity elements, values typically reflect an ideal state of being, while identity elements describe a condition of self. For example, *middle class* is an identity element describing socioeconomic status while *economic security* or *wealth* represents a value. Similarly, describing oneself as Baptist or Jewish is part of an identity, whereas, *spirituality* is a value. Use the Values Clarification Inventory located at the end of the Chapter to assess which values you most identify with.

During your college career, you will experience challenging classes, interactions with peers who may have different beliefs than you, and personal dilemmas. Your current beliefs and values will shape how you view your options and make decisions in these situations. Additionally, these life events can shape or change your current beliefs and values.

Students may graduate with significantly different values than when they entered college. Having an awareness of your beliefs and values and then challenging them yourself or through your interactions with others will contribute to your developing sense of identity, as well as your comfort and competence in a diverse world. Your values and how they differ from your peers represent yet another important aspect of diversity in the complex and dynamic Carolina community.

Check yourself

Values Clarification

The values contained in this list are all worthwhile, but different people are likely to prioritize them differently. Take five minutes to select your top ten values, and identify them with a checkmark. Next, take two minutes to decide upon your top five values, and add a second checkmark to indicate their importance. After completing this exercise, you may find it useful to discuss your results with a classmate, friend, family member, or roommate to see if your actions and choices reflect your core values as well as to reflect upon how your values may be different or similar to others in your community.

_____ Achievement	_____ Freedom	_____ Nature/Environment
_____ Advancement	_____ Friendship	_____ Peace
_____ Adventure	_____ Fun	_____ Pleasure
_____ Balance	_____ Health	_____ Power
_____ Beauty	_____ Help others	_____ Recognition
_____ Caring	_____ Help society	_____ Responsibility
_____ Challenge	_____ Independence	_____ Self-Worth
_____ Change/Variety	_____ Inner harmony	_____ Spirituality
_____ Community	_____ Integrity	_____ Stability
_____ Competition	_____ Justice	_____ Time freedom
_____ Cooperation	_____ Knowledge	_____ Wealth
_____ Creativity	_____ Leadership	_____ Wisdom
_____ Economic security	_____ Leisure	_____ Other: _____
_____ Excitement	_____ Love	_____ Other: _____
_____ Family	_____ Loyalty	_____ Other: _____

Communication and Diversity

To fully engage in relationships and be a participating member of your new community, you must communicate. Communication skills—both talking and listening—are critical to your understanding and appreciation of diversity. It may not always be easy to communicate with someone who is different from you or to talk about those aspects of difference. As mentioned earlier, elements of diversity are tightly connected to the very fundamental aspects of our identity and values. As such, they can represent personal and perhaps sensitive dimensions of our personalities. You may or may not feel comfortable talking about your experiences or identity or hearing about these same issues from others, but these situations provide excellent opportunities to grow and learn. Use the following communication strategies in your daily interactions within the campus community.

> ### Southern Culture
>
> Each fall, Carolina offers *What's the Big Deal About Sweet Tea?*, an event designed to help all out-of-state students learn about Southern culture and become adjusted, comfortable, and successful at the University of South Carolina. Students have the opportunity to meet others from out of state and learn about our student organizations.

The Power of Words

Be aware of the power of language and what you mean when you use diversity terms. In situations where you are introducing yourself using value and identity labels, be aware that others in the group may associate different meanings to these same words—and vice versa. For example, many of us immediately think of race when diversity is mentioned, but we often confuse race with ethnicity. Race is associated with shared biological characteristics, while ethnicity is associated with the environment into which you were born and specifies membership in a group historically connected by a common national origin or language. Refer to the glossary of the top 25 diversity terms to help you develop a more common understanding as you use these words in your conversations.

It Is All in a Name

When you are unsure of the appropriate title (any title) to use when addressing or discussing an individual, it is important to ask for clarification. Does that person prefer the long version of his or her name or a nickname; the term African American or Black to describe race; Hispanic, or Latina/o to refer to ethnicity; Republican or Conservative to identify political views; the name of his or her homeland (e.g., Canada) or a slang term (e.g. Canuck) for national origin? While it may feel awkward at first, a respectful inquiry of someone's preferences will go a long way to help facilitate communication across and about areas of difference.

Beware of Assumptions

Everyday language is a function of our identity and values. Consider how the words you use in conversation suggest your assumptions about gender, sexuality, culture, religion, or power. Is there a way to choose other words that are more inclusive or more sensitive? For example, it may be more inclusive to reference the end-of-semester break as Winter Break instead of Christmas Break. Similarly, it avoids assumptions about sexuality if you refer to someone's partner instead of their boyfriend or girlfriend.

In addition to viewpoints, be aware of the effect of diversity on communication styles. Certain cultures may be more aggressive or more passive in their verbal expressions and body language; others may prioritize written communication over the spoken word. Accents and different word pronunciation or word order can be especially challenging and require you to think of tactful ways to ask for information to be repeated that do not place the speaker in an awkward, embarrassing, or frustrated position. For instance, if you have difficulty understanding a professor's accent, ask for clarification in class by paraphrasing the instructor's comments and prefacing the question with a comment such as, "so I understand you correctly, are you saying…." Or, you may need to explain slang or lingo that is unique to the United States or your region of the country to an international student. It is important to be aware of cultural differences in communication patterns and protocol and be as patient and as inclusive as possible in your discussions.

Awareness Is Key

Maintain an awareness of issues of representation and privilege in discussions of diversity. If you are the only person of a certain viewpoint, particularly if it is one that is widely perceived as being historically underrepresented or a minority position, it can be especially uncomfortable to have open and honest discussions about difference. Gently make others aware of this aspect of the conversation and be open about what that means for the discussion. You should never feel that you are being forced to speak as a representative for a larger group or that you are in a defensive position with respect to your personal history or experiences. Conversely, if you are in the majority position in a particular discussion, do not make the assumption that this equates to being right. Be open to alternate viewpoints.

Do Not Take it Personally

Try not to personalize remarks that are made in discussions of diversity and difference. Although it may be difficult when it feels like someone is attacking who you are or what you believe, it may be healthy to separate yourself from the role being discussed in order to see what the other person is saying. By doing your best to balance your personal experiences with an objective viewpoint, you may be better able to explore and explain your view on an issue than if you adopt a defensive position.

Be Willing to Share

Everything you have encountered in life, including your family history and cultural heritage, contributes to the person you are today. Share with others how your background influenced you. Be proud of the identity elements and values that are important to you and make you unique, and be willing to share them with others. Your participation will likely encourage others—your roommate, hallmates, classmates, and new friends—to share how their background influenced them.

Explore Outside the Box

In addition to your classroom and residence hall experiences, there are other opportunities to explore diversity on campus, including joining student organizations and attending multicultural events and celebrations. You can also explore diversity on your own by visiting websites, reading magazines and books written by and about people different than you, attending workshops on diversity, reading newspapers from other countries, traveling abroad, or participating in service activities. As you look for experiences that will enrich your college experience, consider opportunities, both on and off campus, that will provide new perspectives and increase your awareness about the various ways our campus, community, and world are so richly diverse.

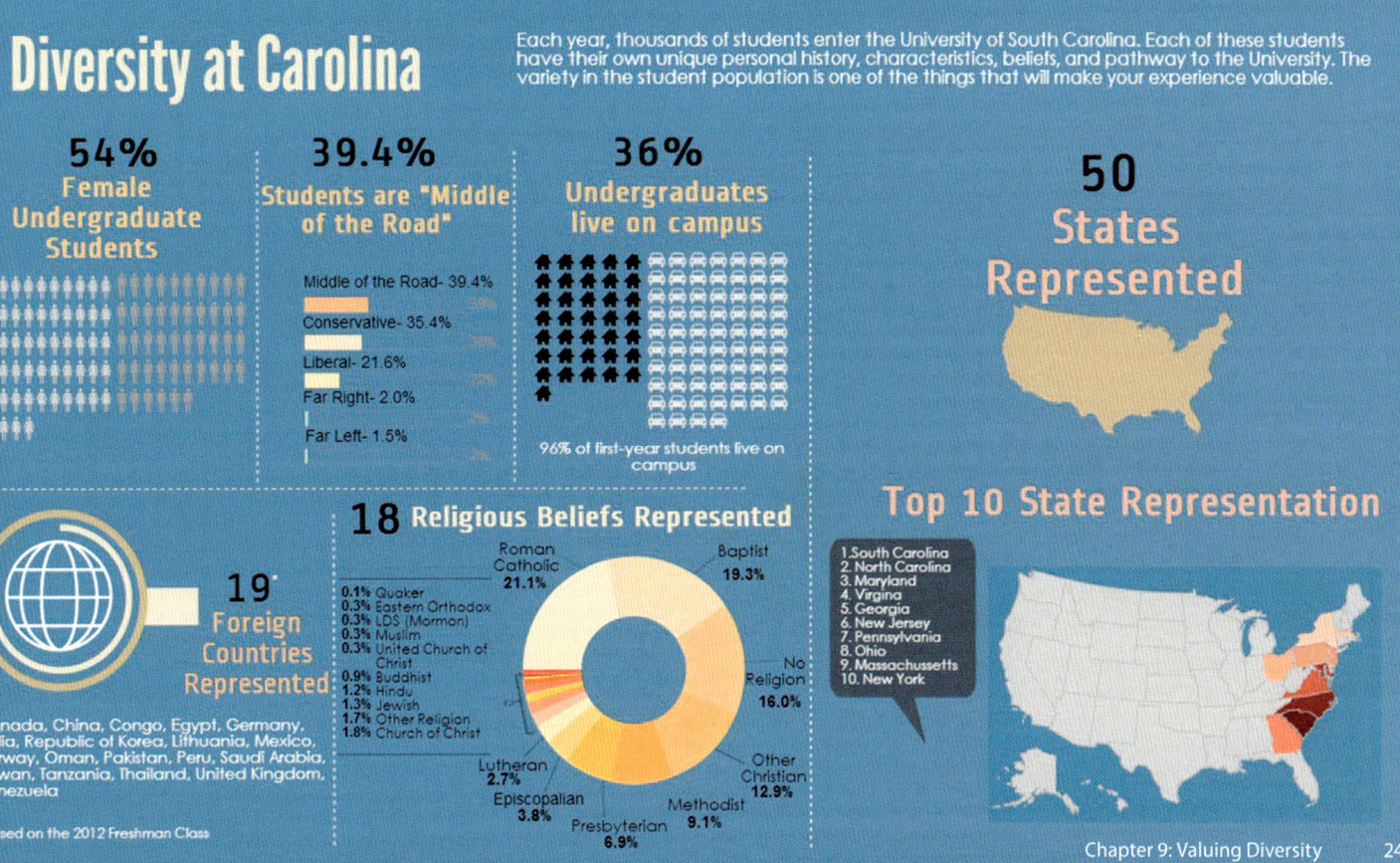

Diversity & Inclusion Terms

This glossary of diversity-related terminology is designed to help students explore concepts of diversity and diverse perspectives. As you explore different aspects of diversity with your class, keep in mind that although we most often think of diversity in terms of racial/ethnic diversity, other forms of diversity are often at play in a college environment and that focusing only on racial/ethnic diversity can often mask and marginalize other aspects of diversity. As human beings, race or ethnicity is only one of many aspects of any individual, and we should explore the other characteristics that define us. In thinking about all of these issues, here are some key pieces of terminology (and definitions) that may be useful.

Ableism   A system of oppression based on the social construction of superior and inferior physicality, which is expressed in individual, institutional as well as cultural forms and functions for the benefit of those deemed able-bodied at the expense of those deemed disabled. [1]

Bias   A preference for or tendency toward a particular viewpoint or outcome. Bias stems from the internalization and institutionalization of particular values, beliefs, and assumptions. Not to be confused with bigotry, which is motivated by ill-intent, bias can co-exist unconsciously with good intentions, but nevertheless result in outcomes that are inclined to favor some groups over others. [1]

Bigotry   Intolerance of cultures, religions, races, ethnicities, or political beliefs that differ from one's own. [2]

Biracial   Of or related to more than one race. Biracial individuals may choose to identify with only one race, especially if they find that they are readily accepted by one group than another. Historically, biracial individuals who had one black parent and one white parent were considered black and were not acknowledged by the white community. [2]

Bisexual   A term used to identify someone who has romantic and/or sexual feelings, attractions, and/or relationships with men and women, not necessarily at equal levels of attraction, and not necessarily simultaneously (a common stereotype). A bisexual person can also be defined as someone who has romantic and/or sexual feelings, attractions and/or relationships with people of any gender (rather than saying both genders). [3]

Disability   Disability is a physical, mental, or cognitive impairment or condition that qualifies under federal and state disability nondiscrimination laws for special accommodations to ensure programmatic and physical access. [4]

Diversity   Psychological, physical, and social differences that occur among any and all individuals, such as race, ethnicity, nationality, religion, economic class, age, gender, sexual orientation, mental and physical ability, and learning styles. A diverse group, community or organization, is one in which a variety of social and cultural characteristics exist. [2]

Ethnicity   The shared sense of a common heritage, ancestry, or historical past among an ethnic group (see Ethnic Group). Ethnicity is a distinct concept from race, as illustrated by the fact that Hispanics, designated an ethnic group in the U.S., may nevertheless be of any race. [1]

Gay   A term that signifies same sex attraction, predominantly pertaining to men, though sometimes used by women-loving-women, and sometimes used as an umbrella term for a community identity that includes, gay, lesbian and bisexual persons. [3]

Gender   Sexual classification based on the social construction of the categories of "men" and "women." Gender differs from one's biological sex (male or female) in that one can assume a gender that is different from one's biological sex. [2]

Identity Group (n.)   A particular group, culture, or community with which an individual identifies or shares a sense of belonging. [2]

Inclusion   The act of creating environments in which any individual or group can be and feel welcomed, respected, supported, and valued to fully participate. An inclusive and welcoming climate embraces differences and offers respect in words and actions for all people. [4]

Intercultural   Term describing intergroup relations across cultural, social and personal identities. The term also refers to global citizenship in that multiple cultural, social and personal identities co-exist in most communities across the globe. [3]

Interfaith   A term that refers to cooperative and positive interaction between people of different religious traditions (i.e., "faiths") and spiritual or humanistic beliefs, at both the individual and institutional level with the aim of deriving a common ground in belief through a concentration on similarities between faiths, understanding of values, and commitment to the world. [3]

Lesbian   The term Lesbian originates from ancient Greece where the homosexual poet Sappho lived on the isle of Lesbos with other Greek women. It is from this isle that the term originates. Homosexual women sometimes prefer the term Lesbian as opposed to the generic term "Gay." This term acknowledges the fact that homosexual women have different priorities and experiences than homosexual men. [1]

Microaggression   "Racial microaggressions are brief and commonplace daily verbal, behavioral, or environmental indignities, whether intentional or unintentional, that communicate hostile, derogatory, or negative racial slights and insults towards people of color." Those who inflict racial microaggressions are often unaware that they have done anything to harm another person. [6]

Multicultural   Multiculturalism is an acknowledgment that, as people, we are culturally diverse and multifaceted, and a process through which the sharing and transforming of cultural experiences allow us to re-articulate and redefine new spaces, possibilities, and positions for ourselves and others. [4]

Multiracial   A term that describes people whose ancestry comes from multiple races, in this case more than two races. [3]

Oppression   A system of individual, institutional, and cultural beliefs and practices that privilege a dominant group at the expense of the subordinate groups. [1]

Questioning   The process of considering or exploring one's sexual orientation and/or gender identity. A term used to refer to an individual who is uncertain of her/his sexual orientation or identity. [3]

Racism   Racism can be understood as individual and institutional practices and policies based on the belief that a particular race is superior to others. This often results in depriving certain individuals and groups of certain civil liberties, rights, and resources, hindering opportunities for social, educational, and political advancement. [2]

Sexism   A system of oppression based on social constructions of gender superiority and inferiority, which is expressed in individual, institutional as well as cultural forms and functions for the benefit of the dominant sex at the expense of others. [1]

Sexual orientation   Sexual orientation is the deep-seated direction of one's sexual (erotic) attraction toward the same gender, opposite gender, or other genders. It is on a continuum and not a set of absolute categories. Sometimes it is referred to as "affection orientation." [4]

Transgender   In the past, used as an umbrella term to describe a broad range of people who experience and express their genders differently from cultural norms. Increasingly, this adjective is used specifically to describe people whose gender identities do not match their sex designation at birth, such as people designated male at birth who identify as women. Some people no longer consider this an umbrella term. [3]

Transsexual   A term used to describe a person whose gender identity differs from that of their physical/biological sex. Transsexuals can be heterosexual, homosexual, or bisexual. [2]

Definitions adapted from the following sources:
[1] http://www.xavier.edu/diversity/Glossary-of-Diversity-Terminology.cfm
[2] http://www.qcc.edu/virtual-multicultural-center/glossary-diversity-terms
[3] http://mcc.osu.edu/posts/documents/identity-terms-and-definitions.pdf
[4] http://diversity.berkeley.edu/glossary-terms
[5] http://www.census.gov/Press-Release/www/2001/raceqandas.html
[6] Sue, D.W., Capodilupo, C., Torino, G, Bucceri, J., Holder, A., Nadal, K., & Equin, M. (2007). Racial Microaggressions in Everyday Life: Implications for Clinical Practice. *The American Psychologist*, 62 (4) 271-286.

Becoming Engaged With Diversity

The University of South Carolina is proud of its diverse population and supports cultural diversity in every way possible. Numerous opportunities exist on campus to learn more about cultures and people different from you. What you learn about differences and similarities in people from different backgrounds will benefit you throughout your life.

Numerous opportunities to explore diversity both in and out of the classroom include

- Interviewing a student who has studied abroad to find out about his or her experiences
- Introducing yourself to international students in your classes. They, too, may be new to campus and often are eager to meet American students
- Asking a nontraditional-age student in your class to study or serve with you on a group project
- Seeking out faculty and staff who have an academic interest in international issues and learn how they entered their field or discipline
- Promoting international programming and events in your groups and organizations
- Volunteering to participate in activities sponsored by or involving international organizations in the community
- Learning a second language
- Becoming a conversation partner with an international student
- Reading biographies of human rights and social activists
- Studying history other than American history
- Reading the newspaper regularly to stay current with local, national, and international issues
- Researching a particular social, ethnic, cultural, religious, or political group
- Attending an event that supports those with various disabilities, or volunteering to aid students with impairments through note taking or proctoring individualized exams
- Taking classes in a wide variety of subjects, such as political science, humanities, women's studies, African American studies, Latino and immigrant studies, or Asian studies
- Asking questions during class discussions if you do not understand the viewpoints of the professor, guest speaker, or another classmate
- Accepting invitations to hear professional speakers through one of the University's many student organizations, academic departments, or other venues

> **Peer Leader Advice**
>
> Use your time in college to make friends with some people completely different from yourself. I have grown so much and learned so much from my friends that have completely different backgrounds and beliefs than I do. My college years have taught me to appreciate the uniqueness of everyone I meet, and I know that an understanding of diversity will be a valuable asset the rest of my life."
>
> - Caroline Hendricks
> Greenville, SC • Senior
> European Studies and Biology

Campus Offices

Several campus offices can help you develop as a member of a particular cultural group and as a member of the South Carolina community. The key is to identify those offices at Carolina and seek out the information and diverse opportunities they offer.

The Office of Multicultural Student Affairs (OMSA) works with students, faculty, and staff to help promote an accepting environment and to assist in fostering an appreciation for our unique human

Did you know?

The SafeZone Ally Project is a program offered through the Office of Multicultural and Student Affairs. A SafeZone Ally is a confidential, trustworthy, and supportive place for students to talk with a trained ally.

SafeZone Allies are trained members of the Carolina Community committed to fighting homophobia and heterosexism while offering support to the members of the gay community on campus.

SafeZone Allies are identified by the SafeZone Ally symbol placed on their door or in their office.

Are you interested in being a SafeZone Ally? Visit their website http://www.sa.sc.edu/omsa/ for more information.

ON THE WEB

For more information on the resources provided by the Office of Multicultural Student Affairs, visit their website:
sa.sc.edu/omsa

differences. The Office provides programs, services, and initiatives for the multicultural development of all students at South Carolina. During the academic year, OMSA coordinates a number of diversity education initiatives, including

- Civil Rights Tour
- Diversity Dialogue Series
- Diversity Retreat
- Student Leadership & Diversity Conference
- R.E.A.L. Talk Series (Relations, Ethnicity, Activism & Leadership)

Lesbian, Gay, Bisexual, and Transgender (LGBT) Programs in the Office of Multicultural Student Affairs, uses outreach, education, advocacy, and collaborative relationships to foster a fair, safe, and receptive climate in which all Carolinians, regardless of sexual orientation or gender identity, are treated with dignity and respect. The program is building a campus wide network of students, faculty, staff, residence halls, student organizations, and academic departments that provide an open door, as well as information and resources, for lesbian, gay, bisexual, transgender, questioning, and ally individuals.

The International Programs for Students Office is dedicated to serving the international education needs of all South Carolina students. The Office provides services and support to international students and to American students who wish to study in other countries. The staff provides international students with pre-arrival information, orientation programs, immigration advising, and personal assistance. The program's study abroad advisors provide guidance to students as they identify possible international academic programs and assist students as they work through the application process and prepare for their time abroad.

Women's Student Services works to build alliances with campus and community groups in order to educate, empower, and mentor female students at the University. They work to educate female students on issues related to personal development, leadership, health and wellness, and safety. Additionally, they provide mentoring to students through the Women's Mentor Network, which pairs faculty and staff women on campus with undergraduate women interested in the same academic area or career path.

Carolina Campus Ministries, an association of ministers and advisors who serve as registered religious workers at Carolina, consists of representatives from a variety of religious traditions who serve the University and the student body in ministry, teaching, and counseling. Each chaplain is available to University students for crisis counseling and spiritual direction.

The Office of Adult Student Services offers adults learners a special place of their own and a staff dedicated to serving their needs. Adult students are provided support for successfully managing issues, such as gaining admission to the University, navigating advisement and registration, and counseling for problems or issues that may arise during their time at South Carolina. The Office also presents three back-to-school workshops during the academic year as well as semi-annual adult student orientations.

The Office of Student Disability Services provides support for students with documented learning, physical, and psychological disabilities. Students registered with the Office may be eligible for a wide range of support services and accommodations, including priority registration, classroom adaptations, test proctors, and note takers. Accommodations are based on the nature and extent of each student's disability.

Student Organizations

As highlighted in chapter 3, Carolina has more than 400 student organizations, including many devoted to promoting diversity at Carolina. These groups provide an opportunity to be exposed to students from many different countries and allow you to gain skills in cross-cultural communication, leadership, and organization. Many religious student organizations have social activities as well as worship services and religious studies events. Student organizations related to specific political parties, religious affiliations, international organizations, or social issues also will help you gain a broader understanding of different views and faiths represented on campus. Attending a student organization meeting is a low-risk way to learn more about the University's diverse student body while you expand your ideas and values.

Listed below are several organizations highlighted by the Office of Multicultural and Student Affairs (OMSA).

The Association of African American Students (AAAS) was founded in 1968 to unify African American students on campus; promote unity among all students and faculty of the University; and motivate the community, members, and University to achieve higher social, educational, and economic status through service projects, cultural programming, and special events. AAAS currently has a diverse general body comprised of more than 500 members, making it the largest organization under the OMSA umbrella and one of the largest student organizations at Carolina. The organization has a full-functioning executive board and seven committees, including Freshmen Council; Cultural Awareness; Special Events; Community Service; Membership; Publicity; and Voices of Color, the organizations monthly newsletter.

Bisexual, Gay, Lesbian Students and Allies (BGLSA) serves to provide information on support and social systems and networks for lesbian, gay, bisexual, and transgender (LGBT) students and allies at the University of South Carolina, as well as to provide a forum for open discussion and positive interaction with the broader Carolina community in order to promote better awareness of LGBT students and allies.

Brothers of Nubian Descent (BOND) is an informative discussion group focusing on the trials and pressures facing Black males today, not only on the Carolina campus, but in the state of South Carolina and the United States. The organization seeks ways to improve all aspects of the lives of Black men by a means of open communication through discussion, planning, and execution. Their goal is to improve the success of Black males at the University while also serving the community. BOND fosters and supports intellectual dialogue by creating a cultural support group.

Chosen Gospel Ensemble was created to provide cultural inspiration at campus events. Chosen sings music that has come out of the African American worship experience.

National Association for the Advancement of Colored People (NAACP) provides a medium for the exchange of ideas to confront issues that face the community and works toward solutions to solve those issues. By educating students, facilitating meetings, and other special events, NAACP strives to make a difference at the University of South Carolina.

ON THE WEB

For more information about BGLSA, check out their website:
web.sa.sc.edu/bglsa

Check out Carolina's NAACP website:
uscnaacp.org

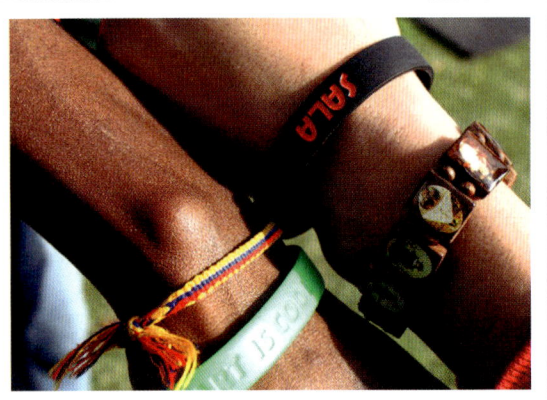

SAVVY offers assistance to multicultural female students looking for a way to maximize their chances at self-improvement and enhance their abilities during their affiliation at the University.

Students Associated for Latin America (SALA) was the first student organization recognized for Latina/o students. SALA's purpose is to promote cultural awareness on campus with regard to Latin American issues, countries, and people.

Services and Programs

In order to produce positive effects upon multicultural student retention and success, OMSA offers a myriad of cultural support services, diversity education initiatives, and multicultural programming. The goal is to help promote an accepting environment, and to assist in fostering an appreciation for each of our culturally diverse populations.

EMPOWER provides a platform for students to challenge stereotypes, to create dialogue about similarities and differences, and to promote cross-cultural awareness and understanding. Members are available to give presentations at meetings and in classes.

LGBT Peer Advocates is a program that trains a group of undergraduate students who give workshops and programs specifically related to the issues related to the LGBTQIA (lesbian, gay, bisexual, transexual, queer, intersex and asexual) community.

The Civil Rights Tour is sponsored by OMSA, NAACP, and the African American Studies Program and educates students about the Civil Rights Movement. The four-day and three-night tour is held annually during the spring semester and is open to all University students, staff, and faculty. The tour departs from Columbia and travels through Alabama and Georgia.

The Diversity Dialogue Series program educates the campus community on issues related to diversity and multiculturalism on a predominately white campus. Dialogues are offered once a month, at 7 p.m., in various residence halls. Bring your friends or come make new ones while discussing current hot topics on diversity, social justice, and what you think is happening in our society.

The African American Male Institute seeks to motivate and empower African American males to assume roles of leadership. The Institute exposes participants to proven strategies for creating greater professional and personal success by promoting academic excellence through mentorship, workshops or seminars, and focus groups.

Minority Student Welcome is an annual event for all incoming first-year students of color. The Welcome offers these students the opportunity to meet one another and leaders of multicultural student organizations as well as interact with members of the faculty and administration.

Minority Assistance Peer Program (MAPP) is designed to assist first-year students of color in their transition to the University by providing them with a trained peer counselor for their critical first semester. The program works diligently to establish positive networks for the student's matriculation—academically, socially, and culturally.

Celebrations and Awareness Events

Each year, the University hosts several cultural celebrations and awareness events, which include

- Hispanic Heritage Month (September)
- Lesbian, Gay, Bisexual, and Transgender History Month (October)
- Native American Heritage Month (November)
- Black History Month (February)
- Women's History Month (March)

You can attend forums and panels, hear nationally known speakers, attend screenings of films, and participate in cultural discussions. Events usually are open to the public and free for South Carolina students. Observances, such as *Creed* & Diversity Week or LGBT Ally Week, offer a variety of events and activities focused on raising awareness and celebrating differences in our campus community. The International Programs for Students Office sponsors World Night, a festival hosted by the international student community that showcases international food, traditional dress, music, and dance from the many countries and cultures represented at the University. International Education Week, also held annually, celebrates opportunities for and benefits of international education and international awareness.

Community Opportunities

Carolina students are fortunate to be located in a vibrant metropolitan city that is also the state capitol. As such, there are many opportunities in the community to become engaged in diversity and appreciate difference. These include cultural events and festivals, visual and performing arts shows, and community organizations. While many of the campus diversity programs collaborate with community partners, it is valuable to also learn what is available in Columbia to complement your experience at the University.

One specific form of community involvement is through service. Many community service experiences offer an opportunity to work with individuals who come from different backgrounds than your own. Engaging in service in the community allows you yet another opportunity to experience new ideas, cultures, people, and backgrounds. As you consider your choices for service outlets, it may also be useful to think of it as an opportunity to expand your exposure to diversity as well.

While you are a student at South Carolina, actively seek opportunities to learn more about the people with whom you live, learn, and interact—both on campus and in the surrounding community. There are many areas of diversity to explore during your college years. Opportunities abound to learn about other cultures, observe how others behave, and, most importantly, learn more about yourself. You have already taken on the challenge to better yourself by enrolling in the University of South Carolina. You took the first step towards promoting a more unified campus community and humane respect for diversity when you signed the *Carolinian Creed*. Continue to challenge yourself to create and maintain an unwavering respect for and understanding of diversity while you are a student and after you leave the University.

Diversity Quiz Answers

1. d   2. True   3. b   4. b   5. d   6. c   7. a   8. c   9. b   10. d

SCENARIOS FROM COLLEGE LIFE

You Believe *What*?

Ben graduated high school from a big town in New England. He was captain of the hockey team and very involved in student government. He hated the cold winters in the north and decided to go down south for college. After applying to a few different schools, Ben was accepted into the University of South Carolina. He was especially excited when he got a scholarship here that gave him in-state tuition. Once August rolled around, Ben made the drive from New England, excited to start his new life in college at South Carolina.

Ben moved into Bates House with his assigned roommate named Mark. Mark and Ben hung out together the whole first week of school. They seemed to be progressing as friends and were getting along well as roommates. Mark was easy to live with and Ben was excited about the rest of the year. He had friends who had horrible roommate situations. Ben considered himself lucky to have Mark as a roommate.

Ben expected that he would face some transitions starting college in a new state so far from home. Still, he was shocked when he arrived in South Carolina and realized how different everyone behaved compared to the north. Many of the guys on campus dressed similarly, wearing kakis and polo style shirts, never without their sunglasses hanging around their neck. Most of the girls dressed up for class and football games. The way that people dressed was not the only difference Ben noticed. Back at home, Ben had friends who came from all different backgrounds and religions. In Columbia it seemed like everyone was Baptist and went to church on Sunday. He finally understood what people meant when they called the south the "Bible Belt." Talking about religion made Ben feel uncomfortable. It was something that was never discussed at home.

One night Mark had some guys over to their room. Mark and his friends were talking about a fellow student who identified as gay. They said he was going to hell and wondered out loud why anyone would want to be friends with this person. They also made references to the possibility of him having a disease because he was gay. While this conversation was going on, Ben was trying to do homework at his desk. The conversation was making Ben uncomfortable. Ben has been struggling with the issue of his own sexuality since middle school. His friends at home all know he was gay and didn't have a problem with it. He hadn't "come out" to anyone in college yet and after hearing his roommate's comments, realized that he would likely not be accepted, even by a person he trusted. Ben wanted to share his secret with Mark but found himself feeling afraid that if he did, he would lose his closest friend on campus.

Processing Questions:

What are the major issues in this scenario?

Similar to Ben, have you felt uncomfortable at Carolina because of a conversation that you have heard or an environment you have been exposed to?

What roles do Mark and his friends play in this scenario? Do you think you have even made others feel uncomfortable because of your actions or discussions?

How can Mark and his friends become more informed on homosexuality?

Are there elements of diversity that you can learn more about? Where can you go to learn more about these topics?

RESOURCES

Adult Student Services 777-9446
   Byrnes Building, Room 605
   http://www.ced.sc.edu/adult/
Carolina Campus Ministries
   http://www.carolinafaith.com/
   http://www.sa.sc.edu/stlife/rrwccm.htm
Community Service Programs 777-7130
   Russell House, Suite 227
   http://www.sa.sc.edu/communityservice/
International Programs for Students 777-7461
   Byrnes Building, Suite 123
   http://www.sa.sc.edu/ips/
Leadership Programs 777-7130
   Russell House, Suite 227
   http://www.sa.sc.edu/leaders/
Multicultural Student Affairs 777-7716
   Russell House, Suite 115
   http://www.sa.sc.edu/omsa/
National Student Exchange Program 777-6731
   McBryde C
   http://www.sa.sc.edu/nse/
   nse@sc.edu

SafeZone 777-8248
   http://www.sa.sc.edu/shs/shvp/safezone.shtml
Special Student Populations 777-4163
   Thomas Cooper Library—Mezzanine Level
   http://www.sa.sc.edu/ssc/ssp.shtm
Student Disability Services 777-6142
TDD 777-6244
   LeConte College, Room 112A
   http://www.sa.sc.edu/sds/
Student Organizations 777-2654
   http://www.sa.sc.edu/studentorgs/
Study Abroad Programs 777-7557
   Legare College, Suite 321
   http://www.sa.sc.edu/sa/
Women's Student Services 777-7130
   Russell House, Suite 227
   http://www.sa.sc.edu/wss/

REFERENCES

Amelio, R. (2008). The four layers of diversity [Electronic version]. *Color Magazine, 1*(18), 6-7.

American Council on Education (2005). *College students today: A national portrait.* Washington, DC: Author.

CIRP Freshman Survey 2011. *Administered at The University of South Carolina.*

Crissman Ishler, J. L. (2005). Today's first-year students. In M. L. Upcraft, J. N. Gardner, B. O. Barefoot, & Associates, *Challenging and supporting the first-year student* (pp. 15-26). San Francisco, CA: Jossey-Bass

Goodman, K. M., Magolda, M. B., Seifert, T. A., & King, P. M. (2011), Good practices for student learning: Mixed-method evidence from the Wabash National Study. *About Campus, 16,* 2–9.

Gurin, P., Nagda, B. A., & Lopez, G. E. (2003). The benefits of diversity in education for democratic citizenship. *Journal of Social Issues, 60,* 17–34.

Light, R. J. (2001). *Making the most of college: Students speak their minds.* Cambridge, MA: Harvard University Press.

National Survey of Student Engagement (2011). *Reported for The University of South Carolina.*

Pryor, J. H., Hurtado, S., Saenz, V. B., Santos, J. L., Korn, W. S. (2007). *The American freshman: Forty year trends.* Los Angeles, CA: Higher Education Research Institute, UCLA.

U.S. Census Bureau (2009). *School enrollment.* Retrieved December 1, 2009, from http://www.census.gov/population/www/socdemo/school.html

Appendix: South Carolina Campus Map

Name (building number)	Location
"The Dodie" Anderson Academic Enrichment Center (189)	H3
Athletic Practice Facility (84A)	E5
Athletics Village Parking (191) Athletics Maintenance	H3
Band and Dance Facility	F3
Baptist Collegiate Ministry*	D4
Barnwell College (18) *Psychology*	C2
Bates House (160) *Residence Hall*	F3
Bates House Cafeteria (F) (161)	F3
Bates West (162) *Residence Hall*	F3
Benson* (159) *Center for Child and Family Studies, Health and Safety Programs*	G2
Biomass Facility (172)	G4
Blatt Physical Education Center (138) *Physical Education, Exercise Science, Pool*	F3
Blossom Street Parking Garage (136)	E3
Booker T Washington Auditorium* (134) *TRIO Programs (Opportunity Scholars, Talent Search, Upward Bound); Theatre and Dance*	E3
Bull Street Parking Garage (117-117A)	E3
James F Byrnes Building (1) *Extended University, The Graduate School, International Programs for Students, International Support for Faculty and Staff, EPI, Judicial Programs and Academic Integrity, Philosophy, Sponsored Programs Management, School of the Environment, Counseling Center*	C4
Callcott Building (115) *Geography*	D3
Campus Ministry Center* *Lutheran, Methodist*	D2
Campus Police (1501 Senate Street) (28) *Law Enforcement and Safety, Security, Campus Police*	B2
Capstone House (F) (39) *Capstone Conference Center, Residence Hall*	D1
Carolina Coliseum (F) (84) *Hospitality, Retail, and Sport Management (Hotel, Restaurant, and Tourism Management; Technology Support and Training Management; Retailing; Sport and Entertainment Management); Mass Communications and Information Studies*	E5
Carolina Gardens Apartments (175)	G2
Carolina Softball Stadium (192)	H3
Carolina Stadium (235)	F8
Carolina Tennis Center (192A)	H3
Challenge Course	F3
Children's Center at USC (133) *Child Development and Research Center*	F2
Cliff Apartments (165) *Kampus Kiddie Day Care Center, Residence Hall*	G3

Name (building number)	Location
Close/Hipp Building (BA) (F) (36) *Moore School of Business, Career Center, Daniel Management Center*	C1
Coker Life Sciences Building (100) *Biological Sciences, Pharmacy*	D4
Colloquium (F) (59)	D2
Colonial Life Arena (158) *Basketball Arena, Ticket Office*	D6
Columbia Hall (40) *Residence Hall*	C1
Computer Center Annex	E4
Currell College* (66) *Criminology and Criminal Justice*	D3
Currell College Annex* (68) *Office of Special Events*	D3
Davis College (62) *Library and Information Science*	D2
DeSaussure College* (11) *Social Work, Residence Hall*	C3
Devine Street Research Center** (228)	E6
Discovery I (230) *Cancer Prevention and Control Program*	D5
Discovery Plaza Garage (231) *Strings Project*	D5
Drayton Hall (78) *Theater*	D4
Earth and Water Sciences Building (89) *Earth and Ocean Sciences, Marine Science, Baruch Institute*	D4
East Quad (135A) *Residence Hall*	E3
Facilities Center (83) *Facilities Planning and Construction*	D6
Field House (186)	G3
Flinn Hall** (6) *Undergraduate Academic Affairs and Counseling*	C3
Gambrell Hall (51) *African American Studies, Social and Behavioral Sciences Lab, Political Science, Institute for Southern Studies, History, Richard L Walker Institute of International and Area Studies*	D2
Gibbes House**	D1
John M Palms Center for Graduate Science Research (114) *Chemistry labs and offices*	E4
Greek Village (148) **Fraternities**: Beta Theta Pi (BΘΠ), Chi Psi (XΨ), Kappa Alpha (KA), Kappa Sigma (KΣ), Pi Kappa Phi (ΠΚΦ), Sigma Alpha Epsilon (ΣAE), Sigma Chi (ΣX), Sigma Nu (ΣN) **Sororities**: Alpha Chi Omega (AXΩ), Alpha Delta Pi (AΔΠ), Chi Omega (XΩ), Delta Delta Delta (ΔΔΔ), Delta Zeta (ΔZ), Gamma Phi Beta (ΓΦB), Kappa Delta (KΔ), Kappa Kappa Gamma (KKΓ), Phi Mu (ΦM) Zeta Tau Alpha (ZTA)	E6
Greenhouse (75)	D3

Name (building number)	Location
Greenhouse #2* (177)	H3
700 Pendleton Street* (082B)	C6
Hamilton College (16) *Anthropology*	C2
Hampton Street Parking Garage (29B)	A2
Harper/Elliott Colleges* (8) *South Carolina Honors College, Residence Hall*	C3
Health Sciences Building (76) *Arnold School of Public Health*	D3
Hollings Special Collections Library (103A)	E3
Honors Residence Hall (F) (113)	E4
Horizon I (236) *Future Fuels Hydrogen Research, IDEA labs*	E4
Horizon Garage (237)	E4
Inventory Central Supply* (81)	C6
Jones Physical Sciences Center (90) *Arts and Sciences, Physics and Astronomy, Women's and Gender Studies*	D4
Koger Center for the Arts (86)	D5
Latter-Day Saints Student Association	E4
Law Center (F) (85) *Law, UTS Instructional Support Center, Distance Education*	D4
LeConte College (60) *Disabled Student Services, Mathematics, Statistics*	D2
Lieber College (74) *Undergraduate Admissions*	D3
Longstreet Theatre (102) *Theatre and Dance*	D3
Longstreet Theatre Annex (101) *Scene Shop*	D3
Maxcy College (9) *Residence Hall*	C3
McBryde Quadrangle** (106–110) *Convenient Store, Fraternity Houses, Residence Hall*	E3
McClintock** (118) *Residence Hall*	D2
McCutchen House (10) *Hotel, Restaurant, and Tourism Management Offices and Lab*	C3
McKissick (15) *McKissick Museum, Visitor Center*	C2
McMaster College (33) *Art*	B2
Melton Observatory* (63)	D3
Motor Pool* (82A)	C6
St Thomas More Center* *Roman Catholic*	D2
School of Music (86A)	D5
National Advocacy Center (27)	C2
Old Observatory** (13)	C3
Osborne Administration Building* (14) *Administrative Offices*	C3
Patterson Hall (121) *Housing, Residence Hall*	E2
Pendleton Street Parking Garage (19) *Vehicle Management and Parking Services*	C2

Appendix: South Carolina Campus Map

Name (building number)	Location
Petigru College (61) *Arts and Sciences*	D2
Pinckney/Legare Colleges* (72) *Fellowships and Scholar Programs, Study Abroad, University Housing Offices, Office of Undergraduate Research, Residence Hall*	D3
Presbyterian Student Center	D1
President's House* (69)	D3
Preston Residential College* (70) *Residence Hall*	D3
Public Health Research Center (156A)	C5
Rec Field Storage (157C)	F5
Rice Athletic Center (190)	H3
Roost (199)	H3
Roost Dormitory (207) *Residence Hall*	H3
ROTC Center (513 Pickens Street) (129) *Aerospace Studies, Military Science (Army ROTC), Naval ROTC, Naval Armory*	E2
Russell House (F) (112) *Student Life, University Bookstore, Student Government, Student Media, Grand Marketplace*	D3
Rutledge College* (67) *Religious Studies, Chapel, Residence Hall*	D3
Senate Street Parking Garage (31)	C2
Sims** (120) *Residence Hall*	D2
Sloan College (17) *Sociology*	C2
South Caroliniana Library (4)	C3
South Quad (135) *Residence Hall*	E3
South Tower (122) *Residence Hall*	E2
Spigner House* (42) *University Dining Services*	C1
Sumter Street Parking Garage (141)	E4
Eugene E Stone III Stadium (187)	G3
Strom Thurmond Wellness and Fitness Center (157) *Support Building*	E5
STWFC Pool House (157C)	E5
Sumwalt College (88) *USC NanoCenter*	D4
Swearingen Engineering Center* (173) *Engineering and Computing (Chemical Engineering, Civil and Environmental Engineering, Computer Science and Engineering, Electrical Engineering)*	F4
Thomas Cooper Library (F) (103)	E3
Thomson Student Health Center (111)	D3
Thornwell College** (12) *Business and Finance, Regional Campuses and Continuing Education, Social Work, Residence Hall*	C3
University Technology Services (139)	E4
Wade Hampton** (119) *Residence Hall*	D2
Wardlaw College (80) *Education, Museum of Education*	D4
Welsh Humanities Building (F) (54) *Confucius Institute; English; Languages, Literatures, and Cultures*	D2

Name (building number)	Location
Welsh Humanities Classroom Building (55)	D2
West (Green) Quad (F) (146A–D) *Residence Hall*	F4
Whaley House (627)	B2
Whaley Carriage House (627A)	B2
Williams-Brice Building (Nursing)* (56) *Nursing, Communication Sciences and Disorders*	D2
Williams-Brice Auditorium (56A)	D2
Woodrow College* (65) *Residence Hall*	D3
819 Barnwell Street* (34) *Quality Research Center*	D1
1301 Barnwell Street (626)	D1
707 Catawba Street* (619) *Film Library*	G7
1200 Catawba Street* (171) *Engineering*	G4
1223 Catawba Street (176)	F4
700 College Street* (83A) *Custodial Services*	D6
720 College Street (83B) *Archives Annex*	D6
1710 College Street* (47) *Institutional Assessment and Compliance*	D1
1714 College Street* (57A) *Student Financial Aid Main Office*	D1
1716 College Street* (46) *Student Financial Aid*	D1
1718 College Street* (45) *University 101*	D1
1728 College Street* (58) *University 101 National Resource Center*	D1
1731 College Street* (38) *Social Work*	C1
718 Devine Street (226) *USC Press Warehouse*	E6
1301 Gervais (636) *HRSM-Integrated Information Technology Program*	B3
1600 Gervais Street *Alumni Association*	B2
1620 Gervais (629)	B2
1800 Gervais (631) *Institute for Mind and Brain*	B1
625 Greene Street (622)	D7
1719 Greene Street** (53)	D1
1723 Greene Street** (44)	D1
1600 Hampton Street (F) (29) *Accounting Services, Advancement Administration, Benefits, Contract and Grant Accounting, Controllers Office, Department of Justice, Employment, Equal Opportunity Programs, Government Relations, Human Resources, Institute for Families in Society, Internal Audit, Payroll, Postal Services, Printing, Purchasing, Salary Administration, University Development, University Press, Web Communications*	A2

Name (building number)	Location
1600 Hampton Street Annex (29A) *Regional Campuses and Continuing Education (Continuing Education Units, Conference and Event Services, Summer Academic Programs, Carolina Master Scholars)*	A2
814 Henderson Street (49)	D1
816 Henderson Street (50)	D1
820 Henderson Street (48)	D1
1420 Henderson Street *Children's Law*	A1
300 Main Street (170) *Engineering and Computing (Civil and Environmental Engineering, Electrical Engineering, Mechanical Engineering)*	F4
516 Main Street (144) *Registrar*	E4
518 Main Street (143) *Bursar, Financial Services*	E4
1321 Pendleton Street (7) *Institute of Archaeology and Anthropology*	C3
513 Pickens Street Annex (129A)	E2
1338 Pickens Street (632)	A2
1400 Pickens Street (638) *Institute of Public Service and Policy Research*	A2
1430 Senate Street (635) *Business and Finance, Cocky's Reading Express*	C3
1527 Senate Street* (28A) *Guignard House*	B2
101 S Bull Street** (202)	H2
105 S Bull Street** (202A)	H2
109 S Bull Street** (202B)	H2
201 S Marion Street** (203)	H2
300 Sumter Street (163) *Engineering Technical Fabrication Facility*	F3
920 Sumter Street (World War Memorial)* (5) *Creative Services, Creative Services Portrait Studio, Magazine Group, News and Internal Communications, Strategic Marketing*	C3
350 Wayne Street (625)	F6
201 S Marion Street (203)	H2
201 S Marion Street (203)	H2

(F) Indicates Dining Facility (Cafeteria/Cafe/Convenience Store) Summer hours may be limited.

Buildings are fully accessible to the disabled unless indicated as follows:
* Limited access: single floor(s) in multi-story building
** No wheelchair access to building

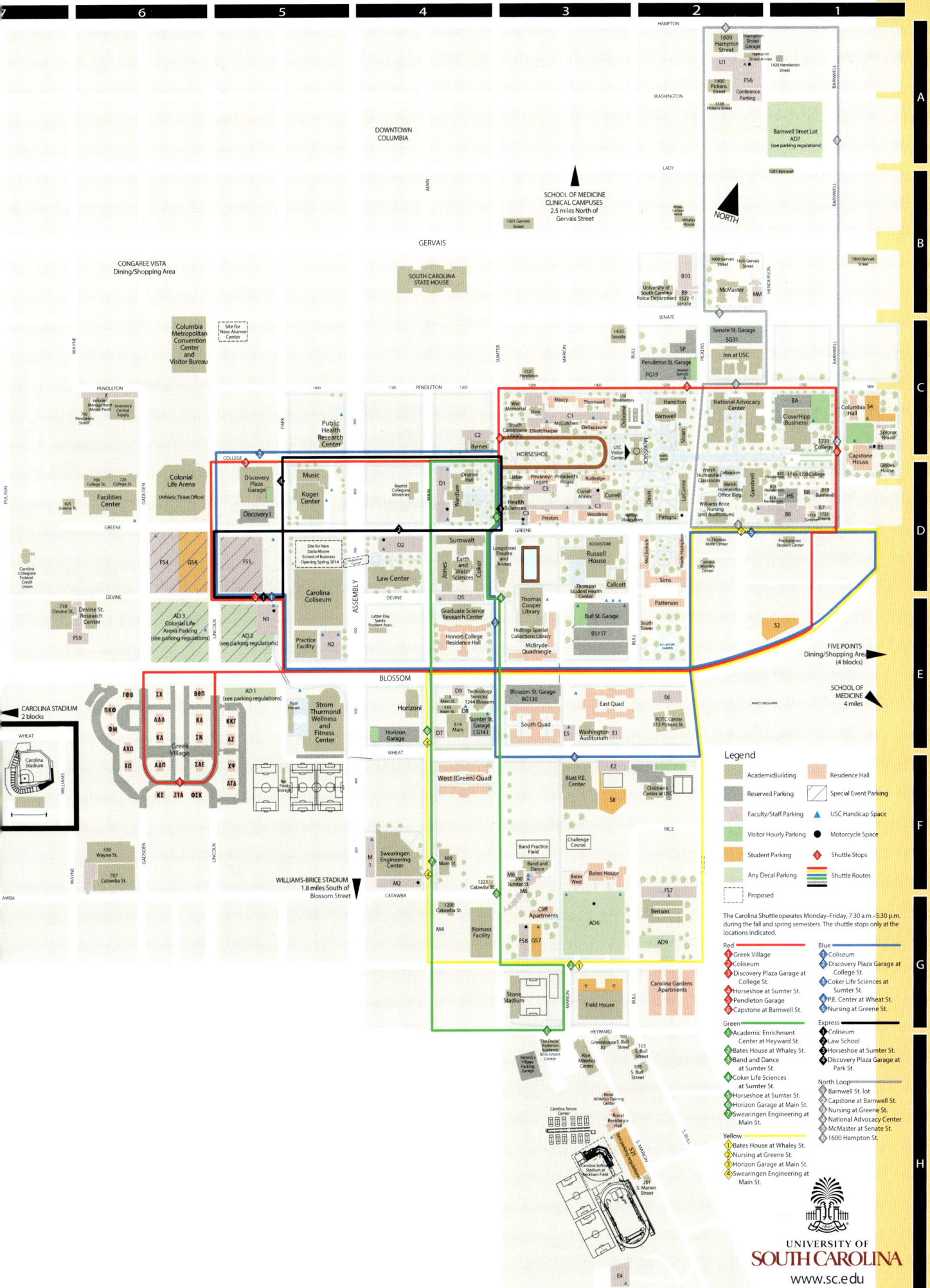

Appendix: South Carolina Campus Map

INDEX

A

academic advisors
    advisee/advisor responsibilities, 141
    Advisement Policies, 146
    Advising Preparation Sheet, 141, 149
    being a good advisee, 141
    course scheduling/planning, 144
    establishing your relationship with your, 127
    how to find your, 142
    Office of Pre-Professional Advising, 143
    requirements for meeting with, 140
academic assistance, 124
Academic Coaching and Engagement (ACE), 48, 86, 98
academic etiquette, 102
academic integrity. *See also* Carolinian Creed
    academic, 171
    Honor Code, 7, 35, 172, 176–177, 179
    importance of, 175–177
    resources, 183
    scenario, 182
academic planning strategies, 139–140
academic strengths, 118
active learning, 102
activities
    charting your, 91
    enhancement, 46
    meaningful, 43
adult students, 251
advisement compared to registration, 142
advisors. *See* academic advisors
advocacy for unsafe relationships, 207
African American Male Institute, 252
African American students, 18, 23. *See also* diversity
    Association of African American Students (AAAS), 251
    first graduates, 19
    history of integration, 25
    Monteith's lawsuit for attendance, 27
AIDS/HIV, 202
AlcoholEdu for College, 199
alcohol use/abuse, 221
    South Carolina state laws, 196–199
alma mater, "We Hail Thee Carolina," 23, 32
Alternative reak program, 56
alumni, 23, 38
American College Health Association—National College Health Assessment (NCHA) of USC, 218
American Library Association (ALA), 157
American Psychological Association (APA), 174, 180, 181
AmeriCorps Programs, 56
anxiety/worrying, 117, 120–121, 216
APO Escort service, 212
article databases, 165
assaults, 195. *See also* interpersonal violence
    reporting, 207
    sexual assault and harassment, 206
    Sexual Assault and Violence Intervention and Prevention (SAVIP), 207, 209, 235
assignments, turning in, 102
athletics programs, 59–60
attendance, 24, 102, 108
awards, 9

B

Barefoot Day, 26
baseball, 27
Behavioral Intervention Team, 220
BGLSA (Bisexual, Gay, Lesbian Students and Allies), 251
bicycle registration, 213
bigotry, 240
Big Thursday, 30
binge drinking, 196
bisexual students, organizations and programs for, 250, 251, 252, 253
Blatt PE Center, 193
blood alcohol content, 196–197
breathing for stress management, 217
Brothers of Nubian Descent (BOND), 251
Bucket List, 39
Bush, George W., 27

C

caffeine intake, 216
calendars
    as part of e-mail account, 88
    tracking due dates, 95
campus engagement opportunities, 50
campus
    historic buildings, 21–22
    Horseshoe, 18, 20
    maps, 20, 257–260
    pre-Civil War, 18
    preservation of historic buildings, 19
    regional, 19
campus health services, 194
campus life. *See also* college life scenarios
    engagement in, 45 (*See also* engagement pathways)
    living on campus, 52
campus offices. *See* resources and websites; specific office by name
campus resources. *See* resources and websites
Campus Wellness, 193
Caravel, 55
Career Center, 66, 128
    JobMate, 131, 133
    Spur Connections, 133
    workshops for job search skills, 132
career path development, 225
    academic advising for, 139
    academic planning strategies, 139–140
    course planning, 144–146
    determining your path, 127
    exploring choices, 128
    four-step model for decision making, 128–132
    four-year curriculum planner, 147
    gathering information for, 135
    job search workshops, 132
    resources, 128, 153
    scenario, 152
    self-assessment worksheet for, 135
    statistics on hiring of new graduates, 133
    timeline for, 133–134
    top skills desired by employers, 134
Carolina Campus Ministries, 250–251
Carolina Community
    community resources, 40
    diversity and, 240, 253
    handbook, 33
Carolina Community student handbook, 33

Carolina Core requirements, 140, 144, 145, 146
Carolina Productions, 50
Carolina Service Council (CSC), 55
Carolinian Creed, 23, 35, 36, 199, 240
CHCD. *See* Counseling and Human Development Center (CHDC)
cheating
    impact of deciding to/not to cheat, 174–175
    plagiarism, 172–173, 174
    statistics on, 171
Chicago Manual of Style (CMoS), 174, 180, 181
chlamydial infections, 201, 202
Chosen Gospel Ensemble, 251
Civil Rights Tour, 252
class rings, 33
classroom issues
    avoiding distractions, 104
    where to sit, 104
Clowney, Jadeveon, 27
Cocky (mascot), 30–31
Cocky's Reading Express, 55–56
college/campus life
    engagement in, 45 (*See also* engagement pathways)
    living on campus, 52
College Laws (1836), 33
college life scenarios
    academic integrity, 182
    cultural diversity, 254
    deciding on career path, 152
    drinking/partying/safety, 234
    eating disorders/helping a friend, 233
    involvement in school organizations, 76
Columbia, South Carolina
    dance, 62
    festivals and fairs, 65
    historical sites, 64–65
    movie theaters, 63
    music, 63
    parks, 63–64
    resources, 65, 77–78
    theaters and arts centers, 61–62
    visual arts, 63
    zoo and gardens, 65
communication
    awareness of others' viewpoints, 246–247
    making assumptions about others, 246
    power of words, 246
    sharing your stories, 247
    taking things personally, 247
    terminology related to diversity, 248
    using titles of address, 246
    with your professors, 105
community. *See* Carolina Community
Community Service Programs, 55–56, 66, 253
Conversation Partner, 58
Cooper, Thomas, 17
Cooperative Institutional Research Program (CIRP), 46
Council of Science Editors (CSE), 174, 180, 181
Counseling and Human Development Center (CHDC), 195, 207, 221
    for help with test anxiety, 117
    services offered by, 218
    Sexual Assault and Violence Intervention and Prevention (SAVIP), 207
    suicide prevention training, 219
    support for sexual assault/interpersonal violence, 207
course sequencing, 144
course work
    balancing, 144, 146
    engagement in, 46
    four-year curriculum planner, 147
    planning, 144–146
    registration procedure, 142
    registration worksheet, 150
    transferring credit hours, 143
    withdrawals from classes, 143
cover letters, 134
credit hours, 143, 145
Creed. See Carolinian Creed
Creed Day, 35
crisis intervention services, 209, 219–220
Cross College Advising (CCA) Program, 139–140
cultural experiences, 33–36, 61, 245–247, 252–253. *See also* diversity
culture, school, 33–36. *See also* Carolinian Creed; diversity
curriculum planner, 147
CUSP (cold, unconscious, slow, puking), 199

D

Daily Gamecock, 23, 33, 51
dance companies, 62, 77
degree requirements, course planning for meeting, 144–145
Department of Leadership and Service, 66
DeSaussure College, 21
digital calendars
    as part of e-mail account, 88
    tracking due dates, 95
dining halls
    abolishment of compulsory attendance at, 24
    Great Biscuit Rebellion, 24–25
disability services, 251
Discover Program, 54
Discovery Day, 54
diversity. *See also* cultural experiences
    awareness and engagement resources, 249–253, 255
    Carolina Community and, 240
    Carolinian Creed on, 240
    communication guidelines, 245–247
    community opportunities for engaging in, 253
    educational value of, 239–240
    exploring, 247
    National Survey of Student Engagement, 239
    scenario, 254
    self-awareness and, 244
    of student population, 18, 239
    terminology related to, 248
Diversity Dialogue Series, 252
Diversity Quiz, 241–243
Diversity Week, 35
Doerpinghaus, Helen, 126
Domestic Study Away, 57–58, 66
domestic study experiences, 58
Dozier, John H., 238
Drayton, John, 17
drinking (scenario), 234. *See also* substance use/abuse
dropping a course, 143
drugs/medications. *See* health and well-being; prescription drugs
drug use/abuse. *See* substance use/abuse

E

eating disorders (scenario), 233
ecological footprint calculator, 225
educational experience, 46
Edwards, Anna, 42
elective courses, 144
Ellet, William, 17
Elliott College, 21
e-mail
    etiquette for communicating via, 105, 122–123
    student account features, 88
emergencies
    alcohol poisoning, 199
    campus call boxes, 212
    crisis intervention services, 209, 219–220
    sexual assault/interpersonal violence, 207
    suicidal ideation, 220
    violence/explosive incidents, 208–209
emergency contraception (EC/morning after pill), 205
emotional wellness, 187, 188, 230
    anxiety, 218
    depression, 218–219
    stress, 214–217, 232
    as a value, 83
    wellness wheel inventory, 228
EMPOWER, 252
Encyclopedia Americana, 17
engagement pathways, 45
    campus engagement opportunities, 49–50, 77–78
    Carolina Productions, 50
    community service, 55–56
    cultural experiences, 61
    discovering Columbia, South Carolina, 61–65
    for diversity, 249–253
    exploring Columbia (*See* Columbia, South Carolina)
    global learning, 56–58
    National Survey of Student Engagement (NSSE), 48
    Office of Student Engagement, 48
    professional and civic engagement, 48
    recreation and athletics programs, 59–60
    research, 53–55
    scenario, 76
    Student Engagement Plan (SEP), 66–75
    student media, 51
English Programs for Internationals (EPI), 58
enhancement activities, 46
environmental issues, 226
environmental wellness, 187, 188, 230
    ecological footprint calculator, 225
    energy and water saving tips, 226
    Leadership in Energy & Environmental Design (LEED), 225
    recycling guide, 227
    wellness wheel inventory, 228
ethical behavior, 171, 176. *See also* academic integrity
etiquette
    academic, 102
    e-mail, 105, 122–123
eustress, 215
Evening Shuttle, 212
examinations. *See* test-taking strategies
Executive Cabinet, 52
Executive Officers, 51
experiences
    educational, 46
    engagement in, 45
    mapping your, 75
    purposeful, 43
expertise, 83

F

faculty
    advisors (*See* academic advisors)
    building relationships with professors, 103
    communicating with your professors, 105
    diversity among, 240
    office hours, 102
    Out-to-Lunch Program, 106
fairs, 65, 77
federal programs, 56
festivals, 65, 77
First Night Carolina, 29
First-Year Reading Experience (FYRE), 29
FitWalk paths, 193
football traditions, 23
    Gamecocks, mascot, colors, 30–31
    Outback Bowl, 27
foreign exchange student programs, 57, 58
four-step model for career planning, 128–132
French House, 58
Freshman Council, 51
Freshman Survey, 101
Friedman, Dan, 2
Friend, Christy, 80
Fundamentals of Inquiry (University 201), 10

G

Gamecocks, 30
Garnet & Black magazine, 51
gay students, organizations and programs for, 250, 251, 252, 253
genital warts, 202
Gentlemen Representing Interacting & Trusting (GRIT), 209
G.I. Bill, 19
global learning programs, 56–58, 66
goals
    for academic advising, 139
    Academic Goal Setting Sheet, 90
    major versus minor goals, 83–84
    planning for achievement of career, 132
    SMART goals, 84
    of University 101, 7
gonorrheal infections, 201, 202
Google Scholar, 168
government, student, 51–52
GPA (grade point average)
    calculating your, 119
    elective courses and, 144
    for peer leadership eligibility, 8, 9
    setting your goal, 83
    and student body office eligibility, 51
    and University 101, 3
    use of social media and, 86
grades
    charting your, 95
    grade forgiveness, 142, 143
    W and WF, 143
Graduation with Leadership Distinction, 44
Great Biscuit Rebellion, 23, 24–25
Green Quad, 23, 225

H

handbook
- *Carolina Community*, 33
- excerpt from 1930s guide, 34

Harper College, 21
hazing, 26, 35
health and well-being, 186, 187, 230
- activity/exercise, 193
- Carolina Dining Services, 192
- Healthy Carolina Farmers Market, 192
- healthy choice icons, 192
- healthy eating, 189
- making healthy choices, 221
- monitoring food intake, 191–192
- nutrition, 189–190
- obesity, 191–192
- offices on campus, 195
- physical effects of stress, 215
- resources on campus, 235
- sexually transmitted infections STIs, 201
- substance use/abuse, 196–200
- wellness wheel inventory, 228

health care services, 194
Healthy Carolina, 187
hepatitis infections, 202
Hispanic Heritage Month, 253
historical sites, 64–65, 77
historic buildings, 20, 26
HIV/AIDS, 202
homosexual students, organizations and programs for, 250, 251, 252, 253
Honor Code, 7, 35, 172, 176–177, 179
- reporting violations, 177

Horseshoe, 18, 20
hospitals, 235
HPV (human papilloma virus), 202
Human Development Center, 195
human papilloma virus (HPV/genital warts), 202

I

identity, internal and external dimensions of, 244
information literacy. *See also* research
- academic integrity and, 171
- definition, 157
- Information Literacy Framework, 158
- USC libraries, 159

information sources, evaluating
- accuracy and reliability, 167
- authority, 167
- currency, 169
- objectivity, 169–170
- relevancy, 169
- using Google Scholar, 168

integration of campus, 25, 27. *See also* diversity
integrity. *See* academic integrity
intellectual wellness, 187, 188, 230
- *Daily Gamecock* puzzles, 222
- ways to enhance, 222
- wellness wheel inventory, 228

International House at Maxcy College, 57, 58
International Programs for Students Office, 250
international study experiences, 57
internships, 66
interpersonal violence
- personal relationship quiz, 210
- in relationships, 206
- relationship violence, 208–209
- sexual assault and harassment, 206, 207
- stalking, 206, 208
- standing up to, 209
- violence/hateful acts on campus, 35

intramural programs, 59–60

J

JobMate, 131, 133
job search workshops, 132
John Paul, Pope, 27
Jones, Thomas F., Jr., 4

K

Kennedy, John F., 27
Kuh, George, 48

L

Lancaster campus, 19
Late Night Shuttle, 212
law enforcement, 195
leadership
- Graduation with Leadership Distinction, 44
- Peer Leader Program, 8, 9
- programs and opportunities related to, 48

Leadership Distinction, 44–45
- in Community Service, 56

Leadership in Energy & Environmental Design (LEED), 225
leadership programs, 48
learning outcomes, 7, 145
learning strategies. *See also* study skills
- active, 102
- application of, 46, 47

LeConte, John, 17
LeConte, Joseph, 17
Legare College, 22
Lesbian, Gay, Bisexual and Transgender History Month, 253
Lesbian, Gay, Bisexual and Transgender (LGBT) programs, 250, 251
lesbian students, organizations and programs for, 250, 251, 252, 253
LGBT Peer Advocates, 252
libraries
- Ask a Librarian service, 164
- Reference Help Desk, 160
- resources, 159
- tips for researching in, 165
- USC's, 159, 171, 183

library research, 114
lice, pubic, 202
Lieber, Francis, 17
Lieber College, 22
listening skills, 112
Longstreet Theater, 18, 27
lying policy, 171

M

Magellan programs, 54
majors
- changing, 139–140, 143
- choosing/declaring your, 128

course planning, 144
mapping your experiences, 75
maps, campus, 20, 257–260
marijuana, 199–200
mascot origins, 30
Maxcy, Jonathan, 20
Maxcy College, International House at, 58
Maxcy Monument, 20, 22
McCutchen House, 21
McKissick, J. Rion, 26, 30
McKissick Museum, 18, 21
media
    campus television and radio stations, 51
    resources for student engagement in, 77
medical supplies/prescriptions, South Carolina PocketRX, 194
memory curve, 104
men's groups, 209
mindfulness, 224
mind map, 75
Minority Assistance Peer Program (MAPP), 252
Minority Students Welcome, 252
minors and cognates course requirements, 144
missed classes, 102
mission statement, 19
Modern Language Association (MLA), 174, 180, 181
Monteith, Henrie D., 19, 27
Moped registration, 213
morning after pill, 205
Moschella, Eric J., 100
movie theaters, 63, 77
museums, 63, 64, 65, 78
music scene, 63, 77
    Chosen Gospel Ensemble, 251

N

National Association for the Advancement of Colored People (NAACP), 251
National Register of Historic Places, 20
National Residence Hall Honorary (NRHH), 53
National Resource Center, 11
National Student Exchange program, 58
National Survey of Student Engagement (NSSE), 48
Native American Heritage Month, 253
newspaper, school, 33. *See also* Daily Gamecock
Nickelodeon Theatre, 63
note-taking, 101, 102
    with fast-paced instructors, 109
    listening for key phrases and words, 109
    listening skills for, 112
    Note-Taking Skills Inventory, 107
    outline method, 110
    reading and lecture notes method, 111
    rereading/reviewing notes, 104
    sentence method, 110
    shortcuts and tips for, 111
    study groups for reviewing, 114
NRHH (National Residence Hall Honorary), 53
NSSE (National Survey of Student Engagement), 48
nutrition/diet. *See also* health and well-being
    eating disorders scenario, 233
    effects of lack of sleep on, 220
    resources, 192

O

Obama, Michelle, 56
O'Brien, Marguerite, 186
Occupational Outlook Handbook (U.S. Department of Labor), 133
occupational wellness, 187, 188, 230
    tenets for experiencing, 225
    wellness wheel inventory, 228
Office of Academic Integrity, 172, 177
Office of Adult Student Services, 251
Office of Multicultural Student Affairs (OMSA), 249–250
Office of Pre-Professional Advising, 143
Office of Student Disability Services, 251
Office of Student Media, 51
Office of Undergraduate Research, 66
Office of Undergraduate Research (OUR), 54, 66
offices, campus. *See* resources and websites; specific office by name
organizations, student, 50, 52, 76, 251–252
outdoor activities, 59, 63–64
Outstanding Advocate for First-Year Students Award, 9
Out-to-Lunch Program, 106

P

papers
    citation styles, 173, 180
    citing sources in, 172, 173–174
    deciding to cite or not to cite, 178
    managing citations, 173
    OWL at Purdue (citation formats), 174
    plagiarism, 172–173
    research strategy for writing (*See* research)
partying (scenario), 234
pathways
    career (*See* career path development)
    engagement (*See* engagement pathways)
    to Leadership Distinction, 44–45
peer leadership, 52, 66
    Peer Leader Program, 8, 9
peer tutoring, 109
personal information, 211
personal relationship quiz, 210
pharmacy, 194
physical health. *See* health and well-being; wellness dimensions
Pinckney College, 22
plagiarism, 172–173, 174. *See also* cheating
planners for time management, 88
police department, USC, 207
policies/regulations/requirements, 127
    academic, 148
    academic load, 140
    Advisement Policies, 146
    cheating and plagiarism, 171, 172–173
positive thoughts, 216
practice testing, 113
preparation
    for advisor meetings, 141
    for class, 109
    for taking tests, 113–117
prescription drugs, 199–200
    South Carolina PocketRX, 194
President's House, 22
procedures. *See* policies/regulations
procrastination/procrastinators, 84–86
    procrastinator's clock, 85
professors. *See* faculty

program offerings, 10–11
Project ID database, 213, 214
protecting your property
 bicycles, 213
 book theft, 213
 residence hall room and personal items, 213–214
Pruitt, Dennis A., 16
pubic lice, 202

Q

questions
 benefits of asking, 102–103
 in class, 109
quizzes. See test-taking strategies

R

rape, 207. See also interpersonal violence
reading assignments, 101, 114
reading comprehension skills, SQ3R method, 112–113
Reagan, Ronald, 27
recreational drugs, 199–200
recreation programs, 59, 77, 195
recycling guide, 227
Reference Help Desk, 160
registration
 advisement compared to, 142
 procedure, 142
 worksheet for, 150
regulations. See policies/regulations/requirements
relationship violence, 206
religious organizations, 224
reporting assaults, 207
requirements. See policies/regulations/requirements
research, 66. See also information literacy; papers
 article databases, 164–165
 assistance with, 164
 breaking down your topic, 160
 Carnegie Foundation designation, 19
 defining your topic, 159–160
 evaluating information sources, 167–170
 evaluating your research question, 161
 into fields of study for career planning, 130
 information required for your, 162
 library, 114, 164, 165
 magazine and journal sources, 163
 Office of Undergraduate Research, 66
 opportunities for involvement in, 53–55
 resources for, 160
 search terms and operators, 166, 170
 type of information needed, 162
 types of sources for, 163
Residence Hall Association (RHA), 53
residence halls
 Green Quad, 23
 opportunities for engagement in, 52–53
 protecting your room and personal items, 213–214
resident mentors (RMs), 53, 199
résumés and cover letters, 134, 136–137
rings, class, 33
Rutledge College, 20, 22

S

safety and transport
 advocacy for unsafe relationships, 207
 campus safety tips, 211
 C=O/D (Crime equals Opportunity over Desire), 211
 evening and late night shuttle services, 212
 protecting your property, 213–214
 protecting yourself, 211
 resources, 235
 scenario, 234
 taxi services, 196–197, 211, 221
 University Safety Committee, 212
 USC Police Department, 207
Salkehatchie campus, 19
scenarios. See college life scenarios
scheduling tools for time management, 87–89
 schedule worksheet, 151
 Weekly Schedule form, 97
scholarships, 9
school colors, 30–31
school newspaper, 33
school songs
 "Fighting Gamecocks Lead the Way," 31
 "We Hail Thee Carolina" (alma mater), 23, 32
security services
 accessing, 164
 campus escort services, 211
 campus shuttle vans, 212
 Division of Law Enforcement & Safety, 195
self-assessment inventories, 129
self-awareness and understanding
 developing, 48, 128–129, 133, 225
 elements of identity in, 244
 for emotional wellness, 214
 engaging in, 131
 reflecting on knowing yourself, 139–140
 values, 244–245 (See also values)
self-plagiarism, 172–173
self-talk, negative, 217
semester at a glance, 88
seminar classes, 3, 4
Senior Capstone Experience (University 401), 10
service-learning courses, 55–56, 66
Service Saturdays, 55
sexual activity, 221
 communicating with your partner about, 204
 contraception methods, 203, 204
 emergency contraception (EC/morning after pill), 205
 USC's parameters of consent, 209
sexual assault and harassment, 206
Sexual Assault and Violence Intervention and Prevention (SAVIP), 207, 209, 235
 on-call services, 195
sexuality, 254
 Bisexual, Gay, Lesbian Students and Allies (BGLSA), 251
 Lesbian, Gay, Bisexual and Transgender History Month, 253
 Lesbian, Gay, Bisexual and Transgender (LGBT) programs, 250
 LGBT Peer Advocates, 252
 resources, 255
sexually transmitted infections (STIs)
 common infections, 201
 symptoms of, 202
 transmission of, 203
SGTV (Student Gamecock Television), 51, 77
Simmons, Timothy, 156
sleep